Revitalizing Relationships

THE RESOURCES OF CONTEXTUAL THERAPY

with inspiration from the pastoral process
and interfaith studies

Catherine Ducommun-Nagy
Hanneke Meulink-Korf
Greteke De Vries

Revitalising Relationships: The Resources of Contextual Therapy with Inspiration from the Pastoral Process and Interfaith Studies

Published by African Sun Media under the SUN MeDIA imprint
Place of publication: Stellenbosch, South Africa

All rights reserved

Copyright © 2023 African Sun Media and the authors

The authors and the publisher have made every effort to obtain permission for and acknowledge the use of copyrighted material. Refer all enquiries to the publisher.

No part of this book may be reproduced or transmitted in any form or by any electronic, photographic or mechanical means, including photocopying and recording on record, tape or laser disk, on microfilm, via the Internet, by e-mail, or by any other information storage and retrieval system, without prior written permission by the publisher.

Views reflected in this publication are not necessarily those of the publisher.

First edition 2023

ISBN 978-1-998951-34-5
ISBN 978-1-998951-35-2 (e-book)
https://doi.org/10.52779/9781998951352

Set in Merriweather Regular 8.5/13

Cover design, typesetting and production by African Sun Media
Cover image: Painting done by © Laliba Ferhat from Algeria

SUN MeDIA is an imprint of African Sun Media. Academic and general works are published under this imprint in print and electronic formats.

Our publications can be ordered from:
orders@africansunmedia.co.za
Takealot: bit.ly/2monsfl
Google Books: bit.ly/2k1Uilm
africansunmedia.store.it.si (e-books)
Amazon Kindle: amzn.to/2ktL.pkL
JSTOR: https://bit.ly/3udc057

Visit africansunmedia.co.za for more information.

Contents

Acknowledgements i

Foreword iii
    Christo Thesnaar

Preface xiii
    Catherine Ducommun-Nagy, Hanneke Meulink-Korf & Greteke De Vries

SECTION I: A Broad View of Contextual Therapy and its Applications
    Catherine Ducommun-Nagy

Prologue to Section I 3

1. **Fundamentals of Contextual Therapy** 7
   Introduction 7
   The core principles of contextual therapy 8
   The general goals of contextual therapy 9
   Giving: A resource in relationships and a resource in therapy 9
   Constructive entitlement 10
   The general fields of applications of contextual therapy 10
   The origins of contextual therapy and its development 12
       Introduction 12
       The systemic paradigm 12
       From early systemic thinking to current practices 14
       Contextual therapy and the newer developments in family therapy 15
       Current practices in family therapy 16
       The move towards eclecticism in contemporary family therapy and its consequences 16
   Contextual therapy as an integrative approach 17

2. **The Five Dimensions of Relational Reality** 19
   Introduction 19
   Dimension I: The dimension of facts 21
       Variables in Dimension I 21
       Mental illnesses as a form of situational injustice 21
       Resources in Dimension I 22
   Dimension II: The Dimension of psychology 22
       Variables in Dimension II 22
       Mental disorders (mental illnesses) and the Dimension of psychology 23
       Resources in Dimension II 23
       Differences between contextual therapy applied to individuals and individual therapy 23
   Dimension III: The Dimension of transactions 24
       Variables in Dimension III 24
       Mental disorders and Dimension III 24
       Resources in Dimension III 25

Multidirected partiality as a resource to promote orderly transactions	25
The implications of the internet and social media in Dimension III	26
Dimension IV: The Dimension of relational ethics	27
Variables in Dimension IV	27
Mental disorders and Dimension IV	27
Resources in Dimension IV	28
Dimension V: The Ontic Dimension	28
Variables in Dimension V	29
Mental disorders and Dimension V	29
Resources in Dimension V	30
The practical use of the five-dimensional model of relational reality	30
The five dimensions as a framework for assessment	30
Five dimensions: One relational reality	30
Changes in life and changes in therapy	31
What is required to perform a five-dimensional assessment?	31
An illustration of the use of the five-dimensional model of relational reality	32
Assessment	32
Resources and interventions	33
When the professional is a pastoral counselor	34
One or more professionals?	34

3. The Dialectic Theory of Personality and its Implications for Practitioners 37

Introduction	37
The relational definition of autonomy and its consequences for therapy	38
Accepting the dialectic theory of the personality, a question or a must?	39
Relational needs according to the five dimensions of relational reality	40
Relational needs and the dimension of facts	40
Relational needs and the dimension of psychology	41
Relational needs and the dimension of transactions	41
Relational needs and the dimension of relational ethics	41
Relational needs and the ontic dimension	41
The six modes of relating	42
1) The intrasubject boundary (no external Other and no internal Other)	42
2) The internal dialogue (no external Other but an internal Other)	42
3) The merger (merger of Self and Other)	43
4) Being the object (Self as the object, Other as the subject)	43
5) Being the subject (Self as the subject, Other as the object)	44
6) The dialogue (Self and Other in an interchangeable position either as a subject or an object)	44
Transitions between the six modes of relating	44
Relational need templates	45
Relational need templates and parenting	46
The place of the therapist in the dialectical theory of the personality	47
Understanding bereavement from the perspective of the relational modes	48

4. The World of Relational Ethics ... 49

Introduction ... 49
- The relational definition of fairness ... 50
- Ethical imagination and its limits ... 50
- Representations of fairness ... 51
- The difference between relational ethics and value ethics ... 51
  - Example I ... 52
  - Example II ... 52
- Religious values and interfaith dialogue ... 52

The origins of relational ethics ... 53
- The contributions of sciences ... 53
- The ethics of responsibility for relationships ... 55
- The intrinsic transgenerational tribunal of solidarity ... 55
- Transgenerational solidarity ... 56
- Transgenerational solidarity and the mandate for therapy and prevention ... 57
- The mandate of therapy and the quality of human survival ... 58
- Contextual therapy and the common mandate of all therapies ... 58

Multidirected partiality, a therapeutic tool and a mandate ... 59
- Goals settings and conflicts of interests ... 59
- The definition of multidirected partiality ... 59
- Multidirected partiality as a mandate ... 60
- Multidirected partiality as a method ... 61
  - Example ... 61
- Order of interventions ... 61
- Multidirected partiality and inclusiveness ... 63
- Limits to multidirected partiality ... 64
- Multidirected partiality: What is required from professionals? ... 64
- The limits of empathy ... 65
- Overcoming our limits to offer empathy and multidirected partiality ... 66
- Co-therapy and supervision as a resource towards multidirected partiality ... 67

The parent-child relationship in the perspective of relational ethics ... 67
- General considerations ... 67
- Children identified as special beings: An honor or a burden? ... 68
- Symmetric and asymmetrical relationships ... 69
- What are children entitled to? ... 70
  - Example ... 71

5. Injustices and their Relational Consequences ... 73

Retributive injustices or relational injustices ... 73
- Introduction ... 73
- Retributive or relational injustices in contextual therapy ... 74
- Relational injustices in the family ... 74
  - Example ... 76

Distributive injustices or situational injustices	76
Distributive injustices in social sciences	76
Societal injustices as situational injustices	78
Overlaps between situational injustices and relational injustices	79
Example	79
Injustices and religious beliefs	80
The relational consequences of injustices	81
Destructive entitlement	82
The difference between the psychology of entitlement and actual entitlement	83
Example	84
The concept of the revolving slate: Who are the targets of our destructive entitlement?	84
Destructive entitlement in close relationships	85
A five-dimensional perspective on discrimination and oppression	86
Example	87
Blocked giving as secondary injustice in the life of the victims of systemic injustices	87
Blocked giving and conduct disorder	88
Helping youths to rediscover the benefits of giving	89
Example	90

6. Parentification and Exoneration — 91

The parentification of children	91
The definition of parentification	91
Infantilization as a form of parentification	92
Full reversal of roles between parents and children	92
Example	92
Life circumstances as a source of parentification	93
Therapeutic strategies to decrease parentification	94
Example I	95
Example II	96
Parentification outside of the parent-child relationship	99
Parentification of adults by adults	99
Parentification of adults and transference phenomena	99
Clients' parentification of therapists and counselors	100
Parentification of clients by therapists	101
Example	102
Subtle forms of parentification of clients by therapists	103
To trust or not to trust? Not trusting as a therapeutic resource	103
Example	103
Forgiveness and exoneration	104
Forgiveness	104
Exoneration	105
Exoneration: The recategorization of parents and the requalification of their actions	106
Exoneration outside of the parent-child relationship	107
The clinical benefits of exoneration	108
The process of exoneration	108
Illustrations of the exoneration process	110

	Example I	110
	Example II	111
	Coming to terms with our parents' shortcomings	113

7. A General Understanding of Family and Group Loyalties ... 115

Introduction ... 115
    The general definition of loyalty ... 115
    Are loyalties visible or invisible? ... 117
    Loyalty as a triadic notion and its systemic implications ... 118
    The role of loyalty in society ... 120
    Loyalty and morality ... 121

Family loyalties and the journey towards autonomy ... 122
    The counterautonomous superego ... 122
        Example ... 123
    The collusive postponement of mourning ... 124
        Example ... 124
    Collusive postponement of mourning and actual losses ... 125
        Example ... 126

Myths about filial loyalty as an obstacle to autonomy ... 126

The clinical manifestations of loyalties ... 128

8. Loyalties in the Perspective of the Five Dimensions of Relational Reality ... 131

Loyalty and the dimension of relational ethics ... 132
    Fairness and reciprocity as determinants of loyalty ... 132
    Loyalty and filial piety ... 132
    Filial loyalty ... 133
    Loyalty to undeserving parents ... 134
    Filial loyalty and its societal implications ... 134
    Decreased family loyalty in modern societies: A threat to traditional support systems ... 135

Loyalty and the dimension of facts ... 136
    Is loyalty based on biological determinants? ... 136
    Loyalty and factual variables ... 136
    Therapeutic perspectives ... 137

Loyalty and the dimension of psychology ... 137
    Loyalty and guilt feelings ... 138
    The psychological variables of loyalty ... 138
    Therapeutic perspectives ... 139

Loyalty and the dimension of transactions ... 140
    Loyalty as an immaterial link ... 140
    Can loyalty be imposed by power? ... 141
    The systemic variables of loyalty ... 142
    Therapeutic perspectives in the case of loyalty imposed by power and control ... 143

Loyalty and the ontic dimension ... 144
    The variables of loyalty in the ontic dimension ... 144
    Therapeutic perspectives ... 144

9. Loyalty Conflicts	**145**
Unavoidable loyalty conflicts	145
Example of ways to handle unavoidable loyalty conflicts	145
Marriage and coupling as a source of loyalty conflicts	146
Family loyalties in arranged marriages	147
Forbidden unions and family loyalties	148
Avoidable loyalty conflicts	150
Avoidable loyalty conflicts in the parent-child relationship	150
Parents' faith and avoidable loyalty conflicts	152
Parents' dilemma over controversial traditional practicess	154
Parents and other adults in the prevention of loyalty conflicts	154
10. Split Loyalties	**157**
Introduction	157
Split loyalties in the case of parental separation and feud	157
Split loyalties in the case of care by relatives-fights between mothers and grandmothers	158
Split loyalties in the case of foster care placement and adoption	160
Guidelines for interventions in situations of split loyalties	160
The clinical consequences of split loyalties	160
First line of intervention: Working with the parents	163
Second line of intervention: Working with the children	165
11. Invisible Loyalties	**167**
Implicit and explicit loyalties	167
Example	168
Invisible loyalties as indirect loyalties	168
Invisible loyalties in the case of complete cut-off from biological parents	169
Example	171
Intergenerational repetitions of negative behaviors and loyalties	172
12. Special Issues Pertaining to Family and Group Loyalties	**175**
Divided loyalties and intergroup conflicts	175
Loyalty conflicts and invisible loyalties in clashes between family expectations and societal expectations	175
Group loyalties and intergroup solidarity: 'us versus them' or 'all of us'?	177
13. The Theory of Change in Contextual Therapy: Treatment Goals and Strategies	**179**
Can contextual therapy be standardized?	180
Contextual therapy: A dialogue of giving and receiving	180
A theory of change: The therapeutic moment as a moment of bifurcation	182
The genogram as a tool to explore the sources of injustices	184
The five dimensions of the genogram and the five dimensions of relational reality	185
Session timing and termination of treatment	188
Concluding message	189

SECTION II: The Contextual Approach in the Pastoral Process and Intercultural Encounters

Hanneke Meulink-Korf & Greteke De Vries

Prologue to Section II 193

Part I 195

1. Contextual Pastoral Care and Counseling (CPCC) and the Dialogical Intergenerational Pastoral Process (DIPP) 195

   Introduction 195

   A contextual intergenerational approach for pastoral care and theology 198
      Pastoral practice and practitioners, in short 198
      'Pastoral', and a definition of pastoral care 200
      Some history: Theologians inspired by contextual therapy theory 201
      Organized dissemination 202
      New input and new terminology 204
      Enduring reliability 206
      Multigenerational homes of wisdom 206
      A plurality of approaches 208

   Amidst diversity of pastoral settings 210
      In newer chaplaincy services 210
      Suffering is not the same as experiencing problems or deficiencies 212
      Ethics of caring 215
      Heuristics of hope 215
      Hans Jonas's heuristics of fear 217

   Working with a dialogical intergenerational perspective 218
      A discipline with a broad orientation 218
      Therapists and pastoral counselors/chaplains: Different domains 219

   Relational life care in the community and the pastoral practitioner's attitude 220
      Multidirected partiality and its possible limitations in a pastoral relationship 220
      A human disposition for multilaterality 222
      The importance of a multi-person perspective 222
      Participation in the community, a relational opportunity 224
      Abuse by a pastor or chaplain and the relational and social effect 225
      An asymmetric responsibility for the client's relational reality 226

   Philosophical and theological outlines 227
      Inspiration comes from several sources 227
      Relational ethics come first 229
      To a theological relational anthropology 229
      The call for justice has priority 230
      How is responsiveness possible? On respond-ability 231
      Trust without guarantee 233

2. A Practical Framework, Related to Religion and Spirituality 235
   The effect of relationality 235
      Spiritual counseling is not enough 235
      A relational focus for approaching the human reality coram Deo 235

Learning this relational focus in life and work	236
On burdens, resources, and a reversal in the counselor's mind	237
Connecting listening, connecting speech, re-engagement in giving	239
Introduction	239
Erica and the J.B. family, a pastoral process	240
Some guidelines as suggestion	243
Guidance in non-family in-group conflicts	245
Can the spiritual dimension be a relational resource?	248
Introduction	248
Relationality in spirituality and in religion	248
Interpretation of life and a transgenerational concern	249
Intergenerational options for proximity and generosity	250
Transmission of religiosity in changing times, its implications for loyalty	250
Changes in religious belonging and options for vitalizing relationships	252
The beliefs of the professional and receptiveness to otherness	253
Loyalty to God?	255
Religion and theology as an obstacle in relational ethics, and pitfalls in counseling	256
Religion as a motivational resource for relational ethics	258
"Where are you?" (Genesis 3: 9)	258
Relational presence activated by indebtedness	260

Part II 263

1. Fair Bridging: Ethics of Caring in Intercultural Worlds 263

Sensitivity to intercultural relations	263
Personal situation	265
Combination of perspectives	267
A few more preliminary remarks	268
Structure of the upcoming chapters	269

2. Wisdom from Interreligious Studies 271

Worldwide	271
Emouna	272
Clashing of social identity groups	273
Stereotypes and prejudices	275
Privileges	277
Privilege check	278
Language	279
Religious literacy	280
Intersectionality	282
Two types of dialogue	283
No dialogue	285

3. **Exploring Intercultural Encounters** 287
   A simple greeting 287
   A five-dimension perspective on Margaret and Nasr meeting 288
      Dimension I: Facts 288
      Dimension II: Psychology 289
      Dimension III: Transactions and systems 290
      Dimension IV: Relational ethics 291
      Dimension V: The ontic dimension 293
   Loyalty 294
   Destructive entitlement 295
   Constructive entitlement 296

4. **Final Remarks** 299
   Insights 299
   Recommendations 300
   Urgent global commitment 301

Bibliography 303

Acknowledgements

In English (and in corresponding verbs in German and Dutch) the verb 'to thank' is related to 'to think'. 'To think' means to keep in remembrance. When someone says: "I thank you", this person says: "I keep you in my thoughts, kindly and friendly." Buber, in a text that he called his testament, explained the layered meaning of this word (Buber, 1967). To be grateful to someone is not only to keep this person in our thoughts and hearts, but also to go out into the world from our hearts as an affirmation of sharing with others.

Although here we shall mention only the names of the people who have been the most directly involved with the writing and publishing of this book, we also want to express our gratitude to the many people in our lives who have contributed to our personal development and our growth as professionals.

We hereby thank in particular:

Alexander Berzin, Rein Brouwer, Henk Meulink, Daniël Louw, Neeltje van Doorn, and last but not least, Christo Thesnaar.

The publisher: African Sun Media, and its team members Melinda Bolton, Anina Joubert, Carla Rautenbach, Lisa Janse van Rensburg, Danie Steyl and Davida van Zyl.

Labiba Ferhat of Algeria and the United Arab Emirates for her permission to illustrate our book with one of her paintings.

And the generous Funds: Stichting Contextueel Pastoraat in Nederland (Ineke Breugem-Verboon, Inge Hoek), KerkinActie, Han Gerlach studiefonds.

Foreword

Christo Thesnaar[1]

From the origin of the development of contextual therapy, its founder Ivan Boszormenyi-Nagy (1920-2007), who was not only a psychiatrist and pioneer of family therapy but also trained in biochemistry and physics, has specifically engaged with other disciplines such as philosophy and psychology to ensure that contextual therapy benefits from the contributions of all these disciplines. The contextual pastoral care approach has followed suit to engage with other disciplines such as philosophy (Buber, Levinas, Rosenstock-Huessy, Theunissen) and theology (Bonhoeffer, Dillen, Van Rhijn) to ensure that this approach benefits optimally from this interdisciplinary engagement. However, in essence, the development of this book is based not only on an interdisciplinary engagement, but also on a truly transdisciplinary journey. Three authors came together to plan and write this text. Catherine Ducommun-Nagy, a Swiss trained psychiatrist, contributes to this book from the discipline of psychiatry, psychotherapy, and family therapy. Hanneke Meulink-Korf and Greteke De Vries are both Dutch Protestant theologians who engage in this task from the field of theology. The three authors focus on the theme of revitalizing relationships by giving, starting from their particular discipline, adding all what can be learned from contextual therapy and pastoral processes. The most significant aspect of this book is that from the outset, it developed within the sphere of relational ethics. Put differently, this relational emphasis is not only very visible in the contents of the book itself but it was also displayed throughout the journey that the authors took to write it.

In line with the transdisciplinary theory, they actively engaged with one another during writing retreats and via Zoom meetings to debate the contents of the book from the vantage point of their different disciplines, and also to ensure that all possible misinterpretations were eliminated. During these face-to-face engagements and also the engagements via Zoom, their focus was on the particular issue at stake and on how each discipline could contribute to the best of its ability to address it as responsibly as possible and on a continuous basis. In their deliberations, they engaged with real-life struggles such as life, faith, religion, culture, tradition, and spirituality in a relational way. During their discussions, the authors also recognized that these struggles are complex and that they cannot be handled just with a simple cause-and-effect paradigm: to avoid the pitfall of oversimplification, transdisciplinary scholars need to commit

---

1 Prof Thesnaar is the leader of the Master program in Practical theology/Clinical Pastorate in the Department of Practical Theology & Missiology, Faculty of Theology, Stellenbosch University, South Africa.

themselves continuously to scientific research. Here, Catherine Ducommun-Nagy brings up some changes in the presentation of the theory of the contextual approach that are based on years of clinical experience and research, as well as continuous interactions and dialogue with Ivan Boszormenyi-Nagy.

Another fundamental aspect of the book is the endeavor by all three authors to connect the theory discussed in this book with practical examples that relate carefully to the life and context of people. In both sections, the authors particularly place the focus on the practice of contextual therapy, pastoral care, and interfaith dialogue in a multicultural context. The clinical examples that they provide as illustrations in these sections are of great value to all who will read it and who are open to learn from it.

The fact that the authors have engaged in this transdisciplinary journey in a relational way while writing this book has truly made it accessible to practitioners in a variety of disciplines such as psychology, psychiatry, family therapy, philosophy, sociology, theology, interfaith studies, and intercultural studies. It will also be valuable to pastors, pastoral caregivers, any kind of therapists, community care workers, youth workers, interfaith caregivers, and intercultural practitioners.

The goal of this book is to place emphasis on positive reciprocity in order to actively steer away from symmetric negative reciprocity like for instance the escalation of revenge. Catherine Ducommun-Nagy reminds us that the ethics of contextual therapy are based on fairness. These ethics speak about humanity and solidarity. They are not based on morals and they are situated within the relationship and not outside of it, as value ethics are. However, this book is more than just about reciprocity. It entails the discussion of other key themes of contextual therapy such as the traditional four dimensions of relational reality, loyalty, etc.

Furthermore, it is safe to say that this new publication in the field of contextual therapy and contextual pastoral care aims at presenting new developments in the contextual approach. In the Section I of the book, Catherine Ducommun-Nagy engages in a detailed presentation of the dialectic theory of the personality and a detailed presentation of the fifth dimension of relational reality, called the ontic dimension, that was introduced by Boszormenyi-Nagy in 2000 (see Chapter 2 of Section I). She introduces a new terminology in the discussion of injustices and in the discussion of exoneration. She also proposes a new way of building genograms, and it will be the first time here that her new method will be presented in a publication.

In reference to the presentation of the dialectic theory of the personality proposed by Boszormenyi-Nagy, Catherine Ducommun-Nagy explains in what way his dialectic view of the Self differs from M. Buber's notion of the I-Thou dialogue. But she also shows that both authors do agree that the Self is inherently dependent on a relationship with an Other to exist as a Self. In contextual therapy, this dependence is defined as an ontic dependence. Usually, the autonomy of the Self is understood as an absence of any dependence on others. Here paradoxically, autonomy is based on relatedness. Indeed, both Boszormenyi-Nagy and Buber agree that autonomy is based on relatedness and on a fundamental interconnectedness between people in the family and in society. This view is critical for the translation of the contextual approach in the African context.

Coming now to the ontic dimension, Catherine Ducommun-Nagy explains that the ontic dimension (dimension V) refers to the determinants of relationships that relate to the intrinsic mutual dependence between the Self and the Other, and to the relational definition of the Self. She indicates that we need to understand that the introduction of this fifth dimension has brought a change to the definition of what constitutes the 'context' in contextual therapy. As she explains, here the context is not limited to the family, as it includes all the people who can be affected by the interventions of the professionals, whether they are in physical contact or not, and all the human beings who are connected through giving and receiving in the present, the past, and the future. This means that the context includes all the current members of a family, the ancestors who have contributed to their lives, partners, friends, and the future generations whose survival depends on a responsible attitude of the current generation. In addition, in the perspective of the fifth dimension, the context is the sum of all the people who depend on one another for the relational establishment of the Self. She also reminds us that there is no hierarchy between the five dimensions. They always co-exist.

As discussed above, Catherine Ducommun-Nagy (2021)[2] brings a new terminology in the discussion of injustices. She renames the terms *retributive injustices* and *distributive injustices*, which Boszormenyi-Nagy borrowed from social and legal sciences and that have consequences for relationships. She prefers relational injustice for *retributive injustice*, as all retributive injustices happen in relationships and *situational injustices* for distributive injustices as a type of injustices that are due to life circumstances and cannot be repaired by anyone. These changes of terminology indeed help to understand the meaning of these types of injustices for relationships and to see that the elements that are at the root of these injustices can affect any of the other dimensions of relational reality. It is critical to understand that the goal is to restore fairness in the relation between all the parties affected by a situation. With regard to relational injustices, the focus should always be on redressing these injustices.

As we are aware, the South African Truth and Reconciliation Commission was committed to reaching this goal. Catherine Ducommun-Nagy indicates that, based on the definition in *Encyclopedia Britannica*,[3] restorative justice is a "response to criminal behavior that focuses on lawbreaker restitution and the resolution of the issues arising from a crime

---

2   This new terminology on injustices was presented for the first time during her plenary presentation *Loyalty and Solidarity* at the occasion of the online webinar *Seeking for Hope*, organized by the department of theology of the Stellenbosch University, South Africa, on 26 May 2021.

3   Heath-Thornton, Debra. "restorative justice". *Encyclopedia Britannica*, 26 August 2018, https://bit.ly/3Lx6NPy (Accessed 15 December 2022).

in which victims, offenders, and the community are brought together to restore the harmony between the parties. Restorative justice includes direct mediation and conflict resolution between the offender, the victim, their families, and the community". She challenges us as South Africans to do research on the possible applications of the guiding principles of contextual therapy or the dialogical intergenerational pastoral process (DIPP) to the field of restorative justice in our context.

Catherine Ducommun-Nagy acknowledges the destructive effect of poverty and discrimination on all the dimensions of relational reality. She indicates some examples of these injustices, such as the lack of clean water or sufficient food, and a lack of access to medical services that have a direct effect on health and life expectancy, etc. She also alerts us to the fact that the Covid-19 pandemic has just exposed these realities to a greater extent. In a few sentences, she manages to articulate the effect of poverty and discrimination in a way that illustrates her understanding. She states the following:

> The stress relating to poverty and discrimination can lead to various kinds of individual symptoms besides symptoms related to post traumatic stress disorder. People may become depressed, or they may get addicted to drugs or alcohol, etc. The systemic consequences of poverty are considerable. It can affect people's abilities to complete their education, forcing them to accept low-paying jobs, which then prevents them to move out of poverty. It can also lead people to engage in delinquent activities as a means of survival. However, most significantly, these situational (distributive) injustices lead to an accumulation of destructive entitlement, which in turn can become a source of relational injustices that have multigenerational consequences. In short, the multidimensional consequences of poverty and discrimination add many new layers of injustices to the original situational injustice, the inequity of the distribution of goods and opportunities.

Another new element in Section I is the introduction of a new terminology in the discussion of the process of exoneration. In the writings of Boszormenyi-Nagy, we have learned that he does not include the process of forgiveness as a therapeutic resource in his approach. Instead, he discusses a process that he calls 'exoneration'. Although there are many understandable reasons why he chooses the term *exoneration*, it is still true that many pastoral caregivers and counselors still struggle with this concept. Catherine Ducommun-Nagy acknowledges that this term can indeed be misleading "because parents remain responsible for the consequences of their actions, whether their children exonerate them or not." To decrease the confusion, she proposes that exoneration should rather be understood as a recategorization of the parents and a requalification of their actions. In terms of this reality, we need to realize that the goal of exoneration is not to absolve parents from their culpability, but to attempt to find mitigating factors and circumstances that can allow for a reappraisal of the degree of their culpability. This reappraisal depends in part on a requalification of the injustices that occurred in the family. This exposition is indeed very helpful.

As already mentioned, Catherine Ducommun-Nagy (2010 a) makes another significant contribution to this book by presenting a new form of genogram that is now based on the five dimensions of relational reality. Her method is to draw a standard genogram and then to encircle with a dimension specific color all people who have played a parental role in one or more dimensions of someone's life. This includes all the people who have been a resource in the dimension of relational ethics and in the ontic dimension. A significant benefit of this multidimensional genogram is that it can be very useful to help people remember the many individuals besides their biological parents who may have contributed to their lives as parental figures.

This new genogram is also extremely useful to visualize what kind of loyalty all these people may deserve based on the discussion of the five dimensions of loyalties that are also presented in this book. She indicates that by now two or three hundred professionals in Europe have had the occasion to build their own genogram in this fashion, and that many of them have started to use this multidimensional genogram in individual therapy and couple therapy, but that most professionals are still hesitant to use it in family counseling because family members could become resentful if they are not encircled with all the colors they expected. She fittingly indicates that this genogram could in fact be used with great success in family counseling as long as the counselor uses multidirected partiality to assist the family members to enter into a dialogue around the use of these colors. She also encourages professionals who may use this multidimensional genogram to present their treatment outcomes in publications, and that this should apply to anyone, including pastoral caregivers and counselors.

It is also very important to note that true to being committed to a contextual approach as well as operating within the principles of transdisciplinarity, Catherine Ducommun-Nagy positions herself with real honesty when she explains in the introduction of Section I what her point of departure is in writing this section. She indicates that she grew up and worked in the context of a homogeneous population in Switzerland and that after she moved to the USA, she spent many years working with the African American population of the inner city of Philadelphia. Of particular interest and very relevant to the South African and African context is that this population is severely affected by racial discrimination, poverty, and violence. She also indicates that she personally experiences faith diversity in her family. Furthermore, she spent time in North Africa to teach and also to visit family members. At the same time, she is clear and honest when she acknowledges her limitations regarding the needs of the South African and African contexts as well as the fact that she has never been to South Africa, nor to any other sub-Saharan countries. However, her experience in working with the African American population and the fact that she has experienced faith diversity does make her contribution on the relational emphasis of the contextual approach of value to the South African and African contexts.

To continue to develop the contextual approach in South Africa and in Africa, we need to ensure that we understand the fundamentals of the contextual approach as well as its core principals, goals, and origins. Catherine Ducommun-Nagy specifies what are these fundamentals in the first chapter of Section I. This should assist us in our responsibility to fully understand the approach before moving to translating it in the African context.

Clearly, the theory and practice presented in Section I by Catherine Ducommun-Nagy provides pastors, pastoral caregivers, spiritual counselors, and leaders in pluralistic networks with a strong framework for dealing extensively with the complex relational issues they encounter in their care and counseling in diverse settings. This is undoubtedly also the expectation of the second section of this book. It is clear that Section I should serve as a foundation for Section II, which is more specifically dedicated to the contextual approach in pastoral care, the pastoral process, and the interfaith dialogue in a multicultural context. It is my wish that all students as well as pastoral caregivers and practitioners will be able to draw inspiration from both sections of the book. It not only engages with real human contexts but also provides opportunities for people to relate to these examples to enable them to transform their lives and contexts. This engagement with the practical lives of people contributes significantly to the richness of the book but also to the fact that it brings hope to people struggling with complex and challenging issues in their lives.

Section II builds on the theory presented in Section I in a special way with its focus on pastoral care within the discipline of practical theology (Hanneke Meulink-Korf) and intercultural encounters within the discipline of interreligious studies (Greteke De Vries). This contribution introduces an approach in service of multireligious and multicultural settings with its scope on 'fair bridging'. It also emphasizes that the contextual approach opens up insights for intra- and interdisciplinary practice theory, practices, and trans-disciplinary research.

In Section II, Part I, Chapter 1, Hanneke Meulink-Korf writes eloquently on contextual pastoral care and counseling (CPCC), which is used in other parts of the world, and on the dialogical intergenerational pastoral process (DIPP) used specifically in South Africa and Africa. As someone who embodies the attitude CPCC or the DIPP requires, Hanneke Meulink-Korf begins her contribution on a personal note to indicate the journey she travelled in developing the CPCC. In her discussion, she indicates with boundless sensitivity that "in relational contexts of specific persons and groups, in concrete acts of trust and fairness, the particulars must be sought and found". She then reflects on the work done by pastoral caregivers in South African with persons and communities deeply affected by various serious injustices, including the ongoing effects of apartheid. She honestly acknowledges that the specific insights and inspirations from African philosophies that are related to the contextual theory are referred to only modestly in this text. However, she states clearly that their challenging views on transgenerational wisdom, social and relational justice, and an inclusive philosophy of life, are relevant to the CPCC and the DIPP.

What I find specifically meaningful is how Hanneke Meulink-Korf presents the assumptions that have played a profound role in the development of her theory, namely "human life as given from beyond; autonomy through heteronomy; personal suffering because of the suffering of others; the other/Other as disturbing countenance for genuine humane encounters; patience and perseverance as relevant for a pastoral relation with someone who suffers; asymmetry in reciprocity as prior to symmetry; responsibility and respondability." She further indicates that although she is personally connected with Christian theology and therefore cannot avoid or hide it in her writings, she nevertheless hopes to inspire and inform the work of pastoral caregivers and spiritual practitioners of any faith tradition, as well as that of those who adhere to a secular philosophy. Presenting these assumptions as well as her starting point contribute significantly to the mature way the theory is presented in this section. In this regard, she is of the opinion that pastoral practitioners always "need to be open to the contributions of other theories, provided that the contextual hermeneutics of the pastoral process as intergenerationally and dialogically directed and orientated on justice, remain at the center."

Hanneke Meulink-Korf focuses in the first chapter mainly on basic principles and hermeneutics that are essential for the CPCC and the DIPP. She argues for an inclusive anthropological theological thinking, with a specific goal to broaden the framework of pastoral, religious, and interreligious practices. The core of the outlines she presents in this chapter is that human reality is a thoroughly relational reality that should always be oriented on fairness, and there should always be a calling for justice. In this regard, she emphasizes caring for others and that it is the other, or the Other, that summons us to responsibility, a heteronomous responsibility. She states: "Giving to others is often without direct reward. But there can be, as an indirect reward, a certain trust that in this way one contributes to the well-being of his neighbor and to a more just human world."

In Chapter 2, Hanneke Meulink-Korf focusses on contextual pastoral care in practice, with attention to religion-related issues. This chapter links the theory and the practice very skillfully to assist pastoral caregivers to be responsible in the way they care for those in need. Apart from discussing the key aspect of relationality, she explains and indicates the importance and practice of connecting listening, connecting speech, and re-engagement in giving. This is well illustrated and demonstrated practically for pastoral caregivers and counselors to learn how to use it in counseling. I personally find the section on religion and theology as an obstacle in relational ethics and the pitfalls that occur in counseling as well as the way religion can be a motivational resource for relational ethics, very insightful for pastoral caregivers and counselors.

The second part of Section II is a contribution by Greteke De Vries that focuses on fair bridging as an ethics of caring in intercultural worlds. Her point of departure is to emphasize that pastoral caregivers and practitioners need to be sensitive in intercultural relations. She states that sensitivity to ethnic, cultural, and religious differences should be essential to contextual caregivers and practitioners. She explains sensitivity within the framework of the contextual theory as not only valuing what is important to others, but also nurturing the human ability to be touched by situational and relational injustices including the ability to contribute to fair relationships, both within one's own cultural group and outside of it.

She lays the foundation for her contribution by indicating the complex relational situations in which people all over the world find themselves due to the emancipation of disadvantaged communities, imperialist and separatist violence, migratory flows, communication technologies, more widely available means of transportation, and individualization – people breaking out of their own social groups. In this regard, she correctly indicates that "Family members struggle with changing relationships, communities disintegrate and they close borders. Many choose solutions to escape these problems that they base solely on their own interpretation of facts, their personal emotions, their desired social structures and on their own perception of relational fairness and unfairness".

Given our past history of racial discrimination that was even later written into law and practiced as apartheid, we as South Africans are well aware of most of these struggles. The depth and devastating effect of this inhuman policy not only affected the previous generations but also will continue to affect future generations. It is still commendable that we have undergone a transition in South Africa in 1994 when the first democratic election was held and we implemented a Truth and Reconciliation Commission (TRC) in the late nineties to assist the nation to attempt to face the effects of the past atrocities on the people of our country. The critical mistake we as pastoral caregivers and practitioners in South Africa can make is to assume that we are already almost 30 years into the so-called new South Africa and therefore we are so used to working in an intercultural context that the content in this Section is not really that relevant. On the contrary, South Africans are currently experiencing the highest level of distrust in all sectors of our country. We are also continuing to struggle with racial tension in the functioning of many of our societies on all levels. The content of this section by Greteke De Vries is not only relevant to South African pastoral caregivers and practitioners, but it is also critical and essential to continue to be exposed to it as we can never take it for granted because it will still take generations to heal the effects of the past on our society. The goal of this section can be echoed as it wants to inspire pastoral caregivers and practitioners to commit themselves to bridge gaps between individuals and communities in multicultural worlds.

As necessary in this section, the author pays attention to the definition of the key terms she will use. She indicates that the "term *interreligious* is used for the academic interdisciplinary field that studies the interaction between different traditional religions, spiritualities, philosophies of life, their narratives, values, and practices. The term *interfaith* or *interpath* is used alternatively, especially in the context of dialogue and organized meetings. The term *intercultural* indicates interaction between people of different beliefs, ethnicities, and cultures."

The focus on interfaith engagement and dialogue is of great value for us as pastoral caregivers and practitioners who work in public institutions as well as in communities. We as South Africans and Africans indeed still have a long way to go in exploring interfaith dialogue. In this sense, we can benefit immensely from the theory and methods for bridging religious, cultural and ethnic divides. More special is that Greteke De Vries engages with these theories and methods from the vantage point of contextual approach, which offers guidelines and practices for working with families in different contexts. The goal of her integration is to deepen our explorations and discussions of perspectives of fairness and injustice in multicultural worlds, which should contribute to increase the sensitivity of contextual caregivers and practitioners and all who contribute to fair bridging. She illustrates how caregivers and practitioners need to go about 'bridging the gap' very practically using the example of Margaret and Nasr, two colleagues from different religious, cultural and ethnic backgrounds. She analyzes the way they greet each other through the lenses of the five dimensions of relational reality. Then she specifically pays attention to loyalty, destructive and constructive entitlement, enriched by observations coming from interreligious studies.

The essential part of Greteke De Vries's contribution is that she demonstrates that fairness in relationships is important for the process of interreligious and intercultural engagements and that all organized interreligious meetings need to be dealt with relationally and ethically.

I want to thank the authors for writing this book in English so that it is accessible for more students in pastoral care and counseling, pastoral practitioners, pastoral caregivers, and counselors throughout the world, especially in Africa. My sincere hope is that this contribution will contribute to the further development of the CPCC and in particular the DIPP in Africa.

Preface

Catherine Ducommun-Nagy, Hanneke Meulink-Korf & Greteke De Vries

We, the three authors of this book were brought together by contextual therapy, the approach founded by Ivan Boszormenyi-Nagy. Two of us, Hanneke Meulink-Korf and Greteke De Vries already had professional contacts and Catherine Ducommun-Nagy had met Hanneke Meulink-Korf during contextual therapy conferences but the three of us met together for the first time only in 2014 at the international conference *Ethics, motivational force and resource in therapy and pastoral care* organized by the Protestant Theological Institute of Cluj-Napoca/Kolozsvár (Rumania). At this occasion, Greteke De Vries presented to the audience the Hungarian translation of Catherine Ducommun-Nagy's French book on family loyalties *Ces Loyautés qui nous libèrent,* (Ducommun-Nagy, 2006, 2014) that had been commissioned by the Foundation for Contextual Pastoral Care in The Netherlands (Stichting Contextueel Pastoraat). Since then, we have been in constant contact and have engaged in dialogue with one another on contextual therapy, its core principles, its practice, and especially its relevance for pastoral care and counseling, as well as intercultural encounters. In this book, we present the results of our cooperative endeavor to colleagues, practitioners and students who are involved in similar disciplines. We hope that our findings will also benefit professionals who come from a wide range of other backgrounds.

But before we go further, we need to explain how this book came about and why it is published in South Africa. In 2017, Prof Thesnaar, a teacher and researcher in the Department of Practical Theology and Missiology at the faculty of theology of the Stellenbosch University, South Africa started a two-years Master Program in Clinical Pastoral Care that has a special focus on the Dialogical Intergenerational Pastoral Process (DIPP). This approach to pastoral care is based in great part on the principles of the contextual approach and Hanneke Meulink-Korf became a guest teacher in this program. As there was a need for new teaching material in English, Prof Thesnaar was interested in a possible translation of *Ces loyautés qui nous libèrent* into English. He asked Hanneke Meulink-Korf to examine if this was possible but Catherine Ducommun-Nagy 's response was negative. She believed that her book, which was originally written in French and in a European context, would not sufficiently address the needs of these students. For this reason, she offered to write a new text not just on loyalties but also on contextual therapy in general. After long discussions between the three of us, and in consultation with Prof Thesnaar, we settled on the idea of writing an entire new book that would also include a section dedicated to contextually inspired pastoral care and interfaith meetings and do it jointly.

We are motivated in our venture by many years of experience in practice, in research and in teaching in a variety of academic and private training programs. To be more specific, Catherine Ducommun-Nagy, the author of Section I, is a Swiss-born and Swiss-trained adult and child psychiatrist who came into contact with contextual therapy very early in her career on the occasion of Boszormenyi-Nagy's teaching tours in Switzerland in the early 1980s. She soon became his interpreter for French language, and later his colleague in the USA, and now his widow after twenty years of marriage. The first author of Section II, Hanneke Meulink-Korf, was one of the first Dutch professionals who invited Boszormenyi-Nagy to lecture in The Netherlands. She and Greteke De Vries, the second author of Section II, are both Dutch Protestant theologians who have been deeply involved in contextual therapy, its practice, and its application to pastoral care and theology for a very long time.

Our commitment to the contextual theory and practice is not merely based on professional choices. Our personal experiences have also been at the root of this preferential orientation. Therefore, each of us will add some biographical information to our writings. We hope that our personal stories will inspire readers to fruitfully recognize their own experiences in our texts.

This book is divided into two interrelated sections. Its common denominator is relational ethics and the five-dimensional model of relational reality developed by Boszormenyi-Nagy in part as an attempt to engage professionals in a multidisciplinary dialogue about therapy and prevention. Section I entails a detailed exposure of the core tenets of contextual therapy and its most recent developments, with special attention to the presentation of the five dimensions of relational reality, an extensive presentation of relational ethics, and an extensive discussion of group and family loyalties. This section entails multiple clinical examples drawn from the author's own clinical and teaching experience.

Both authors of Section II built upon the new inputs of Section I to develop new insights into the contributions of contextual therapy to practical theology and pastoral care. Hanneke Meulink-Korf brings a relational and intergenerational perspective on the hermeneutics of theological and pastoral care practitioners. Greteke De Vries explores dynamics in intercultural relationships in the light of relational ethics. She also introduces the reader to the resources that the contextual approach can offer to interreligious studies and interfaith encounters and to the challenges brought by a growing cultural diversity in an increasingly polarized world. In addition, she alerts practicing contextual therapists and pastoral counselors to the need of acquiring sufficient training on social diversity in multicultural communities.

In his time, Boszormenyi-Nagy was particularly concerned about environmental pollution, and about the human rights of minority peoples. The first decades of the 21st century have presented us with new ecological, economic and political crises, as well as mass migrations due to wars, famines and climate change. These profound changes in society worldwide have led to an increase of fear, distrust, resentment, and social and spiritual disorientation. These have impaired people's ability to show solidarity.

Today, the contextual approach draws our attention to our human tendency to look for culprits and make them pay for injustices that they did not cause. We may indeed turn against 'the others', the ones who stand outside our family and trusted groups. However, we know that an 'us versus them' mentality will be effective for a short time only. Scapegoating only provides relief in the short run, and only for the scapegoaters, of course not for the scapegoats. In fact, this attitude does lead to an acceleration of disintegration of societies. Here is a need for multilateral ethical concern and a demand for accountability on the part of all the parties involved. Furthermore, there is a need to understand the loyalty dynamics that could help groups to move from an 'us against them' to a 'we are all human beings' position.

These problems, as well as the effects of increased globalization, including the disintegration of traditional social relationships, will be considered from the specific angle of relational ethics, with special attention to group loyalty and its effect on intergroup solidarity.

Boszormenyi-Nagy also saw that there is always a risk that "parents will increasingly turn to their children for the fulfilment of their adult emotional dependency needs" (Boszormenyi-Nagy, 1987, 2014). This constitutes a form of parentification. The destructiveness that results from turning to offspring for reassurance may be less visible than the destructiveness that results from securing group cohesiveness by creating scapegoats. Sadly, this serious parentification also has destructive multi-generational consequences. There is indeed a great risk that in turn, these children will use their offspring as a source of compensation for the injustice they incurred as parentified children. Therefore, the mandate of contextual therapy should include the task of educating society about the consequences of unfair burdening and exploitation of children. In our book, professionals will be able to learn about methods of intervention that could help parents to experience indirect personal benefits that come from caring about the needs of their children instead of relying on them as a source of compensation for the hardships they have experienced in their own lives. The fact that generous giving and generous caring benefit both the giver and the receiver is the main source of therapeutic optimism in contextual therapy.

In this book, we seek to provide perspectives and guidelines for the practice of contextual therapists and other contextual practitioners. We also examine the consequences of the vast changes that have occurred in modes of communication because of the Internet and social media and the rapid development in artificial intelligence that are going to affect the practice of therapy, including contextual therapy, and the changes that have already occurred in the practice of family therapy due to the increased influence of neurosciences.

We believe that what we offer will also enrich the insights of psychiatrists, individual psychotherapists and family therapists, whatever school they come from. This is consistent with Boszormenyi-Nagy's wish that his view of contextual therapy as an integrative approach and his definition of the mandate of therapy as caring for the future generations should inform not only contextual therapists but also professionals who are striving for processes of revitalizing relationships.

Finally, we point out that all examples in this book are from real-life situations unless otherwise noted, but all examples are redacted to prevent the identification of any specific individuals.

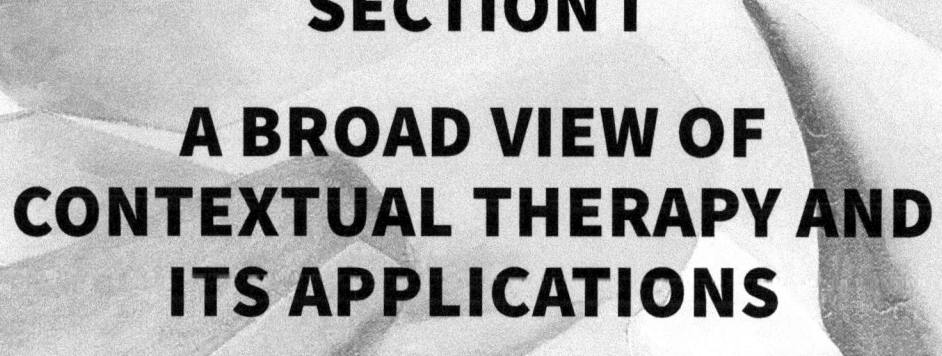

SECTION I

A BROAD VIEW OF CONTEXTUAL THERAPY AND ITS APPLICATIONS

CATHERINE DUCOMMUN-NAGY

Prologue to Section I

As discussed in the preface, Section I is dedicated to the presentation of the fundamentals of contextual therapy and its general uses. This includes a discussion of the theoretical principles that are at the base of any of its applications, its methods of intervention and its general goals. In this section, the focus is placed on the practice of contextual therapy as such, not as much on its applications to other fields. However, the clinical examples that have been chosen to illustrate this section should inform not only therapists and mental health counselors, but also pastoral counselors and to any professionals in the very broad field of human services. It should also serve as a foundation for Section II, which is dedicated to the contextual approach to pastoral care, the pastoral process, and the inter-faith dialogue in a multicultural context. It is my wish that all our readers can draw inspiration from both sections of the book.

As the author of this section, I come to the task of writing on contextual therapy from a rather unique background that I would like to make as explicit as possible to the reader. I am a Swiss-born and Swiss-board-certified specialist in child and adult psychiatry and psychotherapy who also hold a doctorate degree centered on the history of psychotherapy. Early on in my career, I was asked to present a family to Boszormenyi-Nagy on the occasion of his 1980 lecture tour to Switzerland. This consultation became a turning point in my career and the beginning of a professional cooperation that included many facets. I functioned as a co-organizer and co-teacher in the training programs offered by the Institute for Contextual Growth Inc., a private institute that he had founded in Ambler, near Philadelphia, of which I am now the owner and president. I also functioned as an interpreter during his lecture tours in the French-speaking domain for close to twenty years. After I moved to the USA in 1987, I began to teach contextual therapy classes in the Master Program in Couple and Family Therapy that he had founded at Hahnemann University in Philadelphia, often also substituting for him during his European lecture tours. Later, when the Master Program transferred to Drexel University, I continued my teaching on contextual therapy with the rank of Clinical Associate Professor. In addition, for over ten years, I also taught a class in nosology, the science of individual diagnosis, to the program's students and this experience helped to better define the place of contextual therapy in the treatment of mental illnesses. Most importantly, however, our collaboration extended to the co-development of contextual therapy, which included for instance my advisory contribution to *Foundations of Contextual Therapy* (Boszormenyi-Nagy, 1987, 2014: xxi) that was based on my experience in the field of the history of psychotherapy. Given the many levels of interactions we had over thirty years of professional collaboration and twenty years of marriage, it will not be always possible to sort out the knowledge that I have gathered from a systematic study of his writings from the knowledge that I have gathered in decades of dialogue with him. Despite this difficulty, I shall try my best to provide the reader with accessible references whenever feasible.

My presentation of the approach is obviously also informed by my own clinical experience that is based on years of working with adults suffering from severe mental illnesses and children suffering from developmental disorders in Switzerland and then years of work with disfranchised and homeless youths in Philadelphia after my move to the USA. While I shall not mention myself as the therapist, a number of the examples I use as illustrations come from these past experiences.

As already mentioned in our common preface, our case examples have been redacted in a way that prevents the identification of any individuals. My clinical illustrations may involve the description of rather specific elements on which I base my explanations of the approach or its applications, but the reader should not take any of this information as a clue about possibly identifiable people. Not only their identifying information has been changed, but these examples come randomly from two continents at random time periods. Furthermore, the language of the interviews should not be assumed from the choice of replacement first names. They have been chosen to fit in an English language publication, not because of the original identity of the clients. Pertaining to the examples I take from consultations with Boszormenyi-Nagy, the reader should know that these interviews occurred in the presence of a professional audience with the families' full knowledge that these consultations will be used not only to help them but also for teaching purposes.

I hope that theses illustrations will be informative enough to speak to professionals outside of the horizons that are familiar to me: the rather homogeneous population of Switzerland in the 80s and then from the late 80s in the USA, the African American population of Philadelphia inner city, a population affected by racial discrimination, poverty and violence, as well as the more ethnically diverse and better-off population of its suburbs. At the same time, through my international teaching, I have met professionals from many parts of the world. They have helped me expand my knowledge about families and societies. Furthermore, I have been exposed to a great diversity in my family of origin. Although I was born and raised in the French-speaking part of Switzerland, my family of origin have slowly turned into a patchwork family that includes members all the way from Afghanistan to Morocco, with a variety of faiths, Protestants of various denominations, Muslims, and on my side, a deep involvement with Buddhism, and with the Tibetan community in Philadelphia. In addition, I am associated with the Roman Catholic faith through my late husband's family. I can only hope that this level of exposure to diversity has contributed to enlarge my thinking about relationships.

At the same time, I need to acknowledge a limitation that may affect my ability to meet the needs of the South African pastoral counselors who will use this book as a reference on contextual therapy and pastoral counseling. While I have taught extensively in Algeria and spent time in Morocco and the United Arab Emirates to visit family, I have never had the opportunity to travel to South Africa, or to any other sub-Saharan countries. To overcome this limitation, I have done my best to inform myself through readings and discussions with colleagues and friends who have had a direct experience of South Africa.

Coming back now to the context of writing this book, I have seen the invitation to present contextual therapy in a book at this stage of my life as a great opportunity to take a new look at the main aspects of contextual therapy and its presentation. In doing so, I have tried to anticipate the questions of readers who are familiar with contextual therapy and readers who are new to this field. This has led me to pay great attention to present my ideas and my example with sufficient details to avoid as much confusion as possible. Hence, I ask the reader for patience, trusting that my effort will be understood.

As already discussed in the book foreword, I shall introduce new terminology in the discussion of injustices (Ducommun-Nagy, 2021). In brief, Boszormenyi-Nagy distinguishes two kinds of injustices that have consequences for close relationships: retributive injustices, injustices that occur within relationships and distributive injustices, injustices that are related to unfortunate circumstances in our lives. There is now a change of terminology for these two types of injustice. Retributive injustices become relational injustices, and distributive injustices become situational injustices. This proposed change of terminology will be discussed in detail and should contribute to a better understanding of these two types of injustices and their relational consequences. I shall also introduce a new way of thinking and a new terminology in the discussion of exoneration. I trust that the introduction of these new terms and new ideas will be helpful.

Here, I want to express my gratitude to Dr Alexander Berzin, a scholar of Tibetan Buddhism with whom I have been in a long-term dialogue about contextual therapy. Not only, did he advocate for changes of terminology in these two areas, but he also helped me to come up with a better formulation in the presentation of some of the important points pertaining to the dialectic theory of the personality. This resulted in the publication of a joint article in 2019.[1] This is also the place to acknowledge the contribution of my two co-authors, Hanneke Meulink-Korf and Greteke De Vries, to my section of our book. They have not only endorsed these changes in their own texts, but also have helped me to define my new views better, thanks to their patient review of the different stages of my manuscript and thanks to their ongoing constructive comments and suggestions.

---

1   https://bit.ly/41BNytS

Also, in this book, the reader will be introduced to a new form of genogram that I have presented for the first time on the occasion of a family therapy conference (Ducommun-Nagy, 2010a). Since then, I have used it in seminars specially designed for professionals who are interested in presenting their own genogram as a didactical tool to learn more about the five dimensions of reality and the five dimensions of loyalties. Although I have offered these seminars for more than a decade in several countries of Europe, it will be the first time here that this material will be presented in a written form.[2]

---

[2] Professionals who want to discuss this special genogram should make a mention of this book in their references.

Chapter 1
Fundamentals of Contextual Therapy

Introduction

Contextual therapy, also referred to as contextual family therapy, was founded by Ivan Boszormenyi-Nagy (1920-2007), one of the pioneers of the family therapy movement, and it has been enriched over time by the contributions of several of his co-workers and students. All their work cannot be discussed here, but their contributions should be acknowledged. His model offers unique resources that can enrich the practice of professionals far beyond the field of family therapy. Contextual therapy is relevant for couple therapy, individual psychotherapy counseling in general, and especially for the pastoral counselors who have been inspired by contextual therapy in the development of their own approach to pastoral care. This will be the focus of Section II of this book. The principles that form the core of contextual therapy can also be very helpful to address issues encountered by social workers, educators, community workers, traditional healers, or anyone else within the broad field of human services. In addition, principles of contextual therapy can serve as a source of reflection in discussing social issues like systemic injustices, inter-group conflicts, forced migrations due to war or other major crisis, group terrorism, and youth radicalization. Here, the relevance of the model comes from an understanding of the multigeneration relational effect of injustices and from an understanding of family loyalties.

For contextual therapists, what happens in family relationships cannot be explained simply by either the individual determinants that are described in individual therapy and psychiatry or by the systemic factors that are described in classical family therapy. They propose that in addition to all these factors, the way in which we interact with others depends also on our expectation of fairness, reciprocity, and loyalty in close relationships. This notion is at the core of what contextual therapists call relational ethics. Most people who seek therapy bring up questions relating to justice and fairness at some point during their treatment: "Why should I do this for him? He never does anything for me"; "After all I have sacrificed for her, how can she refuse to help me?"; or "Why did this happen to me, it does not happen to other people?" During family therapy sessions, even young children may complain about injustices. Some believe that they are receiving less than their siblings are. Other children may feel that they are asked to do more than their brothers and sisters are.

How do the professionals respond to these kinds of questions? Some may ignore them as irrelevant to their therapeutic goals. For instance, psychoanalysts would not respond, since they focus on the internal world of their client, not on actual relationships or actual events.

Or, if therapists decide to respond to their clients' complaints about injustices, what kind of guidelines should they follow? Should they just advise their clients to accept their losses and move on? Should they encourage them to make claims and insist on getting their dues? How would they know what their clients really deserve?

Since most therapists are encountering these kinds of questions, one would assume that all schools of individual and family therapy have provided their practitioners with a framework to address these issues, but this is not the case. In fact, contextual therapy is a true exception in the world of psychotherapy and family therapy. Not only does it offer a methodology to address relational issues related to fairness and injustices, but the discussion of fairness and reciprocity has also been the central theme of contextual therapy since its beginning. Indeed, within the field of family therapy and psychotherapy in general, the first book to discuss the justice dynamics that are at the core of family relationships was *Invisible Loyalties* (Boszormenyi-Nagy & Spark, 1973, 2014). This early book was at the source of what later developed into contextual therapy. Its subtitle reads: *Reciprocity in intergenerational family therapy*, which underlines the centrality of issues of justice and fairness in families.

Among all counselors, pastoral counselors are especially likely to meet people who come for help because they have experienced losses or injustices. In many cases, the effect of these injustices extends well beyond the individuals who seek help. Since contextual therapy provides unique resources to address these injustices and their relational consequences, it is not surprising that in many countries, a good number of pastoral counselors have become interested in contextual therapy and find more resources in this approach than in any other school of family therapy.

The core principles of contextual therapy

Central to contextual therapy is the definition of relational ethics. Boszormenyi-Nagy writes about the definition of contextual therapy and relational ethics in the following terms: "The empirical basis of this therapy is the experience that, through attention to the issues of merit and fairness in relationships, a deeply relevant dynamic leverage becomes available for therapists" (Boszormenyi-Nagy, 1996: 317). Contextual therapists believe that fair and trustworthy relating in close relationships and in families is a source of healthy individual functioning and resilience at both individual and family levels. They believe that family loyalty can become a source of resilience when family members know that they can rely on one another. They also propose that, in good part, individual fulfilment and relational health result from our capacity for generous giving. Consequently, contextual therapists believe that exposure to injustices, especially within the parent-child relationship, can lead to individual and relational pathologies that can span over several generations. Family loyalties can also lead to various forms of individual and relational pathologies when people experience severe loyalty conflicts or when they can express their loyalty only in indirect and self-defeating ways.

The general goals of contextual therapy

In general, all schools of individual psychotherapy, couple and family therapy, and counseling aim at similar goals: a decrease in individual and relational pathologies, a decreased suffering, an increased level of personal satisfaction, an improved capacity for autonomous functioning, and an increased resilience. This is true of contextual therapy as well. In addition, however, it focuses on goals that are unique to this approach.

Contextual therapists aim at restoring fair and responsible relating between family members and fair giving and receiving between the generations. They also want to help people to find ways to express their loyalty in a direct and constructive fashion instead of expressing it in an indirect and destructive manner. When it comes to parent-child relationships, the most crucial therapeutic goal is to help parents who have experienced injustices in their own lives to find the resources to meet the needs of their children and to refrain from counting on them to be compensated for what they had not received in their own childhood. For instance, an important goal is to help parents to refrain from turning to their children to receive the love and affection that they could not get from their own parents.

Contextual therapists rely on a specific strategy, 'multidirected partiality', to promote fair relating in close relationships. This subject will be addressed in great detail later. By definition, the notion of multidirected partiality can be puzzling, since partiality contradicts the notion of multi-directedness; however, what is meant here is that contextual therapists take a stand of multilateral fairness. They want to offer each family member an opportunity to describe his or her predicament and own expectations in his or her own terms (partiality). At the same time, they make this offer to every person who is involved in the therapeutic process (multilateral fairness). It is assumed that once people are offered a fair chance to present their side, they will become more open to listen to others, and eventually more open to respond to their needs.

This strategy is applied consistently to all types of therapeutic encounters: family therapy, couple therapy, individual therapy, counseling, and pastoral counseling. This principle can also be extended to societal situations in which members of various ethnic or religious groups need to engage in a dialogue.

Giving: A resource in relationships and a resource in therapy

In contextual therapy, the main resource comes from helping people to discover that they can gain something for themselves when they try to meet the needs of others. In contextual therapy, the healing moment is defined relationally as a moment of a dual benefit. It occurs at the moment when a person is willing to make a gesture towards another person. When a person can show generosity to another person, both sides benefit. For the beneficiary of the gesture, the gain is obvious: it is whatever the giver has offered. At the same moment, the giver experiences an indirect benefit from his or her action in the form of what contextual therapists call *constructive entitlement*. In Christian traditions, this form of entitlement could be defined as merit. In Buddhism scriptures, one finds the notion that positive deeds lead to an accumulation of 'merits', and to a better life in the present or the future. In Studybuddhism.com, Berzin proposes to use the term 'positive potentials' or 'positive force' instead of 'merits' since positive actions lead to positive consequences. The notion that positive actions lead to positive potentials in the future fits well with the notion that constructive entitlement earned as the result of acting constructively leads to positive results in the person's life.

Constructive entitlement

Contextual therapists propose that constructive entitlement results in an increase in self-worth, self-esteem, and self-definition that does not depend on the reaction of the beneficiary of the gesture. For instance, when parents are generous enough to give more to their children than what they had received from their own parents, parents earn constructive entitlement, whether their children are aware of their effort or not. In this view, true giving is not entirely altruistic because it leads to some benefit for the Self, but at the same time, calculated giving, i.e. giving with the expectation of a return, including a return in the form of constructive entitlement, would lead to a loss of this benefit.

This indirect gain is now validated by the work of neuroscientists and other researchers who have become interested in documenting the benefits of compassion and altruism for physical and mental health (Ricard, 2015). As a result, generous giving can lead to more positive individual and relational results than an insistence on fair receiving. The fact that generous giving does not require a capacity for altruism is very important. If therapists had to count on parents' capacity for altruism to show generosity to their children, there would not be much hope for changes. Here, however, giving does not require altruism. If therapists can help their clients to discover that they can benefit when they show some generosity to others, there is a realistic hope for positive changes both at an individual and at a relational level. Indeed, even people who do not seem to care about fairness can discover that they befit when they begin to treat others better, and this becomes an important source of therapeutic optimism.

The general fields of applications of contextual therapy

Within the field of mental health, contextual therapy is used as a treatment modality to address the needs of patients suffering from a diagnosed mental illness and their families. While contextual therapists do not believe that this approach as such can cure mental illnesses, they want to address the relational problems that could exacerbate them. Like all professionals, contextual therapists understand mental illnesses in terms of their psychological effect, for instance changes in mood, or cognitive changes. They also understand the effect of mental illnesses on transactions, for instance difficulties in communicating with others.

In addition, however, contextual therapists see mental illnesses as a source of injustices that have long-term negative consequences for the patients and for their families. For this reason, they see the restoration of fairness and trust between family members as an important treatment goal. They do not believe that the restoration of trust between family members can be curative, but they do believe that the restoration of fair relating between family members can become a source of resilience that can decrease the negative effect of these illnesses.

Within the larger field of counseling, including pastoral counseling, and in a great variety of fields, such as social work, education, and nursing, contextual therapy can be used as an approach that can apply to a large range of situations in which individuals experience personal difficulties or difficulties in couple and family relationships. For instance, it can be very useful to address the situation of adolescents and adult children who feel caught between their own aspirations and their parents' expectations. This can occur in many circumstances. They may choose a partner who is not approved by their parents or may engage in a career that disappoints them, etc.

The contextual approach is also very useful to address situations related to the disruption of the parent-child relationship (divorce, adoption, placement due to abuse or neglect, etc.). In all these situations, children depend on adults who may not cooperate with each other, and this can become the source of severe loyalty conflicts.

Another important area of application pertains to the disruption of the giving and receiving between parents and children and the parentification of the children. As already mentioned, parents who have been exposed to injustices may turn to their children to receive what they did not get from the prior generations, instead of being able to meet their children's needs. In all these applications, one of the most important foci of intervention is always prevention. Here, prevention means that contextual therapists and professionals whose work is inspired by contextual therapy want to include the interests of the future generations in their treatment goals and in their interventions.

When used as an approach, contextual therapy can also offer guidelines to address larger societal issues. It can be the multigenerational effect of poverty and discrimination on relationship or the effect of globalization on group loyalties. The approach also offers resources for preventing the violent radicalization of youths, or even for the prevention of forms of terrorism that are based on group loyalty.

The origins of contextual therapy and its development

Introduction

Boszormenyi-Nagy has a unique history that has played an important role in the development of his model of therapy and set him apart from the other pioneers of family therapy (see Ducommun-Nagy, 2002). Here are the most pivotal points that brought him to the founding of contextual therapy. Born in Hungary in 1920, he reports that the impetus to become a psychiatrist came from an experience he had as a teenager vacationing in a small village: he witnessed how villagers harassed a man who was suffering from psychosis just because he was strange. He was struck by the unfairness of the situation: not only was this man hearing voices, already a distressing experience, but in addition, people were cruel towards him. He saw this as a tremendous injustice that he wanted to redress by becoming a psychiatrist and by finding a cure for schizophrenia. He not only succeeded to become a psychiatrist, but also studied biochemistry to be able to engage in research about the biological determinants of schizophrenia.

After arriving in the USA as a political refugee in 1950, he spent six years doing biochemistry research and returned to clinical work only when he realized that he could not reach his research goals. However, his experience as a scientist never left him. He then became the director of a research unit on schizophrenia at the Eastern Pennsylvania Institute in Philadelphia. There he and his team discovered that meeting patients individually was much less productive than seeing them with their relatives. This discovery led him to move towards family therapy as one of the pioneers of this movement. During that time, he discovered that the expectation of fairness and loyalty plays a major role in families.

The systemic paradigm

The pioneers of family therapy, including Boszormenyi-Nagy, shared a common belief about the sources of mental health and illnesses. They proposed that the problems we encounter in the form of individual pathology or relational difficulties need to be explained by supra-individual factors, not only by individual biological or psychological determinants. Since none of the models of individual psychotherapy could provide a theoretical framework for their discoveries, they turned to the general systems theory developed by L. von Bertalanffy (1968). It is a broadening of system theory that describes how the properties of a system emerge from the relationships between its smaller units, not from the simple sum of its parts. General systems theory extended this concept to the interdependence of all phenomena, and it had a major effect in human sciences. The pioneers of family therapy relied on this model to demonstrate that the functioning of a family cannot be explained solely by an understanding of the individual functioning of each of its members. The explanation must also come from an understanding of the ways in which the behaviors of each of these individuals affect the entire family system.

The pioneers of family therapy also relied on cybernetics, which entails the study of communications and "the study of feedback mechanisms and circular causality in biological and social systems" (Von Foerster, Mead & Teuber, 1951). In this view, changes in the family system affect individual behaviors, and changes in individual behaviors affect the family system. Here comes the example of the thermostat. A change in the room temperature (the system) triggers a reaction in the thermostat (the individual) that triggers a change in the room temperature, and so on. In other words, there is a feedback mechanism in which the information about a change in the room temperature triggers a reaction that brings the system back to its prior state of equilibrium, i.e. the chosen room temperature. The change of paradigm from an individual perspective to a systemic one, and the move from a linear model of causality to a circular one was a true revolution in thinking about mental illnesses. The pioneers of family therapy had stopped thinking about symptoms as the result of fixed individual determinants, and they had begun to see them as the result of complex interactions between the parties involved in the family system, or in larger societal systems.

Until then, classical Western psychology and psychiatry had concentrated almost entirely on the individual determinants of our behaviors to explain our individual pathologies and our relational difficulties. As a result, until the emergence of the family therapy movement, the field of mental health was focused entirely on individual treatment methods. Over time, individual psychotherapy had developed into hundreds of approaches, anything from full-fledged psychoanalysis to psychodynamic psychotherapy, cognitive-behavioral therapy, etc. In addition, over the years, the field of psychopharmacology developed enormously to the great benefit of people suffering from severe mental illnesses, but this led also to the progressive abandonment of more holistic approaches to their care.

While the systemic perspective on health and illness was a revolution for European and North American therapists, the view that health and pathology could not be ascribed solely to individual determinants had already a parallel in many cultures. In many societies, traditional healers attribute our individual pathologies and the difficulties we experience to imbalances in our relationship with our environment. It could be imbalances in our relationship with our family, our clan, our ancestors, or even imbalances in our relationship with nature in general. From their point of view, healing requires a restoration of this balance. To reach this goal, they rely on a great variety of methods, in part based on traditional medicine or shamanism, and this can include all sorts of rituals and prayers. Only recently, the resources offered by these multiple traditions have been recognized in the field of mental health.

From early systemic thinking to current practices

Based on their systemic hypotheses, many early systemic therapists proposed that the emergence of psychotic symptoms in one family member could be related to the self-regulating process by which the family system tries to maintain its equilibrium over time, or in other words to maintain its homeostasis. For instance, when youths begin to present psychotic symptoms at the time when they are supposed to reach a news step towards autonomy like graduating from school, or leaving home to pursue their education, their symptoms will prevent them from reaching these new steps: they may have to stop attending school or they may not be able to leave home. The systemic explanation is that these youths are not mentally ill per se, but their symptoms serve a purpose for the whole family. Due to their psychotic symptoms, they cannot move to these new steps. Consequently, the family system is not forced to adapt to change. They then established methods to try to shake the resistance of the system to changes that vary from one school of systemic family therapy to the other. However, in any of these approaches, one problem remained: since the system is an abstract notion, not a person with intentions, the danger of these models was that it was attributing the resistance to changes implicitly to the parents.

While the early systemic family therapists never had the intention of accusing parents of causing their child's illness, it was difficult for these parents not to feel blamed by family therapists, which brought discredit to the family therapy movement in general. Also, because they were postulating that the individuals who presented with psychotic symptoms were not actually sick, most of the early systemic family therapists were against the use of anti-psychotic medications to treat these patients. Their position also closed the door to the integration of the contributions of neurosciences with their model of therapy.

This is where Boszormenyi-Nagy stands apart from all the other pioneers of family therapy: he not only was trained as a psychiatrist, but uniquely among all of the founders of family therapy and any of the later developers of the field, he was also trained as a research biochemist. For him, there are no doubts that schizophrenia and other major mental illnesses have neuro biological bases. For this reason, he was determined to make a place for the individual biological determinants of our behaviors in his model of family therapy. Consequently, he also did not have any objection to the use of psychotropic medication to threat a client's individual symptoms during the course of family therapy treatment. His position and the fact that he made a place for the biological determinants of mental illnesses in his model not only allow for a more integrated view of all the factors that can play a role in mental illnesses, but also places contextual therapy at an advantage for the future. No matter what new explanations about mental illnesses can come from the further development of neurosciences, the model is ready to integrate them without losing its coherence.

Contextual therapy and the newer developments in family therapy

The most significant evolution in the field of systemic family therapy was a move from first-order cybernetics to second-order cybernetics. Von Foerster (1995) differentiated first-order cybernetics as "the cybernetics of observed systems" and second-order cybernetics as "the cybernetics of observing systems". In short, systemic therapists came to the realization that therapists cannot be external objective observers of the family system: as observers, they affect the system, and the system affect them too. This led to the view that reality is co-constructed, and to a move to narrative forms of therapy including the solution-focused therapy or integrative approaches like the open dialogue developed in Finland (cf. open-dialogue.net). One advantage of these approaches is that they involve family members, especially parents, in a much more cooperative way, which constitutes a great improvement by comparison with the older classical systemic models of therapy. From the point of view of contextual therapy, however, these narrative models entail two risks, namely the risk of dismissing factual elements like the biological determinants of mental illnesses, and the risk of relativizing injustices as part of a narrative rather than the sources of actual damages. Also, with these cooperative approaches comes the risk that it becomes more difficult to address situations in which parents in fact do contribute to their children's presenting problem, or to unexpected setbacks in their treatment.

While contextual therapists have pointed out the possible drawbacks of the narrative and cooperative approaches to family therapy, the therapists who have moved to approaches that are based on second-order cybernetics and the postmodern family therapists in general have a tendency to see contextual therapy as outdated. In other words, they see contextual therapy as an approach that is still based on first-order cybernetics like the earlier forms of systemic family therapist. It is true that contextual therapists do formulate hypotheses about the nature of relationships and the origins of pathology and general treatment goals that are not the result of direct results of a co-construction with their clients, and that they use a method of intervention, multidirected partiality, which is consistently applied to all treatment situations. This could induce the belief that contextual therapy is indeed part of the older models of therapy. To the contrary, however, one could propose that contextual therapy is an approach that goes even beyond any of the postmodern approaches.

While not talking about co-construction, contextual therapists define relational ethics, which is so central to the approach, as a form of ethics that requires a dialogue between the parties involved, and they postulate that the definition of fairness can only be intersubjective. Also, their method of intervention, multidirected partiality, intends to promote a dialogue between all the parties involved. Furthermore, contextual therapy is neither past oriented nor focused on the resolution of symptoms. It is resource oriented and in many ways solution focused. People are encouraged to discover for themselves the resources that come from rediscovering what they can get when they are able to treat each other more fairly. In addition, contextual therapy goes even further than narrative and postmodern approaches by postulating that the very definition of the Self is relational.

Here it is interesting to note that when Von Foester was asked to speak on the subject of ethics and second-order cybernetics during a conference on systems and family therapy also attended by Boszormenyi-Nagy (Foerster, 1990), he concluded by quoting a passage from Buber's *Das Problem des Menschen*. The quote begins with the statement that in contemplating the human with the human, one sees a dynamic duality, the human essence. It ends with the statement that the encounter of the one with the other leads each time to a combination of awareness and gratefulness. Von Foester concluded at that point that he could not add anything to the word of Buber, and that it was all what he could say about ethics and second-order cybernetics.

Current practices in family therapy

Currently, most family therapists agree that they need to take the discoveries of neurosciences into account, and these discoveries have led them to new ways of practicing. They no longer believe that the prescription of medication undermines their work as family therapists. Some therapists have moved to techniques that are based on a neuro-psychological model of changes, for instance the use of EMDR (eye movement desensitization and reprocessing) developed by Shapiro (2001). This method has become very popular for the treatment of posttraumatic disorders. Another example is compassion-based psychotherapy, a new movement that is also very successful. It assumes that people should be helped to develop a capacity for compassion because it can bring them great benefit. This is based on the demonstration of the effect of compassion meditation on the brain and the positive effect of this type of meditation on health in general.

The move towards eclecticism in contemporary family therapy and its consequences

While more and more family therapists are adding these new treatment resources to their usual treatment modalities, one problem remains: this has not led to the development of truly new integrative models of therapy. Instead, one can observe that these therapists describe how they use these new resources in juxtaposition with other pre-existing treatment modalities, but in general they do not attempt to fully explore the theoretical implications of these juxtapositions for their model of family therapy.

Also, the newer generations of therapists are also more likely to apply methods that are based on traditional healing practices, including techniques inspired by shamanism. For instance, they may invoke invisible forces, or they may bring their patients into a trance with the hope that they can reconnect with healing forces. Furthermore, most senior therapists and counselors do not abide by a single model of intervention. They integrate all they have learned during their lifetime from various schools of therapy and mentors into a personal way of practicing. This would be true of pastoral counselors who integrate the principles of contextual therapy with their work, and pastoral counselors who are inspired by traditional practices. In general, therapists and counselors who become familiar with a variety of treatment approaches can be better prepared to serve the complex needs of their clients and their families. At the same time, the mixing of various approaches can also lead to significant problems.

When professionals try to use several approaches in the course of a treatment, they often need to shift between different roles. The switch of role and the change of direction of the treatment may be rather confusing for the family. For instance, therapists who try to combine interventions based on strategic family therapy with contextual therapy need to shift between a directive role when they prescribe a task to the family and a cooperative role when they engage the family members in a dialogue. This would be true of a therapist who can also prescribe medications.

In short, when professionals try to incorporate several approaches in their work with clients and families, there is always the danger of eclecticism, the danger of juxtaposing different approaches without sufficient consideration of their effect on the clients and on the course of their treatment. To avoid this, professionals would need to integrate their various practices in a coherent model of intervention, and a coherent treatment plan, which is a difficult task. Here, contextual therapy can serve as a blueprint for future models of therapy since its founder conceived it as an integrative approach right from the beginning.

Contextual therapy as an integrative approach

In his early writings, Boszormenyi-Nagy described his approach as 'intergenerational family therapy', but this terminology was not specific enough for him. He then used the concept *contextual family therapy* to mark the fact that contextual therapists include in their considerations not only the three generations that commonly interact with one another (parents, children, and grandparents), but also the past ancestors whose behaviors and life choices are still affecting us, as well as the generations of the future whose lives will be affected by our behaviors and our decisions, even if we shall never meet them. Later, he began to speak of *contextual therapy* rather than *contextual family therapy* to indicate that his approach could also be applied in the work with individuals, couples, or larger societal groups.

All these elements contributed to shape contextual therapy as an integrative approach. Obviously, like all the pioneers of family therapy, Boszormenyi-Nagy considered all the systemic factors that affect the functioning of families, and they have a place in his model of therapy. This is something contextual therapists should not forget. In contrast with most of his colleagues, however, he was convinced that any good model of family therapy should retain a place for the biological determinants of our behaviors. He also believed that the discovery of the supra-individual determinants of our behaviors did not require a rejection of all the knowledge that had been accumulated by individual therapists, and that family therapists should not dismiss the importance of individual psychological determinants of our behavior. Of course, the main characteristic of contextual therapy is that it gives a central place to the determinants of our behavior that relate to our expectation of justice, fairness, and loyalty in our relationships and to the relational consequences of injustices. Furthermore, Boszormenyi-Nagy followed the existential philosophers in proposing that the Self can be defined only in dependence on a relation with an Other, leading to a relational definition of autonomy.

In short, Boszormenyi-Nagy believed that any good therapy should include an evaluation of all the factors that can contribute to a given clinical situation or to a given presenting problem, and all the resources that can contribute to its resolution. When asked about the future of therapy and about his legacy, he answered:

> I was hoping that family therapists would know all what is needed from psychology or psychodynamics, all what is evolving from systemic dynamics relational factors and therefore be really an integrator of therapies for the benefit of the public, for the benefit of knowledge ... Now, there is a lot of work to be done: the unification of therapies, the intelligent information of the public – what kind of therapy do you really need, what kind of therapy delivers what, what qualifications to look for in therapists – how to understand all of that. I was hoping and I am still hoping that all of this is coming out of the development of family therapy.
>
> *(Video-taped interview with William Doherty during the 1992 AAMFT Annual Conference, Miami, USA. Transcription C. Ducommun-Nagy)*

Chapter 2
The Five Dimensions of Relational Reality

Introduction

As already discussed, contextual therapy presents itself as an integrative approach that try to account for all the determinants that could play a role in relationships and in the therapy process. To this effect, Boszormenyi-Nagy proposes a five-dimensional model of relational reality that is the result of his effort to group in coherent clusters all the factors (variables) that he believes are central to the understanding of individual and family dynamics. For years, he presented his model as a four-dimensional model that entails the dimensions of facts that includes all the givens of a person's life, the dimension of psychology that includes all the individual psychological features of a person, the dimension of transaction that includes all the systemic determinants that influence relationships, the dimension of relational ethics that includes all the determinants that relate to people's mutual expectation of fairness and loyalty, and to the relational consequences of injustices. He later added a fifth dimension to his four-dimensional model, namely the 'ontic dimension', which refers to the determinants of relationships that relate to the intrinsic mutual dependence between the Self and the Other, and to the relational definition of the Self. He introduced this new dimension during a plenary presentation at the occasion of the 2000 national conference of the Hungarian Family Therapy Association (Boszormenyi-Nagy, 2000). The first written presentation of the ontic dimension then appeared in a chapter on contextual therapy in *The Comprehensive Handbook of Psychotherapy* (Ducommun-Nagy, 2002).

The variables that are listed in the dimension of facts and in the dimension of psychology pertain to the individual characteristics of a person, for instance the age of a person, or this person's level of cognitive abilities. In other words, whether the person interacts with others or not, these characteristics always remain present. The variables described in the next three dimensions can manifest themselves only within a relationship. In the dimension of transaction, one cannot talk about triangulation if fewer than three people are involved. Similarly, one cannot talk about loyalty if there is no one to be loyal to, and the relational definition of the Self automatically implies an Other as a counterpart to the Self.

It is also important to note that all these variables co-exist at any given moment of a relationship, and in this perspective, there is no hierarchy between the five dimensions. This co-existence does not contradict the fact that contextual therapists prioritize the dimension of relational ethics both in terms of explanation of relational problems and in terms of therapeutic resources. Also, when Boszormenyi-Nagy (1987, 2014, chapter 19) proposes that the dimension of relational ethics should serve as an overarching dimension that unite all forms of individual and family therapy, he does not mean that this dimension is superior to the other dimensions. He means that all therapists need to care about the relational consequences of their interventions, no matter what form of individual or family therapy they practice.

The introduction of the new fifth dimension has brought a change to the definition of what constitutes the 'context' in contextual therapy. Originally, the term 'context' was used in contrast with the term 'system' to underscore the fact that contextual therapists do not limit their focus of intervention to the people who are part of a given observable family system. They extend their consideration to all the people who can be affected by their interventions, whether they are in physical contact or not, and all the people who are connected through giving and receiving in the present, the past and the future. It includes the current members of a family, partners, friends, ancestors who have contributed to their lives, and the future generations whose survival depends on a responsible attitude of the current generation. Hence, the context defined in contextual therapy is much larger than the family system that is the focus of attention of ordinary family therapists. In its newer definition, the context can also be understood as the sum of all the people who depend on one another for the 'relational establishment of the Self' (see below).

Many teachers of contextual therapy have not followed the changes caused by the introduction of the ontic dimension. Their main argument is that this new dimension does not add anything to the four-dimensional model they are familiar with, and that the dimension of relational ethics already contains all the elements that are now part of dimension V. This is obviously not the position of the founder of the approach.

Conversely, one could easily argue that this five-dimensional model is not sufficient to account for all the factors that affect human lives and relationships. For instance, many people would argue that spirituality is part of the factors that play an important role in our lives and in our relationships, and that it should be given a place as an added dimension in the multidimensional model proposed by Boszormenyi-Nagy. Here, it is important to note that Boszormenyi-Nagy does not include spirituality or religious beliefs as variables in his multidimensional model of relational reality. However, the fact that his definition of good therapy does not include the resources offered by religion, or by any form of spiritual practice means only that he wanted to keep contextual therapy within the confines of mental health sciences, not that he dismisses the importance of religion or spirituality in people's lives. Therefore, contextual therapists should not refrain from inquiring about their clients' religious beliefs and the resources that they can draw from their faith and spiritual practices.

Dimension I: The dimension of facts

Variables in Dimension I

This dimension entails the variables that pertain to all the givens of our life. This includes individual biological givens like our sex, physical appearance, physical abilities or disabilities, the biological determinants of physical or mental illnesses, and so on. It also includes the factual elements of our family history, like for instance our birth order (eldest child, youngest child), the early loss of one of our parents, or our parents' divorce. It includes all the socio-historical factors connected to the time and place of our birth, like been born in a time of peace or war, being born as a national of a stable country or born stateless. It includes our ethnicity and native language, and their consequences for our education and economical status leading to prominence or discrimination, affluence, or poverty, for instance.

Some of these givens are unchangeable and do not depend on our own actions, like the place of our birth, or the early loss of a parent. Other givens can be subject to change. We may grow up as the younger child in our family, but one of the parents may have a child in a new marriage while we are already an adult. Our physical characteristics at birth may be changed thanks to advances in surgery and medicine. People are now able to undertake a sex change. Also, surgeries may prevent people who are born with a congenital condition from becoming permanently disabled. For example, children who are born with congenital cataracts can have surgery to restore their eyesight before they become permanently blind. Socio-historical givens can change rapidly as well. For instance, changes in immigration laws can drastically change the life of people for the better or for the worse, depending on the changes. Another example is the Covid-19 pandemic that has killed millions of people and has abruptly changed the lives and the socio-economic status of millions of people around the world. The same is true of the invasion of Ukraine by Russian troops in early 2022. It not only has brought drastic changes in Europe, but also has led to decreases in food and energy supplies and to economic changes that have affected the entire planet.

Mental illnesses as a form of situational injustice

As already discussed, Boszormenyi-Nagy postulates that, at least to a good extent, major mental illnesses depend on neurobiological and possibly genetic factors, which are all variables in Dimension I. But at the same time, people who suffer mental illnesses are also victims: they have to live with the consequences of the unfortunate combination of the biological determinants that have caused their illness. In other words, by comparison with people who do not suffer from mental illnesses, they are the victims of a situational (distributive) injustice which has then consequences in the dimension of relational ethics. The view of mental illnesses as a source of injustices is unique in the field of mental health.

Resources in Dimension I

The therapeutic resources that belong to this dimension are quite diverse. They entail all the resources of medicine, especially the use of medication. Medication does bring individual benefits that can have a major effect in the dimension of fact, most obviously when a medication is a lifesaving one. Also, many illnesses, and specifically mental illnesses, do lead to difficulties in relating to others. Therefore, psychotropic medications like antidepressants or anti-psychotics not only help the patient who takes them but can also bring positive changes in their way of relating to others.

Surgery can also become a relational resource when people are helped to hear better (cochlear implants), to see better (cataract surgery) or when surgery can correct malformations that can lead to discrimination. For instance, children who are born with a cleft palate not only suffer from significant physical problems (feeding problems, speech impairment) but in many societies they are discriminated, and their malformation becomes a source of shame for their family. Hence these children also often experience low self-esteem. Here, restorative surgery would alleviate many of these problems.

Other resources can come from interventions that can change a person's entire life. For instance, an immigration lawyer or a specialized social worker can help a client to avoid deportation and to obtain permanent refugee status. This would have a direct and permanent effect not only on this person but also on this person's entire family.

In general, contextual therapists are not expected to intervene in this dimension unless they have added professional competences that are relevant in the dimension of facts, such as the ability to prescribe medication, expertise in immigration laws, etc. However, at the same time, contextual therapists need to pay attention to the factual elements of people's lives as a possible source of disparities, the source of situational (distributive) injustices, and then address the individual and relational consequences of these injustices.

Dimension II: The dimension of psychology

Variables in Dimension II

The dimension of psychology includes the variables related to our consciously expressed emotions and emotional needs. It encompasses all the unconscious drives and phenomena that are described in psychoanalysis and object relation theory. Some examples: are transference and counter-transference phenomena, unconscious defense mechanisms, unconscious projections of good or bad qualities onto others, and unconscious psychological processes involved in mourning.

It also includes our attachment style, gender identity, and sexual preferences. In addition, it includes all the variables that connect to our intellectual faculties (limited, average, superior), the level of a child's cognitive development or the amount of cognitive decline in an older person, the cognitive distortions studied in cognitive sciences and cognitive therapy, and ego states described in transactional analysis (parent, adult or childlike), etc.

Mental disorders (mental illnesses) and the dimension of psychology

Even if mental illnesses may have biological determinants, mental disorders by definition belong to the dimension of psychology. In short, mental illnesses cause changes in the emotional or cognitive functioning that can take the form of hallucinations, delusions, depression, suicidal ideations, anxiety, disassociation, memory loss, etc.

Resources in Dimension II

In general, the therapeutic resources associated with this dimension come from improving the individual functioning of people, which in turn can lead to an improvement in their relationships. These resources come from any of the hundreds of forms of individual therapy that are available today. These approaches have been inspired by psychoanalysis, behavioral cognitive therapy, and many other therapy movements. Most of these approaches aim at helping people to develop an insight into the conscious or unconscious motivations that bring them to act in ways that are either dissatisfying or destructive for themselves and for their relationships. In general, individual psychotherapists share many goals in common with contextual therapists: a decrease of pathology (individual symptoms of mental disorders or dysfunctions in relationships), an improved capacity for individuation and autonomous functioning, a greater level of personal satisfaction, and an increased resilience.

Within the dimension of psychology, another type of resource comes from developmental psychology and neuropsychology. Here, one could include the resources offered by specialized education to address the needs of a child with learning disabilities, or the EMDR treatment discussed above to decrease the symptoms of post traumatic stress disorder.

Differences between contextual therapy applied to individuals and individual therapy

In general, contextual therapy differs from individual psychotherapy not only because it focuses on relationships rather than on the inner world of a given individual, but also because contextual therapists do not see a simple increase in insight as a central goal of therapy. In contextual therapy, an increase of insight needs to be translated into a new course of actions. At the same time, however, contextual therapists and contextually oriented counselors can gain greatly from learning as much as possible about all the conscious and unconscious psychological factors that can affect their clients' behaviors and their relational choices.

They also need to learn as much as possible about the possible psychological factors that can affect the therapeutic process. Out of an unconscious need, some clients may see their therapist as an ideal parent while other clients may see their therapist as a parent who will never understand them. Of course, this will affect the course of the treatment. Importantly, some therapists may have a similar unconscious need to see a client as an ideal person or as someone they will never be able to help. Since these kinds of projections and distortions are not rare, contextual therapists and counselors should always remain open to the idea of supervision with a senior practitioner, or as a minimum to peer supervision.

Dimension III: The dimension of transactions

Variables in Dimension III

The dimension of transactions includes all the systemic variables that relate to the functioning of family systems, and all the systemic variables that are involved when individuals or families interact with larger social systems. It can entail their participation in a local community, a church congregation, a club, or an interest group. It also entails the effect of large social systems on the individual and on the family system. This can include the school, health care delivery, political, and military systems, etc. The legal system has a unique effect on families, as it determines what kind of relationships are allowed or not by law, for instance the ban or acceptance of divorce, the ban or acceptance of same-sex marriage, ban or acceptance of racially mixed marriages, or adoption.

More specifically, this dimension also entails all the factors that are described in general system theory, for example the feedback mechanisms that maintain the family equilibrium or the family homeostasis over time. One of the important contributions of Boszormenyi-Nagy in this area is his discovery that the mutual commitment of family members to be available to one another, or in other words their mutual loyalty commitment, is an important factor of family homeostasis, a subject that will be addressed later in more detail.

Here, the variables are the variables that have been described in classical systemic family therapy: the family style of communication (organized or disorganized, including or no double binds), the family style of transactions (coalitions, triangulation), the family structure (flexible, rigid, enmeshed), the family power hierarchy (battle for control versus complementarity, reversal of hierarchy in the case of parentification) as well as the family rules and myths.

Mental disorders and Dimension III

In this dimension, mental disorders have a direct effect on transactions and communication. The effect on communication depends on characteristics of the condition. It could be the pressured speech of a person who experiences a manic episode, the disorganized speech of a person suffering from schizophrenia, the mutism or aloofness of a person suffering from autism, the inability to recognize family members or to recall the contents of a session of the person who suffers from dementia, etc.

Resources in Dimension III

The therapeutic resources connected with this dimension come from changes in the style of interactions or transactions in the family or from changes in the interactions between the family and larger societal systems. The strategies that can bring about these changes are based on the many methods discussed in the classical systemic family therapy, like strategic and structural family therapy and in most of the newer family therapy models available today.

In contrast, contextual therapists do not focus on direct interventions in the family system as a source of changes; but it is obvious that any change in the giving and receiving between family members, any change in their level of trust will have systemic consequences, for instance an improvement of communication. For instance, in the situation of a parentified child, or a child who is enmeshed with one of the parents, the structural therapist who sees this child sitting between the parents and trying to speak for them may tell this child to move to another chair with the understanding that should serve to re-establish a hierarchy between the generation of the parents and the generation of the children. In contrast, a contextual therapist would not intervene directly but instead ask the parents if they were willing to tell this child to move to another chain so that they could sit next to each other as parents. If the parents accept this suggestion, this will give the child the signal that they are ready to work as a parental unit. This would lead to the same changes in the family hierarchy but in addition, the parents would earn constructive entitlement from making the effort to redirect their child.

While contextual therapists are not interested in prescribing tasks, or in commenting on non-verbal communication, they do pay attention to what happens in the session besides the verbal exchanges between the family members. For instance, they may or not ask a family member to comment on their tears or on their laughter, but in any case, these kinds of reactions will give them important clues about the effect of their interventions on the family members.

Multidirected partiality as a resource to promote orderly transactions

In this dimension, one resource to promote order in the family system and to avoid chaotic exchanges between family members comes directly from the use of 'multidirected partiality'. When contextual therapists make sure that each family is given the time to talk without being cut off by others, it brings a structure to the family exchanges. Another strategy that contextual therapists use is to give a voice to the family members who are the more ready to make helpful comments. This brings an added level of order to the session. For instance, if people try to attract the attention of the therapist by cutting into a conversation or by all sorts of non-verbal behaviors, gestures, noises, etc., they will discover that does not distract the therapist from focusing on the person who has been invited to speak. Also, they will quickly learn that if they want the attention of the therapist, they too need to be prepared to make helpful comments, and that creating more chaos will not work.

The implications of the internet and social media in Dimension III

As a last point concerning this dimension, therapists, including contextual therapists, need to be aware of the major effect of the Internet and social media on individuals and families. By now, in large parts of the world, children have access to the Internet at an increasingly younger age. Many children who are too young to learn to read and write already know how to use a mobile phone to access their favorite programs. Many children already have their own mobile phones by the time they turn twelve. No matter how much parents try to control the information their children receive, children are exposed to an incredible number of messages from all sorts of groups and influencers. In addition, children have not been taught how to distinguish real news from fake news. Consequently, they put more credence on the information they receive online than on the information they receive from their parents. This has greatly weakened the boundary that used to separate the family system from all other social systems.

These new ways of communicating through social media have brought people to retreat from direct interaction with one another. This is typical of teens who may sit in the same room but do not engage in any conversation. Instead, they all play online games in which they may compete against each other but only in the virtual world. Parents may retreat from engaging with their children directly, keeping talking on their mobile phones while their children give signals that they would like something from them. Parents may also use programs on their mobile phones as a sort of pacifier when their children begin to cry instead of trying to calm them through direct interactions. Furthermore, many social media impose a very strict limit on the length of messages that can be sent. Now people favor the use of emojis to express their feelings. Over time, this undermines their ability to communicate their feelings verbally.

All these changes in communication have a direct effect on the therapeutic process, and contextual therapists, like other therapists, need to keep abreast of the methods that can be developed to handle the consequences of these changes in communication. We also know that further changes are in sight, especially the introduction of a virtual universe in which people will represent themselves in the form of avatars. It is very difficult to anticipate the consequences of these new developments for actual human interaction and for family relationships, but contextual therapists as well as all other professional in the field of human services need to be prepared to address them.

Dimension IV: The dimension of relational ethics

The dimension of relational ethics, which is so central to contextual therapy, pertains to the discovery of the importance of fairness, reciprocity, and loyalty for any human relationship, but especially for family relationships and other forms of close relationships. It entails all the factors that are related to our expectation of fairness, reciprocity, and loyalty in close relationships, and all the relational consequences of injustices.

Variables in Dimension IV

Here, the variables are connected to the balance of giving and receiving between partners or family members, and to their mutual expectation of fair reciprocity. One variable is the degree of fairness or the degree of exploitation that exists in their relationships. It is important to note that in contextual therapy, fairness is never defined as an absolute. It can be defined only through an actual dialogue between all the concerned parties.

Other variables pertain to loyalty expectations and loyalty commitments inside and outside the family. It can be the degree of loyalty that one shows to a parent, a sibling, a spouse, a child, or any other relative. It also entails the degree of loyalty that one displays to people and groups outside of one's family such as one's loyalty to a friend, teacher, pastor, or group like a congregation, a club, etc. It also entails the degree of commitment that is expected from us by our family members, and by all the groups and institutions we belong to, not forgetting that national governments and their armies do count on the loyalty of their citizens. Lastly, another variable pertains to the way in which the loyalty commitment is expressed: direct expression (direct loyalty), overt disloyalty, or indirect expression (invisible loyalty).

Mental disorders and Dimension IV

In this dimension, the effect of mental illnesses is based on their consequences for the giving and receiving between the family members and between the generations. As we have already seen, suffering from a mental illness constitutes an injustice in comparison with people whose lives are not affected by such illnesses. Hence, it constitutes a situational injustice. In addition, people who suffer from mental illnesses can be the victims of added relational (retributive) injustices when others mistreat them or when society discriminates against them. One of the consequences is that people who are the victims of these injustices do accumulate destructive entitlement, which in turn becomes the source of new relational injustices that can have implications over more than one generation. Depending on the type of mental illnesses, people may also have difficulties in earning constructive entitlement like the depressed person who is too hopeless to care about giving.

Resources in Dimension IV

The therapeutic resources that come from this dimension pertain to all the resources that contextual therapy can offer not only for therapists but also for all the professionals who seek to understand the effect of these expectations on the lives of the people they are trying to help. The discussion of these resources will be the object of several chapters of this book. In short, however, one can say that in this dimension, the main therapeutic resource resides in the fact that contextual therapists can help people to move away from destructive ways of seeking justice and help them to discover what they and others may gain from generous giving. Here, the central strategy is multidirected partiality. Examples of the use of this strategy will be found in several chapters of the book.

Dimension V: The ontic dimension

The 'ontic dimension' could also be described as the 'dimension of mutual becoming', or the 'dimension of relational Self-Other establishment'. This dimension relates to Boszormenyi-Nagy's relational definition of Self that is based on his dialectical theory of the personality presented in *Intensive Family therapy* (Boszormenyi-Nagy & Framo, 1965, 2015). He postulates that the Self is intrinsically dependent on a relation with a Not-Self in order to exist as an autonomous Self, and that this is true for the Other too. "The assumption that the person as a Self depends on a set of matching Not-Self referents implies that he, in turn, has to be a Not-Self referent for others. Part of our relationship with the others is based on our usefulness for their self-delineation" (id: 42). His position agrees with M. Buber (1923, 1970) "At the beginning is the relationship" and with his description of the I-It and I-Thou dialogue.

Boszormenyi-Nagy describes the inherent dependence between the Self and the Other for the definition of the Self as an 'ontic dependence'. He uses the term *ontic* to mean that that this dependence is inherent to the relational definition of the Self, and that nothing needs to be added. As such: "The ontic element in a relationship makes the Other an essential counterpart of one's Selfhood, irrespective of any particular interaction." (Boszormenyi-Nagy & Framo, 1965, 2015: 37) Consequently, this ontic dependence becomes a determinant of relationships.

Boszormenyi-Nagy's dialectic definition of the Self occupies a middle way between an essentialist position i.e. that the Self has an indestructible essence and a nihilistic position, i.e. that if the Self does depend on a counterpart to exist as a Self, the Self as such does not really exist. Boszormenyi-Nagy takes a middle position. He does not deny that the Self exists, but he postulates that it can exist only in dependence on its counterpart, the Other. His view agrees with the notion of the dependent arising of Self and Other that is presented the Middle Way school of Buddhist philosophy.

Variables in Dimension V

In this dimension, the variables pertain to various ways in which the delineation of the Self and the Other can occur. Boszormenyi-Nagy proposes six possible modes of relating to establish a Self-Not-Self contraposition, while Martin Buber's dialogic model includes two modes of relating, namely the I-Thou relationship, and the I-It relationship.

These six modes are listed as follows:

1. The intrasubject boundary (no external Other and no internal Other).
2. The Internal dialogue (no external Other but an internal Other).
3. The merger (merger of Self and Other).
4. Being the object (Self as the object, Other as the subject. An It-I relationship).
5. Being the subject (Self as the subject, Other as the object. An I-It relationship).
6. The dialogue (Self and Other in an interchangeable position either as a subject or an object. (A true I-Thou relationship).

These six relational modes, which will be presented in many details later, can be considered from a few vantage points that can be useful to therapists and counselors. For instance, one could consider these modes as steps in the development of a human being from an infant to a mature adult who can engage in a true I-Thou dialogue with another adult. One can also consider these modes from the vantage point of their implications in terms of exploitation and fairness. The modes that parallel the I-It dialogue in Buber lead to an asymmetry in the relationship and to the risk of unilateral exploitation. The mode that matches the I-Thou dialogue allows for full symmetry and fair reciprocity. However, it is important to note that in the ontic dimension, the focus is on the description of the way in which the Self-Other delineation is established, not on the consequences of these various modes of relating in the dimension of relational ethics or in the dimension of transactions, which they obviously have.

One of the most important consequences of the relational definition of the Self is that it leads to a relational definition of autonomy, which is paradoxical since, by definition, autonomy should be defined by an absence of any dependence. This view of autonomy is quite unique in the world of Western psychotherapy, and it has important theoretical and practical implications that also will be examined in detail later.

Mental disorders and Dimension V

In this dimension, mental illnesses affect the modes in which people operate; for instance, a person who suffers from delusions and who hears voices may establish a Self-Other delineation that is based on an internal dialogue with a hallucinated interlocutor. It is also possible to make a connection between the mode in which people function and some forms of personality disorders.

Resources in Dimension V

The therapeutic resources connected with this dimension come from the resources of the Self-Other dialogue. The dialectical theory of the personality gives a new meaning to the healing encounter between the therapist, or counselor, and the client. Since all therapeutic encounters entail an encounter between a Self (the client) and an Other (the professional), all therapeutic encounters become a resource in the ontic dimension. No one can be cured of an ontic dependence since this dependence is inherent to the definition of the Self. At the same time, all these encounters offer an opportunity for a Self-Other delineation that can help clients to move toward increased individuation and increased autonomy. This increase would not depend on the therapeutic method used by the professional. It would depend on this professional's capacity to engage in a true encounter with the person who seeks help, a true meeting with another human being.

The practical use of the five-dimensional model of relational reality

The five dimensions as a framework for assessment

One of the first steps in any form of therapy, and in any form of counseling including pastoral counseling, is to identify the factors that may contribute to an individual pathology, a relational problem, or in general to the suffering of a person. Whether they are contextual therapists or not, therapists and counselors truly can be helped in their assessments by relying on the five-dimensional model of relational reality. Considering the situation of people who seek help through the lens of these five dimensions gives professionals a much better chance to identify all the factors that can play a role in a given situation and to identify all the therapeutic resources that could be mobilized. For instance, professionals who focus on relationships, including contextual therapists, may overlook the effect of a physical or mental illness on relationships. Professionals like psychiatrists and psychologists who focus on one individual may overlook only systemic elements that can contribute to individual symptoms. Individual and family therapists may overlook the effect of injustices on the functioning of their clients. All this can be avoided if professionals use the framework of the five-dimensional model of relational reality in their assessment.

Five dimensions: One relational reality

As already mentioned, there is no hierarchy between the five dimensions of relational reality. Focusing on one dimension, for instance the dimension of relational ethics, does not decrease the relevance of the other dimensions. Also, a change in one variable in one dimension can trigger changes in any or all of the other dimensions. For instance, the onset of an illness, a change in the dimension of facts, can lead to a depression – a change of psychology, or to a decrease of interaction with family members – a change in the dimension of transactions. It can also lead to a change in the giving and receiving between family members – a change in the dimension of relational ethics, and a change in the mode of Self-Other delineation if the person retreats to an internal dialogue.

At the same time, it is true that one dimension may become more relevant than another in a specific situation. Consider a simple example outside of therapy: people who use a GPS to get somewhere rely on information about the latitude and the longitude of the place they are trying to reach. But this location also has an altitude that could be measured if needed. It is the same here: people may seek help for problems that could be understood without exploring all the possible variables that are part of their relational reality, but these variables are nonetheless present and could be examined if necessary.

For example, if a divorcing couple seek the help of a counselor to discuss a visitation agreement for their children, the counselor will act as a mediator and focus mainly on their present relationship, on their children's need, and on the standards set by courts for visitation rights. This counselor would not need to explore all the determinants that could have played a role in the failure of the couple's marriage. However, if the couple was seeking help to avert a divorce, the counselor would need to proceed to a multidimensional assessment of their situation to identify all the possible factors that could contribute to their marital difficulties, and all the possible resources that could be mobilized to make the marriage more successful.

Changes in life and changes in therapy

As a final point, we need to remember that changes can occur in any of the five dimensions that are totally out of the control of the professionals, but they can have a great effect on the course of the therapy. For instance, a client who has entered therapy because of depression and low self-esteem may suddenly feel better after being recontacted by an old friend. Conversely, a couple who were making good progress in couple therapy may fall apart after one of the partners has become unemployed and end up divorcing despite the couple therapist's best efforts to help them overcome the situation.

What is required to perform a five-dimensional assessment?

It is important to realize that a full five-dimensional assessment requires vast knowledge that cannot be expected from all professionals. It would be too much to expect that all professionals are experts in all the areas covered by these five dimensions. For instance, not all contextual therapists have sufficient training in individual psychology to assess all the individual conscious or unconscious psychological factors that can be involved in a relational problem, or counselors who are well-trained in individual counseling may not be trained to notice the systemic elements that could contribute to maintain an individual pathology, etc. Also, many practitioners are not trained in individual diagnosis. Furthermore, beside pastoral counselors, none of these professionals would be able or in a position to discuss spirituality as a resource or to help people who suffer because they have lost their faith in their religion after a devastating event, like the death of a young child.

What matters here is that contextual therapists and all the professionals who base their practice on the contextual therapy model rely on this framework to account for all the possible variables that can play a role in a given situation. It does matter if they do not have all the answers. Professionals always have the option to seek the help of colleagues if they do not have the sufficient training to assess the relevance of a specific factor. For instance, the professional who suspects that a client suffers from a diagnosable mental illness and could benefit from medication may consider a referral to a psychiatrist for a full evaluation and possible treatment. The family therapist who suspects that a child presents with developmental delays may recommend a full evaluation by a neuropsychologist or a school psychologist to make sure that the child's educational needs are met and to help the family understand the child's possible limitations. Even when contextual therapists are competent to perform assessments in more than one of these dimensions, they may choose to delegate specialized assessments to other professionals to avoid confusing their clients between their role as a therapist focusing on multidirected partiality and their role as an evaluator needing to focus on specific objectives.

An illustration of the use of the five-dimensional model of relational reality

To demonstrate the usefulness of the five-dimensional model of relational reality in clinical practice, we shall consider the situation of a single mother who is raising three children alone and who is suffering from chronic depression. She seeks the help of a therapist not so much because she is depressed but because she is very worried about her oldest daughter who has started to present with symptoms of a conduct disorder. Her daughter has become disruptive at school, getting into fights. In addition, she has started to become defiant toward her mother, refusing to follow her directions, staying out at night, etc.

In this situation, it would not be enough to focus only on the daughter's negative behaviors. To help this mother and her daughter, one would need to examine the situation from a multidimensional perspective. One also would need to understand in what way the mother's depression could contribute to her daughter's symptoms.

Assessment

To proceed to a multidimensional assessment of the situation, the contextual therapist could begin by evaluating the factors that are involved in the mother's depression, for instance a family history of depression that could indicate a biological vulnerability. Then, the therapist could examine if there is any correlation between the mother's condition and her daughter's recent symptoms. At the same time, the therapist would also evaluate the possible individual factors that could contribute to the daughter's symptoms. Also, one need to figure out to what extent the daughter's behavior has been aggravating the mother's depression. This exploration would be based on the systemic notion of circular causality: the mutual influence of the symptoms of the mother on the daughter and vice-versa. One would also need to find out if this single mother can rely on other adults for support or if she is isolated and need to use her daughter as a substitute parent for the younger children or as a confident when she has worries, which would be a source of parentification.

Beginning with the mother, it would be reasonable to assume that some biological factors are involved in her depression. Also, it is obvious that the depression affects her psychological functioning (low self-esteem, helplessness, occasional suicidal ideations). It affects the transactions and the communications within the family (lack of energy, lack of strength to set limits, etc.). Whether or not they were long-lasting issues pertaining to the giving and receiving between the generations in the family of origin of this woman, her illness affects the giving and receiving between her and her children. As she is often too depressed to meet the needs of her children, she relies on her elder daughter to take care of the younger siblings, which places an unfair burden on this girl.

Resources and interventions

The contextual therapist could identify potential resources in several dimensions. For instance, this woman could benefit from treatment with an antidepressant, which is a resource in the dimension of facts. She could also benefit from cognitive behavioral therapy, a resource in the dimension of psychology. The therapist may look at some of the daughter's symptoms as the result of a reversal of hierarchy in the family. Since the daughter behaves as if she were an adult who can set her own rules, the therapist could try to support the mother in setting some limits for her daughter instead of hoping that she would return to more age-appropriate behaviors on her own. This would be a resource in the dimension of transactions.

The specific interventions of the contextual therapist would be based on an understanding of the dimension of relational ethics and an understanding of the ontic dimension. It would begin with understanding the detrimental effect of parentification on the older daughter and understanding the contextual definition of the healing moment. Here, the mother would be encouraged to examine if she could do a little more for her children despite her depression so that her daughter would be less burdened by the task of taking care of her younger siblings. She could also be encouraged to seek resources in her community. For instance, she could be encouraged to contact a social worker who could make sure that the children receive all the services they are entitled to, which would also alleviate the burden on the older daughter.

In any case, whatever action the mother accept to take to alleviate her older daughter's predicament, her effort will earn her constructive entitlement. This will contribute to increase her self-esteem and serve as an antidote to the low self-esteem that is a typical symptom of depression. At the same time, her daughter who has started to engage in a spiral of revenge and antisocial behaviors could be helped if she is acknowledged as a depleted giver rather than a revenge-seeking troublemaker.

Furthermore, as such, the meeting with the therapist would help the mother in an additional way. Whether she sees the therapist alone or during a family session, each meeting will offer her an opportunity for a true encounter with another adult, and an opportunity for Self-Other delineation that does not have to involve her daughter. The same applies to the daughter and the other siblings. Each time, the therapist gives a voice to the children, and encourages them to present their own side, he gives them a new opportunity for Self-Other delineation and a new opportunity to move toward a greater individuation and greater autonomy.

When the professional is a pastoral counselor

If the mother had decided to turn to a pastoral counselor, the contextually inspired pastoral counselor would explore her situation from the vantage point of the five dimensions of relational reality as the contextual therapist would do. However, in addition, the counselor would explore this mother's involvement with religion. Is she someone who can derive strength from her faith or conversely someone who is starting to lose her faith? Is she someone who can rely on the support of a congregation or someone who is cut off from her fellow parishioners? Beside thinking of the resources that could be found in any of these five dimensions, the counselor would also explore resources she could derive from faith or from spirituality in general. For instance, if she indicates that attending services would give her strength but that she is too depressed to meet many people, she could be directed to a small prayer group or even be encouraged to follow services online until she feels strong enough to attend in person.

One or more professionals?

As discussed before, contextual therapists and pastoral counselors may need to rely on a variety of professionals to provide an additional assessment or additional services. If this is the case, they would need to figure out how to incorporate the new information with their own work, or how to work cooperatively with the professionals who would provide the added services. Furthermore, as already mentioned, professionals who have the ability to intervene in more than one dimension need to decide if it is appropriate or not to do so. For example, the contextual therapists who are also psychiatrists, the contextual therapists who are also trained in cognitive therapy, or the contextually oriented pastoral counselors who are also trained in structural family therapy may lose their ability to keep their focus on multidirected partiality when intervening in other capacities or while trying to use other methods of intervention. Some of the professionals who can intervene in two capacities may choose to refrain from involving other professionals because they fear that these other professionals may not have the same treatment goals, which would be counterproductive. Other professionals may prefer to involve other specialists to make sure that they can keep their focus on multidirected partiality and don't confuse their clients by shifting themselves from one role or one method to the other. Here one needs to realize that there is no right or wrong answer. There are only trade-offs.

In the example above, if the mother can benefit from an antidepressant, the contextual therapist who is also a psychiatrist may decide to become the prescribing physician. This would avoid the risk that the mother may have to be referred to a psychiatrist who may have little belief in family therapy, someone who could undermine the therapeutic process. At the same time, the contextual therapist who acts also as a prescribing psychiatrist would need to shift roles regularly. When acting in the capacity of a contextual therapist, this therapist would rely on multidirected partiality to promote a dialogue between the family members, which is a cooperative role. As a prescribing psychiatrist, the therapist would need to shift to a directive role, prescribing a medication, giving instructions to clients, and verifying that the client has followed them. The shift in roles could be confusion not only for the client who needs to take the medication but also for the entire family. The contextual therapist who is also a psychologist versed in cognitive behavioral therapy would face the same issues.

Pastors who engage in pastoral counseling may face similar issues. Very often, pastors counsel people who are members of their congregation, which means that they have a dual role as a counselor and as an officiant during religious services. This role imbues them with a special kind of power that may have implications for their work as counselors. If the people they counsel attribute too much authority to their pastoral counselor, they may have a difficult time to engage in a form of cooperative therapy like contextual therapy, and in this case, it may be helpful to refer them to a pastoral counselor who is less directly involved with their congregation. For instance, this woman may get confused by the dual role of this pastor, or she may feel too shy to discuss personal matters with someone in a position of authority. In this case, a referral to a colleague would be appropriate. Or, on the contrary, this woman may feel freer to talk to her pastor than to anyone else because of the special trust that she has in the pastor. In this case, there would be no need for a referral to a colleague, and a referral could be even counterproductive.

Furthermore, pastoral counselors who are active as pastors of in a congregation need to be attentive to a special problem. If they live in the same neighborhood as their parishioners, they may know much more about the life of the person who ask for help than the pastoral counselor who works in an institution like a nursing home or a hospital. Also, the parishioner who asks for help may know much about the pastors' life. In addition, the life of the pastor may intersect with the life of the parishioner in all sorts of ways. This could limit the pastor's ability to maintain a position of multidirected partiality while acting as a pastoral counselor. For instance, in this example, if the daughter had caused many problems in a youth group that is also attended by the pastor's children, the pastor would have a preconception of the daughter as a serious troublemaker and may therefore be influenced to side with the mother when she complains about her daughter's behaviors. Conversely, if the pastor finds out from his children that this daughter often misses the group meetings because she needs to stay home to take care of her younger siblings, the pastor would be inclined to see the mother as an exploiter and be at risk of siding with the daughter against the mother. The unique position of the pastoral counselor and problems encountered by pastors who function both as pastoral counselors and as leaders of a congregation will be discussed in detail in Section II of this book.

Chapter 3
The Dialectic Theory of Personality and its Implications for Practitioners

Introduction

To understand what is at the core of the 'dialectic theory of personality' is to understand what is at the core of contextual therapy. As already discussed, central to this theory is a relational definition of the Self and consequently a relational definition of autonomy. Boszormenyi-Nagy's relational definition of the Self, and his notion of the inherent dependence of the Self on the existence of another, which he describes as an 'ontic dependence' is based on the position of the existential philosophers in which he includes Martin Buber even if some consider that Buber may not be a true existentialist. As discussed by M. Theunissen, who includes Buber in his book *The Other* (1984), each of these philosophers have their own view of the Other. Indeed, there are some differences between the dialogical view proposed by Buber and the dialectical view proposed by Boszormenyi-Nagy. While these differences may be to technical to interest people beside some specialists of both Buber and Boszormenyi-Nagy, here is a way to think about them. One could try to use the example of a drawing made on a piece of paper. One could say that the existence of drawing (the Self), depends on a 'dialogue' with the paper (the Other). This would be Buber's view. In Boszormenyi-Nagy's dialectic view, the Self is understood as a synthesis of a Self as a thesis and a Not-Self as an antithesis. Here the drawing that one sees would be understood as a synthesis of the trait placed on the paper (the Self as a thesis) and the Not-Self (the paper as an antithesis). However, in the end, both views converge in presenting the Self as inherently dependent on a Not-Self to exist as a Self. What differs also is that M. Buber distinguishes two modes of relating, the I-It mode, and the I-Thou mode, while Boszormenyi-Nagy proposes six modes of relating.

Furthermore, Boszormenyi-Nagy proposes that from a dialectic point of view, transactions can be discussed in terms of their effect on the Self. In any transaction, the agent of the action (subject) is in a dialectical relationship with the object of the transaction. Whether we are the subject of the transaction or the object, each new transaction allows for the establishment of a Self-Other delineation that is necessary for the definition of the Self.

Consequently, the autonomy of the Self depends on the presence of its counterpart, the Other. Normally, by definition, autonomy is defined by the absence of any dependence. This paradoxical view of autonomy sets contextual therapists apart from most individual therapists and from most family therapists. In the Western world, especially in the USA, professionals tend to equate the notion of autonomy with the notion of independence, meaning the capacity to live independently from others. On the other hand, the idea that autonomy cannot be separated from relatedness is much less alien to cultures that recognize the fundamental interconnectedness of people within their families or their society, and do not see the separation between parents and children as necessary evidence of individuation.

The relational definition of autonomy and its consequences for therapy

In most forms of therapy and counseling, the practitioner focuses on interventions that can bring a decrease in individual and relational pathologies. In addition, most practitioners focus also on helping their clients to reach their full potential as autonomous individuals, which is also the goal of many self-help books that focus on the theme of 'learning to becoming oneself'. This applies to contextual practitioners as well. They too want to work on a decrease of individual and relational pathologies. They too want to help their clients to reach their full potential as autonomous individuals. However, here is the huge difference. Contextual therapists believe that autonomy is reached through relating, not through separating.

For most people, professionals and the lay public who read self-help books, the path toward individuation entails a process of separation. For this reason, most people believe that individual therapy is more conducive to individuation than any form of family therapy is. This applies to professionals, especially psychiatrists, who work with adolescents who are enmeshed with their family and unable to differentiate from their parents. In these situations, they believe that family therapy would be counterproductive because it would reinforce the interactions between the parent and the adolescent. They believe that, to promote individuation, the adolescent should engage in individual therapy. If this is not enough, they often recommend attendance of a residential treatment program where the adolescent's individuation would be fostered not only by individual therapy but also by a physical separation from the family. In brief, most professionals equate autonomy with the capacity of separating and living independently.

Contextual therapists do not disagree with the idea that people should be helped to individuate and to reach autonomy. No contextual practitioner would like to see adolescents remaining enmeshed with their family, and not being able to develop into adults who can function autonomously and set their own life goals. However, the big difference lies in the method they use to promote this autonomy. First of all, they do not believe that simple physical separation leads automatically to an increase in autonomy. Also, they do not believe that individual therapy necessarily leads to more individuation than family therapy does. In fact, they believe the opposite. They believe that it is exactly because family therapy promotes relating between family members that family therapy does offer more resources than individual therapy does.

"The allegedly value-neutral therapist can be deeply committed to the desirability of 'separation' from previous especially seemingly unsatisfactory relationships. Often in supporting the ideal of separation, the professional can lose sight of the personal interest of all parties involved ... By contrast, dialectical relational therapists will tend to reduce the seemingly adversary position of close relatives into a mutuality of genuine interests. They have learned that both parents and child would pay significant lasting guilt for an ultimate victory of one over the other" (Boszormenyi-Nagy, 1987, 2014: 144).

Most family therapists who work with teenagers and their families would expect that each family member speaks in his or her own voice, including the youths. As such, this would be an antidote to enmeshment. Contextual therapists go much further. They rely on multidirected partiality, not only to help the youths to speak in their own voice like any other family therapists would to do, but they also engage people to present own their point of view on the giving and receiving between family members. This leads not only to an opportunity of Self-Other delineation between the family members. Furthermore, when they accept to listen to the position of the other members of the family and try to understand it, they also make a gain in the form of self-validation. This gain in self-validation and self-delineation leads to a gain in terms of autonomy. In sum, the dialectic definition of the self and the relational definition of autonomy have major implications for the practice of contextual therapy, and for all professionals who base their work on this approach.

Accepting the dialectic theory of the personality, a question or a must?

Since the dialectical theory of the personality is so central to contextual therapy, it is difficult to understand why this theory has been given so little attention by the teachers of contextual therapy over the years and why many of them still resist introducing the ontic dimension in their presentation of contextual therapy. Not only did Boszormenyi-Nagy introduce this theory in two chapters in *Intensive Family Therapy* already in 1965, but in these two texts, he even presented his approach as 'dialectic intergenerational therapy'. This book also occupies a special place in the history of family therapy, since it contains major contributions by several of the pioneers of family therapy. Furthermore, the article *Relational Modes and Meaning*, first published in 1967, which presents the six modes of relating was considered important enough by its author to be reprinted in *Foundations of Contextual Therapy* (Boszormenyi-Nagy, 1987, 2014). However, it was not included in the Dutch translation of this important book.

But whether or not a number of contextual therapists still don't mention the dialectic theory of the personality nor the ontic dimension in their presentation of the approach, one can easily argue that accepting the five-dimensional model of relational reality is not a just a question of abidance by the latest model of relational reality proposed by Boszormenyi-Nagy. It is a matter of simple logic. Contextual therapists have always known that giving leads to two results: an increase in self-validation, in other words an increase in merits, and an increase in self-delineation. The increase in self-delineation comes from the fact that the act of giving is a transaction that brings together the Self as a subject (the giver) and the Other as the object of the action (the beneficiary). Until the introduction of the new ontic dimension, the only option was to consider that both changes occur in the dimension of relational ethics, but this is a problem because self-validation and self-delineation are two very different processes. To demonstrate that, one could consider stealing instead of giving. It is obvious that stealing cannot lead to any increase of self-validation. However, in terms of Self-Other delineation, both giving and stealing lead to a similar contraposition between the Self as the subject (the giver or the robber) and an Other as the object of the action (the beneficiary or the victim).

In other words, without the possibility of separating self-validation (Dimension IV) from self-delineation (Dimension V), one would miss the fact that whether a relationship is based on generosity or on exploitation, it does not change the fact that it serves as a base for the mutual relational establishment of the Self and of the Other. The same is true of Buber's I-It and I-Thou dialogue. The I-It dialogue implies a certain degree of exploitation, whereas the I-Thou implies reciprocity; but both serve equally at the as a relational establishment of the Self and of the Other.

Relational needs according to the five dimensions of relational reality

Before engaging the detailed exploration of the six modes of relating, it is necessary to focus on another aspect of the dialectical theory of personality. Since we need others to serve as a 'ground' against which we can detach as a 'figure', Boszormenyi-Nagy states that "we are what we need to make of others". Boszormenyi-Nagy also shows that whenever we turn to another person to fulfil a specific need, for instance an emotional need, we also automatically establish a relationship that leads to a Self-Other delineation. This aspect of the relationship is possibly the most important from the point of view of the relational establishment of the Self. We need to relate to others for the fulfilment of all sorts of specific needs. Ultimately, however, our most fundamental need to relate to others is not based on any of these specific needs. It is based on our ontic dependence. Before anything, we need others for the relational establishment of the self.

Relational needs and the dimension of facts

Starting with Dimension I, the dimension of facts, we need others to secure our physical survival. It is obvious that babies could not survive or develop into functional children without the presence of caring of adults. People who suffer from serious physical handicaps would not survive without the help of others. We also need to remember that when people need to rely on a service animal, for instance a seeing eye dog, this animal may become an important 'Other' for the handicapped person, and for this person's family.

Relational needs and the dimension of psychology

Within the realm of psychology, we need others to fulfil a variety of internal needs. It could be our sexual needs that entail biological and psychological components. It could be our conscious need for affection, etc. In addition, psychoanalysts have shown that we use others to fulfil various unconscious needs. We tend to use others as a target onto which we can to project positive or negative qualities that match our internalized parental figures. We also may use them as a target on which to project elements of our own internal world that are unacceptable, for instance anger or shame. The analysis of these unconscious projections and distortions is one of the central goals of psychoanalysis, and other approaches like cognitive behavioral therapy.

Relational needs and the dimension of transactions

From a systemic point of view, we may need others and rely on them to secure our position in a given system. For instance, we need people to be on our side during conflicts. We need people to function as our allies when we engage in battles for control or power, etc. From a dialectic point of view, transactions can be discussed in terms of their effect on the Self. In any transaction, the agent of the action (subject) is in a dialectical relationship with the object of the transaction. Whether we are the subject of the transaction or the object, each new transaction allows for the establishment of a Self-Other delineation that is necessary for the definition of the Self.

Relational needs and the dimension of relational ethics

As far as the dimension of relational ethics is concerned, we need others in our life to gain the special relevance that comes from our ability to contribute positively to the lives of other people. When we care about the needs of others and we can be generous toward them, our positive gestures bring us increased human value, and increased inner security (constructive entitlement). We also need others as a source of redress when we have been victims of injustices. When we have been wronged, we expect redress. If it does not come from the people who have caused us a tort, we may turn to other people with the hope that they could compensate us for the damages that were not repaired by the culprit, which is destructive (destructive entitlement).

Relational needs and the ontic dimension

In the ontic dimension, our ontic dependence and our fundamental dependence on others as counterparts in relational establishment of the Self are central. When we turn to someone to fulfil one of the needs that belong to Dimensions I, II, III and IV, we also automatically establish a relationship with the person. From the perspective of the ontic dimension, ultimately, what matters most is not that the person fulfils any of our specific needs, but that the person serves our need to relate to others as a source of definition of the Self.

This sheds new light on the situation of people who have become severely disabled and who are dependent on a spouse, a close friend, or a family member for their care. In many cases, they not only become unable to respond to the various needs that their caregiver may have, but their disability also puts a heavy burden on the caregiver, and it puts an end to the fair reciprocity that is expected in close relationships. For this reason, many professionals may expect that the caregiver will experience a relief when the disabled person is institutionalized or if this person passes away, but this may not be true at all. From the point of view of the ontic dimension, the disabled person remains a source of Self-Other definition for the caregiver and from this perspective, the caregiver will still benefit from the possibility of relating to this person, no matter how much the relationship is one-sided from the point of view of giving and receiving.

There is even a possible link between our ontic dependence on others and our physical survival. We know that babies who are placed in institutions where they are deprived of any meaningful relationships with adults may simply perish or develop severe forms of autism. We also know that some old people who lose a spouse after a very long marriage can die without any obvious medical reason in the months following this loss. Some people even die following the death of a pet that had become central to their life.

The six modes of relating

1) The intrasubject boundary (no external Other and no internal Other)

Here, the contraposition is established in the absence of any actual relationship. It is established through a contraposition between two parts of the Self. An example would come from people who report that they feel more alive after having cut themselves. Here the contraposition that serves at establishing the Self occurs in the contraposition between the Self that cuts, and the Self that experiences the pain. A similar process could occur when children who suffer from autism bite themselves. This boundary is also established when the Self is defined in terms of an activity, a cause, or an ideology. We hear people say: "Without this job, I would be nothing". These people may completely collapse if they cannot accomplish this task. When the Self is defined in terms of an ideology, people may become so threatened if the ideology that is so central to their Self-definition is challenged that they can become violent toward the people who question it. This may be a possible explanation for the increased expression of violence that is observed on social media. From a diagnostic point of view, this mode could be associated with autism spectrum disorders.

2) The internal dialogue (no external Other but an internal Other)

The second mode, the internal dialogue, relates to the contraposition between the Self and an internal Other that we establish when we think about what we would say to someone who is absent or to a person who is deceased, or when we try to imagine what this person would tell us. People who suffer from psychosis often enter a dialogue with hallucinated people or just hallucinated voices that they take for real. In this case, the Self-Other contraposition occurs between the Self and the internal Other in the form of the hallucinated voice. People who suffer from psychosis often enter into dialogue with hallucinated people or just hallucinated voices that they take for real. In this case, the Self-Other contraposition occurs between the Self and the internal Other in the form of the hallucinated voice. In the internal dialogue, the Self can be the subject, for instance when telling this voice to stop, or the Self can be the object, for instance when receiving orders from this voice. From a diagnostic point of view, this mode can be associated with schizophrenia spectrum disorders, but hallucinations can also be caused by isolation.

3) The merger (merger of Self and Other)

Here the Self and the Other fuse into a unit, a 'we', a two-sum that interact then with external others as third parties. The merger is one of the normal stages in the development of children in which the infant and the mother form a unit. This merger becomes pathological when it occurs between a parent and a growing child, between two adult partners, or in families in which the members are enmeshed with one another. In all these cases, the 'we' unit can interact with third parties either as a subject: "We want them to ...", or as an object: "They want us to ...". Family therapists report situations in which no one in the family is capable of making a personal statement or responding to a question in a personal manner. Each statement begins with "we ...", and each question is answered by "we ...".

4) Being the object (Self as the object, Other as the subject)

It is a form of the I-It dialogue in which the Self is in the position of the It, and the Other is in the position of the I. This type of Self-Other contraposition occurs in situations where the Self serves as a tool for the Other and is interchangeable with any person who could accomplish the same function. In every language there is a difference between terms that just indicate that people are interchangeable and terms that also establish a hierarchy of power within the relationship. For instance, calling businesspeople 'suits' does not have any implication in terms of hierarchy, or power. On the other hand, calling house helpers 'boys' not only denies these helpers an individual identity, but it also places them in a position of inferiority, open to exploitation.

In this mode, the fact that the Self accepts being in the position of the Object and being used by the other may depend on an external necessity. For instance, it could be the simple need of earning money. In this case, it would not matter to the person who needs a job if the workers are treated as people who are entirely interchangeable or not. What would matter is that the job remains available. In other cases, the Self may accept being in the position of the object due to an internal need to be defined by the Other. From a diagnostic point of view, this need would be associated with a diagnosis of a dependent personality disorder. One also needs to remember that it still is better to be an It for an I than to be entirely excluded from any sort of dialogue. This is the case of homeless people who live on the street and become completely transparent to the passers-by who do not even bother to cast an eye on them.

5) Being the subject (Self as the subject, Other as the object)

This fifth mode corresponds to the typical I-It dialogue in Buber's terms. It is the mirror image of the fourth mode. Here the Self is the one who uses the Other as an object, whereas in the other mode it is the Self who serves as an object for the Other. Otherwise, both modes are similar in the sense that they entail the same lack of reciprocity between the Self and the Other. Here the definition of the Self comes mostly from its ability to exert control on the Other, or simply from being able to use the other as a means for a purpose. The restaurant guest who orders a meal does not care who the waiter is; but as such the relationship with the waiter still serves as a source of the Self-Other contraposition that would be lost if this guest had to get this meal from an automatic distributor. The I-It mode is most often associated with the notion of narcissism and exploitation. From a diagnostic point of view, this mode can be associated with a narcissistic personality disorder.

6) The dialogue (Self and Other in an interchangeable position either as a subject or an object)

This mode corresponds to the true 'I-Thou' dialogue in Buber's terms. Here the Self and the Other are in interchangeable positions. The Self can be the subject or the object of the transaction and similarly, the Other can also be in the position of either the subject or the object. In addition to this interchangeability, there is also a true mutuality concerning fairness and responsible behaviors. Another important feature of the true I-Thou dialogue is that it requires that both parties are capable to engage in a dialogue that is free of preconceptions and distorting projections about the partner. It is important to realize that a true I-Thou dialogue cannot be maintained for prolonged periods. Even in couples where the two partners are the most mature and the fairest, they do revert to an I-It mode in many circumstances when one partner ends up serving as a tool for the other. However, as long as the partners' positions remain reversible and as long as they can move back and forth between being an It for an I and an I for an It, the relationship remains fair. A good example comes from sexual relationships: both partners fulfil a role for the other, but as long as both of them receive what they need, the relationship remains fair.

Transitions between the six modes of relating

In the discussion of these six modes of relating, it is important to emphasize that people may switch from one mode to the other in accordance with external circumstances: people may be fully capable of engaging in a mature dialogue with a partner when the partner is present and revert to an internal dialogue when the partner is absent. Furthermore, people who are grieving the loss of an important partner may maintain an inner dialogue with the deceased person and may even occasionally hear his or her voice, but this does not mean that these people have become psychotics. People in prolonged solitary confinement may begin to hear a voice that takes the place of the missing external others, and this can become very distressing for them, but it does not mean that they have become psychotic either. As soon as they are in contact with people again, the voice disappears. Mystics who hear the voice of God, the voice of Holy Mary or the voice of an angel, and shamans who enter a dialogue with invisible entities, or with ancestors do also return to an ordinary dialogue with ordinary people once the mystical episode or the trance is over. They are not assumed to be psychotic, especially if their experience fits into a set of beliefs that is accepted by the social group to which they belong. On the other hand, people who suffer from schizophrenia cannot switch easily from an internal dialogue with hallucinated Others, and often this internal dialogue intrudes into the dialogue that they can have with actual people.

As a final point in the discussion of these relational modes, it is important to remember that Boszormenyi-Nagy wanted to make a clear distinction between his proposed ontic dimension and a spiritual dimension that would need to include the discussion of people's relation to God or to any deity or being that people may worship in their religious tradition. For this reason, this type of dialogue is not included in the presentation of the six modes of relating that he has proposed. One could make the case that this dialogue fits in the description of the internal dialogue, and in this case, the Self could be the subject when asking God for help, or the object of the action, when following God's orders. This dialogue would parallel the internal dialogue that one could have with an internalized parent. At the same time, it is obvious that for believers, the dialogue with God or with any spiritual entity goes well beyond an internal dialogue. For Buber, the relation with God could not be imagined outside of the I-Thou dialogue in which God is the ultimate Thou. His view could probably be endorsed by most people who enter into a dialogue with the entity who occupies a similar position in their belief system.

Relational need templates

Boszormenyi-Nagy speaks of relational need templates to describe that the relational mode in which we tend to operate serves as a template, a mould that determines what place the Other can occupy so that it fits in with the relational mode that we are using to establish a Self-Not-Self delineation. For instance, people who tend to operate in the merger mode may try to bring their partner to operate as a 'we' as well. People who tend to operate in the I-It mode of relating will try to bring their partner into the position of the It.

In a couple relationship, ideally two partners should be able to function in an I-Thou dialogue, and they should be capable of fair mutuality. However, whether they are able to function in this mode or not, the relationship can remain stable if the partners' relational needs are complementary. For instance, people who are very narcissistic and domineering may find partners who are very insecure and willing to accept any role as long as they can be in a relationship. In this case, the relationship is based on an asymmetry and on some degree of exploitation, but as such the fairness is maintained since both partners get their relational need fulfiled. The problem is that this type of complementarity is often only temporary. For instance, the insecure dependent person may enter therapy, become more assertive and start fighting for more reciprocity. In this case, the complementarity would end. Two things can happen then. Either the person who was in the I, exploitative position, can change, and the couple can move to a new more dialogic way of relating, or the relationship will end.

Furthermore, these modes have an implication for the therapist-client relation. All encounters between a counselor and a client leads to a Self-Other delineation in which these modes play a role. For example, clients who operate in the mode of the merger will try to bring the therapist into a merger. Clients who operate in the mode of 'being the subject', an I-It relationship may try to instrumentalize a therapist as a tool to reach a goal. For instance, in some places, the law requires that people who want to divorce need to show that they have attended a fixed number of marital counseling sessions. The idea is that this could avert some divorces. However, if a spouse is determined to get out of the marriage anyway, there is a risk that this spouse may pretend to attend couple therapy in good faith while in fact just waiting to log in the number of sessions required by the law. In this case, the therapist would be instrumentalized as an It, a tool to meet a goal. Conversely, some therapists may also function in this mode. Some professionals may be more interested in using their clients to ascertain their own importance as professional than in helping them, which of course would be very problematic.

Relational need templates and parenting

As counterparts, parents and children are dependent on each other for their self-definition, and the need templates of the parents have formative influence on the relational mode that their children will be able to reach. In the parent-child relationship, ideally, the parents should be able to operate in the mode of the dialogue and they should be able to adjust to the relational needs of their children, which are evolving during their development. On the other hand, if the parents are locked into a rigid mode of relating, their relational needs template will serve as a mould that will permanently shape the relational needs of their children. These relational needs will then serve as a relational need template in future relationships. This can have an effect on the next generations. Fortunately, children can also relate to other relatives or to other important adults who may be able to operate in other modes, and this will mitigate the effect of the relational need templates of the parents. However, this does not always happen.

An extreme example comes from a couple in which both partners had significant autistic traits. They had decided to marry despite their inability to engage in a close relationship. Within the premises of their limitations, they formed a rather stable couple. Eventually, they decided to have a child, but there was one problem: they had never been able to tolerate physical intimacy. They approached a gynecologist who agreed to proceed to an artificial insemination, and a boy was born as a result of this procedure. Unfortunately for the child, while the parents where good providers, neither of them could engage in the type of Self-Other dialogue that was necessary for his development. Also due to their own limitations, they were not interacting with other people who could provide this boy other opportunities for Self-Other differentiation. As soon as he entered kindergarten, it became obvious that he had too many difficulties in relating with adults and peers to attend public school, and that he needed to be referred to a therapeutic treatment center where he was admitted with a diagnosis of autism. While it is highly probable that there was a biological component to his condition, it was obvious that the relational need templates of his parents had contributed to the limitations in his ability to engage in other modes of relating.

The place of the therapist in the dialectical theory of the personality

Another major implication of the dialectic theory of the self is that it gives a new meaning to the healing encounter between the therapist, or counselor, and the client. Since all therapeutic encounters entail an encounter between a Self (the client) and a Not-Self (the professional), all therapeutic encounters promote a Self-Other delineation that can lead to increased individuation and increased autonomy. While no one can be cured from his or her ontic dependence, since it is inherent in the relational definition of the Self, therapy can help people to move from one mode of relating to another and to get closer to an I-Thou mode of relating. This does not depend on the type of therapy, or the level of expertise of the professional. It depends only on the professional's capacity to engage in a true meeting with another human being. This explains why so many different forms of therapy can lead to the same result. Many researchers have demonstrated that what counts the most in therapy is that the therapist is capable of being present for the client, not the technique. For instance, despite their inexperience, therapy students who show a genuine interest in their clients may be able to promote more progresses in these clients than well-trained therapists who sometime hide behind their professional expertise to avoid a genuine dialogue with their clients.

The role of the therapist as a 'ground' for the self of the client needs to be underscored in the new area of Internet-based self-help programs and online therapy sessions. If the therapeutic encounter needs to happen online rather than in person, it will change the dynamics of the encounter between the therapist and the client, but it will not preclude a genuine dialogue between them. On the other hand, Internet-based self-help programs, and self-help programs in general can be very helpful, but they will never be substitutes for the dialogic nature of a true therapeutic encounter.

Understanding bereavement from the perspective of the relational modes

When people lose a partner, they not only may experience the pain of losing a loved one or the pain that comes from all the other possible losses that follow from the death of this partner, but also may experience a deep level of distress that comes from losing their partner as the 'ground' that served a base for the definition of the Self. When this happens, these grievers may become severely depressed and turn to a therapist or a pastoral counselor for help. In that case, the grievers may seek the help of a therapist or a pastoral counselor, but they may not be ready to engage in formal treatment. In this situation, there is a danger that the griever turns to the professional just as a new 'ground' that serves as a substitute for the 'ground' that the deceased partner used to provide.

The danger of supportive therapy is that it becomes interminable since the need of a substitute 'ground' will not change until the griever is able to engage in new relationships outside of therapy. To avoid this pitfall, professionals need to focus on helping their clients to build new relationships that can serve as new sources of Self-Other delineation. They can help their clients to develop strategies to meet new people, or better, they can encourage them to engage in activities where they can help others. In this case, the new relationships would become not only new sources of Self-Other delineation but also sources of self-validation, which could become a powerful antidote to depression. In addition, if the professional is a pastoral counselor, he or she could encourage the griever to re-engage in religious practices and to re-engage in his or her congregation.

Chapter 4
The World of Relational Ethics

Introduction

Boszormenyi-Nagy states that "The ethics of Contextual Therapy is fairness-based rather than value-based. It is not a judgmental, objectifiable opinion or decision. It is a lived 'balance in motion' oscillating between the parties' mutual debts and merits" (Boszormenyi-Nagy, 1996: 373-374). In other words, for him, it is not enough to treat others in accordance with pre-set moral values, no matter how high these values may be. We need to be willing to examine how our acts and choices affect others, and then try to treat others in the same way we would have liked them to treat us.

This view connects very closely to M. Buber's own definition of ethics. He writes about a 'narrow ridge', a narrow space between a universe in which we define what is right and wrong according to our own personal view, and a universe in which morality is defined by others, by outsiders to the relationship. This can go from religious fundamentalism, political totalitarianism all the way to full-fledged nihilism, a total refusal of any values. The narrow ridge between these two universes is the space of the true encounter between people, the space of the true dialogue (Buber, 1947: 184).

Here, it is important to note that many authors are now using the term *relational ethics* in a vast array of fields without any reference to contextual therapy or to the work of M. Buber. The following is cited in the *Sage Encyclopedia of Qualitative Research* "Relational ethics is a contemporary approach to ethics that situates ethical actions explicitly in relationships. If ethics is about how we should live, then it is essentially about how we should live together. Acting ethically involves more than resolving ethical dilemmas through good moral reasoning; it demands attentiveness and responsiveness to our commitments to one another, to the earth, and to all living things" (Given, 2008: 748).

Since the ethics of contextual therapy are based on fairness and defined a form of ethics that is situated within the relationship, not outside of it like value ethics are, the question of what constitutes fairness becomes a central issue. Who can define what is fair or unfair in a given relationship? In contractual relationships, we can set an objective value to what we give and to what we receive. For instance, we can set a price for our work, and we expect to be paid accordingly. If this does not occur, we could seek redress from a court. Here, the definition of justice, or exploitation, is objective. However, what happens in close relationships?

The relational definition of fairness

In ordinary business and professional relationships, relationships are defined by contractual obligations. Here the definition is objective, and one can go to court to obtain redress if a contract is broken. In close relationships, things are very different. The amount of merit of a person and the degree of fairness of a relationship cannot be measured objectively by an observer, for instance the therapist. People have their own views of the value of what they give and the value of what they receive. Also, the amount of merit and the amount of indebtedness that people accumulate keep changing in accordance with what they give and receive over time. In short, each participant to the relationship has his or her view of the degree of fairness of the relationship, and the definition of what is fair or unfair depends on a dialogue between the parties involved.

Indeed, the valuation of what we give and receive is subjective. What value do we give to the time we make to listen to a friend who needs our help? Maybe the call took us away from an important task. Conversely, the call may have given us the chance to talk to someone at a time when we felt lonely. Our friend could not know whether her call forced us to make a sacrifice or whether it gave us an opportunity to feel better unless we speak about it. The same is true for the value of the present we offer to a partner. The fact that the gift has a known price tag does not tell anything about its relational value. Did this purchase require a great sacrifice, or was it a minor expense? Only we can determine that. Similarly, the response of our partner cannot be predicted from the price of the gift. For one person, receiving even a small gift will mean much. Another person may feel that even an expensive gift would not be enough to prove that we care.

If the fairness of a relationship cannot be measured objectively, can it still be measured at all? The answer is that the definition of fairness is intersubjective. It depends on a dialogue between all the people involved in the relationship. True fairness requires that each participant to the relationship recognizes that each of them has the right to a personal definition of what constitutes giving and receiving in the relationship. In other words, each participant to the relationship has an equal right to a personal view of what constitutes giving and receiving in the relationship and an equal obligation to respect the personal views of all the other people who are involved in this relationship. It can be defined by another kind of mutuality, however: mutuality of respect. True fairness occurs when all the participants to the relationship are capable of this mutual respect. In other words, true fairness can be defined as mutuality of respect.

Ethical imagination and its limits

We can try to imagine the side of the other concretely and try to be just, while also keeping our own side in mind. In other words, we can develop the ethical imagination discussed by Krasner and Joyce (1995). Still, our efforts could never bring us to fully understand the other person's perspective on the giving and receiving that has occurred between us.

We shall never know to what level we are indebted to others or how many merits we have accumulated until we hear their side, and they hear ours. This is true for therapists, too. As therapists, we should not rely on our own sense of justice to evaluate the degree of fairness or exploitation of a relationship. We would need to hear how each of the participants to the relationship views the situation. In brief, each person should be encouraged to present his or her side, and to explain how she or he views the giving and receiving in the relationship, something that parallels the direct address described by Krasner and Joyce (1995). At the same time, each person should be capable of listening to the other parties' presentation of the same situation and try to understand their views of the giving and receiving.

It is important to note that people's views about fairness depend on a great number of variables that can be found in any of the five dimensions of relational reality For instance, based on his age and cognitive development, a child may complain that he received less than his siblings simply because the toy that he has received was smaller than the other toys, even if in fact this toy was the most expensive one. Adults' judgment may be influenced by many psychological factors. A depressed person may devalue her own contributions. A person suffering from Alzheimer disease may not be able to credit a caregiver for his efforts, or conversely, this person may stop holding grudges against someone who has been unfair in the past. In short, people will never come to a complete agreement about the exact value of what they have given or what they have received, because it would be simply impossible.

Representations of fairness

In *Invisible loyalties*, Boszormenyi-Nagy proposed the metaphor of the ledger to describe how these debts and merits are recorded, but this image was problematic in two ways. First, the contribution of each of these persons cannot be measured objectively. Therefore, no one can keep a ledger of these people's contributions like the bookkeeper who registers the profits and losses of a company. Also, in close relationships, there is no date at which to balance the accounts like the bookkeeper who issues a report at the end of the fiscal year. For these reasons, Boszormenyi-Nagy adopted as a new image the kind of balance that one finds in marketplaces. It is a balance with two trays that move in accordance with what one puts on each of the trays. Also, the needles that indicate the weight move as soon as there is a change in one of the trays. This gives a better image of what happens in a close relationship where the degree of merit between the partners varies constantly in accordance with their respective contributions to the relationships

The difference between relational ethics and value ethics

We need to differentiate relational ethics from value ethics. Within the world of relational ethics, we act in accordance with our understanding of the direct effect of our behaviors on others. We also try to respond to their realistic needs and expectations. Within the world of value ethics, our decisions and our behaviors are guided by present moral and religious values, not by their actual effect on others.

Example I

Couples who abide by high moral values or religious values may decide to expand their biological family by adopting children instead of having more children of their own. They may do this out of a political or a religious ideal of sharing what one has with the less fortunate ones. Because this is a very noble ideal, these parents may overlook that their decision may affect their own children negatively, especially when the adopted children have special needs and require a lot of attention from their adoptive parents. In this case, it would not be enough to tell the biological children that it is good for them to learn to share. Here, relational ethics would require that these parents take the time to listen to their children's specific complaints and find ways to meet their needs realistically despite their obligations to their adoptive children. For instance, they could make the effort to find people who could escort their adoptive children to some of their therapy appointments so that they can find the time to resume special activities with their biological children.

Example II

Another example comes from people who engage in humanitarian missions that involve a danger to themselves, for instance when they choose to work as medical personnel in a war zone. Their children may suffer from being separated from parents who cannot take them to these dangerous places. These children may also develop a high degree of anxiety that could affect their future emotional development. At the same time, the parents of these volunteers can also experience similar anxiety. To tell these children and these parents that they should be proud to have family members who engage in a noble cause would not be enough. More specifically, relational ethics require that people do not use their moral values as a justification to escape facing their responsibilities toward others.

Here, relational ethics would require that these workers accept to engage in a genuine dialogue with all the family members who could be affected by their decision and try to understand their needs. It may require that these workers accept to lessen their ideals and accept to work in a less dangerous environment to prevent lasting emotional disturbances in their children. At the same time, they would have less responsibility to accommodate the needs of their own parents since these are adults who are expected to have sufficient resources to cope with life's difficulties.

Religious values and interfaith dialogue

We know that moral precepts and religious values vary greatly from groups to groups and religions to religions, and these differences serve to establish a boundary between the group of people who share these values and the people who do not. We know that clashes in values can often lead to severe confrontations between groups when one group begins to see other groups as outsiders who are in the wrong. The same is true of differences in religious beliefs. Over the centuries, they have been at the origin of many devastating wars of religion in many parts of the world.

At the same time, all religions promote values that are very similar. For instance, all religions promote the value of love and kindness, the value of compassion, or the value of caring for people in need. In *Toward a True Kinship of Faiths: How the World's Religions Can Come Together* (2011), the Dalai-Lama proposes that since these values are common to all religions but not exclusive to any of them, one way to promote a reconciliation between religions is to underline their common values. In his effort to promote an interfaith dialogue that would not exclude the non-believers who share these values, the Dalai-Lama proposed the term 'secular ethics' for these common values. Some have argued that the term 'secular' should not be used since it connotes values that would contrast with those of religion, and that the terms 'universal values' would fit better. Indeed, the Dalai Lama is also using 'universal values' and 'universal responsibility' as an alternate to 'secular ethics'. In any case, any of these terminologies gets very close to the notion of relational ethics as defined in contextual therapy and to its mandate, our responsibility toward the future generations.

In the second part of the book, Greteke De Vries dedicates an entire chapter to another way of promoting an interfaith dialogue. Here the avenue is to promote direct dialogue between religious leaders and community leaders at a local community level. This idea is the core principle of the Emouna movement, which is described in detail in her chapter.

The origins of relational ethics

The contributions of sciences

Boszormenyi-Nagy promotes the idea that our capacity for fairness, reciprocity, loyalty, and trustworthiness is necessary to ensure the viability of close relationships over time, and that these capacities are needed to ensure the success of our families through the generations. This is based on his clinical insight. Now his ideas have been confirmed by the work of researchers in fields as diverse as neurosciences, zoology, and economy.

In fact, more and more researchers believe that the capacities described by Boszormenyi-Nagy are anchored in our biological equipment both at a genetic level and at a neurobiological level and are common to all of us. If they are correct, we are programmed for reciprocity, cooperation, and loyalty, and this does not depend on the level of our moral development or on the degree of our mental health. If indeed relational ethics in a broad sense is an inescapable determinant of our behaviors toward others, this should have implications for all family therapists, not only for contextual therapists.

Neuroscientists have shown that our brains are equipped to remember what people have done for us and what we have done for them, which serve as a base for our evaluation of what they own us and what we own them, even if as discussed before this evaluation is not objective. We have also developed a capacity for mirroring, empathy (our ability to feel the same as someone else), and sympathy (our ability to perceive the feelings of someone else even if we do not experience the same feelings). Furthermore, in general we try to avoid experiencing unpleasant feelings. Children who have been taught to experience shame, an unpleasant feeling, when they do something wrong like lying are more likely than others to try to avoid the behaviors that have triggered these unpleasant feelings.[1] All these factors play a very important role in our relationships. For more information on them, see *The Neurobiology of Human Values* (Changeux et al., 2005).

Neuroscientists have indeed confirmed Boszormenyi-Nagy's hypothesis about the indirect benefits of our generosity toward others. The research initiated by Richard Davidson (Goleman & Davidson, 2017) shows that meditation on compassion leads to brain changes, and, in general, has beneficial effects on the immune system and blood pressure. More specifically, Inagaki, Ross and Lauren (2018) have shown that, in humans, offering support to others may activate neural regions that in animals are shown to relate to parental care. Giving to others also decreases the activity of the amygdala. Since the amygdala is a brain structure that is related to the flight and flee response and its activation leads to an increase of stress hormones and blood pressure, a decrease in its activity resulting from giving to others would have a health benefit.

Furthermore, several authors in the field of economy, like Kaplan Thaler and Koval (2006), have been able to demonstrate that being 'nice' to others can be a winning proposition when it comes to individual benefits. They have used different methods to demonstrate that fair sharing may bring better returns than selfish grabbing when it comes to individual profit.

We know that traditional societies tend to place great emphasis on the maintenance of a fixed social order and much less emphasis on the implementation of social justice. Still, most of these societies place great emphasis on giving and receiving. Mauss (2016), a prominent French anthropologist, believes that the exchange of gifts exerts a crucial social function in archaic societies. His ideas have influenced many researchers like Godbout (Godbout & Caillé, 2000) who believe that, in the act of giving, what counts is not the possibility of a return but the establishment of a relationship and the possibility of trust between the people who exchange gifts.

For a long time, the general opinion was that our capacity for morality, our humanity, was just a thin cover hiding much deeper-rooted tendencies to use power and aggression to establish our ground against others, a tendency that we had inherited from animals. This was for instance the position of Freud (1930, 1961). Over time, many researchers in the field of ethology, zoology, and social sciences have challenged this view. By now, most researchers believe in a continuum between our capacity for morality and altruism and the qualities that have evolved in a variety of species over time. All these ideas are illustrated

---

1   While most modern educators advise against using shaming as a method of education because it can lead to low self-esteem, it is also true that accepting the notion that children have the right to do whatever comes to their mind without any consideration for others has also lead to serious negative consequences in society.

best in the work of the primatologist De Waal (1996, 2006). When it comes to humans, the journalist and social historian Bregman (2020) argues that humans are fundamentally mostly decent, and that more recognition of this view would likely be beneficial to everyone.

The ethics of responsibility for relationships

In the world of relational ethics, the degree of fairness of a relationship can be measured in terms of fair giving and receiving, or in terms of a mutuality of respect for the views of others. Not only that. It can also be defined people's mutual acceptance of responsibility for the relational consequences of their actions. In symmetrical relationships, for instance in couple relationships, the definition of fairness depends on a dialogue between the parties involved, but what is the definition of fairness in the parent-child relationship? Fairness toward children cannot be defined by this kind of reciprocity. It needs to be defined in terms of the parents' willingness to accept the responsibility to care for their children, and to think about the long-term consequences of their actions.

The intrinsic transgenerational tribunal of solidarity

The degree of fairness in the parent-child relationship has implications not only for the children, but also for the next generations, and ultimately is assessed in terms of what Boszormenyi-Nagy has defined as the 'justice of the human order', by analogy with Buber's 'human order of being'. Injuries to this order are measured in terms of 'existential guilt', which is incurred by people who know that they have injured an order that is at the foundation of all human existences, theirs included. This notion connects with the notion of an 'intrinsic transgenerational tribunal of solidarity', also known simply as 'the transgenerational tribunal'. Boszormenyi-Nagy writes: "The tribunal stands for the outcome of consequences from posterity's vantage point and thus it represents the "integration" of the sum total of all vertical and horizontal merit ledgers ... In a way the tribunal represents a dialogue between each of us and humanity as a whole – the justice of the common order." (Boszormenyi-Nagy, 1996: 378).

In this perspective, it behooves us to protect the future generations from destructive expectations coming from past generations, for instance the expectation to discriminate against a certain group. We also need to find out what resources our predecessors had been able to mobilize in the face of adversity and to learn from it for the benefit of the next generations. In short, we need to use discrimination to make sure that what we transmit to our children will contribute to the survival of the next generations, and to the survival of humanity in general.

This tribunal can be considered as a sort of court of justice that is intrinsic to all relationships. Using the analogy of computers, one could envision it as a background program that is always on and monitors the consequences of our actions for others, and vice-versa, the consequences of their actions for us. This monitoring would apply not only to our current interactions. It would also evaluate the consequences of our actions for the next generations. Furthermore, since the consequences of our actions are reverberated through the network of all possible people who could be indirectly affected by what we do, this monitoring would also extend well beyond our families, our close relationships and our lifetime.

Boszormenyi-Nagy states: "There are no feedback mechanisms that could regulate the interactions between us and the next generations. Not only our children, but our great grandchildren whom we may never meet will have to live with the consequences of our choices sometimes long after we are gone. There are no feedback mechanisms to bring corrections to our behaviors. We are the only ones who are responsible to care about the survival of the next generations". He states then: "I propose that these interpersonal consequences constitute the most important aspect of close relating, and this is the basis for both relational and therapeutic ethics" (Quotes transcribed by C. Ducommun-Nagy from a videotaped presentation by Boszormenyi-Nagy in San Francisco in 1985).

Transgenerational solidarity

Boszormenyi-Nagy proposes that the judge is *transgenerational solidarity*. This would include not only solidarity to the not yet born members of our families and our groups, but also inter-group solidarity, solidarity with the future inhabitants of our planet in general, and some degree of interspecies solidarity. In line with Jonas' thesis in *The Imperative of Responsibility – In Search of an Ethics for the Technological Age* (1984), he believes that the introduction of modern technologies does not have the same effect as the introduction of new technologies in the past. These new technologies can affect the future of humanity, and this is not limited to weapons of mass destructions like nuclear weapons. Today, many new medical technologies can affect the future of humanity, for instance medically assisted reproductive technologies that would include artificially induced genetic changes. Artificial intelligence, which can appear benign at first sign, can also affect the future of humanity in ways that are still hard to imagine. While we cannot be held personally accountable for the potential damages caused by any of these new technologies, we have the obligation to care about the interests of the future. Do we care about the future of not only our family but also about the future of humanity, or not? Do we do things that give the future generations a better chance to survive, or not? We could do this for instance by getting involved in groups that demand more accountability from politicians and scientists, more accountability for the future of our planet. In short, transgenerational solidarity also includes universal solidarity, and universal responsibility.

Of course, this transgenerational tribunal does not issue rewards and sentences like an ordinary tribunal would. Do people who exploit others and do not care about posterity receive a kind of sentence in the form of existential guilt that could then result in some forms of self-sabotage or psychosomatic symptoms? Could people also incur an indirect punishment by being exposed to the destructive entitlement of people who have been the victims of their unfair demands? It would be difficult to demonstrate that people who do not care about posterity will automatically pay a price for that. However, it is not unrealistic to think that people who care about the consequences of their actions for the future generation do get a reward in the form of constructive entitlement, and freedom from existential guilt. This means that we can earn constructive entitlement through our efforts to move toward universal solidarity and universal responsibility. This notion becomes then a source of optimism about the future.

The model of the transgenerational tribunal of solidary brings together the realm of justice that is specific to close relationships and family relationships, together with the realm of justice that pertains to a much larger field, the field of our interconnectedness with humanity in general, and our responsibility toward the future in general. This second notion is very close to the notion of universal responsibility, which is the cornerstone of secular ethics that has already been discussed. It is also connecting with the notion of *Ubuntu* which can be defined as 'I am, because we are', or as 'the belief in a universal bond of sharing that connects all humanity'.

Transgenerational solidarity and the mandate for therapy and prevention

Boszormenyi-Nagy believes that a great risk for future generations comes from the increasing burden that society places on children. In modern societies, parents become increasingly isolated due to major changes in their families. More and more children live in nuclear families. Fewer and fewer parents can get the support from extended families to raise their children. This is due to many social and economic factors like the migration to big cities, or the migration to a new country. Also, with an increasing level of divorce, many more children live in single-parent families. In addition, parents, isolated or not, can become bewildered by fast and unforeseeable changes, like the massive changes brought by the Covid-19 pandemics. Consequently, these children are deprived from an extended support system, and in many cases, they become the sole source of trust and affection for their depleted and isolated parents. These children not only are exposed to a serious injustice, but also will become depleted like their parents. This will result in further injustices and further damages to the next generations. Boszormenyi-Nagy associates the progressive deterioration of the parent-child relationship over the generations with the notion of entropy in physics, a tendency of physical systems to move to an increased level of disorganization over time.

Conversely, he believes that the resource that can prevent an ever-increasing exploitation of the future generations comes from helping parents to discover that in caring about the needs and the rights of their children, which of course is good for the children, they can gain constructive entitlement in the form of self-validation and self-delineation, and this gain becomes a resource for the parents as well. In short, parents do not need to be capable of altruism to be good parents; they just need to be helped to discover that they can gain something for themselves when they make the effort to do a little more for their children. For him, this is the major source of therapeutic optimism. He associates the notion of constructive entitlement with the notion of 'negentropy' proposed by the physicist Schrödinger in 1962: it is defined as the capacity of all living systems to move toward an increased level of organization, which is necessary to sustain life.

The mandate of therapy and the quality of human survival

In accordance with the discussion of our responsibility toward the future, Boszormenyi-Nagy also explored the mandate of therapy in the context of the quality of human survival. However, first we need to examine the ethical implications of therapy and counseling in general. In individual therapy, therapists contract only with one person and do not include the interests of other people in their treatment contract. Most couple therapists focus entirely on the two partners, and do not include their children in their consideration, even if they may be the most affected by the result of the treatment. Furthermore, couple therapy can even influence the couple's decision to have children together or not, but it is very unlikely that couple therapists would include the interests of unborn children in their consideration. We generally assume that therapists who treat families always include all the family members in their treatment contract. However, this is not automatically the case. First, more often than not, they work with subgroups. There are many examples of that. A family therapist may receive a remarried mother with her husband, their common children, and her children from her first marriage, but they may omit to include these children's father in their consideration. When children are placed in foster care, the family therapist may see the children with their host parents, and not include the biological parents in any of the treatment sessions, etc. But, both from a systemic point of view, and from an ethical point of view, this would be a mistake. Therapists and counselor should care about all the people who could be affected by the consequences of their interventions, whether they are present or not in the meetings, whether they know them or not, and this care should include the interests of the future generations as well.

Contextual therapy and the common mandate of all therapies

Boszormenyi-Nagy insists on the notion that contextual therapy is not simply a school of family therapy, but that it is searching for the common denominator of therapy as a whole: "Currently, the integration of biological therapy, individual psychotherapy, and systemic family (relational) therapy can only be empirical and fortuitous, rather than rational. The three methodologies may coexist with one another in a treatment plan, but they are mutually non-translatable. Yet, considering the inevitable interlocking between individual and relational realities, selective reliance on any of these three approaches would be oversimplifying and reductionistic. I propose that through transcending the realms of biological, psychological, and systemic transactional regulations, we arrive at the sphere of the ethics of responsibility for the long-term consequences of relating. Without this indispensable foundation, relational reality cannot be understood" (Boszormenyi-Nagy,

1987, 2014: 295). He concludes in postulating that all the possible forms of therapy from individual to family therapy can be united through one mandate, the mandate of caring and fitted under one single umbrella, the umbrella of transgenerational solidarity.

Multidirected partiality, a therapeutic tool and a mandate

Goals settings and conflicts of interests

As discussed above, ideally, all therapists should include the interest of posterity in setting treatment goals, but this is often not the case. Individual therapists establish treatment goals with one client only and they do not assume responsibility for the effect of their interventions on family members or other people. Couple therapists contract with the two partners who seek help and need to set treatment goals that are agreeable to both parties, and here as well, the contract does not include others like the couple's children. If the partners get into an argument during a session, the therapist will refuse to side with one partner against the other and will remain neutral.

However, what about family therapists and counselors who want to work with an entire family? It is obvious that they cannot expect that all the family members will enter therapy with the same expectations, the same interests, and the same goals. How should the diverging interests of the youth who wants to be granted more autonomy and the parent who is not ready to grant it be addressed? Some family members may even refuse to attend family therapy. Is it still possible to proceed with family therapy without them, or is family therapy contraindicated in these cases? When family members cannot agree on common goals, family therapists can be tempted to solve the difficulty by setting their own goals for therapy based on what they consider healthy for the family. In this way, they can escape the trap of siding with anyone. However, in most cases, this 'neutrality' still amounts to some form of siding. For instance, if the family therapist believes that the issue that causes problems is the lack of autonomy of the youth, this therapist could try to help this youth to leave home at the cost of ignoring the needs of the parents. This would amount to siding with the youth against the parents.

The definition of multidirected partiality

For contextual therapists, the only alternative to address the conflicting interests of the family members is to engage them in a dialogue about the treatment goals in which they can express their own views and describe their own expectations and at the same time also help them to make space for the views of other members of the family. This requires a different attitude from the family therapist. It can be neither unilateral nor neutral. This is where Boszormenyi-Nagy has coined the term 'multidirectional partiality', which appears in an article published already in 1966 (see reprint in Boszormenyi-Nagy, 1987, 2014). Soon after that, he also began using the term 'multidirected partiality'. While both terms are exactly equivalent, the current tendency is to use the second one: multidirected partiality. Both terms entail a contradiction. By definition, partiality entails the notion of unilaterality. How can there then be such a thing as multidirectional partiality? The answer is in the timing: it is a successive offer of partiality to each and all of the persons who can be affected by the therapy process. It is also a tool that can be used to promote interpersonal dialogue outside of therapy.

Multidirected partiality as a mandate

One needs to understand multidirected partiality as an ethical stand and a treatment strategy that is applied to all the treatment situations that are met by contextual therapists and all the diverse situations that are met by contextually inspired professionals, including pastoral counselors. It is based on an attitude of 'multilateral fairness'. However, this type of fairness should not be confused with the attitude of universal compassion or universal love that is promoted by the great world religions, nor is it based on a general humanistic attitude. As individuals, many contextual therapists chose this approach because it was compatible with their religious convictions or their humanistic views. However, here, multilateral fairness has to be understood in a more limited fashion. Here the rationale for the use of multidirected partiality and multidirected fairness and for multidirected partiality does not come from any of these universal values. It comes from the understanding of the functioning of family systems. In business, one of the main jobs of marketing consultants is to help the firm for which they work to beat the competition. Consequently, these consultants could not offer their services to competing business without being accused of disloyalty to the first company. This does not apply to the situation of contextual therapists. Ultimately, in families, no one gains from truly winning over the others, nor from causing seriously damages to each other, since this would have a negative effect on the family system of which they are part. This remains true of ex-spouses who have children together. Even if their relationship remains very contentious, they will not gain from destroying each other, since this would have a negative effect on their common children. Hence, ultimately, both would lose.

Also, in adopting a position of multilateral fairness and inclusiveness, contextual therapists avoid the risk that family loyalty pushes family members to become protective of each other in the presence of a stranger, the therapist, and begin to refrain from discussing their true feelings or needs. If they feel that the therapist is genuinely interested to help all of them, it becomes easier for them to discuss their own personal goals without having to be protective of the others. In families, people may have very diverging interests.

As a stand, multidirected partiality is based on the therapeutic mandate of caring about all the people who can be affected by the therapeutic process, with special consideration of the future generations. The therapist needs to offer each and all the family members a fair opportunity to present their side and their aspirations, and the therapist needs to offer each of the family members a fair chance to earn constructive entitlement by helping them to accept to consider the position and the needs of other family members, especially children.

Multidirected partiality as a method

As a method, multidirected partiality requires that the contextual practitioners give an equal opportunity to each of the family members to present his or her own view of the situation that has brought the family to seek help, their own expectations, and their own view of the way they are treated by others. More specifically, they should be asked to present their own views of the giving and receiving that occurs in the family: what they believe they have given, what they believe they received or did not receive, what injustices they experienced, who can or cannot make up for them. After having offered all their attention to this person, which is a form of giving, the practitioners will be in a better position to ask this person to give attention to the positions expressed by the other family members. During the entire course of therapy, the main tool of the therapist remains multidirected partiality.

Now to an important question: in what order should the therapist offer partiality to the family members? This cannot be learnt from a textbook; it only comes from experience. However, there are guiding principles that can help answer this question. A very first step in the first meeting with a family is to raise the question of names: how people want to be addressed. Each society has its own conventions about the use of names, and about the level of formality that is appropriate. In some societies, especially in the USA, therapists and clients may address each other by first name. This may be unthinkable in other societies. In many cases, professionals and clients will address each other according to their local habits, but it still is worth checking whether this works for everyone or not. For instance, some children may object to be called by their nicknames and may ask to be called by their official names, or vice versa. These issues need to be addressed at the beginning of the first encounter with the family, not only for practical purposes, but also because the way people address each other has relational consequences that are not limited to the person who is addressed. This discussion also applies to chosen pronouns.

Example

Here comes the example of a consultation with a young mother who has entered therapy because she wants to become a better parent and regain custody of her daughter. The consultation is attended by this young woman and her mother. She has introduced herself by her first name and her mother as "my mom" (her daughter is not present). Here is the consultant's response: "If I use your first name, than you are the daughter, but here you are coming as a parent, not as a child, so it would make more sense to call you 'mother' and to call your mom 'grandmother'." To this, the young woman replies: "Yes, this is a good idea. It will remind me why I am here."

Order of interventions

Especially at the beginning, professionals need to offer their partiality first to the people who are in the most difficult predicaments, to the people who have experienced the greatest degree of injustices, to the ones who are the most vulnerable, or the less likely to be able to present their side without receiving special support. This may apply to people who have difficulties in communicating due to a specific impairment, and it also applies to children. Even small children should be given an opportunity to speak and to tell what is in their minds in their own terms. However, at the same time, professionals should not allow parents to put their children in the spotlight and force them to explain why the family are seeking help. This task belongs to the parents. Not only the children who are asked to talk first are in effect parentified, but it may place them in a loyalty conflict if the therapist asks them to speak about issues that the parents do not want to address. If the parents refuse to respond to the demand of the professional, one could begin by giving them credit for the fact that they may be exhausted by the situation and that they may wish that someone could take some burden off their shoulders. This fair recognition of their predicament may be enough to help them to talk. One can also remind them that if they do not present their own view of the situation, it will be even more difficult to help them.

Another avenue to help such parents is to ask them to give an example of a time when their child has been available to them, a time when the child has expressed concern for them or done something to help them. When indeed the parents see their child as the wrongdoer, this question will take them by total surprise, and their first response will be a dismissal. How could you think that our child does anything for us? Parents may have a hard time to produce any answer, but if the professional insists and provides some potential example, parents will end up remembering a time when their children indeed have done something positive for them. This change of view is important. First, it will indicate to the professional that these parents are still capable of fairness. Also, parents who can see their children as capable of giving will feel better as parents. They did not raise children who are only troublemakers but children who are also capable of fair giving, and this should boost their image as parents. In turn, this can help them to accept more parental responsibilities. The children, too, will be taken by surprise. How could a stranger whom they meet for the first time, cares to try to see them in a different light? If their children had a negative attitude toward therapy, this would change their view and motivate them to work with the professional.

These early questions are very important because they set the stage for the therapeutic process. However, it would be too much to provide the reader with a full array of the questions that can be raised during the course of an entire treatment. A French author on contextual therapy has attempted that (Michard, 2017). An example of such questions may be: "Who do you think has given more to the other, you or your partner?" Reading such questions may be helpful as a source of inspiration, but if one uses them in the sessions, one may be prevented from hearing people's spontaneous statements about their own views of the situation. In many cases, it is more productive to pay great attention to what people say and then follow up with questions.

Multidirected partiality and inclusiveness

Contextual therapists extend their partiality to all the people who can be affected by their interventions, whether they are present, absent, deceased, or not yet born. They also include all the people who have contributed to the giving and receiving between the generations. This may sound unrealistic but let us examine how this is possible. Some people may not be able to participate in the treatment session because of geographical obstacles. They may live too far away. Some people are cut off from their families by migration and may never be able to reunite with their relatives. However, in all these types of cases, the obstacles could be overcome using one of the various systems of online meetings, unless some of the family members live in countries in which communication is controlled by the state, where communication with the outside could place them in danger. In this case, one can remain partial to them at least by asking the accessible family members about their view of these absent relatives, about their view of what these people may feel or expect and their view about what they may owe them. There are also situations in which the cut-off is required by the law. It can be the case of people who are banned from contact with an ex-spouse after episodes of domestic violence, or people who are incarcerated. Even if these people have been sentenced as wrongdoers, they still deserve some consideration as human beings and as parents who could still do things to make their children's lives better (see the example later in this section).

Multidirected partiality is not limited to people who are alive. One can extend fairness to a deceased ancestor whose positive contributions have been overlooked by the family, or one can ask people to think about the rights and the needs of the generations to come. Professionals can also offer partiality to a long-deceased parent, especially parents who are viewed very negatively by their children for a good reason; for instance, parents who have been abusive or neglectful. To reach this goal, the professional may ask the family member some questions about the deceased parents to see if this person's life predicaments could have triggered their destructive entitlement. In many cases, especially when the children were removed from the parents' care at an early age, there may be too many unknown elements in these parents' life history to come to a clear conclusion, and the therapist may be able to produce only some hypotheses about the injustices they may have experienced. However, even so, this could be helpful. Just the simple hypothesis that parents may have struggled with injustices that could have let them to turn toward their children with unfair expectations or led to treating them harshly could already bring changes. It would help the present family members to move toward a new narrative about these parents: a narrative of unfortunate circumstances rather than a narrative of personal meanness. This would constitute a first step into the exoneration process that we shall soon examine as one of the important therapeutic resources in contextual therapy.

Limits to multidirected partiality

Like any other professionals, contextual therapists should consider the systemic constraints that can affect their work, especially the legal constraints that can set limits to what they can offer to their clients. Here is an example of a situation in which a mistaken understanding of multidirected partiality ended up causing damages not only to an entire family, but even to the therapist: owing to an episode of incestuous behaviors of the father toward his adopted teen daughter, this family consulted a psychologist who was contextually oriented. The father was very sorry about this episode and very motivated to get help. The therapist believed that since the father had stopped his behaviors and had entered therapy voluntarily, multidirected partiality toward the father required that his actions would not be reported to child protective services as required by law. This ended up badly. One day the teen had to miss a class because of a family therapy session. The teacher asked her why she needed to attend therapy, and she briefly explained the situation. The teacher, who was also a mandated by law to report abuses, contacted the child protective services to make sure that the situation had already been reported. Since this was not the case, the court was notified. The judge ordered the immediate removal of the teen from the home, and she was placed in a residential treatment facility. The father received a suspended sentence. He could stay at home, but he was prevented from any access to his daughter, including participation in family therapy. Furthermore, the treating psychologist received a blame from the national psychology association, with a potential risk of exclusion. If this therapist had immediately reported the situation to the child protective services as required by the law and been able to show the father's willingness to get help, the judge most likely would have authorized the therapist to proceed without removing the teen from her home, and the family therapy treatment indeed could have been successful as anticipated by the therapist.

Multidirected partiality: What is required from professionals?

Multidirected partiality requires two capacities: a capacity for multilateral fairness and a capacity for empathy. 'Empathy' is an important ingredient in human relationships in general. Without any capacity for empathy, it would be hard to imagine that we could function as contextual professionals or as any professionals in the field of human services in general. However, it would be naïve to believe that we can always be able to empathize with anyone, in any circumstances, and that we always offer people the unconditional positive regard that is at the core of Rogerian psychotherapy (Rogers, 1951). At the same time, there are methods to increase our sensitivity to others, which can come from focused training (see Berzin *Developing Balanced Sensitivity*, 1998).[2] We can also participate in programs like the Emouna program described by Greteke De Vries in Section II of this book. Still, empathy has many kinds of limits.

---

[2] Also available at https://bit.ly/3HbEVy0

The limits of empathy

It is not possible to empathize with people who have behaved in ways that are horrifying by any human standard. The only door that remains open to offer them partiality is a realistic humanism: no one is born a monster. From this position, one can then try to look for any residual human qualities that these people may still have. One can also hope to build on these remaining qualities to try to help these people to re-engage in some forms of giving to others. However small the gesture may be, it can lead to a slight increase of humanness in this person. This is important, especially if the person has children. The slight increase in humanness will not change the past, but it may be just enough for the children to feel less ashamed about their parentage, which in turn can have positive consequences for the future generations.

Empathy also has its limit when people have a life experience that is very far from our own experience. We can tell someone: "I know what you feel" or even: "I really feel for you", but what does it mean when we say it to the man who has lost his sight, or to the woman who is permanently bound to a wheelchair? We can try to develop sensitivity to their predicament. We can try to eat in the dark as an exercise to increase our sensitivity to the predicament of blindness, or we may know what it means to be bound to a wheelchair if we have to use one for a short time after surgery, but their world will never be ours. It will always remain difficult to empathize with them authentically. In these cases, it is much more honest to acknowledge our limitations. For instance, one could say: "I have had to use a wheelchair once, so I have some ideas about what the world looks like when one cannot stand and when one depends on others for many things, but for you, what is the most important, the most difficult, the most unfair, or conversely, do you see any resource in your situation that people may overlook?".

It is even more difficult to show authentic empathy to people who have been exposed to situations that go beyond the limits of our ordinary imagination, like people who live in situations of total devastation after a war or a natural disaster, or who are survivors of genocides. We can try the best to develop sensitivity to their predicament, but we shall never really be able to put ourselves in their shoes, no matter how hard we would try. In this situation, we can only try our best to understand their life by learning as much as possible about all these situations through meeting people who talk about their life experiences in public or privately. We may read about their lives or watch movies that illustrate their predicaments. This is better than burdening our clients with the added task of educating us about their life circumstances. However, in the end, in all these situations, the only thing we can do is to acknowledge the fact that we have been spared these tremendous hardships, and act with humility toward the clients who have had such difficult life experiences.

In some situations, the reverse could occur. Some therapists may have experienced a degree of affluence and privileges that cannot even be fathomed. An example is the person who reported that she grew up in her parents' palace and that she needed a bicycle to commute from her private quarters to the dining hall. She may have a harder time than other therapists to understand the life of ordinary children. Conversely, many professionals have gained their qualifications after a hard struggle against adversity. Some have grown up in families where they have experienced abuse or abandonment. Some may have experienced poverty or discrimination. Some may have begun their studies after a tragic accident that left them permanently disabled, like the pastoral counselor of a nursing home who started his studies after he had become paralyzed from the neck down following a sport accident when he was a teenager. Professionals who have been exposed to such serious hardships may have difficulties to extend empathy to clients who complain about a life that appears much easier than theirs.

Overcoming our limits to offer empathy and multidirected partiality

In all situations in which our natural empathy reaches its limits, we can still rely on multidirected partiality. Empathy belongs to the dimension of psychology. Multidirected partiality and multilateral fairness belongs to the dimension of relational ethics. Relational ethics behoove us to make sure that we give a voice to everyone who is reached by our interventions, whether we can empathize with them or not. However, multidirected partiality is also not automatic; it may reach its limits in several circumstances. One of the limitations comes from a lack of knowledge about the life of the people we meet. It may be difficult to offer partiality to people if we do not know what the premises of their lives are. If we are not familiar with the kind of constraints that are placed on family members, we may not be able to see how it affects the giving and receiving between them. Also, we may try to encourage them to give to others in ways that are not available to them.

Another crucial element is that if we do not know enough about the socio-historical circumstances in which families have evolved over time, we may miss the elements of their ancestors' life that could explain their behaviors and consequently their consequences on the next generations. For instance, in the current time, especially in Europe, it is increasingly more common for couples to have children without being bound by any official ties, and their children do not incur any legal consequences for the fact that they are not born within a marriage. However, this was not the case in the past. Often these children were removed from the care of their unmarried mother, and they could not inherit from their biological fathers. If one forgets these historical elements, it may become very difficult to understand the injustices that a grandparent born in these circumstances may have incurred and that may explain the grandparent's inability to care about the needs of his or her own children. For this reason, the more professionals can learn about the socio-historical background of their clients' families, the more they will be able to offer their partiality to all the family members.

The World of Relational Ethics

Co-therapy and supervision as a resource toward multidirected partiality

Another way to increase our ability to be partial to people is co-therapy. In many cases, our co-worker may have a different scope of life experiences and knowledge that can expand our possibilities to offer partiality to our clients. When our limitations come from visible or invisible prejudices against a specific group or even against the practitioners of a given religion, we owe it to our clients to try to overcome these prejudices through various means, for instance by participating in interfaith meetings. Contextual therapy supervisors and supervisors in general need to be very attentive to these issues.

A more serious limitation to multidirected partiality comes from our own experience of injustices. How can we truly be fair to people if people have not been fair to us? This would require an extensive discussion of the nature of the injustices that we can incur and a detailed discussion of their relational consequences. But in short, when we are blinded by our own experience of injustice to the point of becoming unfair to our clients, the only remedy comes from supervision. In this case, the supervisors need to apply the same method of multidirected partiality that is used in therapy. They need to begin by extending their partiality to the supervisee and then a result from this fair crediting helps the professional to extend more partiality to his or her clients.

Professionals who have experienced split loyalties in their families may also have difficulties in maintaining multidirected partiality, especially in working with couples. When the partners begin to fight, it may remind them of their own childhood. They may feel torn again or they may experience a high level of anxiety. In both cases, it may be difficult for them to maintain a position of multidirected partiality.

The parent-child relationship in the perspective of relational ethics

General considerations

In general, contextual therapy has focused its attention on to the parent-child relationship as it presents in nuclear and extended families in North America and Europe, but it has also given consideration to a number of other forms of families: single parent families, matrilineal families in which grandmothers raise the children of their single daughters, families where parents have remarried, and more recently the new type of families that can be created because of medically assisted reproduction involving donors. (Ducommun-Nagy, 2010a). Contextual therapists have also considered the problems that can occur in families with mixed ethnic, racial, or religious backgrounds. Furthermore, contextual therapists have paid great attention to the effect that social injustices and discrimination can have on families. On the other hand, one of the shortcomings of contextual therapy up to now is that it has not addressed some of the forms of family relationships that can be found in many other parts of the world, or the beliefs that could be related to them. For instance, in some cultures, the relationship between a child and an aunt or an uncle may be more significant than the relationship with a mother or a father. Also, children may be given roles that do not exist in an ordinary Western society.

Contextual therapists should not assume that because they understand the workings of relational ethics, they can understand any family, any parent-child relationship, in any environment and in any culture. This is not true. For this reason, it is important that contextual therapists and all other kinds of therapists or counselors try to learn as much as possible about the culture and the religion of the people with whom they are working. Courses on ethnicity can be very helpful, but at the same time, one needs to remember that the courses themselves occur in a certain ethnic background and for this reason, the courses themselves can entail a certain degree of biases. In addition, when professionals learn about the specificity of a certain group through a course on ethnicity, they may develop pre-conceptions that can later become an obstacle in their work with families coming from this group.

Contextual therapists, and especially pastoral counselors can develop an understanding of groups they are not familiar with through programs that encourage meetings between community leaders of different backgrounds in programs like the Emouna program, which is discussed in the second part of the book. In some specific situations, professionals may go further and want to invite cultural mediators into the treatment sessions to foster a better contact with the families with whom they are working.

Children identified as special beings: An honor or a burden?

In many societies, some children are identified as special beings very early on. They may be recognized as part of a lineage of people who have special powers or special functions in their societies, for instance shamans. They can also be recognized as the reincarnation of a known ancestor. In Tibetan Buddhism, it is not rare that a child is recognized as the reincarnation of a highly accomplished religious figure, as was the case with the Dalai-Lama. When children are recognized as special beings, in any kind of tradition, anywhere is the world, they automatically benefit from a special status. Often this special status gives them access to a special education or special training that would not be available to their siblings. Also, these children's special status gives a special social status to their entire family. In short, the recognition of children as special beings appears to be a benefit for everyone. However, at the same time, this special status comes with a number of expectations and restrictions. These children may be raised separately from their family. They may not be allowed ordinary childhood activities like playing with other kids. In the case of children who are recognized as the reincarnation of a highly developed monastic, they may be sent to a monastery at an early age, ordained early and then expected to live their entire adult life as monastics. Furthermore, in any tradition that attributes special powers to these children, they may be expected to perform rituals. When people turn to these special children for blessing, it automatically changes the hierarchy between adults and children. Does this amount to the same kind of parentification that one sees in families?

In brief, one could raise a valid question: could these special children be the victims of some level of injustices? In most cases, within a given society or a given faith, people would not raise this question, but what about contextual therapists? We can assume that from the point of value ethics, the life of these children would not be considered as unfair. From the point of view of relational ethics, the only way to assess the level of injustices that these children may incur would come from a dialogue between them, their parents and/or their caregiver, and such a dialogue is unlikely to occur, except maybe in the case of teenagers who may begin to rebel against the future that is expecting them. Most important in these situations is that contextual therapists and counselors in general learn to recognize their own biases, for instance the Western view that children should not be imposed any roles that restrict their lives as children.

Symmetric and asymmetrical relationships

From the point of view of contextual therapy, the only true existential asymmetry in relationships is found in the parent-child relationship. Children come into life because of the actions of the people who have conceived them. Children do not create their parents, and they cannot choose to enter the word or not. Therefore, there is a fundamental asymmetry of responsibilities between parents and children, and this asymmetry has an existential basis.

One could argue that over the life cycle, parents and children end up giving and receiving in a relatively symmetrical manner. In the early years, children are vulnerable and need care. Giving flows from parents to the children. When children become adults, they often give as much to their parents as they receive from them. Later in life, the parents may become vulnerable, and they may need to rely on their children as caregivers. However, in the end, these temporary changes of position in the giving and receiving do not affect the asymmetrical nature of the parent-child relationship.

On the other hand, the relationship between friends and partners is characterized by the fact that each party has an equal option to enter the relationship and to leave it. The relationship is symmetrical in terms of responsibilities. This applies even if one of the partners is more emotionally dependent on the relationship than the other is, or if there is an inequality of power.

Therapeutic relationships belong to the same category, even if there is an obvious asymmetry of functions: therapists are there to help their clients, not the reverse. Also, during therapy, the client may regress to an infantile position and see the therapist as a parental figure. In pastoral counseling and spiritual guidance in general, there is an added asymmetry because the pastor or the spiritual leader has access to the sacred, and to forms of power that are not available to the people who consult them, for instance the empowerment to bestow blessings.

The ethical imperative of caring also brings an asymmetry into the relationship between therapists and clients. Therapists have the obligation to care about their clients, while clients do not have the obligation to care about their therapists. Still, the relationship between the client and therapist or the pastoral counselor is defined by an agreed-upon contractual relationship, and it does not entail the existential asymmetry that exists between parents and children.

What are children entitled to?

While, in general, the definition of fairness needs to be the result of a dialogue between the parties involved, in the case of children, fairness needs to entail recognition of their basic rights. According to the UN Convention on the Rights of the Child, children's basic rights include a right to life, survival, protection from violence, abuse or neglect, the right to an education that enables them to fulfil their potential, a right to express their opinions and be listened to, and very importantly, the right to be raised by their parents or at least to have the least restricted level of relationship with them. It is not clear what this means for children who have been adopted or who have been conceived with the help of a sperm donor, an egg donor, or a surrogate mother, but the general tendency is to place growing emphasis on children' rights to have information on their genitors.

When children are separated from their parents due to abuse or neglect, or when their parents are incarcerated, it is often difficult to find a balance between their right to be protected, their right to have some level of relationship with their parents, and their parents' rights to have contact with their children. The situation is especially difficult in the case of parents who are incarcerated, especially if the incarceration is a consequence of their mistreatment of the child (severe physical abuse or incest).

People who work in child protective services encounter this problem all the time and struggle to find the right answers. In many cases, they become doctrinal. Professionals who work with children who have experienced severe abuse often believe that these children should be shielded from any contact with their abusive parents, even if the meetings are supervised to prevent any risk of new abuse. They also believe that the meeting with the abusing parent may trigger new memories of the trauma, which would be detrimental to the child's development. The danger of this position is that when workers have a very negative view of the parents, it can force children to show their loyalty to their parents by pushing away the people who try to help them. Other workers may decide that, since children often remain loyal even to abusive parents, it is useless to impose a separation and they may as well allow the children to stay with their parents or at least to have much contact with them This position entails the risk that the children can be exposed to further harms. In both cases, the decisions of the worker are based on a doctrinal position that can have a detrimental effect on the children he or she is supposed to protect.

Instead, in all these circumstances, contextual therapists propose to rely on multidirected partiality to figure out what the most realistic approach to the situation is, and what kinds of contacts children may have with their parents without jeopardizing their safety or well-being. Here, partiality toward the children means to give them the opportunity to express their needs, their wishes, or their fears in their own terms. And partiality to the parents is not based simply on giving them the opportunity to present their justifications for demanding to have contact with their children. Here, partiality to the parents would need to include something else: it would need to include their right to earn entitlement by trying to meet their children's needs to the best of their abilities.

Example

Here is an example that pertains to a teen who was removed from his parents' care at birth because he was conceived right before his parents were sentenced to a long jail term for having jointly sexually abused his older sister. The two children were placed in separate foster homes so that the boy would not have to learn what happened to his sister, and he was never told why he could not meet his parents.

Years later, the parents, who had been living separately since their release from jail, decided to divorce. The clerk who prepared the divorce agreement included a clause about visitation rights, not knowing that the parents had been deprived of their parental rights. The error was overlooked by the judge, who signed the divorce decree. The mother immediately seized the occasion to claim her right to visit her son. In anticipation of her visit, the foster parents finally told the boy the entire truth about his past, presenting his mother as a monster. When he met her for the first time, he was in a state of great confusion and his distress increased at each subsequent visit. It soon became obvious that the visits could not continue. The judge who had signed the divorce degree could not correct his error unless the visitation could be deemed detrimental to the boy by a psychiatric expert.

Based on contextual therapy principles, the expert relied on multidirected partiality to assess the situation. The teenager was seen alone first and begged the psychiatrist for help: he wanted his mother out of his life at least until his majority. Then the psychiatrist saw the mother alone. She looked depressed and worn by life. She reported that she was unable to work and living on the minimal disability benefits that she was receiving from the government but that was trying to keep busy by knitting socks for a charity organization. This made her feel good. Since she was happy to be able to do something for others, the contextually oriented psychiatrist asked her if she was interested in hearing what her son needed from her. She accepted. During the joint session, the son was able to spell out clearly that it was too hard for him to see her and that he wished that she could step out of his life at least until his majority. She was able to hear that.

Since it was clear that a continuation of the visits was detrimental to the child, the expert offered two options to the mother: sending an expert report to the judge indicating that the visits needed to be terminated or letting her write a letter to the judge stating that she was renouncing her rights in the interest of her child, which would be a gift to her son. She agreed to do that. From a transactional point of view, whether the psychiatrist sent a report to the judge, or the mother wrote to him, the result would be the same: the visits would stop.

However, in accepting to meet her child's needs even only once, this mother was turning into somebody who was capable of giving, and this was a major change in the dimension of relational ethics. In accepting to write a letter in the interest of her son, she was not only avoiding being officially labelled a bad mother once again, but also able to earn constructive entitlement, which could become a resource in her own life. This was a big change for her son, too. He was not only relieved of the burden of the visits, which was what he had asked for, but also no more the child of a woman who was only known in the community as a monstruous mother. Now, he was the child of a woman who could care about his needs, even if only once. This made a huge difference for him.

In short, in this situation, the partiality to the mother was based on her right to give. It was not based on the notion that parents have an automatic right to have contact with their children, no matter what they have done. The partiality to the child was based on his rights to be protected but also on his right to have a parent who is given an opportunity to show some caring.

Chapter 5
Injustices and their Relational Consequences

As already mentioned before, Boszormenyi-Nagy distinguishes two kinds of injustices that have consequences for close relationships: 'retributive injustices', injustices that occur within relationships and 'distributive injustices', injustices that are related to unfortunate circumstances of our lives. He borrows these two terms from social and legal sciences but uses them in a way that is specific to his approach. Here the reader will be introduced to the new terminology that was announced earlier in the book, i.e. the introduction of the term 'relational injustices' as a replacement for retributive injustices and the term 'situational injustices' as a replacement for distributive injustices. For the sake of understanding, the old terms will occasionally still be mentioned in parenthesis, especially the term distributive justice when the situational injustices are based on an inequity of chances.

Retributive injustices or relational injustices

Introduction

In general, as a legal term, retributive justice is defined as a form of justice that is concerned with punishing or rewarding an individual. By consequence, a retributive injustice would occur if an individual who has caused damage to someone escapes punishment, or if an individual is not rewarded for his or her contributions. In contrast, distributive justice concerns the domain of distribution of goods in a society, and distributive injustices are defined by the lack of equity in that distribution, or the lack of equal opportunities for its members. Consequently, distributive injustices cannot be traced back to the wrongdoing of a single identifiable individual, as is the case in retributive justice.

The notion of retributive justice is associated with the notion of 'talionic' justice, a word that comes from the Latin *talis*, meaning 'such'. This means that the wrongdoers should receive such a punishment that it precisely matches the injuries or damages that they have inflicted upon their victims, an eye for an eye, a tooth for a tooth.

Miller (2009) shows retributive justice is not as primitive as some people may present it. He states: "Trading eyes for eyes is not so much about indiscriminate, unthinking violence as it is carefully calculated attempts to match punishment to crime." He also describes: "The more ancient and deeper notion that justice is a matter of restoring balance, achieving equity, determining equivalence, making reparations ..." There is also a similarity in the description of the process that leads to the restoration of justice in societies that use retributive justice, and the process that occurs in contextual therapy when therapists address injustices within close relationships. In both cases, the restorative process is based on fostering dialogue between all the parties involved, and both aim at restoring equilibrium in the relation between all the parties affected by the situation. Miller's comments help establishing a bridge between the notion of retributive justice in social sciences, and the way this term is used in contextual therapy.

Retributive or relational injustices in contextual therapy

In contextual therapy, 'retributive justice' does not pertain to crimes and punishments. Here, 'retributive injustices' pertain to people's unfair treatment of each other and to their damaging behavior. Within family relationships, retributive injustices pertain to situations in which one person is the victim of damages that have not been repaired by the partner or the parent who has caused it. This occurs in situations in which the wrongdoer does not recognize his or her unfair or damaging behavior. This occurs when the wrongdoer is not able to offer redress due to external circumstances: it can be a lack of material resources, an illness, an advancing age, or because the wrongdoer has died without repairing the damage. Lastly, this also applies to situations in which a person's contributions have not been recognized by the partner or the child who has benefited from them. Since all these injustices are injustices that occur within relationships, the term *retributive injustice* chosen by Boszormenyi-Nagy is now replaced by the term *relational injustices*. This new term should help the reader to better understand this category of injustices.

To a certain extent, in the case of relational injustices, the therapeutic goals of the contextual therapists have similarities with the goals of 'restorative justice'. Restorative justice is a new model of justice that has been central to the South African Commission on Truth and Reconciliation. According to its definition in *Encyclopedia Britannica*,[1] restorative justice is described as a "response to criminal behavior that focuses on lawbreaker restitution and the resolution of the issues arising from a crime in which victims, offenders, and the community are brought together to restore the harmony between the parties. Restorative justice includes direct mediation and conflict resolution between the offender, the victims, their families, and the community". It is worth noting that up to now, there has not been any research on the possible applications of the guiding principles of contextual therapy to the field of restorative justice, but this could be productive area of exploration.

Relational injustices in the family

In couples, the two classical examples of relational injustices are the exploitation of one partner by the other, or the refusal of a partner to recognize the contribution of the other. In parent-child relationships, a frequent source of relational injustice comes from the child's exploitation by the parent. It can take many forms, from blatant sexual exploitation to all kinds of subtle destructive demands. For instance, parents who experience marital

---

[1] Heath-Thornton, Debra. "restorative justice". *Encyclopedia Britannica,* 26 Augustus 2018. https://bit.ly/3Lx6NPy (Accessed 15 December 2022).

difficulties and turn to their children for comfort or use them as confidents instead of turning to other adults for help. Parents can also turn to their children to receive the unconditional affection that they did not receive from their own parents while growing up. This form of exploitation is a classic example of parentification of the child by the adult. In the case of the parent-child relationship, the exploitation is amplified by the asymmetry of the relationship: children have no chance to escape their parents' exploitation simply by leaving the relationship, which an exploited adult could do.

The parent-child relationship is by nature asymmetrical. Children are entitled to care and protection from exploitation by virtue of their vulnerability. They do not need to earn it, and the parents' failure to provide this care constitutes a relational injustice. At the same time, when they grow up, children should be willing to acknowledge their parents' care and commitment. Filial loyalty is one of the most common expressions of this acknowledgment, and failure to offer this commitment would amount to a relational injustice.

It is important to note that relational (retributive) justice does not allow for substitutions. The father who has abandoned his child remains liable toward his child for this abandonment even if the child is raised by a devoted stepfather. The same is true for merits and rewards. Parents who have gone through many sacrifices to give their children a good education are entitled to receive some recognition from their children once they have become adults. These children should not assume that they could be discharged from acknowledging their parents' efforts just because they have already received the praises of other people who have underscored this dedication.

In general, in close relationships and family relationships, the definition of what constitutes a relational injustice, or an acceptable redress depends on the definition of what people consider fair or unfair, and what they consider loyal or disloyal. Therefore, the task of the contextual therapist is not to define what constitutes fairness or exploitation but to use multidirected partiality to promote a better dialogue about these issues among family members.

This strategy does not apply if the perpetrator of the injustice commits an act that constitutes a crime under the law. For instance, incest is considered as a criminal act in most countries, and in most countries, health professionals, pastors and teachers are mandated reporters who need to report child and elder abuse to the authorities. It is not the job of the therapist to decide whether a father's sexualized behavior toward his daughter meets the full criteria of incest or not. The court must establish if a crime has occurred or not, and then decide if the perpetrator should be sentenced to jail or possibly be ordered by the court to attend therapy. In these cases, contextual therapists need to abide by the recommendations of the courts, but contextual therapists can still be helpful to address the relational consequences of a crime for all the parties involved, and in some less clear-cut cases, they can be helpful to determine what the damaging part of the relationship between the parent and the child was, and what to do about it.

Example

Here is an example of a situation that was presented to Boszormenyi-Nagy who saw the family for a consultation. A teen girl had accused her father of sexual abuse but retracted her accusation immediately after her complaint had been filed with the court. The judge did not simply close the case. He ordered the family to undergo treatment because he believed that the girl's need to accuse her father had to be the result of serious problems within the family. Indeed, the assigned family therapist soon discovered that the girl's mother was weakened by genetic illness that had already taken the life of one of her siblings. Also, the children were at risk to carry the same gene, and there was no way to test them. They had to live with the possibility that at some point of their life, they could get ill like their mother. This teen was shaken by this realization much more than her younger brother who had not yet fully realized what could happen to him. She started to act out, specifically started to dress in a provocative manner and to give herself the appearance of someone much older. As a result, she easily could have passed as a young adult. At the same time, her father was very scared at the thought of losing his wife and very needy. He had noticed how attractive his daughter had become and was very worried that he could lose control. On her side, the girl too had begun to feel unsafe in their relationship. The mother was aware of the danger of the situation but she was too ill to have the strength to do much about it. Soon it became evident that her accusations had served a goal. It had brought outsiders into the family at a moment when the situation had become dangerous. The judge was right in his decision to order the family to attend therapy.

The parents were able to recognize that, indirectly, their daughter had brought help to the family at a moment when they were unable to seek help. Their willingness to acknowledge her contribution was a great step in fostering new trust within the family. The father was able to describe that in his attempts to keep a safe distance from his daughter, he had to stop expressing any affection toward her. The daughter then described that during this period, the most frightening experience for her was not the fear that her father could act out, but that he did not love her anymore, and she was now reassured that this was not the case. The work then focused on the parents. They were encouraged to seek couple therapy to explore in what way they could maintain a satisfying couple relationship despite the circumstances.

Distributive injustices or situational injustices

Distributive injustices in social sciences

To approach the notion of 'distributive injustices' or in the new terminology 'situational injustices' in more details, and to better understand their clinical implications, it is useful to return to the definition of 'distributive justice' in social sciences. Depending on what theory of distributive justice one examines, the definition of distributive justice, and the path to achieve it will vary. Here, it is helpful to rely on an article in which the author,

Knight (2014), evaluates the respective merits of these theories in the example of post-apartheid South Africa. He discusses three main theories of retributive justice, beginning with the 'utilitarianism theory'. He presents it as a model of distributive justice that is based on the maximization of overall societal well-being and posits that an action is good insofar as it increases overall welfare, and bad insofar as it decreases overall welfare that is represented by Bentham (1970). Then he discusses the theory proposed by Rawls (1999) as a theory that is based on fairness expressed in terms of equal basic liberties, fair equality of opportunities, and ways to resolve inequalities that should benefit the least advantaged group. Lastly, Knight evokes the theory of 'luck egalitarianism' as exemplified by Temkin (1993). It postulates that it is unjust for some to be worse off than others through no fault or choice of their own, but there is no injustice if the inequality is the result of an individual's choice.

The definition of distributive injustices in the theory of luck egalitarianism is the one that comes the closest to Boszormenyi-Nagy's own definition of what constitutes distributive injustice. For him, too, it is unjust for some to be worse off than others are through no fault or choice of their own. He uses the concept of distributive injustices to describe situations in which a person suffers detriments that cannot be traced back to the wrongdoing of any specific individual or any specific group. It can be anything from being born with a handicap or a genetic illness, or the early loss of a parent, or the loss of housing in an earthquake. Since these injustices comes from unfortunate circumstances, not from any intentional act, they can also be described as *situational injustices*, a new term that will be used as an alternate to distributive injustices. In any case, whether one talks about distributive injustices, situational injustices, or just bad luck, the fact is that for no faults of their own, people who are victims of such adverse events are worse off than people who have been spared from similar experiences.

One of the main characteristics of situational (distributive) injustices is that they cannot be repaired by anyone. People cannot sue their genes for causing a disease; they cannot sue parents who died early for making them orphans; they cannot sue the earth for shaking. They must live with these injustices. Whether parents lose a baby due to cancer or to famine, the injustice of losing a child comes from circumstance that are not under anyone's direct control. Both are situational injustices and these parents cannot turn to anyone to obtain redress for their loss. This would be very different if the child had been killed by a reckless driver. Depending on the laws of the country, the culpable driver could be incarcerated and forced to pay a large sum of money to compensate the parents for their pain and suffering.

In many situations, people cannot even name the injustices they have been exposed to. They only act in a way that reflect a certain degree of destructive entitlement. For instance, a youngster who suffers from diabetes may become very demanding toward his siblings, which may cause fights between them to the point of requiring a professional intervention. Neither the child nor the parents who seek help for the family would think of the diabetes as an injustice. However, once the therapist start to ask questions, this will change. For instance, this child may be asked what he thinks about not been able to eat the same nice birthday cake that his siblings receive for their birthdays? Does he see this as unfair? The response usually comes very quicky: of course, this is unfair. Soon, it becomes clear to everyone in the family that indeed his diabetes is a source of injustices for which no one is responsible. Once the therapist has been able to show partiality to this youngster, it become easier to ask him to listen to this siblings' complains and to help him to become less demanding. Conversely, his siblings may start to become more understanding of his predicament, and therefore a little more patient, which will also help improving the situation.

Societal injustices as situational injustices

In the case of social inequalities, the factors that lead to these inequalities may be extremely complex and can change over time. To the extent that in many cases, they can still be traced back to the decisions and the actions of some people or some group at an identifiable moment of history, they could be regarded as a form of relational injustices. Also, the victims of social injustices can take to the streets or use their voting rights to try to force political changes that could bring more justice to them, but as individuals, they will never be in direct control of the processes that could lead to a decrease of these injustices. As evidenced in the case of post-apartheid South Africa, it is a long and difficult process that involves many parts of society. Since people who have been the victims of social inequalities and social discrimination cannot expect to obtain redress within a predictable time frame, or may die before they see any changes, they end up at the same place than people who have been the victims of other kinds of adverse events, in other words the victims of situational (distributive) injustices.

Poverty and discriminations always have a negative effect on all the dimensions of relational reality. To name a few, a lack of basic resources like clean water, or sufficient food, and a lack of access to medical services have a direct effect on the health and life expectancy, and this effect becomes even more significant at the time of pandemics like Covid-19. The stress relating to poverty and discriminations can lead to various kinds of individual symptoms beside symptoms related to posttraumatic stress disorder. People may become depressed, or they may become addicted to drugs or alcohol, etc. The systemic consequences of poverty are considerable. It can affect people's abilities to complete their education, forcing them to accept low-paying jobs, which then prevents them to move out of poverty. It can also lead people to engage in delinquent activities as a means of survival. However, most significantly, these situational injustices lead to an accumulation of destructive entitlement, which in turn can become a source of relational injustices that have multigenerational consequences. In short, the multidimensional consequences of poverty and discrimination add many new layers of injustices to the original situational (distributive) justice, the inequity of the distribution of goods and opportunities.

Overlaps between situational injustices and relational injustices

Example

Here is an example of a clinical situation where the domains of distributive/situational injustice and retributive/relational injustice overlap: a young woman who had just completed her secondary education had just received the confirmation from a geneticist that she suffered from a minor form of a genetic illness that can manifest itself by minor symptoms or instead can affect the entire functioning of the person.. In her case, she had been very lucky and was not at risk of any future deterioration. But still at the follow-up consultation with the geneticist she was so depressed that the geneticist decided to refer her to a psychiatrist.

At the first interview with the psychiatrist, she reported that she was not depressed because of her diagnosis but because of her father's rejection. Based on this information she had received from the geneticist, she announced to her parents that she was renouncing the idea of having children in the future. Instead, she wanted to devote her life to genetics. When her father heard her decision, he became outraged and began to attack her. Neither she nor her mother could understand his reaction. She became very depressed because she loved her father and did not want to upset him. At the same time, she believed that her decision was right. She had learnt from the geneticist that her disease was probably the result of a spontaneous mutation since it was not found in her family. However, this did not make any difference for her future children. Each of them would be exposed to a fifty percent risk of inheriting this mutated gene, and there was no way to predict how severely they could be affected by it. She believed that she could not in good consciousness expose innocent beings to such a risk.

Based on this initial information, the consultant offered to see her with her parents. What she had not told yet was that her father was severely handicapped. He arrived at the consultation using crutches and visibly tired from walking a short distance from the car to the office. When asked about his condition, he reported that his legs got paralyzed as the result of an infection he had contracted as a child. He always tried to live as normally as possible despite his condition. He mentioned that from an early age on, he had been determined to build a family. He believed that he had succeeded in being a good father despite his handicap. For that reason, he could not understand why his daughter, who did not suffer any physical impairment due to her condition, could refuse to become a parent. He was hurt by the fact that she was refusing to continue the family that he tried so hard to build despite all the obstacles that he had to overcome to marry and become a parent.

As the daughter was encouraged to present her side, she made the following point: her father was handicapped, and this had many practical consequences for the family, but he never had to worry about transmitting his condition to his children. She was in the opposite situation. Indeed, she would have the physical ability to raise children without *any difficulties. However, if any of her children were to inherit her disease, especially in a more severe form, she would have to live with the terrible burden of knowing that she was responsible for the child's suffering. She believed that the only way to behave as a responsible parent was to renounce having children. The consultant was able to show to the father that in renouncing to have children, his daughter was not disloyal to him. In fact, she was showing her loyalty by abiding to a goal that had be central to his life, the goal of being the best parent possible despite adverse circumstances. Unfortunately, in her case, this meant renouncing parenthood. The father was surprised by this formulation but agreed that indeed there was some truth to it. This acknowledgment was sufficient to give his daughter hopes about an improvement of their relationship, and this helped her to start recovering from her depression.*

In this example, the father and the daughter were both victims of a situational (distributive) injustice. Both of them suffered from a disease, and no one can be held responsible for it. However, due to factual differences in their origins, these two diseases had different relational consequences. The father's illness was due to a virus, and it could not be transmitted to the next generation. The daughter's illness was caused by a mutated gene. No one was responsible for this mutation, but now she had a responsibility to spare the next generation from its consequences, a responsibility that her father did not have.

Injustices and religious beliefs

Many people will turn to their faith to find explanations for the injustices that they incur and to find the resources to overcome them. For the faithful, within Judaism, Christianity and Islam, God is trusted as a just God. In Islam, among the many names of Allah's names one can find for instance The Just, The Equitable. People who have faith in God or Allah will often accept the hardship they are experiencing as a test of their faith. Some of them may rely on the belief that they will be rewarded in Heaven: "The lasts will be the firsts." In any of these cases, they will be able to accept unfair events in their lives with more fortitude than people do who do not have the same faith.

When people believe in reincarnation, they may understand the unfortunate events that occur in their present life as the consequences of their negative actions in their past lives. Consequently, they will try to engage in positive actions in this lifetime to avoid the repetition of unfortunate events in the future. Other people may believe that what they experience is a punishment for their disregard of an invisible entity, like an ancestor or a local god. Consequently, they will end up taking greater care to honor these entities.

In short, people who believe in what one could describe under the general term of divine or cosmic justice may be much more able to accept their lot than others may. Their beliefs may also motivate them to remain fair to others, no matter how people treat them. However, it can also happen that people who have strong faith may lose it if they are hit with severe injustices: "Why did God do this to me? It cannot be a just God." In these cases, one could say that they become the victims of a double damage: the damage that was at the source of the injustice, and the indirect damage to their faith.

When it comes to the discussion of people's faith, there is a big difference between contextual therapists and contextually inspired pastoral counselors. In Europe especially, therapists are expected to operate within the premises of laicity and refrain from discussing matters of faith with their clients. They should not discuss their clients' faith nor bring about their own faith. Of course, pastoral counselors are at the opposite end of this requirement. They are there to address their clients' faith. However, based on the principles of contextual therapy, both therapists and counselors are united by a common denominator: their interest for the relational consequence of this faith. Without infringing on the boundaries of their profession, contextual therapists are not only allowed but also encouraged to ask clients who are facing injustices if they have relied on religious explanations or on any kind of other beliefs to deal with these injustices, and if this has been helpful or not.

Even people who seem most acceptive of their fate may still harbor some hope to receive compensation for their misfortunes within the realm of actual relationships. "The quest for an objective human justice has long preoccupied people's mind. Through their religious systems, human civilizations have created their idiosyncratic notion of justice ... [but] in ordinary instances, the private sphere of close relating absorbs much of the ricocheting impact of life injustices. Small children and often pets are captive shock absorbers of these forces. They become scapegoats and silent hostages to the frustrations of the adult world" (Boszormenyi-Nagy, 1987: 308).

The relational consequences of injustices

People who have been victims of injustices have the right to seek justice, but in many cases, they cannot obtain redress from the people who have wronged them. People may not see that they did anything wrong. People may refuse responsibility for the consequences of their actions, even if they know that they have caused harm to people. In other cases, the person who has committed an injustice is not able to repair it due to his or her own life circumstances. Some people die before having offered any redress to the people they have wronged. Conversely, some parents who were not available to their children when they were young try to make up for the past by becoming over-giving later in their life, but unfortunately, this does not undo the injustices that the children incurred earlier in their lives. This can be seen in parents who lost custody of their children due to drug addiction and become sober later in life and are then reunited with their children. Often, they try to make up for the past by becoming over-indulging parents, but this does not erase the fact that their children had to spend a good part of their childhood in foster care. This injustice cannot be repaired through gifts; it must be acknowledged by the parents.

Since fairness and reciprocity are two of the central human preoccupations, it is not surprising that people who are the victims of relational injustices that are not repaired by the people who have committed them, and people who are the victims of situational injustices are not likely to simply ignore them. People who grew up in families where they could experience fair and trustworthy relationships will have a better capacity to deal with injustices later in life than people who have already experienced injustices during their childhood, because injustices are cumulative. However, very few people can accept injustices as part of the hazards of life and simply move on.

People who have been wronged may simply become revengeful. They may seek to take revenge on the people who have hurt them in a very visible fashion, and if no one can be identified as the perpetrator of the injustice, they may develop a revengeful attitude that can affect all their relationships. The dynamics of revenge and counter-revenge is a well-known phenomenon that can have disastrous effects on individuals and groups over generations. Conversely, other people may not want to become revengeful and try to find explanations for these injustices through their faith.

Destructive entitlement

It would be difficult to argue against the idea that people who have been wronged are entitled to redress. However, what happens when the perpetrator of the damage refuses to recognize it? What happens when the person who has caused the damage has died before repairing it? What happens when people accept responsibility for the injustices when it is already too late to repair the damages they have caused? What happens in the case of situational injustices when there is no one to turn to for redress? In all these cases, most people, even people who have seemingly accepted their lot, are tempted to seek some forms of compensation from people who have nothing to do with the situation. In seeking redress from people who do not owe them anything, the victims of past relational or situational injustices do commit new relational injustices. No one should be asked to provide restitution for damages that they have not caused, and this becomes very destructive to relationships. In other words, people are entitled to obtain redress, but they have no right to cause harms to others in seeking it. This is the predicament of 'destructive entitlement' that is also at times described as *destructive overentitlement*. What is meant here by overentitlement is that the people who have been wronged appear to act as people who are overentitled, people who claim more than their dues. What happens is not that the people who seek redress from past injustices are asking for too much, but the problem is that they become blind to the fact that they are committing an injustice themselves. From their own points of view, they are just asking for their dues. At the same time, from the point of view of the third parties who are expected to make up for these past injustices, these people's demands are unfair because they are not responsible for what happened to them in the past.

In short, for the better and for the worse, our expectation of fairness and loyalty in our relationships is a major determinant of our behaviors. This can lead us to cooperation and generosity. It can also lead us to revenge and exploitation. The antidote to this situation is to help people discover what they can gain from showing generosity to others and earning constructive entitlement instead of trying to get their dues in a way that damages relationships.

The difference between the psychology of entitlement and actual entitlement

Here, it is important to distinguish between the 'psychology of entitlement' and the 'actual entitlement' that is earned by contributing positively to the life of others, or the entitlement that is based as a right to seek redress for actual injustices. In other words, one needs to make the distinction between a 'sense of entitlement' that depends on the psychology of the person and an 'actual entitlement' that is defined according to the dimension of relational ethics. Here, there is a parallel with the notion of 'psychological guilt' versus 'existential guilt', meaning the psychological guilt that people may experience whether they have actually committed a reprehensible action or not and the existential guilt that comes from knowing that one has caused an actual harm. The psychology of entitlement and guilt depends on many factors. People can be manipulated into feeling guilty about things for which they are not responsible. People who suffer from depression may accuse themselves of hurting people or failing them while they have not done anything wrong. They may also be convinced that they are worthless and that they don't have the right to get anything. Conversely, people who have accumulated destructive entitlement don't feel guilty when they ask too much from others. Often they are described as people who 'behave entitled'. In short, there is a discrepancy between people's feelings of entitlement or guilt and the actual degree of their entitlement or guilt as measured according to relational ethics. However, when people present themselves as overentitled, it is important to remember that their psychological attitude of 'overentitlement' is very often connected to actual past injustices that need to be recognized before they can be helped to come to more realistic expectations in their current lives.

Most people have experienced some variations of unrepaired injustices in their lives, from minor ones to very serious ones, and the consequences of their destructive entitlement vary greatly based on their beliefs, their past life history, and their own mental features. People who have grown up in families where they were treated fairly may be more resilient in the face of injustices later in life. Siblings who have experienced similar injustices while they were growing up together may have different reactions. One may be able to refrain from relying on destructive entitlement, the other not. The difference can come from slight differences in their early life experience, or it can also be due to differences in their psychological makeup. In general, people who suffer from mental illnesses like a bipolar disorder, an attention deficit hyperactivity disorder, or any kind of substance abuse disorder that increases impulsivity are more likely to act destructively without thinking of the consequences of their behavior. However, in general, experience shows that destructive entitlement may lead anyone to act before having the time to think about the negative consequences of their actions for other people and themselves. It is almost as if there is a calculator in the brain that operates independently from the part of the brain that does the rational thinking.

Example

Here is the story of Kate and her car. Kate had noticed a dent in the bumper of her car when she arrived at the parking lot. There was no way to find out who had hit her car. She decided to consult her regular mechanic for advice about the repair. He told her that it was just a matter of banging the bumper back into shape, a two-minute job that he could do himself, and that he would not charge her since she was an old client. Kate agreed. Soon after she left the car shop, she noticed something odd. She had not given the mechanic any tip. Not only was she normally generous with tips, but this time a tip would have been definitively well deserved. It then became clear to her that she was still thinking about the person who had caused the damage: she was entitled to have her car repaired without having anything to pay for it, and this blocked her from acknowledging the help of her mechanic. Here, the consequences of her destructive entitlement are very limited. To make up for her failure to acknowledge the help she had received from the mechanic, she could simply give him an extra tip on another occasion.

However, in other circumstances, the consequences of destructive entitlement can be tragic. The newspapers reported that a young man had shot a woman in the stomach simply because she refused to give him one dollar, the money he was missing to buy a beer at the corner store. Fortunately, the woman could be saved. It obvious that no one, including this young man, would ever argue that a bottle of beer has more value than the life of an innocent passer-by. However, for people who have experienced repeated injustices, and who present with added mental health issues, including drug and alcohol dependence, the denial of a simple request can have catastrophic consequences, even mass shooting in certain cases.

The concept of the revolving slate: Who are the targets of our destructive entitlement?

In his early writings, Boszormenyi-Nagy proposes the image of the 'revolving slate' to illustrate how people seek compensation from past injustices. The image is that of a blackboard that can be flipped from one side to the other. By this, he means that in family life, people who have not received what they were entitled to get from their parent may turn to their partners or children to be compensated for their parents' shortcomings. When people shift the burden of the repayment of the debt to a substitute, they also indirectly close the account with the original debtor. This can come from a realistic evaluation that they will never get anything from the original debtor. If it is the parent who is spared of further claim, the shift to a substitute debtor could also be understood as an indirect expression of loyalty to the parent. One also needs to note that the phenomenon of the revolving slate is not limited to the parent-child relationship. People who have been wronged may turn to substitute debtors in other circumstances also.

In fact, to explain this phenomenon, it may be easier to use another image, that of the simple slate that some shopkeepers still use to keep a record of what clients owe them if they cannot pay right away. When the clients come back to pay, they wipe the slate clean. These shopkeepers accept the risk that some clients may disappear without clearing their debts. If they were fool enough to present the slate to one of their remaining customers, hoping to get their money back that way, the client would just laugh. However, this is different in family life, people who have not got want they deserved from parents will indeed try to pass the slate to others, partners, or children. They will not be stopped by the reality that it does not make sense to expect people to repair damages that they have not caused.

In many cases, the negative effect of destructive entitlement is mitigated by the immediate reaction of the people who are exploited in the process. People who had to be over-responsible when they were growing up may develop the tendency to pass some of their workload to co-workers to do, but it will not take long before these co-workers react. People who have been short-changed by society may decide that it is time for them to get nice things by looting luxury stores. But they also know that if they are caught by the police, they will end up with handcuffs around their wrists, not expensive watches or diamond bracelets, and this may be enough to detract them from stealing.

Destructive entitlement in close relationships

There are several reasons why people turn their destructive entitlement toward spouses, family members, or close friends rather than strangers. The most obvious reason is the reaction of complete strangers. Most of them will refuse to respond to unrealistic claims. Even if some strangers may respond out of simple kindness or for some other reasons, it is unlikely that their goodwill will last for very long if they sense that they are exploited. This is different in family and close relationships in which people are bound by all sort of ties, anything from the strong emotional attachment to the legal ties created by marriage, or the blood ties that connect family members. In all these situations, it makes it very difficult for people to simply put an end to relationships that have become exploitative. This exploitation becomes a source of destructive entitlement. The result is that people begin to turn their destructive entitlement toward each other instead of getting out of the relationship.

Another factor that brings people to turn to close friends, spouses, or children to get some compensation for past injustices is the fact that people who are in close relationships tend to use each other as a target of unrealistic projections. Cognitive therapists know that in close relationships, we lose the capacity to see our partners as they are. We begin to see them through the lenses of all kinds of distortions and projections that have an origin in some deep psychological needs. For instance, people may idealize their partners as the ideal parents they are longing for. For similar reasons, the people who are the targets of these projections may lack objectivity. They may respond to unrealistic demands of a partner out of a need to idealize the person and not see his or her flaws, or out of a fear of losing this person's affection, etc. Children are not spared from these kinds of projections. One can observe new parents already projecting things on babies who are barely a few minutes old: "She looks just like my mother, she will never love me", or conversely: "He looks so strong, I know he will always be there for me." Often, parents will not even remember theses immediate reactions, but they can continue to flavor the parent-child relationship over decades.

A five-dimensional perspective on discrimination and oppression

It would not be realistic to review all the possible individual and relational consequences of social injustices, especially the consequences of discrimination and oppression. However, the model of the five dimensions or relational reality is useful to order them in relevant categories. For instance, we can think about the factual consequences of segregation. It can result in a decreased life expectancy if people are cut off from the medical resources available to the dominant group. Oppression can result in psychological traumas. People who have been exposed to traumatic situations because of oppression and violence often suffer from a post traumatic stress disorder, and they are vulnerable to depression, or drug and alcohol addiction. Consequently, they become less available to their children. Children may also grow up feeling ashamed of their origins. Of course, oppression and discrimination have major consequences on the dimension of transactions since they are based on the power and the control that the oppressor exerts on the oppressed. It also has many other systemic consequences that can affect the parent-child relationship. For instance, fathers and mothers may be forced into living separate lives, which would prevent them to function as a parental unit. Women who are denied access to education due to discrimination often live in poverty, and they have much fewer resources to raise their children than other women have. Children may be forced into adult roles early in their lives.

For contextual therapists, discrimination and oppression need to be examined from the point of view of relational ethics. Any violation of basic human rights, any type of discrimination against ethnic or religious groups, and any form of oppression based on race, gender, or sexual preference result in relational (retributive) and situational (distributive) injustices. They constitute a relational injustice in as much as it is often possible to identify the people and the groups who are at the origins of these violations. At the same time, they constitute a situational injustice since these discriminations are often based on the physical features the victims are born with, for instance the color of their skin, or on their place of birth and their ethnic belonging, in other words on the factual determinants of their lives.

The tragedy of discrimination and oppression is that it not only harms the people who are the direct victims of these violation, but also can cause harms to relationships that can last for several generations after the actual discrimination or oppression has stopped. People who have been the victims of these injustices can be caught in the predicament of destructive entitlement, which can lead to problems in couple relationships, and to the destructive parentification of children that can span over several generations. These victims may also turn their destructive entitlement against members of their own community, which is an added tragic consequence of past and ongoing societal injustices.

Example

One example of this tragedy comes from Guadeloupe, a Caribbean Island that is an overseas territory of France where the Covid-19 pandemics led to a severe social unrest. The French government decided to impose vaccination on all the medical personal of the country, and employees who refused to comply lost their jobs. Whether or not the measure was medically needed, the issue is that thousands of health workers lost their jobs in France and its territories. In France, many of these dismissed workers took to the streets to protest. In Guadeloupe, the situation escalated when, as a form of protest against the French government, the dismissed workers organized themselves to block access to hospitals and health care facilities serving their own population, putting many of their own people in danger. This triggered the reaction of the local authorities, but soon these authorities got themselves divided between the people who wanted to use force to open access to these facilities and the sympathizers of the movement who did not want to intervene. Over time, the situation escalated to a very serious social unrest. From the point of view of contextual therapy, what seems to have happened is that many of the workers who had refused to follow the order to get vaccinated did so because they considered this measure as an imposition by the country that has colonized them, not by the country they belonged to as French citizens. In short, it is realistic to see the situation as a result of their destructive entitlement, a destructive entitlement that is the result of a past history of colonization, discrimination and oppression.

Blocked giving as secondary injustice in the life of the victims of systemic injustices

When people who have been the victims of systemic injustices get caught in the cycle of revenge or in the spiral of destructive entitlement, they not only hurt others but also become the victims of an additional injustice. One of the most insidious results of injustices is that people who are caught in the predicament of destructive entitlement are blocked in their capacity to give to others, which in turn deprives them of the opportunity to earn constructive entitlement. Consequently, they have fewer chances to gain the inner self-esteem and the inner freedom that they would need to have to succeed in their lives. This constitutes an added great injustice that is often overlooked not only by professionals but also even by the very people who are the victims of this additional injustice. They may have forgotten what they got for themselves when they were still able to give to others.

In short, possibly the greatest harm caused by discrimination and oppression is that generations after generation, it can deprive people of the fundamental right to give, and it deprives them of the opportunity to earn the constructive entitlement that could serve as a resource to reach their own goals and to succeed in life. For this reason, it is extremely important to regard the people who are caught in the destructive cycle of revenge and destructive entitlement not simply as wrongdoers but also as people who have been wronged twice, once by the social injustices that were inflicted on their group, and a second time by the fact that they have been harmed in their capacity to give. This acknowledgment can be the most important step in helping people to get out of the cycle of revenge and destructive entitlement, the first step in helping them to re-engage in positive contribution to society and to begin earning constructive entitlement.

Blocked giving and conduct disorder

Youths suffering from a conduct disorder often come from families that have been exposed to a variety of hardships that often include poverty and discrimination. By definition, a conduct disorder is characterized by a series of behaviors that are evocative of negative reciprocity and destructive entitlement: a refusal to care about the rights of others and to abide by the rules of society, a tendency to physical violence, a tendency to steal or to deceive people, etc. Youths who present with these kinds of behaviors can be blocked in their ability to give to others simply because they have experienced too many injustices, or because their generosity has been exploited.

It is important to keep in mind that the indirect benefit that comes from generous giving can reach a limit. If a giver is taken for granted, or asked to give more and more, there is a risk that the giver begins to build up destructive entitlement. We know that young children have a natural tendency to make small gifts to their parents and that they enjoy doing things for them. However, if parents take advantage of this natural tendency to ask more and more from their children, especially through parentification, these children's capacity to give will come to a standstill. Instead, they will begin to claim their dues in ways that are destructive, grabbing what they want without asking people for permission, or even beginning to steal from people. Also, they will begin to refuse to care about the rights of others. In many cases, they will stop refusing to respect adults, especially their parents and teachers, and they will stop following their directions. In short, these youths will end up presenting the characteristic symptoms of a 'conduct disorder'.

Because of their bad behaviors, these youths may be kicked out of school, or they become truants, roaming around with other youths, and getting into trouble. In other cases, they begin to become violent at home, which may force their parents to ask for their placement in a residential treatment facility. Often the youths perceive these measures as unfair punishment, and this gives more fuel to their destructive entitlement. Over time, these youths may engage in behaviors that become punishable under the law. They may begin to use drugs, or to join violent groups. Consequently, some of these youths end up in juvenile detention centers. Also, since many of the youths who are diagnosed with a conduct disorder often do not finish school and do not acquire the skills necessary to get stable jobs, they are also at risk of becoming homeless once they become young adults.

Helping youths to rediscover the benefits of giving

Therapists often become very discouraged by these youths and very pessimistic about their future. They believe that since these youths tend to refuse to accept responsibility for their behaviors, they are not likely to be willing to engage in therapy even if their behaviors get them into trouble. When these youths end up in residential treatment facilities, they are often overmedicated, which is also a sign of the hopelessness on the part of psychiatrists who do not know how to deal with them. Even some contextual therapists express discouragement about these youths. They wrongly believe that since these youths do not care about the rights of others, they live outside of the world of relational ethics. In fact, nobody lives outside of the world of relational ethics. Like everyone else, these youths expect fairness and reciprocity in their relationships, and this is what lead them to engage in negative reciprocity: "No one cared about my rights, why should I care about the right of others?". In many cases, they are parentified children who had been exploited by their parents. Here, the first step to help youths get out of the damaging spiral of destructive entitlement is to acknowledge them as hurt givers.

Since most people who work with these youths see them as wrongdoers, these youths are taken by surprise if one asks something like the following: "I hear that you are going in a lot of trouble because you are doing bad things to others (here could come some details), but tell me about the last time that you tried to do something good? Tell me about the last time you tried to help someone?" Some youths who are so used to been seen as ruthless takers may dismiss the question. This is the moment when it is important to insist: "Maybe this takes you by surprise, but I don't know anyone who has never done something nice for someone else. Maybe it has been a very long time ago since this happened. Maybe you were just a small kid but try to remember." "Did you ever make a little drawing that you wanted to give to your mom or to you dad, or was there a time when you gave a little help to someone?" After a while, the youth will usually come up with an example. Then the next question could be: "Did it feel good, did you enjoy it?" The usual answer is yes. Then, from there, the therapist can move to tell the youth: "In this case, it is not fair to you that now you are no more able to care about other people." This statement usually surprises the youths even more. From there, the therapist can use a two-pronged approach, giving the youth acknowledgment for past injustices and at the same time supporting the youth in re-engaging in activities in which he or she can begin to help others. One trap to avoid is to begin to point out to the shortcoming of the parents, because this would trigger the loyalty that youths still often have even for parents who have failed them. In this case, they could become protective of these parents and reject the therapist. These youths can also rediscover the positive effects of giving in other circumstances than therapy.

Example

Here is an example of a teen who was admitted to a residential treatment program with a diagnosis of conduct disorder. The program entailed a behavioral component. The youths were given points for good behavior. If they had enough points at the end of the week, as a reward, the staff took them for an outside activity of their choice, for instance going to a cinema, to a pool, etc. For weeks, one of the girls struggled to get enough points to be able to participate in these outings. Each week, she had a good start but eventually she would lose her points because of some acting-out behavior. The chaplain of the program had organized an activity for the youths who had earned enough points to go out and who wanted to do something different than just going to a fun place: she was taking them to a homeless shelter to bring toys and play with children who were living there with their homeless parents. On one occasion, one of the youths who was usually participating in this activity was not available, and she asked the staff if she could take someone else with her. This answer was that this girl could go if she wanted. She had not enough points for an outside activity, but she was trying, and she would most likely not cause any problem. In fact, this girl was so moved by the predicament of these little kids and so happy to be able to do something for them, that this triggered a complete change. From that day on, she never failed to earn her behavioral points and keep them. This was striking because of her prior failure. She had never been able to earn enough points to participate in fun activities. Now that she could use these points to go to the shelter to help kids, she was not losing them anymore. In short, being able to give was a bigger motivator for her than trying to get fun rewards like the permission to go to movies.

(For more about this story, see Ducommun-Nagy, 2003)

Chapter 6
Parentification and Exoneration

The parentification of children

Children are not only entitled to receive appropriate care as defined above, but from the point of view of contextual therapy, they also deserve to be spared from unrealistic tasks and unfair expectations. Many parents struggle with past unresolved issues. It can be a disappointment with their own parents, a history of exploitation, or they may have personal vulnerabilities coming from physical or mental health conditions, etc. Parents own their children to try to find a way to overcome these issues so that they do not become a burden for their children. Unfortunately, this is not always the case. Many parents who have experienced injustices may have accumulated too much destructive entitlement to retain enough generosity to spare their children from the unfair task of making up for past injustices. Clinical evidence shows that parents indeed turn to their children as a source of love and understanding when they did not get this love and understanding from their own parents.

The definition of parentification

Boszormenyi Nagy has introduced the notion of 'parentification' in the field of family therapy already in *Invisible loyalties* close to fifty years ago. In a strict sense, parentification is the process by which an adult tries to place a child in the position of the parent. For contextual therapists, the main source of parentification is the parents' need to turn to their children to get from them what they were missing in the relationship with their own parents. This leads to a significant degree of reversal in the giving and receiving between the parent and the child. It can also entail a change in the family hierarchy, with the child assuming a position of power over the parent. This happens when parents give up their parental responsibility and expect their children to become the decision makers.

At this point in time, parentification is a subject that has generated an enormous volume of publications. It has been explored from a large variety of perspectives, not only contextual therapy. This includes the perspective of psycho-dynamically based psychotherapy, systemic family therapy, and especially structural family therapy. It has also been considered from a socio-historical perspective. There is a common denominator between all these perspectives: the parentification always entails a reversal of the function of the parent and the function of the child, and it also entails a reversal in the family hierarchy. But only contextual therapy look at this reversal in terms of a reversal of giving and receiving between the generations.

One of the reasons that make children vulnerable to parentification is that they are not able to set limits to their parents because of their existential dependence on them, and because of their spontaneous tendency to offer them their loyalty and their love. Children are also motivated by their need to be perceived as good children by their parents. In any case, children can easily be parentified, with all the negative long-term consequences that parentification can entail.

Infantilization as a form of parentification

Many family therapists may believe that children who are infantilized by their parents escape parentification, but this is not true. When parents infantilize their children by doing everything for them, and by not expecting them to behave in an age-appropriate manner, the result is that these children will not reach autonomy as soon as children who are not infantilized. Hence, they will remain available to respond to the needs of their parents for a longer time than other children will. This explains also why in families in which one of the siblings suffers from a mental handicap or a physical handicap that affects the child's capacity for autonomy, this sibling is the one who is parentified and not the siblings who are the more competent.

Full reversal of roles between parents and children

In some other circumstances, parentification entails a full reversal of the roles of parents and children. For instance, when parents are severely addicted to drugs or alcohol, they may stop assuming any parental responsibilities. They leave their children to care for themselves and for their younger siblings. Furthermore, in these families, children may have to step in as the sole responsible adults and set limits to their own parents. A child may need to hide the keys of the family car to make sure that a parent does not take off while seriously intoxicated. Another child may need to hide needles to prevent a parent from overdosing; another may need to call the police to stop a violent parent from beating the other.

All these situations are already extremely unfair to the children. However, even more unfair is that these children are often blamed by their parents for assuming a parental role as if they were usurpers who had seized the power for themselves and should be punished for that. In the end, these children not only are deprived of their own right to be raised by responsible parents, but also may be the victims of this added injustice. In any case, they do accumulate destructive entitlement, and inevitably, this will have an effect on their future relationships, and an effect on the next generations.

Example

Here is the example coming from a consultation with Boszormenyi-Nagy (see also Ducommun-Nagy, 2018). The family had consulted a family therapist because the son, a young man in his early twenties had severe angry outbursts toward his teen sister.

The situation had become so severe that the parents decided to seek the help of a family therapist. The father had a past history of alcoholism that he had refused to discuss with the family therapist. He believed that he was a responsible parent and that his past alcohol abuse was not relevant to the present family problem. But at some point during the consultation, he finally admitted that he had drank heavily while his children were growing and that it must had an effect on his son. He remembered an incident when his son caught him in the kitchen trying to get a drink before leaving for an excursion with the family. His son looked at him with such disapproval that it forced him to put the bottle down. In talking about it, he realized that his alcoholism had put an unfair burden on his son: it had forced his son to behave as the responsible parent. As the son heard his father acknowledging that, he immediately turned to his sister: "See, I was the one who had to carry this burden, and this protected you. You owe me respect for that, and I deserve it." In brief, his bursts of anger against his sister came out of his expectation to be credited for what he had done for the family. At the same time, she had no clues about what he was expecting from her. However, in the session, she was able to tell him that she was sorry for what he had to do and now understand that indeed this had shielded her from some of the effects of their father's alcoholism. In sum, both the father and the sister were able to give credit to this young man, and his contributions were also recognized by his mother and his older sister, who were also present in the session. As soon as this happened, he began to relax. It is obvious that the change that occurred in the session was to translate into a significant improvement in the relationship with this sister.

When parents are willing to acknowledge the damages they have caused by parentifying their children, it will not remove the harm that this parentification caused at the time, for instance the harm to these children's capacity to trust adults. At the same time, this acknowledgment can have a great effect on these children's future relationships by decreasing their urge to seek redress in an unfair manner. On the other hand, when parents have built up too much destructive entitlement to be capable of fairness toward their children, the parentification will continue to have destructive consequences over time.

Life circumstances as a source of parentification

There are circumstances in which children need to assume responsibilities beyond their age due to circumstances that do not depend on their parents' unfair neediness. Parents may have to depend on their children at a time of a crisis like a major illness. In other cases, parents do not have professional qualifications necessary to hold a good paying job and they need to work many hours in low paying jobs to be able to bring enough money to the family. In these cases, they often may have to ask their children to manage on their own, or to take care of the youngsters.

For multiple reasons, immigration puts a special burden on parents. It can be that they are limited to accept low-paying jobs due to a lack of skills, or because they do not speak the language of the host countries. They can also become the victims of discrimination, etc. Children of immigrants may have to assume all kinds of responsibilities beyond their age. For instance, they may have to serve as translators and intermediaries in all kinds of settings (school meetings, medical appointments, etc.). Parents who are socially isolated by immigration and cut off from contact with their family of origin may also turn to their children as confidents of all their worries.

Furthermore, when families live in very dire conditions, lacking proper shelter, access to water, food, or basic medical care, or when families are displaced and live in overcrowded refugee camps, children not only may suffer from all sorts of deprivations, but sometimes also are the only ones who can bring some help to the family. Here is an example of a young Syrian refugee in Turkey who was only ten years old. He was interviewed by journalists. He told them that he had got a job in a carpet factory because people were looking for young boys with very fine fingers. His parents were both highly trained professionals, but they could not find any employment, and his tiny income was the only money the family could count on. The parents felt very bad to have to rely on their son, but at the same time were very thankful for his help. The boy told the journalists that he was sad to have to miss school but very proud to be able to help his family to survive.

When circumstances force children to act beyond their age, they may gain something from this experience. These children not only may acquire competences that they would not have acquired in other circumstances, but also may develop a strong self-esteem and inner confidence that they would not have acquired if their lives had been less demanding. In this sense, one could say that parentification can have some benefits, but this depends on the degree of demands that is placed on the children and on the degree of acknowledgment that they receive from their parents or from society.

When parents are able to recognize the contribution of their children, and the children are proud to be able to help their family, they will still suffer from the situational injustice caused by their life circumstances but not from the consequences of unfair exploitation by their parents. On the other end, parents who have had a very difficult life may have accumulated too much destructive entitlement to be capable of fairness toward their children. In this case, the parentification becomes clearly destructive for the child. However, in any case, whether parents can remain fair or not, it does not change the fact that both parents and children remain the victims of situational injustices: having to survive in much harsher circumstances than other people. Also, the degree of injustices to which the children are exposed does not depend only on the degree to which they are parentified, but also on the response of society to the miseries of these families.

Therapeutic strategies to decrease parentification

Professionals cannot expect that the victims of injustices will be able to see the unfairness of their demands only by hearing what it does to others. Here, the limitation is the blindness caused by their destructive entitlement. The most effective strategy to help them to accept responsibility for their destructive expectations is to bring up their side first. If the professional can acknowledge the unfairness of the situations that were at the root of the original injustice, they are already providing some redress to the victim.

Example

This example is taken from a consultation of Boszormenyi-Nagy with a family who came for treatment due to the destructive behaviors of the older son, who was only nine years old and had already been diagnosed with a conduct disorder. At the beginning of the session, the mother was very anxious, and very soon, her so-called very destructive son climbed onto her lap, holding her hand and caressing her cheek. When the consultant asked her if there were indeed moments when her son tried to help her, her answer was shocking. She stated that her son would never help her. Instead, he would always bother her, and she could not make him stop unless she would give him a few coins. At this moment, many professionals would have been tempted to ask her to see the absurdity of her statement, since it was so obvious that the boy was trying to help. Many people also would have tried to credit the child for his contribution to undo the injustice created by his mother's statement.

The consultant chose another avenue. Since he understood the mother's response to his question and her total blindness to her child's effort as clear evidence of destructive entitlement, he did not ask to consider the unfairness of her statement. Instead, he asked her if she could remember situations in which she had tried to do something for her parents and was overlooked. Before moving further, the consultant took care to state that he was not interested in blaming parents, and that her parents might have experience difficult things too while they were growing up (multidirected partiality).

She immediately came with a very precise example. As a girl, she had tried to help her mother by preparing for the visit of an aunt while her mother was still at work. She went shopping, cleaned the apartment, and set the table nicely. Instead of being thanked by her mom when she arrived from work, she was scolded for having put aside her schoolwork. The sharpness of her memory about the details of the situation indicated how much she had been hurt at the time. At the end of this exchange, the therapist asked the boy if he had listened to his mother's story and if he understood it. He shook his head to say yes. He had spent the time of the discussion drawing and spontaneously brought one to the consultant. The consultant complimented him for his drawing and asked him if he wanted to show it to his mother. The boy said yes. He then asked the mother if she would like to look at his drawing. She not only responded positively to the consultant's suggestion, but also complimented her son, asked him if she could keep the drawing, and thanked him when he gave a head signal showing that he agreed. Immediately after this exchange, she added that when he was born, she was sure that he would always be there for her, that he would be her savior, and that is why she named him Emanuel – the savior.

At that moment, it became clear that this mother had turned to her son from the day of his birth to receive from him all the unconditional love and attention that she had missed in her family, which of course was not only an unfair demand on the child but also an impossible one. Consequently, this child became destructively entitled, asking too much from his teachers and school comrades, and exploding in anger when he did not get what he wanted. Of course, the mother's new description of her son was in total contradiction with what she said about him at the beginning of the session; however, the consultant refrained from any comments. What counted here was the fact that this mother had been able to earn constructive entitlement by complimenting her son and by giving him a chance to offer her his drawing.

In helping the mother to acknowledge the contribution of her son, the consultant had accomplished two goals. The mother was given an opportunity to earn constructive entitlement, and this new experience could help her to become more generous toward her son in the future. The boy was credited for his contributions, which could decrease his own reliance on destructive entitlement. Only after this long exchange, the consultant moved to give a voice to the father who had felt helpless in the face of the conflicts between his wife and their son. The little brother was given a voice, too. He did not have much to say, but he showed signs that he was happy about what had happened during the session.

In the example above, the consultant was trying to remotivate the mother to show fairness to her son by using a two-pronged approach: acknowledging the past injustices in her life and offering her an opportunity to give when he asked her if she wanted to comment on her son's drawing. This gesture may appear too small to bring any changes, but this is not true. No matter how small a gesture may be, it will still lead to a slight increase of constructive entitlement, inner freedom, and inner self-esteem. As people begin to experience the benefits that come from even a small gesture, they will be more likely to behave in a more generous fashion on subsequent occasions, and less driven to rely on their destructive entitlement. At the same time, the people who are treated a little better will be more likely to respond more positively.

Example II

The second example comes from the work with a young woman, Kierra, who had been admitted to a homeless shelter after having lost housing due to her inability to pay her rent. She came from a family affected by poverty and drug use. Because of her parent's addiction, she had to take care of her younger siblings, and she left home as soon as she could. She moved in with her boyfriend and soon she decided to have a child with him. She believed that a baby would give her the love that she had not received while growing up. She was not thinking about her responsibility to raise a child (the need to be loved by a baby is a frequent factor in teen pregnancies). Soon after the birth of her baby daughter, her boyfriend was incarcerated for drug-related charges. She also got into trouble. She became neglectful of her daughter. The little girl was removed from her care by the child protection agency and placed in foster care with an aunt of her boyfriend.

Parentification and Exoneration

To regain custody of her daughter, she needed to prove that she was visiting her regularly, and that she was able to obtain a job and proper housing. She was also asked to attend parenting classes. None of this happened, and the family court judge became impatient. The aunt had offered to adopt the girl, and the father agreed to this adoption. The judge gave Kierra an ultimatum: if she did not begin to work on the goals he had set, he would terminate her rights and allow the adoption. Within three months, she needed to show at least that she had attended all the required parental classes and resumed regular visits to her daughter, whom she had not visited for several months.

The staff at the homeless shelter was puzzled by her ambivalence: on the one hand, she was telling everyone that she wanted to regain custody of her daughter, on the other hand, she was not doing what the judge was expecting from her. She was encouraged to see the consultant psychiatrist, who was also a contextual therapist, to figure out what was happening.

After hearing her story, it became clear to the consultant that Kierra had been parentified while she was growing up, and now she was not able to give her daughter what she deserved as a little child. Before her birth, she had parentified her as the little child who would provide her the love and understanding that she had not received while growing up. In this aspect, she was in the same position as the mother of the example above. At this point, she was not parentifying in a direct manner, but still, she did not feel the pressure to get her life in order as soon as possible. It was almost if she believed that this little girl should have the patience to wait until she was ready. One thing was clear: she was parentifying the judge. While everyone was telling her that the judge would abide by his warning, she still believed that he would give her more time to do what he had asked for. She spoke of him as if she knew that he would show her the patience that parents show toward a beloved child. In other words, she spoke of him as the good parent who would make up for the help and the patience she had not received while she was growing up. Of course, this was not going to happen. At that stage, the consultant took two steps.

The first step was to acknowledge what she had missed in her life, and to acknowledge that indeed she would deserve that people make an extra effort to make up for that. However, that this was not realistic, a simple example can be considered. If she had collected coupons to get a rebate on something, she would be entitled to get the merchandise for less. However, if the coupons had expired, she would have to pay the full price. She could not expect the cashier to give her the merchandise for the rebate price, and surely, she could not expect the cashier to pay the difference out of his or her own pocket. She would have to pay the full amount or leave the merchandise in the store. She fully agreed with the story. Indeed, there were only two options.

Now, coming to the story of her daughter, what was the parallel? Well, she was in fact expecting that she could have a relationship with her daughter without having to meet the requirements of the judge, as if the judge owed her a rebate on what he had said he *expected. As a person, however, he did not owe her any rebate. Furthermore, her daughter deserved a parent who was able to accept all the responsibilities relating to raising a child. She could not be a parent on rebate, picking and choosing what she was willing to do for her daughter. So, in the end, the story was the same. There were only two options. She would have to pay the full price of being a parent, or she would have to accept to the adoption and accept to possibly lose all contact with her daughter. At this point, the aunt was still obligated to accept her visits. If she became an adoptive parent, she would have the right to decide to cut her off entirely if she chose so.*

Now the next question: what could make her believe that she was entitled to this 'rebate'? In fact, in a certain way, she actually was entitled to it. She had done much for her siblings. In a way, she had served her years as a parent at an early age, and now she was entitled to retire. Maybe she was already in the same place of grandparents who are happy to see their grandchildren when they have the time and energy, and who are not expected to be responsible for their grandchildren like parents are. So, from this point of view, it would be fair to her to not ask her for more. However, her daughter was needing more. Where were they to go from there? The consultant had acknowledged the injustice that she had incurred in been parentified while at the same time asking her to recognize that her daughter was entitled to be raised by a parent who was capable of consistent parenting. The consultant left the question open and offered to see her again if she wanted.

She soon asked for a second meeting. At the second appointment, she told the consultant that she had decided to try to meet the judge's requirement and that she had already registered for a parent education class.

Kierra's decision probably hinged on several factors. One factor was the acknowledgment of the injustice she had incurred in being parentified, and the recognition that this gave her a certain degree of entitlement, but that in relying on this entitlement (the rebate) she was depriving her daughter from a responsible mother, and she was depriving herself from a daughter.

The other factor was the honesty of the consultant, telling her the plain truth that there were only two options and that both were costly: either she had to lose her daughter, or she had to give twice, once when she was a young parent for her siblings, and now again as a parent for her daughter. One thing the consultant did not do was to give her a lesson in morals, telling her about her obligation to be a good parent. Given her history, this not only would have been useless but also would have put an extra burden on her. On the other hand, in recognizing her predicament fairly, the consultant was undoing some of the unfairness to which she had been exposed. This recognition could help her to choose the path of giving instead of insisting on her right to get what she wanted. The hope was also that if she chose the path of giving, she would also begin to earn constructive entitlement, and this indirect gain would make up for the cost of having to give more to the future than what she had received from the past.

The main point of these two examples is to remind us that it is possible to remotivate parents to care about the needs of their children despite their destructive entitlement. While destructive entitlement leads people into a destructive spiral of exploitation and retaliation, constructive entitlement leads to a constructive spiral of increased fairness and increased trust. This is crucial in the case of parenting. If parents who have experienced many injustices in their lives can be helped to discover that they can gain from trying to be generous to their children despite the circumstances, one can remain optimistic about the fate of future generations.

Parentification outside of the parent-child relationship

Parentification of adults by adults

In a broader sense, the phenomenon of parentification also occurs in relationships that involve adults only. In all these situations, the expectations are the same. The adult who has missed something important in the relationship with a parent tries to turn adults into parental figures, into parents who love them unconditionally, or into parents who take responsibilities for all the important decisions of their life, etc.

Within families, people can parentify a relative who is in the same age group, for instance a sibling or a spouse. At work, people parentify colleagues. They may defer all decisions to them, or they may expect the same patience from them than they would expect from an understanding parent. In ordinary life, people who are parentified by other adults usually set a limit to this parentification when it places unrealistic demands on them. A popular poster that people often place in the kitchenet of offices reads: "Your mother does not live here, wash your own dishes." In couple relationships, things are different. In many cases, the parentification is reciprocal: each partner tries to turn the other into the parent who was missed, the parent from whom something is still expected. In addition, in love relationships, the partners often turn to each other to satisfy their regressive needs, i.e. their need to return to the position of the baby who is taking care by a loving parent. As long as both partners have the same needs and the same willingness to respond to the needs of the other, the relationship can be fulfilling despite its component of mutual parentification. On the other hand, if the relationship turns into the unilateral exploitation of one partner by the other, the relationship usually ends in a break-up.

Parentification of adults and transference phenomena

Another component of parentification comes from the fact that people unconsciously transfer the childhood feelings that they had toward their parents onto adults who are part of their lives. Consequently, they unconsciously relate to them as parental figures. Here is the story of a middle-aged woman who had begun to attend therapy at an outpatient clinic. She was treated by a young female therapist. She kept reporting to her how relieved she was that she did not to have to work with "this young guy", another therapist whom she had met in the building. In fact, this therapist was a senior staff member, who looked clearly older than his junior colleague. Over time, it became obvious that this woman was addressing her therapist as an idealized mother, not as someone who was barely older than her own daughter, and she was not aware of this.

Most individual therapists, especially therapists who qualified in psychoanalysis or psycho-dynamically oriented therapy, are familiar with these transference phenomena. Furthermore, therapists who have studied to become psychoanalysts and some other therapists are required to engage in didactical therapy so that these unconscious phenomena do not interfere with their work. Also, in many cases, ordinary people go for therapy, being psychoanalysis or cognitive therapy, to gain an understanding of the mechanism that leads them to see people in a distorted way and consequently experience difficulties in their relationships.

Contextual therapists neither focus their work on the analysis of transference, like psychoanalysts do, nor do they try to help their clients to deconstruct what they project on their clients, like cognitive therapists do. Nonetheless, they are very attentive to the relational consequences of these distortions in terms of loyalty or in terms of injustices. Out of loyalty to their parents, some people may present their parents in an idealized fashion, and project all the negative feelings they may have toward them onto other people: a spouse, a friend, or even a therapist.

These projections, negative or positive, can easily become a source of injustice. Indeed, the person who is constantly idealized as a rescuer incurs an unfair burden. Similarly, the person who constantly is described as someone who is insensitive is also the victim of an injustice. In these situations, contextual therapists try to use multidirected partiality as a tool to give a voice to the person who is affected by the distortions, and not only a voice to the person who is at the source of the distortions. Also, contextual therapists are better equipped than other professionals are to address the parentification that results directly from the clients' destructive entitlement.

Clients' parentification of therapists and counselors

Any therapy and any form of counseling inevitably entails a certain degree of parentification of the professional that is inherent to the form of asymmetry that is involved in the relationship with the professional. The parentification of the professional can also be due to the unconscious elements discussed above. However, in many situations, this parentification is due also to the destructive entitlement of the clients. When clients have not received what they expected from their parents, they may place unrealistic demands on the professional and often insist on special treatment. Clients may parentify their therapists as ever-available caring parents. Consequently, they insist on getting special attention from the therapist and special privileges. Some clients may insist on getting special access to the therapist (a private phone number), a special schedule (asking to be seen after hours or on weekends). They may ask for a reduced fee, or for free extra-time, etc.

In general, it does not help clients to agree to these kinds of requests: when people have missed things early in their lives, no matter how much they receive later, it will never entirely make up for early injustices. These clients will get much more from an acknowledgment of the injustice that they had incurred in the past than from any of the concessions that therapists may be willing to make to meet their demands. Also, these clients should be helped to rediscover their own strengths, including the strengths that come from being able to show generosity to others.

When clients have a valid reason to ask for an accommodation, the professionals may be tempted to accept their request, but this can lead to another problem: an accumulation of destructive entitlement on the side of the therapist. For instance, a client who was coming to the office during regular hours may ask to be seen after hours because of a change of schedule at work. The therapist may be willing to accommodate this request to prevent an interruption of therapy. If the therapist who has agreed to see a client after hours begins to hear complaints at home for being late for dinner, the therapist may eventually turn to the client and say in an abrupt manner: "Please understand that I cannot keep our schedule because my family is affected by my late returns." It is not the client's responsibility to care about the needs of the family of the therapist. It is the responsibility of the therapist to make sure that what he or she offers to a client can be sustained for as long as the clients still needs therapy, or else to take the responsibility to decline the client's special request. In this example, the therapist who has family obligations could have referred this client to a colleague who has routine evening hours. The same would be true of the therapist who has agreed to see a client for a lower fee. This therapist may eventually become impatient with this client and express this impatience by paying less and less attention to the client during the sessions, which is of course detrimental to the treatment.

Parentification of clients by therapists

It is obvious that it is not admissible that therapists and counselors turn to their clients to get what they were seeking from their own parents, but as everyone else, they unconsciously may tend to transpose some of the features of the relationship with their parents onto their own clients. Also, as everyone else, they may accumulate destructive entitlement. One of the problems is that their destructive entitlement in itself can become an obstacle to the self-awareness that would be required to refrain from the potential exploitation of their clients. For these reasons, it is very useful if training programs use the inspiration from contextual therapy to help their students to address these issues as part of their training. This can be done in a variety of ways. It would be difficult to ask students to engage in their own didactical family therapy, since it would require the involvement of their entire family, which is not realistic. However, in most family and counseling programs, students are expected to become aware of the effect of their own family issues on their work as therapists. In fact, most programs do ask their students to present their genogram (a graphic representation of their family) as part of their training. Here, the genogram could be used to explore the giving and receiving between the generations, and to examine the effect of injustices on the family members, including the student, and then encourage the students to explore the resources that come from giving. Training supervisors and supervisors in general should also be aware of these elements and capable of detecting the situations in which therapists maybe use a client as a source of compensation for past injustices.

Example

Here is an example of parentification coming from a need of recognition that was revealed during a session of family therapy supervision. The family therapy student had come to the session prepared to present a video-taped session of her work with a family. Owing to a conflict of schedule with a colleague, the supervisor had not been able to obtain the usual TV set needed to watch tapes and told the student to proceed with her presentation orally. The student became frantic and said,: "I wanted to show you how well I am working, and now you will not be able to see what I have accomplished with the family in this session." The supervisor tried to calm the student down, telling her to explain what she had done. However, she responded that this would not be enough to show how good she was in that session. At this moment, the supervisor stopped her, realizing that the urgent subject was not the discussion of the family but the discussion of the student's need of recognition. She had tried to parentify the supervisor as an approving parent and felt rejected when she was not given the opportunity to present her videotape. Also, she needed the family to show improvement to meet her own need of approval. This was a subtle form of parentification as if the family members should be the good parents who gave her an opportunity to succeed. This incident forced her to face this issue, which was a must if she wanted to become a good and fair therapist.

Abuses of the therapeutic situation, like the sexual use of a client or the financial exploitation of clients, not only constitute a clear violation of professional codes of ethics, but in many cases also an infringement of the law. These obvious cases of abuse require interventions by professional organizations, or even prosecution, and these are not discussed here. The statistics of the American Association for Marriage and Family Therapy pertaining to complaints against its members show two elements. The first element is that the most frequent infringement of the association's code of ethics comes from therapists who become sexually involved with clients. Studies show that this infringement often occurs after a recent loss or recent divorce. Here, it is likely that the infringement could be a consequence of the destructive entitlement. The second element is that among the therapists who commit this type of infringement, a good number are therapists who had a background in religious studies, or who were trained at faith-based counseling programs. It should be surprising since these therapists would be assumed to abide by high moral values that would prevent them from engaging in inappropriate relationships with clients. However, it is possible that this assumption of high moral values prevents faith-based training programs and pastoral counseling programs to sufficiently address the risks of infringements of professional codes of ethics by their students, which they could do by discussing the risks of relational exploitation that can be triggered by destructive entitlement.

Subtle forms of parentification of clients by therapists

There are other situations in which the parentification of the client is not caused by the neediness of the therapist. In these cases, the parentification occurs inadvertently when therapists put some burdens on the clients that should belong to the therapist, and often the burden is not obvious at all. These subtle forms of parentification can take many forms, but in many cases, the parentification results from an inappropriate offer of trust. Of course, therapists, especially contextual therapists, place great emphasis on restoring trust between family members. Also, in general, therapists tend to believe that when they tell a client: "I trust you", it will boost their client's self-esteem. However, there is a danger. This statement entails an expectation that the client will respond to this offer of trust by behaving in a trustworthy manner. This amounts to a subtle form of parentification. When a therapist tells a client: "I trust you that you won't hurt yourself", this offer of trust may be more of a burden to the client than a form of help, because indirectly it means: "I need to trust you so that I do not have the burden to worry about you". Here, the parentification would come from expecting the client to behave in a way that alleviates our task as responsible therapists.

To trust or not to trust? Not trusting as a therapeutic resource

When we work with clients who have a history of serious aggressive behaviors, we should be able to approach these clients with realistic humanism, ready to help them but not minimize their dangerousness. We owe it to them to create an environment that is safe for us, not to expect that they owe it us to control their aggressive impulses. For instance, we could make our office a safer place by removing anything that could be thrown at us. Good parents would not tell a child: "I need to trust you that you are not going to play with the sharp knifes in the kitchen", and then leave them around. They will make the effort to store them out of the reach of their children. In therapy, we owe it to our patients to make sure that we do not offer them our trust indiscriminately, and that we do not burden them with unrealistic expectations of trustworthiness. It is also important that we can show clients that we are not gullible, and do not accept to believe whatever they tell us when they try to deceive us. In these cases, we would lose our own trustworthiness if we did not challenge the veracity of their stories.

Example

Here is an example of young woman, Jonnie, who was admitted to a homeless shelter shortly after her discharge from a treatment center with a prescription for anti-anxiety medication. Upon her admission, she asked to see the consultant psychiatrist immediately for a renewal of her prescription. The staff at the homeless shelter knew her from prior stay.

She had been admitted several times, and on each of these occasions, she had returned to the streets after only a short stay. She had never tried to participate in the program that the shelter was offering to try to keep homeless youths off the streets. The staff believed that she was not taking her prescribed medication but that she wanted a new supply to be able to make some money by selling it on the street. The psychiatrist was warned that Jonnie could not be trusted. During the consultation, Jonnie explained that she needed medication right away because the doctor at the treatment center had prescribed medication for only a week. While this was possible, this did not appear true since most psychiatrists write prescriptions for a month supply. The consultant made a remark about this, but Jonnie remained adamant that she had received medication for a week only, and that she should be believed. The only way to know if she was telling the truth or if she was making up a story to stash pills and possibly misuse them was to call the pharmacy that filed the prescription to find out how many pills had been prescribed. When the consultant asked Jonnie for the name of the pharmacy, she got furious. Here is what ensued: "I tell you the truth, why don't you trust me?" The consultant answered: "What you don't see is that if I call the pharmacy, it is a win for both of us. What I want is to check facts. If you told me the truth, great. If I was right that you got medication for a whole month, not a big deal. I have not given you my trust, so I cannot lose it and we can still go on a good basis. On the other hand, if I give you my trust and don't call, and later find out that I was right, we both lose. This is the end of my trust in you, and on your side, you are short-changed because you deserve better than a doctor whom you can manipulate." This last point really took her by surprise, and she was actually quite moved to hear someone caring about her rights to be helped. Although she had indeed lied about her medication as the staff had suspected, this dialogue brought a big change in the attitude, and she began to show interest in the programs of the shelter. This change would not have occurred if the consultant would have offered to trust her indiscriminately.

Forgiveness and exoneration

In contextual therapy, one of the best ways to help people out of the spiral of destructive entitlement is to help them to gain an indirect benefit in the form of earning entitlement through generous giving. However, there are other avenues that help people to break free from the destructive consequences of unrepaired injustices: one is forgiveness, and another is exoneration. These two notions need to be examined in detail to understand in what ways they differ, and what the clinical consequences of these differences are.

Forgiveness

In psychotherapy, forgiveness is usually defined as a conscious decision to let go of feelings of resentment or vengeance toward a person or a group. Forgiving is an act of giving that is entirely under the control of the forgiver. It does not require any dialogue with the wrongdoer, nor a reappraisal of his or her deeds. In other words, it does not depend on the degree of culpability of the wrongdoers, nor on their willingness to make amends for their deeds, but only on the decision of the forgiver. This puts the forgiver in a position of control over the forgiven. This becomes a therapeutic resource in as much as the acts of the wrongdoer stop defining the life of their victims. At the same time, this position of superiority can have detrimental consequences when it blocks the dialogue with people who would have been willing to amend for their negative actions.

In fact, In Judaism and Christianity, there is a relational element to forgiveness. In Judaism: forgiveness cannot be granted unless the wrongdoer seeks it by taking full responsibility for his or her negative actions and fully repents them. In Christianity, one cannot expect to be forgiven unless one is capable of forgiving others.

Worthington (2018),[1] a psychologist and author who has spent his career studying forgiveness, describes four types of forgiveness. The first two types apply to situations in which the forgiver has been the victim of an injustice or an offense. The forgiver may be a person who offers forgiveness to the person who has caused the damage. If a group, not only an individual, is the victim of an injustice, the forgiver could be someone who is appointed by this group to offer forgiveness to the group who has committed the offense. Another type is self-forgiveness, which occurs when someone blames him- or herself for failing to abide by some predefined standards. The last one is divine forgiveness, which is granted to the person who has committed an offense against the divine. Worthington reminds us that forgiveness has been practiced for thousands of years by the members of religious groups that value forgiveness and by many people who did not have any specific religious beliefs. He also mentions that, within the last twenty years, over three thousand articles on forgiveness have been published, and that many are composed of multiple studies.

In the field of family therapy, Terry Hargrave (see Hargrave & Zasowski, 2016) introduced the theme of forgiveness already in the 1980s. He later wrote on contextual therapy, and more recently developed his own new approach, restoration therapy, which entails components of forgiveness (Hargrave & Pfitzer, 2016).

Forgiveness also applies to larger societal issues. The idea that forgiveness is a necessary step in the process of healing and reconciliation has been central to the entire process set in motion by the Truth and Reconciliation Commission that was established in South Africa after the end of apartheid. There is vast literature on that specific subject, which is exemplified by the writings of Archbishop Desmond Tutu on forgiveness (see for instance Tutu & Tutu, 2014).

Exoneration

In contrast to all the authors who write about forgiveness, Boszormenyi-Nagy does not include the process of forgiveness as a therapeutic resource in his approach. Instead, he focuses on what he calls 'exoneration'. Many therapists have struggled with the

---

[1] https://bit.ly/3NfoeWr

concept of exoneration for a good reason. In English, the word exoneration can have two possible meanings. It could mean relieving someone from a burden. For instance, people can be exonerated from having to pay taxes if their income is very low. It can also mean exculpating, meaning relieving someone from the burden of an accusation. Courts do make a difference between pardon and exoneration. For instance, the presidents of some countries have the privilege to pardon people. The people whom they pardon have been judged to be culprits. Otherwise, they would not need to be pardoned. People who are exonerated do not need pardon or forgiveness because the courts have decided that they were not culpable of any crime.

But what about the parents who have caused damages to their children? They are culpable of having committed actions that were detrimental to their children. Why should they be absolved from any blame? Furthermore, parents remain responsible for the consequences of their actions, whether their children exonerate them or not. The term *exoneration* is indeed somewhat misleading because in contextual therapy, exoneration should not be understood as a full exculpation of the parents but as a reappraisal of the degree of their culpability.

For Boszormenyi-Nagy, the main difference between forgiveness and exoneration lies in the fact that forgiveness does not require a reappraisal of the degree of culpability of the wrongdoer, while exoneration does. He is also concerned that forgiveness could entail an unhelpful aspect of arrogance: "I can forgive you, I am better than you are." Furthermore, one of the limitations of forgiveness is that one cannot forgive people who have hurt one for the damages that this hurt has caused to others; for instance, if this hurt has limited our ability to function as parents. He believes that the clients who show the most improvement in therapy are not the clients who are able to forgive their parents but the clients who are willing to learn enough about their parents' life to understand the origins of their detrimental behaviors, and then based on that, are able to exonerate them. (For more on the discussion of the difference between forgiveness and exoneration, see Ducommun-Nagy, 2010b)

Exoneration: The recategorization of parents and the requalification of their actions

In fact, the process of exoneration could be even better understood as a 'recategorization' of the parents and a 'requalification' of the injustices that have occurred in the family. When family members are caught in a negative spiral of destructive entitlement and parentification over several generations, one needs to search for the event or the situation that could have been at the source of the original situational (distributive) injustice that has triggered the cascade of relational injustices. It could have been a war, a natural catastrophe, a forced migration, or it could have been a time in history when the family had been exposed to hardship due to poverty, racial discrimination, etc. It could also be any adverse event inside the family, for instance an illness, an untimely death, etc.

Once people begin to understand that their parents did not act out of malice but out of a misguided effort to seek redress for past relational injustices or situational injustices, this new understanding enables them to recategorize their parents. They can remove them from the category of pure wrongdoers, the perpetrators of relational injustices, and place them instead in the category of people who are not just wrongdoers but also the victims of past injustices.

But this goes further. Once people who try to exonerate their parents come to the realization that all family members, themselves included, have been the indirect victims of an original situational injustice over which no one had any control, it leads to a requalification of the injustices that they incurred themselves. They are not as much the victims of the relational injustices committed by their parents, but much more the victims of the original situational injustice that has affected the entire family, an injustice that no one can repair. This becomes a fact of their life, no more a relational issue. This realization can bring even more definitive changes than an exoneration that is based solely on an identification of the attenuating circumstances that could explain their parents' destructive behaviors.

Exoneration outside of the parent-child relationship

Exoneration does not have to be limited to the exoneration of parents. It can be extended to siblings, partners, friends, or even to total strangers. However, there is a great difference. People who have been wronged by perpetrators with whom they do not have irreversible ties, like the tie that exists between parents and children, do have a choice. They have the option to simply get these people out of their life and never think about them anymore. They may choose to maintain a relation with them and decide to forgive them, and they may derive a significant benefit from their actions. They may even want to find a way to exonerate them, but this would not bring as many changes in their life than the exoneration of a parent would.

Blood ties and legal ties between parents and children are irreversible. Children cannot divorce their parents or ask to void an adoption. Also, parents and children are connected by all kinds of conscious and unconscious psychological ties. No matter how much damage they cause, parents remain the crucible that gives shape to their children's identity. Also, no matter how bad the parent-child relationship is, parents and children also remain connected by some forms of loyalty ties, often costly invisible loyalties. In short, parents and children are bound by all kinds of ties that do not depend on their personal preferences.

For all these reasons, people who see their parents as unredeemable, bad people can only have a negative image of themselves, and this can have negative consequences in many areas of their life. Conversely, the people who can shed a new light on their parents by understanding their own predicament, and by finding some redeeming elements in their life, will incur a direct benefit from recategorizing these parents. They become the children of people who have understandable shortcomings, not the children of hopelessly bad people, and this is much better for their self-esteem.

The clinical benefits of exoneration

In general, a contextual therapist regards the process of exoneration as something that happens in the dimension of relational ethics. Trying to understand one's parents is a form of giving. Therefore, people who are willing to make the effort to understand their parent's predicament gain constructive entitlement, with its associated benefits in the form of increased self-validation, increased self-delineation, and increased inner freedom.

It is obvious that forgiving has great benefits that should not be dismissed by contextual therapists. We already know that forgiving does help the forgivers let go of their grudges and move on with their lives. Furthermore, since forgiving is a form of giving, it does lead to an increase in constructive entitlement that benefit the person who forgives and can already serve as an antidote to destructive entitlement and already benefit the next generations. But unlike exoneration, forgiveness does not result in the recategorization of the parents nor to the requalification of the injustices that occurred in the family.

The process of exoneration

Since contextual therapists believe that the exoneration of parents constitutes an important step in the treatment process, they strive to encourage clients to engage in this process as soon as it seems feasible. When clients are not ready to try to shed new light on their parents, contextual therapists may suggest a moratorium, asking their clients for the permission to come back to this subject later on in the treatment. It is important to understand that one should not expect young children to be pushed to engage in the exoneration of their parents. They deserve understanding from their parents. It would be unfair to push them in the reverse position, i.e. to ask them to understand their parents' predicament or to accept their justifications for their unfair behaviors. At the same time, it may be helpful if the professional mentions some redeeming features in the parents' life. It would indicate that they are capable of offering them some partiality, which will decrease the risk that their children push the professionals away from remaining loyalty to their parent. On the other hand, some teenagers and young adults may benefit from beginning to engage in an exoneration process, but professionals need to proceed slowly. They need to take the time to verify if this process does not turn into an unfair burden for them, too.

The exoneration process can begin in several ways. Therapists can propose family therapy sessions to foster a dialogue between adult children and their parents during which these children could learn more about the parents' own predicaments. However, one of the limits of such a dialogue is that the parents may use the situation to try to justify their behaviors, and to try to escape responsibility for their past actions. Here, therapists need to rely on multidirected partiality to make sure that the parents do not overlook the children's side, and conversely, that the children do not simply dismiss what their parents try to tell them.

Sometimes, also parents or grandparents who have been severely traumatized avoid talking about their past experiences, which creates not only a gap of information between the generations but a stagnation in their relationship since children will not be able to understand their parents' side if they do not know what has happened to them. Here the professional who has a knowledge of historical events that have affected the parents can be partial to the parents' need to remain silent and at the same time partial to the children's need to make sense of their parents' experiences and behaviors. This situation has been encountered often in the families of holocaust survivors, but it could occur in the families of people who have been the survivors of genocide in other parts of the world. A gap of information between the generations can also occur when a parent is silenced by his or her own shame about a situation, or when loyalty prevents parents from revealing what their own parents did. Here again, progress can be made if the professional is capable of multidirected partiality.

There can be many reasons why parents cannot be included in the therapeutic process. They may be unwilling to participate in family therapy sessions. They may refuse any discussion about the past. They may be willing to talk, but only outside of a formal setting, or they may be totally unreachable for many possible reasons. People may not know who their parents are if their mother does not know who their father is, refuses to talk about him, or if the child was abandoned at birth. Parents may have totally disappeared out of people's lives. Parents may be dead. In all these cases, therapists can still encourage their clients to learn more about their parents' lives by collecting whatever information they can get about them. Sometimes the information can come from relatives, sometimes from public records. Sometimes the information comes by chance only when people suddenly come across someone who has some information about their past. Sometimes it happens when someone, even a total stranger, begins to disclose information about a person's family that has been kept secret until that point. It could be the actual identity of a parent, the suicide of a relative, a bankruptcy, an incarceration, etc.

Experience shows that often the original situational injustice that has triggered the ensuing relational injustices occurred a long time ago, not rarely in the generation of the great grandparents or even in some cases, one generation earlier. This is a problem. Over time, information get lost between the generations. No matter how hard people try to get information about the past, it is often difficult for people to get information about past relatives beyond the generation of their grandparents. Often, information can get lost when families have moved away from the areas they originally came from. This is not only the case when families migrate from one country to the other. It can also occur when families move from the villages of their ancestors to the big cities. In some cases, the professionals themselves may have some knowledge about socio-historical factors that are not known or not remembered by their clients, and this can help them to understand the predicament of their ancestors. But once this knowledge of the past is gone, it becomes much more difficult to return to the sources of these injustices.

Illustrations of the exoneration process

Example I

The first example comes from a family who had been referred for treatment after a report of child abuse. The girl, Anna, had reported in school that her mother was hitting her. Her parents were divorced, and she lived with her mother and a younger brother. In general, the mother was a responsible parent who was able to take care of her children's needs. At the same time, she had hit Anna on several occasions. She knew that it was not right to hit children, but she believed that Anna needed to be punished for refusing to obey immediately when she had asked her to do something. She was much more patient with her son. When asked about her own growing up, Anna's mother told the therapist that she had been born in a family of farmers who lived an isolated village. She explained that her parents were still living on their small farm with her brother (Anna's uncle), who was disabled. He was born with Down syndrome, and he had never been able to live independently. Anna's mother reported that her father was somewhat distant, but otherwise she did not see any problems in their relationship. On the other hand, she had a difficult relationship with her own mother (Anna's grandmother). She described her as a woman who was never available to respond to her needs. Instead, she was always asking much from her. While she was growing up, she had to perform many chores in the house, and she had very little time to herself. Later, her mother continued to rely on her for all kinds of help, and never expressed any gratitude for that. Over time, Anna's mother became tired of the situation. She put an end to her mother's unending demands by stopping all contacts with her and by stopping visiting the family.

From the point of view of contextual therapy, it was evident that Anna's mother had been parentified. She was asked to do too much (a relational injustice). Now she was expecting Anna to obey her and do whatever she was asked to do without raising any questions (an example of destructive entitlement). Based on the principle of multidirected partiality, the therapist wanted to offer his partiality to the grandmother as well. He asked Anna's mother if she had ever talked with her own mother about her experience of raising a child with Down syndrome. She was taken aback. She not only had never talked with her mother about this, but also could not see why it would matter.

The therapist responded by asking more precise questions about the family situation: what did Anna's mother know about the way her parents reacted when they found out about their son's condition? Were they able to rely on each other? Could they talk to anyone in the community? Did they receive support to raise their special-needs child? Anna's mother had never discussed this with her parents, but she could report that life was in fact quite hard for her parents. They were running the farm without any outside help, and it did not bring much money. Also, at the time, there was very little help for families raising a child with disabilities, especially since the family lived on an isolated farm, like her parents did. It was also a time when there were still many superstitions in villages about children born with disabilities: maybe the parents had done something wrong and they were being punished by God, etc.

After this exchange, the therapist simply mentioned that based on this information, it was quite likely that Anna's grandmother had felt overburdened by the task of raising a child with special needs in these circumstances. Could Anna's mother see that? She was quite surprised, but she agreed that this was indeed possible. She added that it did not change the fact that her mother had asked too much from her. However, now, she could begin to see that why her mother had to rely on her. She did not have many choices. In other words, Anna's mother was able to accept the idea that her own mother did not exploit her out of malice but because she was overwhelmed by the situation. In Boszormenyi-Nagy's original terms, Anna's mother was beginning to exonerate her own mother. In the new terminology, she seemed willing to recategorize her mother: she was willing to remove her from the category of wrongdoers and place her in the category of people who had been the victims of unfortunate circumstances.

It is important to remember that the recategorization of the wrongdoers does entail a requalification of the injustices that occurred in the family. In this example, Anna's mother was not only the victim of her own mother's unfairness (a relational or retributive injustice). All the family members were the victims of situational injustices that had at least two components: the situational injustice stemming from the random genetic condition that affected Anna's uncle, and the situational injustices stemming from historical and geographical circumstances: the lack of supportive services, and the old prejudices of the community.

It is always difficult to know when people can reach the point of fully exonerating their parents, but in this example, Anna's mother had already made a clear step in this direction. She did this by accepting to respond to the therapist's question, and she was able to hear his point about the predicament of her mother. In doing that, Anna's mother was already indirectly giving to her own mother and therefore beginning to earn constructive entitlement. Recategorizing her own mother as a person who was the victim of a situational injustice, not as simply an unfair parent, would help her to be less frustrated about their relationship. Therefore, she would also become less likely to expect too much from Anna and to hit her when she did not respond immediately to her expectations.

Example II

Here is a second example of the process of exoneration: here, the process began during therapy, but the actual exoneration occurred at a moment that could not have been predicted by anyone. Jane was a successful professional but she had experienced many difficulties in her personal life. She was suffering from chronic depression and had attended therapy with several individual therapists and psychiatrists without much success. She knew that she had a very difficult relationship with her mother, complaining that she had never received any love from her, but she was adamantly opposed to any offer of family therapy. Still, she accepted to give some information about her family situation.

Jane's maternal grandmother had been diagnosed with schizophrenia and hospitalized when Jane's mother was very young. She never returned home and remained institutionalized for rest of her life. Jane's grandfather could not raise his daughter alone and she grew up in foster care.

In contextual terms, Jane's mother had been the victim of a situational injustice. In the historical time when Jane's grandmother was diagnosed with schizophrenia, her condition was considered incurable, and she was institutionalized permanently. This constituted a situational injustice for not just this poor woman, but for Jane's mother and Jane herself: their mother/daughter relationship had been affected by the fact that her mother had been deprived from receiving the care of her own mother.

Jane did not speak much about her father. She mentioned only that he was a responsible parent and that they had a fairly good relationship. He had died unexpectedly and her mother had remained a widow with only little financial resources. Jane had a brother who was married and had the responsibility of his own family. As a single woman with means, she was the one who was expected to support her mother. She was refusing to do this, feeling that she did not owe her mother anything. She believed that her mother should return to work and support herself but she was worried that she could not be hired: she had some past work experience as a clerk, but this was long before this kind of jobs required the use of computers. Since Jane was very competent in this area, she decided to invite her mother for a few lessons. She had no intention to get closer to her. On the contrary, she believed that this would guarantee that her mother would get a job and not need her in the future.

Even if Jane's intention to help her mother came out of a personal need, self-protection, it still allowed her to interact with her mother in a new way. She was able to have a glimpse of her vulnerability as a new widow and aging woman and she was able to develop a little empathy for her, but this was not enough to change their relationship. However, the big change occurred unexpectedly.

Jane and her mother were invited to celebrate Christmas at her brother's home. Jane brought presents for everyone, including a small one for her mother. She did not feel happy about having to buy a present for her mother but could not see herself not doing that. However, this was not true for her mother. She had come with gifts for her son and his family, but none for Jane. Jane described that this was a revelation for her. She did not become angry. She just realized the enormity of the situation. Her mother was not even able to give her the kind of small gift that any person who is invited to a Christmas party brings to make sure that everyone gets something. Jane described that as soon as she realized this, she suddenly began to see her mother as someone who was profoundly damaged: a girl who could not expect to receive any gift from her own mother and a girl who had been raised without her love.

Jane reported later that this sudden experience reminded her of trying to use binoculars. At first, one sees two blurred pictures, but once the lenses are adjusted, the two pictures merge and one sees only one very sharp picture. For years, she had seen her mother as a someone who did not even deserve to be called mother. More recently, she was able to see her as someone who was vulnerable. Now these two pictures had merged into one. Now, she was able to see her mother just as she was, a woman who had been damaged by life and who could not do more than what she was doing. Jane reports that this new way of looking at her mother was liberating. Now, she could deal with a factual situation. She could stop wondering why her mother did not show her any affection while she was able to be affectionate toward her brother. He was not in a similar relationship with her. It was the mother-daughter relationship that had been damaged over two generations.

In this second example, one can see that the exoneration process has led Jane to a recategorization of her mother whom she could finally see not just as the perpetrator of a relational injustice, her lack of giving to her daughter, but also as the victim of a situational injustice, the damages to her life that were caused by her own mother's mental illness and the social prejudices surrounding her condition. Jane was also able to requalify the injustices that she had been the victim of. She was not just the victim of a relational injustice, her mother's inability to give, but in fact, the victim of the situational injustice that had affected everyone, the illness of her grandmother for which no one was responsible.

But this were not the only changes. What Jane describes in using the metaphor of the binoculars is that this recategorization of her mother also brought a realignment of internal objects, a deep change in the dimension of psychology. She had spent her life separating two internal objects, a bad mother, the mother she had, and an ideal mother, the mother she wishes she could have had. Once she was able to exonerate her mother, these two internal objects, the bad and the good mother, merged into one, a mother as an internal object that was neither all bad, nor all good.

Coming to terms with our parents' shortcomings

Up to this point, we have considered forgiveness and exoneration as part of the process of the healing process in therapy and counseling, but all of us need to come to terms with our parents' shortcomings. Maturity requires that we reach a point in life where we can accept our parents for what they are or what they have been. If our parents had serious shortcomings, we need to accept that parents who were not able to meet our needs when we were growing up are very unlikely to be able to meet our needs later in our lives. We have discussed destructive entitlement as a source of injustice to third parties, but if we turn to aging and sick parents to get back what we did not receive from them while we were growing up, we are almost doing the same. Since these aging parents are so different from the parents who failed us, it is almost as if we were in fact asking strangers for redress. In this case, what we can still do is to offer our parents a chance to earn entitlement by letting them know what they could still do for us in their current circumstances, but this offer would have to come from a position of generosity, accepting that they may totally dismiss our offer. It would be immature to make this offer with the expectation that they could finally meet our needs.

Even the best parents can never fully meet the needs of their children. Sometimes, people even blame their parents for having done too much for them, for having been too protective, etc. In short, no parents are perfect, and no parents are able to fulfil all the needs of all their children. At some point in life, we need to be able to stop rehashing their shortcomings and stop dwelling on the injustices of the past. We need to accept to close the account we have with our parents and begin a new relationship with them that is not constantly tainted by our expectation for redress. This can lead to the same changes involved in exoneration.

In addition, at the moment when we can stop looking at our parents through the lens of our unrealistic expectations, we shall also be able to see what we received from them, even if this was only little. Furthermore, we shall often be able to discover that our parents had qualities that we could not see as long as we were blinded by our grievances or by our disappointment. Often, these may be not only qualities that could serve as a source of inspiration in our lives, but also qualities that could be bring benefits to the next generations.

Here comes the example of a man who had suffered from the shortcomings of a father who had seemed unable to meet his needs, especially when he was a young child crying for help. This man had known all along that his father had a decreased hearing capacity, but he had never thought about it as a factor that had affected his parenting abilities. Once he realized that, of course, his father could not hear him cry since he was partly deaf, he was able to exonerate him. His father was not just the perpetrator of a relational injustice, his lack of responsiveness. He could be recategorized as the victim of a situational injustice, the illness that had caused his hearing loss, a situational injustice that had consequences for both of them. This also changed his perspective on his father in another way. Instead of only seeing him as someone who was unavailable, he suddenly realized that in reality, he had been very devoted to his family, always trying to be as good a provider as possible despite his handicap. This man then discovered that his own personal quality, his commitment to the welfare of others, did not come from nowhere, but from his father. Without realizing it, he had been loyal to his father all along by cultivating this trait in himself. This realization became an added source of inspiration in his determination to work toward the welfare of others, in his case not as a parent, but as a friend and as a scholar who wanted to make his knowledge readily available to the next generations. This example should remind us that we can benefit the future generations in many different ways, not just by becoming good parents.

Chapter 7
A General Understanding of Family and Group Loyalties

Introduction

The purpose of this chapter is to present the notion of loyalty as it is understood in standard contextual therapy, with the addition of some new perspectives. The goal is to help professionals in the field of mental health, pastoral counseling, social services, and education to be better prepared to identify situations in which family and group loyalty plays a role in their clients' individual or relational difficulties and to be better prepared to intervene in these situations. When people talk about loyalty, it can cover many things, and loyalty can be defined in many ways. In society in general, the discussion of family and group loyalties comes up in a vast array of domains: social and political sciences, history, anthropology, evolutionary biology, etc. It would be impossible to cover all these areas, but we shall examine some of the things we can learn from these other fields and discuss some of the contributions that contextual therapy can make to the understanding of group loyalties in general.

The first part of the chapter includes a discussion of the definition of loyalty in general, its specific definition in contextual therapy, its systemic implications, and a discussion of its determinants according to the five dimensions of relational reality. The chapter continues with a presentation of the various forms of individual and relational problems that can be related to loyalty: loyalty conflicts, split loyalties, invisible loyalties, including the loyalty factors that can contribute to intergenerational transmission of destructive behaviors. This will include a discussion of the interventions that can be used to address these issues. The chapter concludes with a discussion of loyalty as a source of resilience and a source of individual autonomy.

The general definition of loyalty

In the discussion of loyalties, priority will be given to the definition of loyalty that is used in contextual therapy, but it remains useful to consider the main ways in which loyalty can be understood. The word itself is associated with the notion of law and legality. The definition of loyalty in English language dictionaries may vary slightly from one dictionary to the other, but the common point is that loyalty is defined in two ways: it is defined as the quality of the person who is loyal, and being loyal is defined as the quality of the person who is capable of abiding to a promise, to an oath, etc. In other words, it refers to the quality of the person who is capable of faithfulness. In this sense, there is a close association between the notion of loyalty and fidelity. Also, loyalty can be defined by its object. In this sense, it is used to define faithfulness to a government, an institution, a cause, etc.

Loyalty to a person or an organization can be affirmed by a pledge. One of the most common pledges that people take is the pledge of fidelity that partners take during their wedding ceremony. When the loyalty to a government, an army, or an organization is affirmed by a formal pledge, one may speak about a pledge of allegiance rather than a pledge of fidelity. Indeed, many groups require their new members to take some form of pledge to formalize their commitment. This could be the formal pledge that new U.S. citizens take during their naturalization ceremony. It can be the pledge to serve the interest of a firm, and in this case, the pledge may take the form of a non-compete agreement, which usually entails the promise to refrain from disclosing trade secrets and the promise to refrain from working for a rival company for a determined length of time after leaving a job.

Most of the authors who write about loyalties in social or moral sciences raise the same question: what are the factors that bring us to be loyal to others? Many see loyalty as a psychological attitude, and in this case, they see attachment as one of the important factors of loyalty. They see loyalty as based on a shared emotional bond, a shared experience, a shared nationally, ethnicity, and also on shared religious beliefs or shared myths. They also ask: can loyalty be conceived of outside of a relationship? Most agree that it is not the case. Loyalty is specific to social relationship. Even if loyalty can be conceived as a commitment to a cause or an ideal rather than a commitment to a person or a group, implicitly it still includes a commitment to the people who engage in the same cause or the people who share the same ideal. All these authors agree on one thing: loyalty leads to a selection between the person or the group that benefits from this loyalty and all the other people or groups that are not the recipients of this loyalty. "Rather than talking about faithful adherence to a group, I think it is clearer to regard loyalty to a group as involving acting in such a way that shows that one regards its members as warranting more consideration than people not in the group. Particularly important is that someone who is loyal to a group regards avoiding or preventing harm to the members of the group as more important than avoiding or preventing a similar harm to people not in the group." (Gert, 2013: 4).

This agrees with the definition of loyalty that is found in contextual therapy. However, one big difference is that, in contextual therapy, loyalty is presented right away as a triadic notion, a notion that cannot be dissociated from the notion of loyalty conflict. Boszormenyi-Nagy (1987, 2014: 98) states that: "loyalty to one's parents is founded on the most substantial earned merit [the merits of the committed parents], and any later loyalty is subject to conflict with our primary, filial loyalty. The teacher, the friend, the spouse or the therapist are all candidates for conflicting loyalties." Hence, for him, the notion of loyalty conflict is inherent to the definition of loyalty. In its definition in contextual therapy, loyalty is understood as a form of commitment that is based on fairness and reciprocity, and it is anchored in the dimension of relational ethics: fairness behooves us to place the interests of the people who have shown the biggest commitment to us before the interests of the people toward whom we are less indebted.

Most authors who discuss loyalty in the field of social sciences agree that loyalty can also become a source of problems when people have multiple loyalties that conflict with one another, but they see loyalty conflicts as a secondary consequence of loyalty, not as part of its definition. Furthermore, they emphasize the psychological determinants of loyalty, and they give much less attention to reciprocity and indebtedness as determinants of loyalty.

Are loyalties visible or invisible?

Since, in contextual therapy, loyalty is defined as a preferential commitment to a person or a group, one cannot talk about loyalties in the absence of a choice between two persons or two groups. From this point of view, people may be registered members of a political party, but this would not tell anything about their loyalty to this party until there is an election. This is the time when they are faced with a choice. Out of loyalty to their party, they may decide to vote for their party's candidate even if they find more qualities in the candidate of an opposite party. This vote would be a direct expression of loyalty. Instead, they could choose to vote for the candidate of the opposite party whom they like better. This would be an open expression of disloyalty to their party. Or they could decide that they should not give their vote to the candidate of their party whom they do not like, but that they should not go as far as giving their vote to the opposite candidate. Consequently, they will choose to abstain from voting. In this case, their own party will accuse them of disloyalty, but indirectly they would have remained loyal to it since the other party did not make any gain either. Here, contextual therapists speak about invisible loyalties as a synonym for indirect loyalties.

Another example comes from soccer matches. During the off-season, when no matches are played, nothing distinguishes the supporters of one club from the supporters of a competing club. In other words, their loyalty to their favorite club is not visible. However, this changes as soon as the season opens. People will begin to wear all kinds of things that have the logo or the colors of their favorite club, hats, scarfs, t-shirts, etc. In short, their loyalty to their favorite team becomes very visible. During international championships like the world soccer cup, people begin to show their loyalty to their national team in a direct manner commonly by decorating their windows or their car with their national flags. Many immigrants to a new country remain loyal to their old national team and show it directly by displaying the flag of their old country. Some other immigrants may be torn because they would like to show support for the team of their old countries but at the same time, they do not want to create conflict with neighbors, colleagues or even friends who support the team of their host country. Consequently, they may decide to refrain from displaying anything. This does not mean that they have suddenly lost their interest in the championship or stopped supporting their old national team. Here it is the absence of the flag of their host country that becomes an indirect or invisible evidence of their loyalty to their old team. In this understanding, invisible loyalties are synonymous with indirect loyalties.

However, invisible loyalties can also be understood not only as indirect loyalties, but also as invisible expressions of loyalty, meaning behaviors that would not be understood as an expression of loyalty until one understands their purpose. This is what Boszormenyi-Nagy and his team discovered when they began to observe the families of patients who suffered from schizophrenia in the late 1950s. A detailed discussion of this kind of invisible loyalties and examples will be provided later in the chapter.

Loyalty as a triadic notion and its systemic implications

Whether one talks about loyalty or allegiance, the main point is that by definition, loyalty is a triadic notion. One pole of the triangle is occupied by the person who needs to make the choice; the second pole by the group or the person who is the beneficiary of the commitment; and the third pole by the rest of the people, the groups and the persons who are not offered the same commitment. Here, we speak about a simple triangle, which is described in geometry. This has nothing to do with the notion of triangulation that is familiar to systemic family therapists. From a systemic point of view, the significance of loyalty is that it establishes a network of connections between the people who are bound by a mutual commitment, and this network of connections contributes to hold the group together. "In families and non-family groups the most fundamental loyalty commitment pertains to the maintenance of the group itself" (see Boszormenyi-Nagy & Spark, 1973, 2014: 40). Furthermore, this loyalty commitment establishes a boundary between the group of people who are connected through their mutual commitment, and all the other people who are not included in this commitment. Consequently, each time group members show loyalty to other group members, it reinforces the boundaries of this group vis-à-vis any other groups, and this in turn contributes to reinforce the stability of the group. In other words, loyalty becomes an important factor of homeostasis in families and in groups.

System theorists have taught us a long time ago that families are more than the sum of all the people who are part of them. Indeed, over the generations, family members come and go, but families continue. People are born, others die. New people join through marriages, some leave through divorce. Some people disappear after a complete cut-off. Others are accepted as family members in the absence of any biological or legal ties. These system theorists have also postulated that stability of open systems like families depend on mechanisms that maintain the equilibrium of the systems over time. One of their hypotheses is that families are held together by shared myths, common rituals, or common patterns of behaviors. Families are also held together by irreversible blood ties, emotional attachment, and legal ties that may be reversable or not. In many countries, marriages could not be dissolved until divorce was allowed; in general, adoptions cannot be dissolved even when adoptive parents and children become estranged.

Boszormenyi-Nagy does recognize the many factors that bind family members together, including the shared myths described by his colleagues, but his main contribution to the field of family therapy was to postulate that what ensures the stability of the family system over time is the mutual commitment of each of the family members toward each other, especially the commitment that exists between parents and children. In other words, the stability of the family system over time is based on reciprocal solidarity and loyalty. This commitment may be expressed in very direct ways by statements like "No matter what happens, my family will always come first". Or, conversely, this commitment may be expressed only in an indirect, invisible way. In this case, it can be inferred only from some behaviors. For instance, people who have decided to cut off all relationship with their family often remain surprisingly ready to attack the outsiders who would make negative comments about their family. In families, loyalty is not limited to the parent-child relationship. Siblings or more distant relatives can also be bound by loyalty.

Since loyalty contributes to stabilize groups, disloyalty can present a serious threat to the integrity of any group. Families are less vulnerable to defection of group members than ordinary groups are. As discussed above, family members are tied together in ways that are not found in ordinary groups. For various reasons, people may try to cut all ties with their family, but they will remain connected by blood ties and legal ties. In many countries, people cannot legally drop their family name, nor can parents fully disinherit their children.

In families, the punishment of disloyal members may take many forms, from subtle psychological blackmailing to physical threats. Parents may threaten to disinherit a child who wants to engage in a career choice that is not approved by the family. They may cut all ties with a child who has rejected their religion, or they may threaten harm to the child who tries to engage in a relationship that is not approved. However, at the same time, parents and children know that they will remain tied together in one way or another, and that they will never be able to totally break loose from one another.

In non-family groups, the group members may be bound by emotional ties, by commitment to a common goal, and their interactions may be an important source of Self-Other definition, but they are not bound by irreversible ties like family members are. Consequently, these kinds of groups are more vulnerable to disloyalty and defection than families are. Groups that are not based on family ties may enforce loyalty by having the group members take a formal pledge and by exerting various kinds of pressure on the people who may think of leaving. This may include serious threats or attempts to isolate the group members from contact with outsiders. This is often the case in sects.

In traditional societies that are based on traditional units, like clans, disloyal members may be punished by banishment from the group, which could threaten their survival if they are left to fend alone in a hostile natural environment. Totalitarian regimes very often require absolute loyalty of the population to the leaders and their party. Here, dissidents, who are labelled as defectors, can be punished by being deprived of all sorts of human rights, all the way to imprisonment or death. In most armies of the world, defectors are sentenced to death because if they were followed by others, it could lead to a disintegration of troops' unity. Conversely, many armies do not kill the enemies they have captured, not because they want to be good to them but because they serve a purpose. Their presence as enemies contributes to reinforce the boundary of the troops as a unit and therefore contributes to secure its cohesion.

In families, family reunions serve as a test of family loyalty. The reunions may center on important events, like weddings, funerals, or the baptism or circumcision of a child. In these cases, people may attend the family gathering not only out of family loyalty but because they also need to fulfil societal expectations that go beyond the boundaries of the family. When the reunion does not have a major purpose, for instance when family members are invited to join a family picnic, people's attendance is truly based on their commitment to be part of the family, not on any other factors. If family members accept to put aside the plans that they have made with other people to attend an event like that, it means that they are truly motivated to show loyalty to their family, and this contributes to the stability of the family system. One could also cite the examples of people who are committed to attend functions organized by their ethnic group, being a ball, a parade, or any other event. Each time they respond to the invitation of their ethnic group, they redesign the boundaries of their group by contrast with all the other ethnic groups that could exist in their community.

The role of loyalty in society

It is possible that the notion of family loyalty may not apply entirely to societies in which the definition of what constitutes a family diverges from the standard definition of the family that was used by the pioneers of family therapy, i.e. the standard Western post-World War II nuclear family. It is also possible that the word 'loyalty' does not translate well into some languages. However, it would be difficult to imagine any societal group that could function without some expectation of reciprocal commitment between its members, and without some expectation that these group members would place the interests of their own group before the interests of any other groups. This is true for families, clans, or any other kind of human groups.

It is even very likely that our capacity for caring and for loyalty is at the source of our success as a species. Loyalty has probably played an important role in the survival of early human groups that not only needed the cooperation of all the group members to accomplish various tasks, but also needed to rely on their members' commitment to protect one another from outside attackers. When people know that they can rely on the loyalty of their family members or group members, they feel more secure in their personal endeavors, and they are more resilient in the face of adversity. From this point of view, loyalty does become a source of resilience, both at an individual and at a group level.

At the same time, at an individual level, loyalty can have negative consequences. People may be caught in severe loyalty conflicts that result in a variety of individual and relational symptoms. Also, when people and groups are bound by loyalty, the attack on one person or one group becomes an attack on all. Here, instead of the saying: "The friends of my friends are my friends" one could say: "The enemies of my friends are my enemies." Over the course of history, nations have formed alliances that at times had devasting consequences. The worst example comes from World War I, which caused the death of so many millions people: the original situation that led to the onset of the war could have had much less devastating consequences if the nations of the time had not form alliances that bounded them to engage on one side or the other of the original conflict.

Loyalty and morality

One serious question raised by social and moral scientists is the following: is loyalty compatible with morality, or not? If loyalty is based on gratitude, being loyal should be regarded as a moral virtue, but here is the main question: is it moral or not to give priority to a group over another one? Is there a risk that loyalty can bring us to act blindly without questioning the negative consequences of our actions for people outside our group? Can loyalty lead us to engage in reprehensible actions like lying to protect a friend, or worse, killing out of filial loyalty? Indeed, all of us are concerned by the moral dilemma that comes from the tensions that exist between our loyalty obligations to our families, our loyalty to our partners, our personal aspirations and general moral principles. These various types of loyalty conflicts will be reviewed in detail later.

We know that there are no easy solutions to these dilemmas. For Gert (2013), the problem starts with the fact that loyalty entails a selective (discriminatory) element. He reminds us that the general concept of morality entails the obligation of impartiality, i.e. the moral obligation to refrain from favoring one group over the other. When this is the case, by definition, loyalty would always lead to a violation of morality. However, he offers a more nuanced solution by defining that "loyalty is morally acceptable only when acting loyally does not involve justifying violating a moral rule". He lists a series of common moral rules that are usually agreed upon like, for instance not killing, not causing pain, not deceiving, etc. He is clear that society may interpret these rules according to circumstances, for instance by not seeing killing as immoral during wartime, but in general, loyalty cannot justify a breach of these general moral principles. For instance, loyalty to a family member who needs an organ transplant could not justify killing someone to obtain this organ. However, according to him, as long as loyalty does not require intentionally harming someone else, favoring one group over the other would not contradict morality. For instance, the parent who sees two children drowning would not contradict any moral rule by trying to save his or her own child first. Similarly, impartiality is not required when it comes to moral ideals. Out of loyalty, one can choose to dedicate time or money to promote a specific cause or to support a specific organization without violating any moral principle. These guiding principles are useful to orient us when we need to help people who are caught in a moral dilemma around issues of loyalty in their family or in their life in general.

Family loyalties and the journey toward autonomy

We know that the structures of families vary enormously from one society to the other, and it is also affected by all kinds of external detrimental and positive factors that are not under the control of parents. All these conditions play an enormous role in shaping the parent-child relationship, but one thing does not change: all these parents and families have a common task, which is to nurture their children and teach them the skills needed to become adults who are capable of taking care of themselves and of raising a new generation of children.

A major step in this journey is the moment when the young has become independent enough to leave the family. It can be a moment of joy for the parents who feel that they have succeeded in their task. It can be a moment of relief for the parents who have experienced parenthood as a burden and who look forward to regaining their own freedom. Or it can be the moment of a huge loss for parents who see their child as their sole source of trust or as their sole reason for living. However, in general, the most common reaction of parents is one of ambivalence: a sense of accomplishment mixed with a sense of loss. This is the same for the children.

To overcome this ambivalence, both parents and children need to engage in a mourning process which as a minimum should entail a capacity to mourn the loss of the prior form of relating. Parents and children may move at a different speed (non-synchronicity) or misinterpret where the others are in the process, and this can be confusing to professionals. For instance, teens may tell their therapist that they cannot wait to leave home for college but that they are worried because their parents will feel upset about separation, while their parents would tell the same therapist that they cannot wait to see their child move on. However, in some situations, parents have a much bigger ambivalence toward letting a child become autonomous. It can go to the point of an unconscious wish that this child remains forever in a symbiotic relationship with them. This occurs typically when parents have been unable to mourn the loss of their own parents, whether they had a parent who was never available or a parent who died early.

The counterautonomous superego

In his effort to account for the family dynamics that he was observing in families of young adult patients suffering from schizophrenia, Boszormenyi-Nagy had discovered that these patients' psychotic symptoms could be understood as a response to the parents' unconscious need to keep their child in a symbiotic bond. He coined the term 'counterautonomous superego' by analogy with the superego described by the psychoanalysts to describe how children internalize their parents' and society's normative messages in the form of taboos. They also describe that people experience psychological guilt when they infringe these taboos. Here, he describes that some parents who are especially needy unconsciously transmit the message to their children that autonomy is a bad thing. This parental message is then internalized in the form of a counterautonomous superego. Consequently, any infringement of this internalized directive of the parents becomes a source of psychological guilt that can lead children to sabotage their chances to reach autonomy. In predisposed children, this guilt can even lead to a psychotic breakdown.

Example

To illustrate the concept of counterautonomous superego, here is the example of a young woman, Rita, who had developed very severe psychotic symptoms as a young teen (for a more detailed story, see Ducommun-Nagy, 1999). She was hospitalized several times, but she never stayed at the hospital for very long. Her parents had an amazing ability to tolerate her symptoms and to take care of her at home, even when she was acutely delusional. They were also very engaged in her treatment and very willing to attend family therapy. The mother had been parentified as a teen, but she did not see the relevance between her role in her family of origins and her place as a parent. At the same time, she admitted that when her daughter was born, she had a sudden and strange impression that this daughter would never leave her. She did not have the same impression when her two younger children were born. At one point Rita had improved enough to begin thinking about taking a small paying summer job, the first time she could earn some money. During this time, she was occasionally seen individually to discuss her medication treatment. During one of the individual sessions, she reported a recurrent dream: she was leaving home, walking on the street toward another house but, each time she was beginning to walk, she was stopped by a big barking dog on the way, and she had to retreat. Her dream was discussed, and it became clear to her that it had to do with her fear of hurting her parents if she was moving ahead in her life.

At the next family session, she was helped to bring up the subject of the job. At first, her parents believed that this was not a realistic idea and that she should return to the summer camp for youth with mental health issues that she had attended the summer before. However, Rita came up with an offer: she would still attend the specialized program but for a shorter time and then work but also for a shorter time. In proposing this solution, Rita was considering her parents' needs, showing loyalty to them directly and realistically, which freed her from experiencing the unconscious guilt over hurting her parents by seeking more autonomy.

The collusive postponement of mourning

Boszormenyi-Nagy introduced the concept of the 'collusive postponement of mourning' in conjunction with the notion of the counterautonomous superego to account for the systemic implications of the mourning process. When parents and children are not able to engage in the mourning process necessary to engage in a new phase of their relationship, family members may show their loyalty to one another by unconsciously protecting one another from the task of engaging in a mourning process. "Family members can choose between either investing in their autonomous life goals with energy, and rewarding other members for originalities and creative intuitions, or conversely consistently rewarding allegiance to a never-changing system" (Boszormenyi-Nagy, 1987, 2014: 71). This is the place where Boszormenyi-Nagy speaks of a 'collusive postponement of mourning'. In other words, the family members unconsciously 'collude' with each other to postpone any changes in the family system. Here, the world collude does not reflect any bad intentions and should be only understood from a systemic point of view. From a systemic point of view, as long as at least one of the family members acts in a way that slows down the process of growth and individuation, the entire system is protected from true changes. Even if the person who had stalled the mourning process was able to change, it would trigger a counter-reaction in another family member, and the result would remain the same: as a whole, the family would continue to resist the change, and the family would not be able to move on to a new step.

Example

To return to Rita's story, originally, the person who was experiencing difficulties in seeing Rita making steps toward autonomy was clearly the mother. Rita's father seemed less burdened by past issues and appeared less ambivalent about Rita's reaching more autonomy, but the following example shows that this was only an impression. Despite her serious illness, Rita had attended a specialized school and later she had returned to her local public school. She was still very fragile, but her mother who had made great strides in overcoming her ambivalence about Rita's autonomy had decided that Rita should attend the end-of-year school dance like all the other students. She asked a young man who was very reliable to escort her, and she was optimistic that Rita would manage to attend the pre-dance dinner and maybe stay for the dance. However, soon after arriving at the venue, Rita got very anxious and asked her companion to take her back home. As the two arrived, Rita's father told them that he was sure that she would have needed to return early and that he had prepared a dinner for them (he was the cook at home). Instead, he could have just helped his daughter to calm down and encouraged her to try to return to the event.

This is a good example of collusive postponement of mourning. As the mother made a move to help Rita to reach more autonomy, the father made a counter move in anticipating Rita's failure.

Collusive postponement of mourning and actual losses

While most therapists and counselors do not work with patients suffering from schizophrenia, learning about the different processes that can block people from accepting the inevitable changes brought by life and block them from reaching their own goals can be very important for any professionals. Any actual or anticipated loss can be a source of distress and can lead to a collusion to avoid the mourning that would be necessary to accept this loss. The loss is not limited to the moment when a child leaves home, and it can take many forms. It can be the actual death of a family member, or the announcement of a permanent handicap in a child born with a birth defect. It can be the announcement of a terminal illness. It can be the loss of a home country after migration.

In any of these moments, a professional may encounter families in which all family members but one accept the loss, and the professional may be lured into believing that this is the person who needs help, but in reality, the situation can change as soon as this person is helped in his or her mourning process. Suddenly another family member may begin to fight the loss in a way that brings the family to the same place.

Pastoral counselors may encounter families in which one adult family member is inconsolable about the loss of his or her last surviving parent. Now, the siblings need to come to a decision about the choice of a gravestone. This person may not be able to participate in a discussion that will give a concrete reality to this loss. However, if this person musters the strength to accept this loss, thanks to the help of the counselor, and now accepts to participate in this discussion, it would not be surprising if one of the other siblings will come up with a reason for postponing a final decision about the gravestone. Consequently, the family as a whole would still be spared from dealing with this final concrete step in the mourning process.

Medical professionals may have to tell parents bad news about a child. It could be the announcement that a child is born with a condition that will preclude this child from reaching normal developmental milestones, that a child has suffered from an accident that will cause a permanent disability or that the child suffers from an illness that cannot be cured. In each of these cases, the parents will have to come to the painful realization that many of the objectives they had in mind for their child's future will not be reachable. In some cases, both parents try to avoid this pain by thinking that either the professionals have made a wrong diagnosis, or that their child could still be cured. However, more typically one parent, the so-called more reasonable parent, accepts the reality presented by the professionals while the other begins looking everywhere for ways to defy this prognosis. It could be anything from alternative medicine to pilgrimages. The professional and the so-called more reasonable parent may then try to convince the other parent of the futility of this effort. However, if the parent who was looking for other forms of help gives up his or her search, the so-called more reasonable parent suddenly takes over and becomes the one who goes on a quest for improbable treatments. The result is they protect each other from fully engaging in the mourning process that would be necessary to engage fully in the pursuit of goals that could be reachable despite their child's condition. Also, parents who appear cooperative with the professionals about the treatment of their child may suddenly resist their recommendations when this could lead their child to acquire more autonomy.

Example

Here is an example of a teen who had become blind and had to attend a specialized residential school. The program had two focuses: one was to help children achieve their academic goals, and the other was to prepare them to become as autonomous as possible despite their handicap. The parents were very pleased with their son's teachers who had high academic expectations for him. However, things changed when it came to the second goal. The students were expected to learn the use of a mobility cane so that they could begin to move around independently. As soon as the school staff referred the teen to the mobility specialist, the parents complained about this decision: they argued that their son was not ready for this step and that he could have an accident if he began to move around with this cane. This took the staff by surprise, since the parents had always been very open to the staff's proposals. Very soon the boy began to say that he did not like his mobility teacher and that he did not want to work with him anymore. This was a big setback for his treatment team. Here, the idea of working more cooperatively with the parents would not work. They were clearly not ready to see him gaining more independence.

In this situation, contextual therapists would use multidirected partiality to address the conflicting needs of all the parties involved: the school staff, the parents, and the youth. Specifically, they would begin by acknowledging the parent's dedication, and only then move to explore the origins of their ambivalence about their child's progress toward autonomy, i.e. pushing him toward academic achievements, but blocking him from becoming more independent on a practical level.

In short, family loyalty can lead people to collude to protect each other from pain in ways that not only stall the mourning process but also prevent people from finding constructive ways to adapt to inevitable changes and losses. However, loyalty can also become a resource. If parents and children can reassure each other that they will remain committed to the relationship, no matter what changes life brings about, they will have much less urges to collude to fight these changes out of a fear of losing their relationship, especially in the case of children leaving home.

Myths about filial loyalty as an obstacle to autonomy

The discovery of the systemic implications of loyalty is one of Boszormenyi-Nagy's main contributions to the field of family therapy. At the same time, his ideas have led to several misunderstandings, especially to the myth that family loyalty constitutes an obstacle to our autonomy because it ties us to our parents in a way that prevents us from reaching our individual goals. For this reason, many individual and family therapists believe that to reach our personal goals, we need to liberate ourselves from the tethers of family loyalties.

Nicole Prieur (2022), a well-known French psychologist and family therapist, goes even further. For her, one cannot become oneself without having to betray one's parents, and she coined the word 'ethical traitor' to describe children who refuse to respond to the possessive needs of their parents or to their destructive expectations. She is right in believing that it is ethical to behave in a way that is protecting our welfare and the welfare of the next generations. We have already seen that the mandate for posterity, a very important concept in contextual therapy, behooves us to figure out what is the best way to respond to our parents' expectations without endangering our future and the future of the next generations. However, we do not need to become traitors to achieve that. If what counts the most for our families is that we remain part of the family system, we are already loyal to our parents when we take the relation seriously enough to examine what we owe them and what they realistically deserve from us. Furthermore, in some cases, we could in fact betray our parents by doing exactly what they want.

Consider the example of a successful professional woman. Her parents supported her throughout her studies, but they objected strongly to her idea of going abroad to pursue her career. She decided to respect her parents' wish and she never left. The family came from a very traditional society in which men were hesitant to marry a professional woman like her. Her parents, who were hoping for grandchildren, told her that they regretted that she had not defied them. They had come to realize that she would have had many more chances to find a partner with whom to build a family abroad than in the society in which they were living. Since on her side, she was missing having her own family, it was hard to hear that she would have been more loyal to her parents if she had refused to yield to their objections instead of accepting their demands.

What therapists often forget as well is that there are many ways in which we can express our loyalty to our family, and this does not require the sacrifice of our individual aspirations. Among all the ties that bind us to our parents and families, the ties formed by loyalty are the most flexible ones exactly because there are so many ways to demonstrate our loyalty to them. If we can reassure our parents of our loyalty in ways that are realistic for us, and at least minimally acceptable for them, we shall be freer to reach our own goals. In contextual therapy, offering our loyalty to others is a form of giving that brings us an indirect gain in the form of constructive entitlement as well as self-delineation. From this point of view, one could say that to be able to offer our loyalty to others should be viewed as a right, not only as an obligation.

The task of contextual therapists is not to discourage their clients from offering their loyalty to parents who may or may not deserve it, but to help them to offer it in a manner that remains compatible with the interests of both parents and children. It is often possible to help these children to find ways of expressing their loyalties in a direct and non-self-sacrificial manner. This will give them more freedom to reach their goals than a simple refusal to respond to their parents' realistic needs will. For instance, if our aspiration is to engage in a profession that takes us far away from our parents, we could offer to commit to a weekly online meeting with them, or we could commit to return home for regular visits. If we have left our homeland to live in a more affluent country, we could send money back home to support our family, which is something that many immigrants do. All of these actions should count as direct expressions of loyalty, but for our parents, this may not automatically the case. Sometimes, no matter what we try to do, our parents will continue to see our departure as an expression of disloyalty. But at the end, whether or not our parents accept our offers as a valid expression of loyalty, our sincere effort to find ways to remain available to them should least reassure them about our commitment to remain part of our family.

Similarly, if we decide to practice a religion that is different from the religion of our family, we may try to reassure our parents that we shall continue to respect the core values of the religion that they have transmitted to us. All these efforts may not always satisfy our parents but will reassure them that at least we are not entirely removing ourselves from the family system. Also, in trying to remain committed to our parents and trying to care about their needs even if we cannot fully respond to them, we shall still earn constructive entitlement. This should also help us to reach our personal goals. In short, loyalty may set us on the path toward an authentic autonomy much more than any attempt to get rid of our family loyalty.

The clinical manifestations of loyalties

An exploration of all the situations in which family and group loyalties become a source of individual pathologies or relational problems requires a discussion of all the situations that could lead people to seek treatment with a mental health professional. In contextual therapy, we distinguish the following types of loyalty-related problems that can lead to individual or relational symptoms: avoidable and unavoidable loyalty conflicts, split loyalties, invisible loyalties, and loyalty-related intergenerational repetition of detrimental behaviors. These specific clinical manifestations of loyalties are dealt with in specific chapters later in the book. Contextual therapists and contextually oriented pastoral counselors should be the best equipped to address these situations, but all professionals can learn about loyalty dynamics and about interventions that can be used to help people to find the way to express their loyalties directly and non-sacrificially.

As already discussed, loyalties can be expressed in various direct, indirect and invisible ways. Whether loyalties become a relational resource or a source of individual or relational pathologies and distress depends on a great number of factors. We know that the notions of loyalty and loyalty conflicts are inseparable due to the very definition of loyalty. By definition, loyalty behooves us to give special consideration to the people or the groups toward whom we are indebted. Since we are indebted not only to our parents, but also to the many other people who have been committed to us at different times of our lives, we are bound to experience unavoidable loyalty conflicts. They are part of our daily lives.

A General Understanding of Family and Group Loyalties

Most of us manage to deal with these ordinary loyalty conflicts on our own. We may share our dilemmas and discuss our questions with a partner or a friend who can give us good suggestions, and fortunately, in most cases, we do not need the help of professionals.

However, there are situations that lead to more distress and push people to seek professionals help. Some people may be overwhelmed by too many demands coming from too many sides. Some people may be caught in the predicament of split loyalties. We usually think about the children of divorced parents who are expected to show their loyalty to one parent by rejecting the other parent. However, adults can be caught in the same predicament, with one major difference: they do not depend on their feuding parent for their daily existence. Other people may struggle because they do not know how to respond to their parents' expectations without having to abandon their own individual pursuits. It can be anything: the choice of a partner, the choice of a career, the conversion to a new religion, anything that their parents do not approve. Some may resent these demands and try to cut themselves off from their parents but still do not succeed in reaching their own goals. Some people may abandon their plans because they feel guilty or disloyal, but they remain frustrated by the situation.

Some people seek help because they realize that they reproduce the destructive patterns of relating that they experienced in their family relationships but do not know how to change them. Finally, some people may be caught between the expectation of their family and the expectation of the groups to which they belong, for instance a political or religious group, or any other group that expects their loyalty. In all these situations, people tend to have a fairly clear understanding that the problems they experience are related to loyalty issues before they seek the help of a professional, in some cases a pastoral counselor.

Conversely, people may seek the help of mental health professionals for symptoms or relational problems that do not appear to be related to loyalty issues but in fact may be. In these cases, the task of the clinician is to establish if their client's symptoms are indeed the manifestations of a full-fledged diagnosable mental illness or the result of unresolved loyalty issues. For instance, people who are caught in severe loyalty conflicts can present with individual symptoms of anxiety or depression, even at times suicidal ideations in the case of split loyalties. Self-destructive behaviors, including substance abuse or professional failures, could be related to invisible loyalties. Either loyalty conflicts or invisible loyalties can trigger relational difficulties between partners. Children whose parents are in a serious feud and who are caught in the predicament of split loyalties may become suicidal or may present serious behavioral problems, including a true conduct disorder. Children who are cut off from their biological parents after a foster care placement or an adoption may also present with significant behavioral problems related to invisible loyalties.

Even when the client's symptoms may not have been triggered by unresolved loyalty issues but by an actual diagnosable mental illness, mental illnesses can decrease people's ability to handle loyalty conflicts or their ability to deal with the conscious or unconscious expectations of needy parents. This inability can become a new source of anguish that aggravates the already present condition. Therefore, it is important that all clinicians, not only contextual therapists and contextually oriented pastoral counselors, learn about family and group loyalties and their clinical implications.

To address clinical situations that may involve loyalties, professionals need to be able to identify what types of loyalties may be involved, and in which dimension their main determinants are located. It is also necessary to learn to identify other factors that could play a role in the situation, for instance parentification and destructive entitlement with their multigenerational consequences. The general task is to help people to discover that they are neither doomed to renounce their individual goals to remain loyal to their family, nor doomed to express their loyalty in invisible and self-defeating manners. In short, they need to help people to find a way to express their loyalty directly and constructively. Since showing loyalty to others is a form of giving, it becomes a source of constructive entitlement and a source of Self-Other delineation that becomes a resource on the path toward autonomy.

There are situations in which contextual therapists and pastoral counselors may not be able to fulfil all the treatment needs of their clients whose problems are at least partly related to loyalty issues. A client may suffer from a depression that is severe enough to require the intervention of a psychiatrist who could prescribe an antidepressant. A client who is in recovery from drug or alcohol abuse may need to attend a recovery program, etc. In many cases, the other professionals may have no awareness that these clients' presenting problems may be related to loyalty issues. However, this would not prevent the contextual therapist or the pastoral counselor to continue working with this client on loyalty-related issues. If possible, they should try to educate their colleagues about their hypotheses about the possible correlation between the client's symptoms and unresolved loyalty issues and try to work cooperatively with them. If such a dialogue is not realistic for all sorts of reasons, the contextually oriented professionals would still be able to help their clients. Helping clients to express their loyalty to their parents and family directly and non-destructively is never contra-indicated. Moreover, if these clients' distress and symptoms decrease following the interventions of the contextually oriented professional, it would be a good surprise for the other professionals involved in the situation, and this may lead them to want to learn more about family loyalties.

Chapter 8

Loyalties in the Perspective of the Five Dimensions of Relational Reality

If we want to help people who seek our help for individual or relational problems that could be related to loyalty issues, we need to understand all the conscious or unconscious factors that bring them to show loyalty to others. Contextual therapists postulate that the main determinants of loyalty belong to the dimension of relational ethics (Dimension IV), but this does not account for all the reasons that can bring someone to place the interests of a given person or a given group before the interests of other people or to respond to their needs before responding to the needs of other people. This preferential attitude has determinants that can be found in any of the five dimensions of relational reality. In addition to its determinants in the dimension of relational ethics, it can be anything from blood ties (Dimension I), an unconscious internalization of parental expectation (Dimension II), a fear of retaliation (Dimension III), or the need to relate to some specific people as a source of Self-Other delineation (Dimension V). Furthermore, the way in which loyalty is expressed can be influenced by variables that are found in any of these five dimensions. For this reason, we can speak of the five dimensions of loyalty, as has been done for almost twenty years (Ducommun-Nagy, 2006). However, loyalty based on an emotional attachment or loyalty based on a fear of retaliation may not be considered as a true loyalty if one defines loyalty solely as commitment based on indebtedness.

For example, loyalty to parents can be the result of various combinations of actually recognized indebtedness, emotional attachment, unconscious guilt, overt fear of retaliation if not abiding by the parents' expectations, or the need to relate to the parents as a special source of Self-Other delineation that is very important in terms of identity formation. Loyalty between gang members can be explained by several factors. Youngsters often join gangs after a life full of abandonments and traumatic experiences. In their case, loyalty to gang members could be explained by several factors, including the need to find figures of attachment in the gang leaders, serious threat of retaliation in the case of defection, a need to find sources of Self-Other delineation, and still possibly some level of true indebtedness for having received acceptance or support.

In short, only after we have identified all the factors that can bring people to offer their loyalty to others, we shall be able to help them when this loyalty becomes an obstacle that prevents them from reaching their life goals and succeeding in their relationships. Since relational ethics are central to the understanding of family and group loyalty, the presentation of these determinants will not respect the usual order of Dimension I to V but begin with Dimension IV, the dimension of relational ethics. This will include a discussion of filial loyalty and its implications for individual autonomy as well as the concepts of counter-autonomous superego and the concept of collusive postponement of mourning that have already been presented in the discussion of loyalty and autonomy.

Loyalty and the dimension of relational ethics

Fairness and reciprocity as determinants of loyalty

As already discussed, for contextual therapists, the primary determinant of loyalty lies in the dimension of relational ethics. Loyalty is based on fairness and a special form of reciprocity. Being loyal to someone does not mean that we are just returning a favor as in "you helped me, I help you". Loyalty requires us to be willing to give a priority to this person's needs over the needs of other people, and to be ready to do this even at a cost to ourselves. For instance, it is one thing to offer to drive a friend to an appointment if this friend's car is under repair and if this friend helped us in similar circumstances in the past. It is another thing to accept to cancel an appointment with someone else to be able to meet this friend's need. Here, our willingness to reciprocate would require a choice, which may have a cost. In this example, we would have to deal with the complaints of the other person who may feel let down.

Coming back to Gert's definition of loyalty, he adds that "loyalty requires an individual to be willing to make significant sacrifices to avoid causing harm to the group or to prevent or relieve harm suffered by members of this group. However, it is a matter of controversy whether loyalty to a group requires a refusal to harm the group or a willingness to prevent or relieve harm to members of the group when this involves causing a greater harm to others not in the group" (Gert, 2013: 4). He also states that "Acting as if harm suffered by one group or one of its members is more important than harm suffered by those not in one's group is not acting out of loyalty if one is motivated by fear or greed ... A test of loyalty is whether, when one refuses to harm the group or its members or act to prevent harm to the group, one would still act in that way if one believes that no one knew or would find out how one was acting" (Gert, 2013: 6). This means that if we favor someone over someone else to avoid hurt or retaliation, or just to make some personal gains, our action is not based on loyalty but on our personal interest. This does not mean that loyalty cannot bring any returns: we know that when we show loyalty to a person or a group, it is likely that in return these people will show loyalty to us. Loyalty can have mixed motives, but true loyalty requires that we do not count on this return to begin acting. In short, loyalty must be based on past gratitude, not on hope for future returns.

Loyalty and filial piety

In China and in large parts of East Asia, the notion of loyalty is associated with the notion of filial piety. Many of these societies are still directly influenced by the vision of society that was proposed by Confucius (551-479 BC), a Chinese thinker who was contemporary to the

Greek philosophers who have influenced Western societies for close to 2500 years. "While Western approaches to ethics have traditionally emphasized individual ethical agents and their actions, Confucian thought aims instead at nurturing human relationships. Loyalty, accordingly, figures centrally in the Confucian worldview, for it is an indispensable ingredient in the achievement of this goal" ... "According to Confucius, loyalty begins at home. The family is the first society that the child encounters and relating to other members of the family is the initial political life" ... "Confucians do not believe that their emphasis on family loyalty slights the larger social order. Filial piety, for them, is essentially political, for it is the prelude to good citizenship generally" (Higgins, 2013: 23-24).

Higgins then concludes "The Confucian message is that human beings cannot live fully human lives without being able to depend on one another. Indeed, without the network of relationships that defines him or her, a human individual is less than a person. Loyalty from the Confucian perspective amounts to vigilant effort to sustain the relationship in which one is embedded. Loyalty is central to the ethical aim of supporting the human world and enabling it to flourish and yet it is neither abstract nor general in practice" (Higgins, 2013: 36). According to this worldview, it becomes clear that loyalty is fundamentally a relational resource and not the negative force that holds us back from reaching our full human potential as it is too often represented in the universe of Western psychotherapy and family therapy.

Filial loyalty

In the Chinese perspective, loyalty to the parents requires that parents and children act according to their roles: the father must act like a proper father and the son like a proper son. Loyalty also requires that parents be respected and that the ancestors be honored. These two expectations are found also in many traditional societies all over the world.

For contextual therapists, the parent-child relationship is embedded in the dimension of relational ethics. In ordinary situations, the parent-child relationship begins with the parent's gift of life. It is followed by the parents' commitment to provide for their children and place their needs before the needs of other people, often including themselves. This commitment meets the definition of loyalty. One could say that filial loyalty begins with parental loyalty. Children have the right to receive care, but nonetheless, the fact that they receive this care leads to a certain degree of indebtedness.

Ordinary relationships are based on simple reciprocity. People tend to repay each other by offering something similar to what they have received from them. However, what could children offer to their parents that equals everything they have received from them, including life? Furthermore, parents transmit to their children many things that they have received from prior generations. Also, caring parents do not stop giving to their children only because they have reached adulthood. Often, they remain available to help them much later in their life, for instance in stepping in as babysitters for their grandchildren. In addition, they may also benefit their children by leaving them assets when they die.

In short, the parent-child relationship is fundamentally asymmetrical, and children can never fully repay the debt they have toward their parents in a direct, measurable manner. Instead, in the parent-child relationship, the repayment takes the form of filial loyalty. Children can also repay their parents by caring for the next generations. The next generation deserves this care anyway, but in addition, most parents feel rewarded by the success of their offspring. They are gratified to see that whatever effort they made in raising their children, this effort was not lost. Furthermore, no parents want to see the next generations fail, since it could imply that in one way or another they have not been good enough parents, and no parents want to be seen like that. In short, we are most loyal to our parents when we succeed in our lives and give a chance to the next generations to succeed, not when we give up our individual goals to abide blindly by their expectations.

Loyalty to undeserving parents

Some children may argue that they have not asked to be born and do not owe anything to their parents, but this is rare. Experience shows that the majority of children tend to show loyalty to their genitors, no matter how little they know about them or how little these parents have done for them. Some children are born as the result of an anonymous gift of sperm or eggs. They will never know who these people are, and these donors will never know if their gift resulted in the birth of a child or not. But these does not stop some these children to try to express their gratitude to their unknown genitors for their gift of life. But what about children who are the survivors of a failed abortion or a failed infanticide? What would be the gift of life of parents who did not want their baby to live? At the same time, we know that some children can remain loyal to their parents even if they had murderous intentions. From the point of view of relational ethics, this does not make much sense. What would they owe to such parents? But the ontic dimension offers a possible explanation. All of us have the need to establish a relationship with our biological parents as a special source of Self-Other differentiation that has no direct substitute. Therefore, we are likely to offer our loyalty to our genitors as a way to establish a link with them no matter if they have never been part of our life or if they have endangered our survival.

Filial loyalty and its societal implications

Filial loyalty implies that children accept to give priority to their parents' needs and interests over the needs and interests of other people. However, how they do that varies from one family to the other, from one child to the other. One child may be willing to join the family business, another child may endorse the same political cause as the parents. In short, one can say that loyalty obligations can be repaid in many kinds of currencies. Still, one common expression of this filial loyalty is that children accept to take care of their aging parents, even if it has a cost for themselves and even if it causes conflicts in other relationships, like in the children's marriage.

In traditional societies all around the world, people cannot count on society to provide a safety net for them when they cannot meet their own needs anymore. They must rely solely on the help of their families. This is especially true for the elderly. Furthermore, in vast parts of the world, hospitals are not equipped to provide patients with basic necessities or basic personal care. Family members are expected to bring them food and to take care of their personal hygiene. Often this help comes from the patient's children. Hence, in these societies, any infringement to the expectation of filial loyalty constitutes not only a relational injustice but also a threat to the entire social system that hinges on family loyalty.

Decreased family loyalty in modern societies: A threat to traditional support systems

In many societies, the whole traditional system of care has come under threat as the generations of young people have no choice but to move to big, sometimes huge cities in the hope of employment. These young people do not have many options besides leaving the older generations to fend for themselves in the villages where their families come from. In addition, with globalization and massive exposure to information from around the world through the Internet and social media, the younger members of traditional societies are increasingly exposed to Western values of individualism and individual success that go against the traditional values of respect for the older generations and filial loyalty. This change has led many young people, especially young professionals, to seek success far away from their families, and consequently, they are no more available to take care of their elders. In India, where parents typically have relied on their children for their old age, people have suddenly realized the need of building homes for the elderly who are left to live alone after their children have left.

Young people who focus solely on their personal goals and totally dismiss their obligations toward their parents may experience some backlashes from their lack of loyalty in the form of a variety of individual symptoms or relational problems. Also, some other people may feel truly torn when they realize that they may cause serious hurt to their parents if they try to pursue their own aspirations, but they do not know what to do about it.

It is true that it is rarely easy to balance the expectations of our families with our own personal aspirations. If we are lucky, we may have parents who have tried to refrain from burdening us with unrealistic expectations, and parents who have tried to sort out what they wanted to transmit to us, or even parents who have expectations that are very compatible with our own personal aspirations. However, in most cases, one of the big tasks of our life is to sort out what we owe to our parents, what we do not owe them, and to figure out how to balance their needs with our needs and with the needs of the people who are part of our lives, like our love partner, spouse, children, work partners, etc. Some people manage to accomplish this task early in their adult life, but for some it remains the task of an entire lifetime. This is also the place where people turn to professional help. In this

Loyalty and the dimension of facts

Is loyalty based on biological determinants?

If it is true that our capacity for fairness, reciprocity, and caring has roots in our biology, then we have to assume that our capacity for loyalty must have some roots in our human biological characteristics as well. Furthermore, does the fact that we tend to show more loyalty to our closest relatives than to distant ones, and more loyalty to relatives than to pure strangers mean that we are biologically programmed to favor people with whom we have biological ties over strangers? This is much less clear. This hypothesis was raised by a scientist, R. Dawkins, who proposes in his book *The Selfish Gene* (1976) that we may be genetically programmed to help our closest relatives because if we help them even at a cost to ourselves, it increases the chance that our own genes are transmitted to posterity. This hypothesis is unprovable, but not impossible. We also know that children seem to have an urge to offer their loyalty to biological parents they will never meet and to non-deserving biological parents. It is unlikely that this need is related to a simple genetic connection between the children and their parents but most likely to their need to maintain a relationship with them as a source of Self-Other definition (Dimension V).

Loyalty and factual variables

Many factual determinants can influence the expression of loyalty. Starting with biological determinants, sex at birth, physical features, health and illnesses, congenital or acquired disabilities, factors like life expectancy, infertility, etc. do play an important role in determining how people may be able to express their loyalty.

Children who have many natural assets may be able to show their loyalty to their parents by fulfilling many of their dreams. Conversely, children who suffer from a handicap may not be able to meet the expectations of their parents but may be able to fulfil some of their unspoken needs. For instance, children who are born with a Down syndrome have a limited ability to reach any of the steps that other children reach easily, but they are exceptionally capable of showing affection to people. This could fulfil the expectations of parents who have been deprived of affection while growing up.

At times, a child who exhibits some special features or innate talents may be destined to a special role in the family or in the society. In some societies, this child may be identified as a future shaman or as the reincarnation of an ancestor. In Tibetan Buddhism, a child may be identified as the reincarnation of a spiritual leader. When these special children become adults, some may want to move back to an ordinary life, but this may be considered disloyal to their family and the religious society of which they are part.

In the case of adoptions, the children's physical features have consequences in terms of loyalty. When adoptive children look very much like their adoptive parents, they may be complimented about it: "You look just like your father" or "You look just like your mother". Children who receive this kind of compliment may have the urge to show their loyalty to their biological parents and may need to respond: "He is not my real dad" or "She is not my real mom." Conversely when the children's physical features show that they could only have been adopted, people may ask them: "Who are your real parents"? In this case, children often show their loyalty to their adoptive parents by answering: "Why do you say this? They are my parents." Depending on the child's answer, the adoptive parents may be hurt, or they may be reassured of the child's loyalty. However, in either case, the children's physical features become an important element in the children's need to remain loyal to both sets of parents.

In traditional societies, gender and birth order may determine the way in which people can express their loyalty to their family because of the fixed roles assigned to men and women and the fixed roles assigned to elder siblings (see also loyalty and the dimension of transactions).

Therapeutic perspectives

In this dimension, the task of the therapist is first and foremost to identify the factual determinants of loyalty that may play a role in a given situation and to consider this variable in the discussion of the various ways in which people can try to express their loyalty directly and constructively. For instance, people who suffer infertility, and people who are part of same-sex couples will not be able to respond to the expectation of parents who want to see their bloodline continue. However, they could express their loyalty by committing to give them grandchildren through medically assisted procreation or through adoption.

Loyalty and the dimension of psychology

As already discussed, in a strict sense, loyalty is based on merits and indebtedness, but attachment and other positive or negative emotional factors like attraction, fear or guilt play an important role as a sustaining factor of loyalty in families, couples, and groups. When people have a strong emotional investment in a relationship, for instance the relationship with their parents or their partners, they will place the interest of these people before the interest of anyone else, whether they truly deserve this loyalty or not.

Young children respond to the expectations of their parents more so than to the expectations of strangers, and there are many reasons for that, but it is obvious that attachment plays a major role. Indeed, children who present an attachment disorder may not make such a distinction and respond indiscriminately to anyone who has shown the slightest interest in them. In many cases, people feel both attached and indebted to their parents. Here, whether their loyalty to them is based on attachment or on indebtedness would not make much difference. However, in other cases, people may remain loyal to even undeserving parents out of emotional attachment and this may prevent them to offer their loyalty to other people who would have deserved it based on their merits, for instance the devoted stepparent who has tried to make up for the shortcomings of a biological parent.

It is hard to know at what stage of their cognitive development children begin to understand the concept of loyalty as such, but loyalty can be expressed without having to think about loyalty as a concept. We know that even very young children are already attuned to their parents' needs and try to adjust to them. When parents cannot agree on what they ask from their child, even very young children react to the situation with distress, which seems to relate to a very early experience of loyalty conflicts. By the time children begin school, they begin to have a concept of loyalty that plays a role in friendships. Often, children form groups of friends who are expected to be loyal to each other, which also means that they are punished if they engage in friendships outside of the group. Another basis of loyalty is the identification with the group members, and a need for acceptance and approval.

Loyalty and guilt feelings

As already discussed in the presentation of the counterautonomous superego, which is of course part of the dimension of psychology, some of these adults may unconsciously harbor guilt feelings that are the result of the unconscious response to the parents' own unconscious wishes. Furthermore, among adults who seek the help of therapists, many report that they are still longing to get their parents' approval or their parents' recognition of their devotion.

There are also situations in which adults can be clearly manipulated into experiencing guilt feelings. This can happen when parents blame children for failing to love them, or when they blame them for causing them pain. Some of these children are actually extremely devoted to their parents. Here, the guilt feelings may be another expression of loyalty to their parents. Instead of seeing their parents as people who blame them unfairly, they blame themselves for not having done enough to please them.

The psychological variables of loyalty

The expression of loyalty is affected by several psychological variables. We have already seen that the degree of attachment between people may vary from one relationship to another. Mental illnesses affect the way in which people can express their loyalty. For instance, people who suffer from a major depressive disorder may be too hopeless to take any actions or to make any choices. People who suffer from delusions may express their loyalty to their family in bizarre ways, for instance by trying to protect family members from the attacks of a dangerous enemy that is only imaginary.

According to object relation theory, all of us internalize our actual parents as either idealized parents or bad parents and eventually we should be able to see them as they are in reality, neither totally good nor totally bad; in other words, we need to be capable of ambivalence toward them. However, while this process is not completed, we may unconsciously project our internalized parental images onto people who are close to us: partners, colleagues, or therapists, and even onto our actual parents. Through the lens of these projections, we may see some people as ideal parents, and some as bad parents.

Boszormenyi-Nagy assumes that the direction of these projections may be influenced by loyalty. We may spare our actual parents from scrutiny by seeing them as ideal parents and instead see other people as the bad parents. Professionals need to be aware of these projection mechanisms and of these distortions. They should not assume that the way people present their parents or significant people in their lives in therapy correspond to an objective reality. Also, people may see their therapist in a way that is far from objective, saying: "I know that you will never understand me" or "I know that you are the only person who will ever understand me".

Therapeutic perspectives

In general, the main therapeutic goal in the dimension of psychology is to bring people to reach an increased level of insight. The methods may vary. In psychoanalysis, it is the interpretation of dreams and the interpretation of transference. In cognitive therapy, it is the deconstruction of projections, etc. In contextual therapy, the focus is placed on exploring options to act more than on insight, but any exchange between the professional and the client that brings new perspectives can also bring an increase of insight.

For instance, in the case of the young woman's dream about the dog chasing her back home, the discussion with the therapist allowed her to give a meaning to the dream, a discussion that may have been similar in other approaches, but the goal was not only to give her insight into the meaning of this dream but also to explore actions that could free her from her unconscious guilt over moving toward more autonomy, which was her offer to find a compromise between her wish to work and her parents' anxiety about it. In short, therapists can explore two avenues to help people who experience these kinds of guilt feelings and who still struggle to get their parents' approval. One avenue is to help them to find ways to express their loyalty in a direct, realistic way that is non-sacrificial. The other is to help them to engage in an exoneration process, to try to understand the origins of their parents' inability to give them credit, and to accept their parents' limitations as a matter of fact.

Loyalty and the dimension of transactions

As already discussed, family loyalty contributes to establish a boundary between the family system and all other surrounding systems, and it contributes to maintain the homeostasis of the family system. With regard to the systemic dimension, loyalty can be expressed by not challenging its habitual patterns of transactions or by accepting to share its common values, its religion, its myths. In many cases, the family myths entail narratives about other groups that are described as friends or enemies. Family members are then expected to abide by these narratives that serve to maintain the boundaries between the family and other groups. Also, family myths often serve to protect the reputation of the family after a suicide, an incarceration, or anything that could bring shame to the family. Family members who try to challenge these myths are often accused of disloyally, and they often retreat to avoid being punished. In all these cases, professionals should venture with caution and not push these clients to ask too many questions about the past unless it can be done in a way that the other family members can perceive as helpful.

At the same time, many families follow rules that have become irrelevant simply because the family members never thought of challenging them. Consider the example of two families of farmers who were each other's only neighbors in a very isolated area. The two families had no contacts at all. This surprised the new wife who had arrived from the city to marry the son of one of the farmers. She could not understand the situation and raised questions. She heard that it all began with a dispute between the grandfather of her new husband and the man who was living in the other farm. They stopped talking to each other, and that was the end of the contact between the two families. Both men were long dead, and there had been several changes of ownership of the other farm, but nothing had changed. It took the arrival of an outsider to challenge the rule of not talking to neighbors. Once people realized how obsolete it was, they resumed contacts to the satisfaction of everyone. During therapy, the family therapist becomes this outsider who can raise questions that help people to abandon habits that have become detrimental or simply obsolete.

Loyalty as an immaterial link

One particularity of loyalty is that it does not automatically require an actual direct transaction between the individuals who offer their loyalty and the beneficiaries of the loyalty. When loyalty is expressed by a direct gesture like a visit or a call, it automatically brings people in a direct interaction. Currently, we can keep in touch with family members and friends across the world, thanks to all kinds of electronic ways of connecting with one another that are not only widely available but cheap. However, for generations, when people left their country to begin a new life in a faraway land, they had very little hope to maintain contact with their families. Mail was very slow and phone calls impossible or extremely expensive. Early immigrants were trying to keep their language and all kinds of family traditions. Their loyalty to their old world was their way of bringing all these absent people into their lives without having to be in direct communication with them.

Also, people who leave their countries as political refugees often come from oppressive regimes that often punish their families severely if they maintain contact with them. This was the case for Boszormenyi-Nagy when he left Hungary as a refugee. He reports that he tried to remain loyal to his parents in two ways. The first way was to work as hard as possible to achieve something his parents could be proud of, at times at a cost to himself and to this relationship with other people in his life. He obviously succeeded to become one of the leaders of the family therapy movement. Also, once he had become an American citizen, he decided to keep his long family name, something that was not very practical in America where people like short and easy names. The only concession he made to this tendency was to drop the accents on his first and last name and his decision should be respected by the too many people who are mistakenly reintroducing these accents in writings about him. (Wikipedia is not always right).

Furthermore, there is an obvious situation in which loyalty serves as an immaterial connection between people: the separation by death. It seems that all human societies from the earliest times on have created rituals around the death of their members, anything from funeral rites, prayers for their sake, commemoration ceremonies, to full-fledged worship of ancestors. All of these are expressions of loyalty that establish a link between the absents and the presents. In brief, the reasons that lead people to want to offer their loyalty to an unreachable family member may vary. It could be indebtedness, guilt, or the need to relate to parents as a source of definition of the self. However, the result is the same. Loyalty can connect people with one another, even in the absence of any actual interaction. This is one of the most overlooked aspects of family loyalties, and possibly also one of its biggest resources.

Can loyalty be imposed by power?

In its strict definition, loyalty can be understood only as a form of commitment that results from our indebtedness toward people or groups who have been available for us. It is based on fairness and reciprocity. People have a right to expect our loyalty as a fair return for their own commitment toward us, but they have no right to extract it from us by threat or by manipulation. Furthermore, if we were to place the interests of a person or a group before the interests of others out of fear of retaliation, we would act out of self-protection, not out of loyalty.

However, even if we can agree with Gert (2013) that loyalty extracted by threat is not real loyalty, it is rare that threat is the sole factor that leads us to accept to adhere to the demands of a group and accept to protect their interest. In most cases, our willingness to show loyalty to people out of attachments or even out of indebtedness exposes us to the risk that these people begin to manipulate our loyalty to their advantage. For instance, gang members who are told that they will be killed if they try to leave the gang usually did not join this gang under duress. Young people may often join gangs out of a desperate need for support and recognition after an experience of traumatic relationships while growing up, abuse in their family, rejection by society, etc. Therefore, to a great extent, they may be loyal to the gang not only because of fear of retaliation if they were not, but also because of their need to belong.

Children can be manipulated into remaining loyal to their parents exactly because their natural loyalty to their parents can be exploited. We have seen that parents may have unconscious needs that result in an unconscious guilt or conscious guilt feelings in their children. However, parents may use guilt as a tool to keep their children from leaving them. For instance, some extremely needy parents may threaten suicide when their children plan to move away from the family or when they plan to get married. The very likely result is that these children may abandon their plan because it would be too hard for them to risk bearing the guilt of having caused the death of a parent. These kinds of manipulations exist also between adults, like the spouse who threatens suicide as a way to discourage a partner from leaving.

Other parents are less focused on issues of physical separation but more on the respect of rules and traditions. They may threaten to cut support to children who refuse to follow a path that they have chosen for them. They may threaten to disinherit children who stop abiding by the family traditions, including the family's religion. Some parents go further; they may even threaten to kill the children who engage in relationships that the family consider as forbidden. In fact, we know that some young people, especially young women, do get killed by family members because they have engaged in a premarital relationship that tarnishes the honor of the family. Young people, including men, can be threatened because they want to engage in a couple relationship with a partner who belongs to an ethnicity or a religion that is totally unacceptable to their families.

In cults and sects, the loyalty of group members is often enforced by a combination of psychological manipulation by the group leader and by threats of exclusion or some form of curse. It is also enforced by cutting the sect members from any communication with outsiders, in a way by abiding by the etymologic definition of the word sect: to separate. This is also true of families who belong to communities that feel threatened by their surrounding environment. For instance, some American Amish families who by tradition abide by their own interpretation of the Bible and live without using any of the amenities of the modern world like electricity, telephones, cars, etc. have moved to the jungle of Yucatan in Mexico to prevent the younger generations from the temptation of joining the modern world that was surrounding them in the USA.

The systemic variables of loyalty

While loyalty as such can have a great effect on the functioning of the family system, the expression of loyalty can also be determined by the many systemic variables that relate to larger social systems. Poverty, wars, and oppressive political regimes may push people to migrate, which, as we have seen, affects the ways in which people can express their loyalty to their families. The choice of societally acceptable expressions of loyalty can be determined by the form of society in which people are born. As already mentioned, in traditional societies, sex and birth order may determine the way in which people are expected to show their loyalty to their family. In many cases, the older son becomes the inheritor of the family assets: a farm, a business, or a trade. This son is then expected to express his loyalty to his family by accepting this legacy. The younger sons who are deprived of this inheritance are more or less free to pursue their own goals. In these societies, the burden of caring for aging parents often falls on the elder daughter, who may be expected to remain single while her younger sisters may be free to build a family if they want it. In other societies, this burden may fall on the daughter-in-law, and her husband is expected to make sure that she abides by this requirement. In situations in which women are left alone to raise children as single parents, the eldest boy is often expected to show his loyalty by assuming the role of a family leader. The eldest girl is expected to show her loyalty by taking care of the younger siblings. In any of these cases, children who do not have any siblings may be left alone to respond to multiple demands, which can amount to a great burden.

Therapeutic perspectives in the case of loyalty imposed by power and control

What professionals need to retain from all the situations discussed here is that people's loyalty to others can be based on a fear of retaliation. When this happens, they should not minimize the danger that their clients actually can be hurt or even killed if they encourage them to disregard the warning that they have received from their family or the group to which they belong. For this reason, professionals need to refrain from questioning children who have been the victims of abuse, especially incest, until they are placed in a safe environment, for instance in foster care or in a residential home. Otherwise, these children will either refuse to talk out of a fear of retaliation, or if they talk and then return home, they may indeed be beaten by their parents, who will accuse them of disloyalty. While it is crucial to protect these children, it remains important to help them to find ways to express their loyalty to their parents directly and non-sacrificially. Otherwise, the risk is that they express their loyalty indirectly and destructively by rejecting the people who are trying to protect them, including the residential staff or foster parents who serve as parental substitutes.

When expressions of loyalty are determined by stereotypes about roles or by rigid societal expectations, therapists can help their clients to engage in a discussion about these stereotypes with their parents and siblings to explore if there is a place for more flexibility and more individualized ways to manifest their loyalty to their family.

Loyalty and the ontic dimension

In the perspective of the ontic dimension, family relationships are very important for the relational establishment of the Self. Family members serve as a unique source of Self-Other delineation. No matter what happens in the relationship between family members who are connected by blood ties, these ties will always exist. Therefore, family members serve as a unique source of Self-Other delineation. Each family member can be in the position of the Self who depends on an Other, another family member for the relational establishment of the Self. Conversely, this same family member can serve as the Other, the ground, for another family member as the Self. "From this ontic dependence of all members on their relationship with one another arises a main component of the superordinate, multi-person level of relationship systems. The sum of all ontologically dependent mutual dyads within a family constitutes the main source of group loyalty." (Boszormenyi-Nagy & Spark, 1973, 2014). Here, the children's loyalty to their genitors may be the result of a special form of ontic dependence that does not allow for substitution (see above).

The variables of loyalty in the ontic dimension

The only variable in this dimension is the manner in which the loyalty is expressed. If loyalty is expressed directly, it brings the loyal person as the Self into direct contact with the Other, the beneficiary of this loyalty. In another case, the loyalty is expressed indirectly, and it serves as an immaterial link between the Self as the loyal person and the Other as the beneficiary of this loyalty in the absence of any tangible interaction between the two.

Therapeutic perspectives

Here, the main point for professionals is to understand that people may offer their loyalty to others because they serve as an important source of Self-Other delineation, not because they are indebted to them. When children show loyalty to non-deserving parents, they should not be discouraged from this, but instead encouraged to show their loyalty directly and non-self-sacrificially.

Chapter 9
Loyalty Conflicts

Unavoidable loyalty conflicts

As we have already discussed, we are bound to experience 'unavoidable loyalty conflicts' simply because we cannot respond to all the needs and all expectations of the people who deserve our loyalty at the same time. We are forced to set priority, and in doing so we may hurt the people who rely on our availability, our parents, the members of our family of origin, and many other people. Sometimes, these other people have been more committed to us than our own parents have been. It could be a spouse, a friend, a partner, a colleague, or just someone who has been there for us at a time when we needed it. We are also indebted to the groups that have welcomed us, for instance the congregation or the religious group to which we belong. All these people and these groups deserve our loyalty. Furthermore, our children deserve our commitment, and sometimes our obligation toward our children may decrease our availability to our own aging parents, and this may also become a source of loyalty conflicts.

To resolve unavoidable loyalty conflicts, we can reassure all these people that we care about them and that we are committed to treat them as fairly as possible. Most reasonable people will appreciate our effort and understand our predicament, since everyone is bound to experience similar types of loyalty conflicts. Also, if they see us trying to abide by our commitment at a cost to us, including the cost of feeling bad for hurting someone's feelings, they will know that we are trying to be trustworthy. Therefore, they will be reassured that in time we shall also show loyalty to them. If we were just helping the people who had been the nicest to us, or the people who would reward us the most for our loyalty, we would give reason to our parents and our partners and friends to worry about our willingness to remain loyal to them.

Example of ways to handle unavoidable loyalty conflicts

Let us take the example of a married couple preparing to celebrate Christmas. Here, the parents of the wife and the parents of the husband hope to see them for Christmas but they live in different places and cannot travel. Whose parents should the couple visit? If they decide to visit the parents of the wife, the husband will feel disloyal to his parents, or vice-versa. If they decide that each of them should go to visit their own parents alone and spend the holidays separately, they will feel disloyal to each other. And what if the spouses were expected to spend Christmas with the members of their congregation, or if they had children who begged them to stay in town to be able to spend Christmas with their little friends? Of course, here we could exchange Christmas for any important celebration in any religion and in any culture. The details may be different, but the issue would remain the same: how to respond to the conflicting expectations of people who deserve our loyalty.

To take the example above, if the distances are not too big, the couple may travel to spend Christmas eve with the parents of the wife, and Christmas day with the parents of the husband. Or maybe they may offer to visit one set of parents for Christmas and the other for Easter and alternate the sequence the next year, etc. In this example, and in any other cases of loyalty conflicts, people may or may not accept the solutions that we have found to meet conflicting obligations and honor conflicting commitments. In some cases, the two sets of parents may be satisfied by the solutions proposed by the couple. In other cases, one set of parents may accept the proposed solution but the other may not, or both may resent the idea of alternate visits, which would then put the couple in a much more difficult situation. At times, adverse circumstances can become a resource. As families were not able to get together during the Covid-19 pandemic, families began to organize online meetings. For some families, this forced experience may have turned into a long-term solution to celebrate holidays with family members who live far apart.

When parents become too demanding of an exclusive loyalty, the spouses may not be able to respond to their expectation and begin to experience guilt feelings or distress, and this is the time when they may seek the help of professionals. If possible, the therapist or counselors should invite the parents and use multidirected partiality to help their clients and their parents to re-engage in a dialogue with the hope that they can come to an agreement about which forms or expressions of loyalty could be acceptable to them besides a demonstration of exclusive loyalty to the parents. However, in any case, spouses who try to find solutions to meet their parents' expectations will earn constructive entitlement, whether or not their parents accept these solutions or recognize their efforts.

Marriage and coupling as a source of loyalty conflicts

Couples struggle to balance their commitment to each other with their commitment to their family of origin in daily life. Also, one tends to forget that marriage as such always represents a major shift of loyalty between *vertical loyalties*, our loyalty commitment to the prior and future generations of our family of origin, and *horizontal loyalties*, our loyalty commitment to people of our generation, like our spouses, partners, friends, or anyone else we may be indebted to. This switch is a major step for most families. In many demonstration family therapy interviews that included teen children, Boszormenyi-Nagy asked a question that sounded rather insignificant to the audience. He would ask a parent: "Are you interested in your children's friends?" or "Are your happy when your children get invited over by their friends?" He would ask the teen: "How do you think your parents accept your friends?" These apparently simple questions gave a picture of the degree of difficulties that these young people may experience in trying to balance vertical and horizontal loyalties. The more the parents indicate that they welcome their children's ability to form peer relationships, the less the children would have to struggle to find a balance between their vertical and horizontal loyalties once they are ready to engage in a couple relationship.

In modern societies, more and more couples live together outside of the formal commitment of a marriage or any form of civil union. For all practical purposes, these couples are often treated as married couples by society and by their families of origins. If this is indeed the case, nothing should change if at some point they decide to formalize their union by a marriage or by another form of public commitment, especially if they do this only for some kind of practical reason like social benefits or naturalization. However, this is not always true. In several cases, the 'new spouses' begin to experience relational problems that they had never experienced before they formalized their union, leading in some cases to an actual break-up.

A possible explanation is that some people live together without a formal commitment not because it has become a new norm in many modern societies, but because of unresolved loyalty issues. For instance, parents who clearly express that they do not like their children's partners may not object to the relationship as long as they believe that it is not 'serious'. In this case, it may be much easier for the partners to live together without being married than to face a conflict with their parents. However, the conflict will become unavoidable if they marry or if they have a child together with or without getting married, since parenthood creates an irreversible tie between the two parents.

In other situations, parents appear to endorse their child's choice of a partner but give subtle messages that their relationship represents a loss for them. A father may tell a daughter: "You are right, if you were to get married, I would gain a son-in-law, which would be nice but still I would have to lose you." The mother may add: "Yes, I like your boyfriend, but don't forget that I shall cry on the day you get married." Some children may see these kinds of comments as only a touching expression of love, but in some others, it may trigger an unconscious guilt. In this case, they may try to avoid a permanent commitment with their partner, or they may push this partner away as a form of invisible loyalty to the parents. In such a situation, the solution is to help people to express their loyalty to their parents in a more direct and less self-defeating manner.

Family loyalties in arranged marriages

In many traditional societies all around the world, marriages are still arranged between families, and the degree to which the young people are let free to accept or reject the choice made by their parents varies considerably from one society to another. In general, people in modern Western societies, including therapists, tend to consider arranged marriages as an infringement on people's fundamental right to make their own decisions about their lives without any outside interferences. Of course, everyone should agree that child marriages are unacceptable, and that young people should not be forced to marry against their will.

However, from the point of view of contextual therapy, arranged marriages as such can bring benefits to the spouses because it will be easier for them to balance their vertical and horizontal loyalties if their respective parents not only endorsed them as a couple but have contributed actively to their union.

In traditional societies, whether marriages are arranged or not, couples often meet because they belong to the same social and cultural background. In this case, their families of origin share common traditions, common values, and the same religion. In these situations, it will be easy for them to meet the expectations of their respective families because they would be similar, which will diminish the risk of loyalty conflicts. In addition, once they become parents together, it will be easy for them to reach an agreement on what they want to transmit to their children.

In modern societies, many people have the occasion to meet and to engage in couple relationships without having much in common besides their mutual attraction. They may come from different countries, with different traditions, different languages, different religions, etc. They may often live very far from their family of origin. In these cases, they will have much work to do not only to overcome their differences but also to find a way to balance their loyalty to each other with their loyalty to parents who may have very different expectations of them. As people become more isolated, it is more frequent for single people to rely on dating services to meet a partner. All these services try to match people according to all kinds of individual criteria, and to a good extent, people who meet through these services may in fact succeed in forming stable couples because they have compatible individual needs and expectations. However, none of these services focuses on exploring family loyalties, for instance by asking something like: do your parents endorse your effort to find a partner? Would they approve of the kind of partner you are looking for?

Forbidden unions and family loyalties

While couples who live in traditional societies may experience the benefits from arranged marriages, couples who decide to choose a partner against their parents' wishes may experience problems that are much more severe than problems that people in a more modern society experience. When people seek advice about a relationship that is disapproved by their parents, especially when the parents clearly indicated that there could be dire consequences if they went against their wishes, professionals need to exert great caution. They should not encourage their client to defy their parents and simply go ahead with the disapproved relationship. In some cases, this could entail an actual serious risk, even the risk that the parents may have their child or the child's partner killed, which of course would be horrible. While these kinds of crimes are very rare, professionals should not forget that they can happen anywhere in the world. As more and more families coming from traditional societies migrate, they bring with them traditional views on marriages and couple relationships that they may impose on their children even more rigidly than families who have remained in their original traditional society. It is their way of remaining loyal to the world that they had left.

When couples try to unite against the express will of their respective parents, or when their parents' expectations are incompatible with the needs of their partners, they may experience a clash between vertical and horizontal loyalties that appears insurmountable. The world literature is full of stories that center on this theme. A classic example of this in literature is William Shakespeare's tragedy *Romeo and Juliet*, which was published in 1597, has been translated in over 25 languages, and has been staged in over 25 countries only in the last decade. It is about two young lovers who meet their death after trying to unite despite the feud of their two families. In the end, the grief over the loss of their death brings the two families to reconcile. It is also the central theme of many movies. In the French language, the notion of loyalty conflict is often associated with the notion of the 'Cornelian dilemma' in reference to the famous tragedy of Pierre Corneille, *Le Cid* (1637), which remains one of the most famous texts of French literature. In this tragedy, the hero, Rodrigue, is torn between two obligations: the obligation to avenge his father who has been offended by his lover's father, an offense that would demand his death, and the obligation to protect his lover, Chimene, from experiencing a terrible grief by sparing her father, but in this case betraying his father. Rodrigue decides that his gratitude to his father obliges him to avenge him (vertical loyalty) and that this has to take precedence over his obligations toward his beloved one (horizontal loyalty).

If a dialogue with the parents remains possible, the professionals who encounter such situations should try to invite the parents and use multidirected partiality to give a voice to both the parents and the young adults, but this is rarely possible. In some cases, the young people may resolve to accept their parents' rule and accept to renounce the disapproved relationship. In other cases, however, they may refuse to give up their relationship, and if this puts them in danger, they may escape from the area where the parents live and try to begin a new life somewhere else. When therapists become involved in this kind of situation, the most important consideration is the safety of the young people. Trying to contact their parents would be dangerous. However, at the same time, these therapists or counselors should help these two young people or the person who has fled alone to escape an imposed marriage to find ways in which they can still remain loyal to their parents in a direct and safer manner, for instance by engaging in a profession that would be approved by the parents to avoid the risk of invisible loyalty. In their case, their invisible loyalty could be expressed in becoming less cautious and in exposing themselves to the risk of being found by their parents, which could have catastrophic consequences.

Avoidable loyalty conflicts

In general, people who expect our loyalty do not owe it to us to agree with each other on what they expect from us. It is our job to figure out how to handle their contradictory expectations. However, this is not true in the case of children. Children not only deserve to receive the care of committed adults who are willing to provide for their needs, but they also have the right to be protected from unfair burdens. They deserve to be protected from the burden of trying to resolve loyalty conflicts that would be totally avoidable if the important adults in their life were willing to work on harmonizing their expectations and set common goals.

Children can also experience avoidable loyalty conflicts when their parents have discordant expectations, or when their expectations clash with the expectations of other important adults in their life, for instance the expectations of foster parents, residential childcare workers, or teachers. When adults cannot work together for the good of the children they care for, the children are left alone to figure out how to respond to their contradictory expectations, which is a form of parentification that can lead to an accumulation of destructive entitlement.

Avoidable loyalty conflicts in the parent-child relationship

Children are placed in an avoidable loyalty conflict when their parents cannot agree on what they expect from them. In some cases, children who are much too young to have an awareness of true loyalty conflicts may already react to their parents' inability to work as a team and in these cases, one can observe very subtle forms of parentification already. Swiss researchers have spent years studying the triangle formed by the child, the father and the mother. These researchers have demonstrated that even very young children react with distress when the parents are unable to agree on how to engage the child in play (Fivaz-Depeursinge & Philipp, 2014). In this case, one could say that the distress comes from the fact that the child is placed in a loyalty conflict. Even surprisingly young children try to find a way to get out of this predicament. Consider the example of a toddler who tried to substitute his parents' inability to work together by beginning a song and moving his arms like an orchestra conductor to try to make his parents sing along. In a way, this child was already parentified, meaning that as a toddler, he already had to try to find a solution to address his parents' inability to work as a team.

When couples come from very different backgrounds, from different countries with different languages and religions, and when they have very little in common besides their attraction to each other, they will have to work hard to establish common grounds for their life as a couple. If they manage to do that, they will also be able to build a common ground for parenting together. For instance, these couples need to decide what language will they speak together, what language will they speak with their children, what traditions they will follow, and in what religion they will raise their child. Some parents may like the idea of exposing their children to a diversity of languages and traditions, which could become a source of enrichment for their children as long as there are no conflicts in the family.

Professionals forget that children may experience loyalty conflicts in situations that appear totally trivial. For instance, whether children use a fork and knife to eat or take food with their fingers does not make much of a difference. The same for sipping soup from a bowl or eating it with a spoon from a soup plate. However, eating habits are an indication of ethnicity, and parents who come from different cultures need to agree on what eating habits they want to transmit to their children. But they can also agree to allow their children to try different ways of eating (you can use a soup plate at school and a bowl at home). When children get these kinds of directives, they not only may adjust to eating in a variety of ways, but this may also be fun for them. However, things can change rapidly if their parents get divorced. Suddenly, the mother could tell a child: "You had better not ask for a bowl. Now that your father is gone, you are going to use a plate like normal people do." Out of loyalty to the father who is put down, this child may decide not to eat soup anymore, which may then infuriate the mother. This is just an example. Any action of daily life could become a source of disparaging comment on the part of either of the ex-spouses. In these cases, children not only may experience loyalty conflicts, but also their loyalty will be split, a predicament that will be discussed later.

At the same time, many parents who live separate lives after a separation or a divorce may still be able to work together as parents, and often they make commendable efforts to protect their children from experiencing loyalty conflicts. They try to agree on as many points as possible, for instance on big issues like education, or on practical points like the schedule of the visits, the level of contact with other family members, including grandparents, the celebration of holidays and birthdays, etc. In this case, the children are protected from avoidable loyalty conflicts but not from unavoidable loyalty conflicts that result simply from the fact that they cannot be with both parents at the same time.

Even the most cooperative ex-partners are still likely to make comments that indicate that they are missing their children when they are spending time with the other parent. Parents will make comments like: "It is too bad that you have to go already", or "It is too bad that you will not be there next week", or "I love you, I shall miss you", etc. Each of these sentences tell the children that they are valued, and they do not entail the slightest criticism of the other parent, but still the children will get the message that this parent is pained, which will trigger some guilt, and lead to a certain degree of loyalty conflict.

Sometimes, ex-partners who sincerely try their best to work together as parents feel hurt because despite their best efforts, their children complain about their situation and at times begin to show some signs of destructive entitlement. They may begin to refuse to follow directions, or to care about others. The reality is that these children may still perceive their situation as unfair. For instance, many children resent the fact that their little comrades are spared from the experience of having to shuttle from one household to the other. Their resentment may be even bigger if they have half-siblings who can live at home with both parents. Professionals who meet such parents should credit them for their efforts, and this in turn will help them to acknowledge the burdens that their children experience. When these children see that their parents understand their predicament, they will be less likely to complain or to act out.

Parents' faith and avoidable loyalty conflicts

When couples do not share the same faith, they will need to work out a solution that could work not only for them but also for their children. For this reason, it is important that professionals who meet these couples, pastors and priests who are expecting to celebrate mixed marriages, as well as pastoral counselors and other professionals, need to understand the loyalty implications of the couple's decision pertaining to religion. In marrying, some people convert to the religion of the other, and some retain their own religious practices. Other couples solve the issue of religion by dropping any religious practices or by engaging in religious practices that are totally alien to their family of origin. Couples who manage to find solutions that work for them and that are at least in part acceptable to their family of origin will have a better chance to succeed as couples. Therefore, premarital counseling of mixed couples should not be limited to foster a discussion between the future spouses but should include a discussion of their position toward their parents' views and a discussion of their parents' expectations. In as much as it is feasible, it may be very productive to include them in some of the premarital counseling sessions. Also, couples who are able to find a solution to deal with their different religious backgrounds will be able to spare their children from experiencing avoidable loyalty conflicts.

We also know that even when the future couple belongs to the same religion, the preparation of the wedding ceremony can trigger some disagreement between the future spouses, and a lot of pushing and pulling between the two families of origin who may get into an argument about anything from the size of the wedding party to the texts and music that should be used during the religious ceremony. All these things may be rather trivial. People will quicky forget about the hymns that were sung during the ceremony. The wedding dress will disappear in a closet. However, at the same time, the ability of the future couple and their respective families to reach an agreement about all these things is an important predictor of the success of the marriage.

Some mixed couples may not be prepared to deal with their differences. They do not get married or if they do, they skip a religious marriage. They may continue to practice their own faith and do not engage in any discussion about the religion in which to raise their children. They assume that when they grow up, their children will figure out for themselves what they want to do about religion. Also, some parents may refrain from making any decisions about their children's religion, not because they are not able to deal with this issue as a couple, but simply because they truly believe that children deserve the right to make their own choices.

There are situations in which the parents have rejected the religious practices of their own parents. In this case, the grandparents may put pressure on the grandchildren to endorse their faith, which could also put them in a difficult bind. For example, grandparents can try to have a child secretly baptized against the will of parents who have abandoned their Christian practice, or they can try to involve the children in traditional practices that are unacceptable to Christian parents. In any of these situations, the children are caught in loyalty conflicts that could have been avoided if the adults had the courage to speak openly about their disagreements and tried to agree on what to expect from the children. If not, children will have to invent their own solutions to avoid these loyalties conflicts. Here, it could be lying to suspicious parents, assuring them that they never went anywhere with their grandparents while in fact having attended a church service or a traditional ceremony with them.

In short, even when parents tell their children that they will be entirely free to choose what they want, they forget that they may still give signals that they would be happier if their children choose their side rather than the side of the other parent, and that the two families of origin may put some pressure on them, too. When children begin to feel that their choice may be disloyal to one family or the other, they often try to escape the loyalty conflict by rejecting both options. For instance, once they become teenagers or young adults, instead of opting for the faith of one of their parents, or the faith of one of their grandparents, they may end up getting interested in a religion that is entirely alien to their family, for instance Islam or Buddhism when the families come from a Christian background. Other teens who find themselves in a bind may end up rejecting the idea of religions altogether. In any case, their decision is not based on a true freedom of choice but on their attempt to get out of a conflict of loyalty that would have been avoided if their parents and grandparents had been able to come to an agreement about what religious tradition to transmit to the next generation.

Professionals, especially the pastors and pastoral counselors who may meet with couples who come from different religious backgrounds should be very attentive to these issues and help parents to understand that giving children the freedom to decide what religion to choose or what traditions to follow is not a true gift. They should help these parents to realize that they will give more to their children by accepting the responsibility to work on a solution that is acceptable to both of them and then let their children know about their decision. Of course, this changes later. Once the children become adults, they will make their own choices, and the parents need to be prepared to accept them.

Parents' dilemma over controversial traditional practices

As an important note to the issue of conflicts between parents and their families of origins over the issue of religions and traditional practices, one big and difficult subject is the excision of girls. It is far beyond the scope of contextual therapy to address the multiple systemic elements that play a role in the maintenance of a practice that is considered illegal in many countries, but professionals may meet parents who are caught in a difficult dilemma. They are expected by their families to abide by this tradition, but at the same time they are aware that this practice is cruel, that it may lead to all kinds of medical problems, and also that they may be punished for not protecting their daughters from a procedure that is considered a serious form of child abuse.

When parents experience this kind of dilemma, professionals may help them by showing them that in wanting to protect their daughters from this practice, they are not disloyal to their family of origins in as much as they want to protect their health and give them the chance to become themselves mothers without the risk of obstetric complications due to the procedure. In some cases, they may be able to educate their relatives about these dangers. Once they get the determination to protect their daughters, they could be helped to feel less disloyal to their family of origin by helping them to find constructive ways of keeping their family's traditional practices, for instance by making the effort to transmit the stories, the traditional language or music of their group to the next generations.

Parents and other adults in the prevention of loyalty conflicts

One needs to remember that children depend not only on their parents but also on the many other people who play an important role in their lives: anyone from other family members like grandparents to various kinds of caregivers, like day care workers, teachers, or other parental figures like foster parents, residential care workers, etc. Some of these adults may come from a different culture and speak a different language than the parents, which happens frequently when families relocate in a new country. These adults may have their own view of what the children in their care should do and achieve. Here it is important that all these adults can agree on a minimum of rules and expectations.

For instance, parents may have become vegetarian. What should they do if the grandparents insist on feeding their children meat because they believe that children who do not eat meat will become ill? They may feel disloyal to their own parents if they were to deprive them of all contacts with their children. Would they then let the children eat meat once in a while when they visit the grandparents? They may. Would they then put the responsibility on their children to refuse meat? This could leave the children in a bind: having a fight with their grandparents or else eating meat and lying to their parents that they did not, which also would be difficult. Consequently, they may try to find pretexts for not visiting the grandparents, for instance saying that they feel sick, etc. In short, they may begin to present with symptoms that could appear unexplainable if one does not know about loyalty dynamics, unexplainable belly aches, angry outbursts, panic attacks, etc.

The primary responsibility to protect children from unnecessary loyalty conflicts falls on the parents. They are the ones who should make sure that their children are not caught in a bind between their expectations and the expectations of other adults. Parents who catch a nanny trying to teach their child something they disapprove of may not even engage in a discussion. They may just fire her. When it is grandparents who do not respect the view of the parents and try to impose their own view on their grandchildren, parents may struggle because of their own loyalty to these grandparents. One clinical leverage in such a situation is that both the parents and the grandparents have a common investment in the health and success of the children and seeing them getting ill because of their conflicts may motivate them to resolve their disagreement. Also, when parents and grandparents make a sincere effort to find solutions for the sake of the children, they will earn constructive entitlement that will benefit them, too.

Chapter 10

Split Loyalties

Introduction

We have already shown that the notion of loyalty conflicts is inseparable from the notion of loyalty. Does this mean that the notion of split loyalties is also inseparable from the notion of loyalty? This is not the case, and here is the difference. We are bound to experience loyalty conflicts because we have multiple commitments that we cannot always honor at the same time, often for simple practical reasons. The people who rely on our loyalty may resent the fact that at times, we appear to give more attention to other people, but it does not imply that they resent the other people we are committed to. Our parents may wish that we spend more time with them and less with our partner and our friends, but it does not mean that they resent them as persons. In fact, they may like them much. In this case, since our parents do not ask us to reject these people to prove to them our loyalty, our loyalties are not truly divided. We could say the same of many situations in which people expect us to show more loyalty to them than to other people without having any bad feelings toward them.

The situation changes if the individuals or groups who expect our loyalty are in a warfare with one another. When one person or one group demands our exclusive loyalty and forces us to prove our loyalty by abandoning any form of loyalty to another individual or group that they hate or despise, and if in addition, the other person or group expects the same exclusive loyalty from us for the same reasons, our loyalties become truly divided. In short, split loyalties are the result from an extreme version of loyalty conflicts. While loyalty conflicts as such may not be avoidable, but what could change is the attitude of the people who expect our loyalty and put us in the predicament of split loyalties.

Split loyalties in the case of parental separation and feud

People usually think about the predicament of split loyalties in the case of children whose parents are involved in nasty divorces or long custody battles. These parents are in a warfare of mutual mistrust and mutual accusations. They not only often force their children to take a side, but also in addition, in most cases, demand exclusive loyalty of their children. However, this can also happen outside of divorce situations. The parents may never have married, or not even lived together, but they can still have a very contemptuous relationship that puts their children in the middle. Same-sex parents do experience the same relational problems as other couples and may end up in a contemptuous separation and bitter fight over the custody and the visitation rights pertaining the children they have raised together. In many countries, the non-biological parents of the couple's children do not have legal rights over them unless they have legally adopted them, but whether or not these non-biological parents have formal parental rights or not, they may engage in a bitter battle for visitation rights with their former partner. Also, if the same-sex couple relied on a friend as a sperm donor or if one of the men has conceived the couple's children with a woman friend, these biological parents may get into serious conflicts with the same-sex couple for several reasons. Some may rescind their agreement to stay away from the children's life and begin to claim visitation rights, or they may claim the right to a closer relationship with the member of the couple with whom the child has been conceived. In any of these cases, if the conflict between the adults escalates, the children may be caught in a true predicament of split loyalty. On the other hand, anonymous genetic parents like sperm donors would not the child in the predicament of split loyalty since they would have no way to know whom they may have engendered.

What all the situations have in common is that the children are expected to show their loyalty to this parent by siding with this parent, accepting to believe all the negative things this parent is saying about the other, and mainly by not displaying any evidence of loyalty to the other parent. If both parents have the same expectation, children are placed in an impossible bind: for instance, the child of divorced parents may hear the mother saying: "Do not even think of wearing the t-shirt your father gave you" while the father is saying: "Do not even think of calling your mother while you are with me". How can the child show his or her loyalty to either parent? This is a small example of what children may be exposed to. Sometimes during custody battles, a parent may expect a child to testify against the other parent, or the child may be asked to tell the judge with whom he or she wants to live while both parents pressure on him or her to make the 'right choice'.

Children, as well as adults who have parents who have spent an entire lifetime trying to recruit them in their battles with each other, can be caught in this predicament. Also, the death of one parent may not relieve the child from this predicament. The surviving parent may still harbor the same expectation of exclusive loyalty at the cost of loyalty to the deceased parent, and the child may still remain under the influence of similar expectations that were expressed by the deceased parent. The only difference is that adults have more resources to take a stand and refuse to be manipulated than children are who are still completely dependent on their parents.

Split loyalties in the case of care by relatives-fights between mothers and grandmothers

When children are raised by family members, the contentious relationship leading to split loyalties is not the relationship between the parents, but the relationship between the parents and the family members who have become caregivers. Many grandparents step in as caregivers when their children need help to raise their own children. Most parents are grateful for the help they receive, but it is not always the case. There are many circumstances in which parents resent the fact that their own parents step in as caregivers, and they get into a contemptuous relationship with them. Also, when both parents die in an accident, or when both die of an illness like AIDS, there is a possibility that both sets of grandparents fight over the right to raise their surviving grandchildren at the exclusion of the other grandparents. Here, their possessiveness and demand of exclusivity may be exacerbated by their respective grief over the loss of their child. This too places the grandchildren in the predicament of split loyalties.

However, here, the most common example of split loyalty comes from the feud between mothers and their own mothers, or possibly the maternal and paternal grandmothers. One of the most common examples of these situations is the case of mothers who are drug addicted and have to relinquish the care of their children to their own mothers. In some cases, the children are simply abandoned to the grandmothers; in other cases, they are removed from the care of their mothers by child protective services and subsequently placed with their grandmothers. In the case of drug addiction, the addiction can be the result of a cascade of precipitating factors that have affected the family for generations, including the situational injustice of poverty, discrimination, poor educational resources, unemployment, life in a drug-infested area affected by systemic violence, etc. Because of all these injustices, parents and grandparents may be caught in a multigenerational cascade of destructive entitlement and parentification. In these situations, it is not unusual that the fathers of the family are absent. Some die early in violent, often gang-related incidents, many become involved in drug dealing and end up in jail for various reasons. Consequently, generation after generation, women become single parents who may see their children as a source of affection or support. Consequently, these mothers and grandmothers may begin to compete for their loyalty.

In addition, if child protective services become involved and remove the children from the care of the mothers due to neglect or abuse, the mothers who have lost custody of their children may be jealous of their own mothers who can live with them, or they may try to fight against the grandmothers in court to regain custody of their children. Consequently, these mothers may try to alienate their children from their grandmothers by telling all kinds of negative things about them. Also, they can be very vocal in telling their children that they are the ones who deserve their loyalty, not their grandmothers. The grandmothers also may have bad things to say about their addicted daughters who may have caused them all kinds of worries and troubles: their lives may have been in danger due to overdoses or because they were the victims of violent partners. These addicted mothers may have stolen money from their own mothers to buy drugs, etc. They also may have a very negative view of the children's father. For all these reasons, the children may be blamed by their grandmothers when they try to show loyalty to their mothers or to their absent fathers. In short, all these elements place the children in the predicament of split loyalties.

In South Africa and other countries, an enormous number of children have come into the care of their grandmothers because of the devastating effect of the AIDS epidemic. Many of these grandmothers become overwhelmed by the task of having to raise too many of their grandchildren, which is often the case in families in which several members of the same generation become too ill to raise their children or die of AIDS. Even when there was no contentious relationship between them and their AIDS-infected children, these grandmothers who are overburdened may begin to make disparaging comments about the ill parents who have placed them in this situation. This could add to the risk that children are placed in the predicament of split loyalties.

Split loyalties in the case of foster care placement and adoption

When children are removed from the care of their parents and placed in foster care with non-relatives due to neglect or abuse, the parents who have lost custody of their children may deeply resent the decision of the child protective services. Consequently, they may try to sabotage the relationship of their children with their caregiver in a similar manner than the drug-addicted mothers. In turn, foster parents who become attached to these children and who may be dismayed by what the parents did to their children may try to discourage these children from showing any loyalty to their parents: "Why should you make a drawing for your mother, you know she always misses her visiting times"; or "I hope you are not going to turn out like your father", etc. Consequently, the children's loyalties can be split. However, in the case of foster care, the children's possible loyalty to their foster parents is not based on as many factors as their loyalty to even non-deserving parents. Also, children are often moved from one foster home to another before they can develop deep ties with their caregivers.

It must be noted that childcare workers in institutions are less likely to discourage children to show loyalty to their biological parents because they do not have the same degree of investment in the relationship as foster parents do. However, at times, they may try to recruit the children to take their side if they are in a battle with other staff members. This could also place the children in a situation of split loyalties, but here again, their loyalty to the various staff members is usually not as strong as their loyalty to their parents.

In situations of adoption, children are not usually caught in a full predicament of split loyalties, since their biological parents are usually absent from their lives, but adoptive parents can be extremely critical about them, which can the children in a very difficult predicament and lead to invisible loyalties rather than split loyalties (see below).

Guidelines for interventions in situations of split loyalties

The clinical consequences of split loyalties

Children who are caught in the predicament of split loyalties often suffer a lot. No matter what they try to do to satisfy their feuding parents, their mothers and grandmothers, or their parents and foster parents, they are bound to fail since the sole way to satisfy one of these feuding adults is to shun the other. Their despair over the impossibility to ever show loyalty to one of these adults without being punished for it by the other can lead them to depression and suicide. Instead, it can also lead them to an escalation of violent behaviors toward both parents. In part, this may be the result of their destructive entitlement. They are indeed the victims of a great injustice, which may lead them to seek revenge and to stop caring about the rights of others. This violence can also be the result of a desperate attempt to treat their parents equally. If they cannot be equally loyal to both of them, they may try consciously or unconsciously to re-establish this equality by treating both of them very badly. In many cases, these youths end up with a diagnosis of Conduct Disorder.

These youths may also try to re-establish a balance between the parents by becoming equally disloyal to both of them. For instance, some teens may engage in gangs, to the dismay of both parents. They can also convert to a religion that both parents consider as completely alien, like Islam or Buddhism for Christian or Jewish parents. Also, young people who cannot offer their loyalty to both parents may offer it to gang leaders. Or especially if they come from Muslim families, they may become radicalized and offer their loyalty to terrorist organizations like ISIS.

From a systemic point of view, it is important to note that when there are two or more siblings in a family, some of them side with one parent, the others with the other parent. There may be many reasons that bring a child to side with one parent rather than the other: age, gender, living arrangements, etc. These siblings may even engage in a bitter fight with each other because of "I cannot believe that you still talk to our father" (or our mother). However, from a systemic point of view, the result is that as a sibling unit, they have remained loyal to both parents. Therapists who work with such families should not get fooled into believing that the children's attitude toward each of the parents is a permanent one. If for some reason, one of the children who was always on the side of one parent changes camp, it is very likely that another child who was staunchly again this parent changes camp too and begins to take this parent's side.

Professionals meet children who are caught in the predicament of split loyalties in all kinds of circumstances. Professionals in the mental health field and in school counseling see children who are referred to them for a variety of problems: deteriorating school performances, depression with or without suicidal ideations, disruptive and aggressive behaviors meeting the criteria for full-fledged conduct disorder or not, etc. Specialists in mediation regularly receive referrals from lawyers and judges who try to help parents to agree on custody matters. Obviously, marital counselors meet many couples who are also parents who may recruit their children in their disputes. Pastoral counselors may be asked to see youngsters who experience behavioral problems or couples who are in a serious feud, and feuding mothers and grandmothers. Social workers may be involved when children must be removed from the care of their parents to protect them from neglect, abuse, or intra-familial violence. The same workers may be mandated to supervise the visit of parents who for some reason or another are not allowed to see their children by themselves. Other social workers may get involved with parents who are engaged in serious custody battles. Often during these battles, one of the ex-spouses alleges that the other spouse is abusing the children as a means to gain full custody of the children, and social workers are then asked to investigate these allegations.

Helping children who are caught in the predicament of split loyalties is never an easy task, and there is no standard way to proceed. Much depends on the nature of the presenting problem, the nature of the referral, the scope of practice of the professionals who are involved with them, and the resources available in the area where the children live. For instance, children who are acutely depressed and suicidal may benefit from psychiatric hospitalization, but there are many places in the world where this kind of hospitals do not exist. Also, in many places of the world, there are no organized foster programs, only orphanages, and children who have to be placed outside of their parents' home need to be placed with relatives.

In general, there are no exact rules about whom to invite during therapeutic interventions related to split loyalties. Some parents are too angry with each other to be able to sit in the same room. Some are still willing to meet. Some adolescents want to be seen alone at first. Of course, contextual therapists recommend that the entire family is invited, but no matter who attends the sessions, multidirected partiality should remain the main tool of the therapist/counselor. Also, no matter what approaches people use, the goals remain the same. The first goal is to ensure everyone's safety, especially when children become suicidal and when there is a high risk of intrafamilial violence.

In some cases, the depression and risk of suicide are evident. In other cases, it is clear that the child has never presented any evidence of depression. However, even then, a simple sentence may be helpful to exclude this risk entirely: "I want to ask you a question that may have nothing to do with you, but I still want to ask it. I have met children who have become so discouraged about trying to be a good kid for both parents that sometimes they are even thinking that it would be better if they were dead. Did this ever come to your mind?" If the answer is no, great. The therapist may even praise the parents for having a child who is not struggling with this kind of issues. If the answer is yes, this can help the parents to see how difficult the situation is for the child, and this may motivate them to work together in therapy.

Professionals also need to evaluate another risk, namely that a desperate parent may kill a child or commit a murder-suicide. This can happen when a parent who is haunted by hatred against the other parent may want to kill their child to punish this parent, or parents can become desperate over the loss of custody of a child to such an extent that they want to commit a murder-suicide. Any professional who believes that such a risk exists needs to contact the appropriate authorities to ensure the protection of all the people involved. Fortunately, most situations do not involve this kind of risk.

First line of intervention: Working with the parents

Here, the main goal is to help the parents to work more cooperatively and to help them to be less demanding regarding their child's exclusive loyalty. The first step is to understand what may have led them to their children in the predicament of split loyalties.

Often, both parents come from families in which they were parentified, and both of them hoped to receive from their partner what they had been missing while growing up. Consequently, very soon, they start to make unrealistic demands on each other. In short, they become the victims of their reciprocal destructive entitlement, and the relationship quickly deteriorates. The parents begin to blame each other for all kinds of things, and their relationship is dominated by mutual resentment, whether they decide to separate or not. These needy parents also tend to parentify their children. The more their relationship deteriorates, the more each of them turns to their children for love and support, and the more they compete for their loyalty. If they decide to divorce, they often engage in bitter court fights with both trying to gain exclusive custody of their children. Their battle could be understood as the battle of two needy and jealous children seeking to obtain the exclusive love of an idealized parent. Understanding parents this way may help professionals to remain capable of multidirected partiality in a situation in which the parents' attitude is often difficult to tolerate.

In any case, from the point of view of contextual therapy, the goal is to use multidirected partiality to try to remobilize these parents' capacity to show some generosity to their children. Here, generosity would entail the recognition that children have the right to have a constructive and peaceful relationship with both parents, and the willingness to begin working more cooperatively with the other parent for the sake of the children. To get there, professionals should rely on multidirected partiality and on the guidelines that have been proposed in the discussion of destructive entitlement and its consequences.

When parents are too angry at each other to accept working together for the sake of their children, two strategies may be helpful. The first strategy is to try to help the parents remember a time when they still had a positive view of each other, maybe just very early in their relationship while they were still only dating. This intervention may be tried while their child or children are present. If they are present, the advantage is that they could hear that at some point the parents were sharing something in common and this would allow them more freedom to show their loyalty to both. However, even if the children are not present, the change of mindset of parents who can finally remember good things about each other would already help the children.

If this does not work, parents can be reminded that no matter how much they dislike each other, no matter how hard they try to eliminate the other out of their life and the life of their children, they will remain bound together by biology. They will be reminded of each other for the rest of their lives through the physical features of their children, for instance the eye or hair color of the ex-spouse, and the same would be true of their grandchildren in the future. Also, if their children get hurt by their battles, they may renounce having their own family, and both parents will be equally deprived of a descendance. Sometimes, people who are very focused on preventing any contacts between their child and their ex-spouse are surprised when they realize that there is no escape from the genetic ties that connect them through their children, and this can help them to become more tolerant of each other.

In the case of children who are raised by grandmothers in a context of poverty and multiple social injustices, mothers and grandmothers could be brought together, and the therapist or counselor could offer partiality to both of them by showing them that they are both the victims of systemic injustices that have deprived them from receiving what children deserve. Once both receive this kind of acknowledgement, it will be easier to ask them to consider the interests of the children and to help them to earn constructive entitlement by trying to work toward a more cooperative relationship. Here, one important preventive measure to decrease the risk of multigenerational parentification, destructive entitlement, and ensuing split loyalties is to offer support to children who are parentified not only because of the needs of their mothers and grandmothers, but also often by the harsh circumstances in which they live. Often, they have to assume responsibilities that are beyond their age. Here, afterschool programs, community programs, and church youth programs in which these children can get the attention of benevolent adults could decrease the level of their destructive entitlement, which in turn could decrease the risk that they later parentify their own children. Also, these programs could offer a neutral environment where their loyalty is not constantly solicited by feuding adults.

When the feud occurs between the parents and people who act in a professional capacity like residential childcare workers or paid foster care parents, it is the job of these people's supervisors to intervene as soon as possible. Here, multidirected partiality becomes an important resource as well. The parents and the caregivers should be encouraged to express their concerns with the hope that once they are given the chance to present their side of the situation, they will also become more willing to respect each other. This in turn should decrease the risk of true split loyalties. However, if the foster parents are the ones who induce the split, it would be best to place these children in a new home. In some places, foster parents are required to receive some training before they can become accredited as foster parents. People who train them should think of including training on family loyalty in their curriculum. Once the future foster care parents realize that they too have most likely experienced some kind of painful loyalty conflicts in their own lives, they will become less likely to place the children they care for in a similar predicament. Childcare workers should receive similar training and ideally, adoption agencies should provide a similar training to future adoptive parents.

Second line of intervention: Working with the children

The second line of therapeutic interventions pertains to the children. If the children begin to show signs of distress, especially suicidal ideation, consideration should be given to hospitalization or placement in a residential treatment facility for their own protection. In several cases, the parents do accept these proposed measures, since it is often easier for them to accept that their children are moved to a neutral environment rather than concede victory to the other parent in a custody battle. In other more dire situations, if the parents cannot agree to a placement, it may be necessary to involve child protective services to make the decision. In any case, preference should be given to residential treatment centers that offer comprehensive services that meet the individual treatment needs of the children, their educational needs and that can also provide family therapy.

If at least one parent is still capable of understanding that children have the right to express their loyalty to both parents, the situation becomes less desperate for the child. For this reason, judges should be encouraged to make custody decisions based on an evaluation of the parents' tolerance of each other. Preferably, they should award custody of the children to the parent who is the more willing to accept contacts between the children and his or her ex-spouse.

Older teens can be helped in a more direct way, which is based on gaining insight into their parents' limitations. One could begin by asking these teens a simple question: what would they do if they were themselves the parents of two kids who were fighting over a cake, each insisting on getting the entire cake and leaving nothing to the other. Would they accept that, and give the whole cake to one of the kids, or would they scold them, telling them that they need to learn to share? Most of these teens will agree that these two kids need to learn to share. One could then proceed to show them that their parents are in some ways like these two kids. Both are hungry for love and affection and want to grab all what their children can give without sharing anything. If the solution is to tell the kids that no matter what they ask, they need to get used to sharing, the same should be true for their needy parents: they should learn to share. In short, these teens should be told that they have the right to show their loyalty to both parents, no matter how much each of them may complain. This strategy can be liberating for these teens even if it implies a certain degree of parentification since it requires that they act in a more adult way than their parents.

Chapter 11
Invisible Loyalties

Implicit and explicit loyalties

In the general public, people may think of invisible loyalties in situations in which a person is not allowed to express his or her loyalty directly and explicitly. For instance, people who are living in a totalitarian regime would pay a heavy price for showing loyalty to their religious group or to a forbidden political party. For this reason, they may choose to refrain from wearing any signs that could identify them as members of that group. However, the absence of an explicit expression of loyalty would not automatically mean an absence of loyalty. It would only mean that the loyalty to this forbidden group must be kept invisible. One could also say that their loyalty remains implicit as long as they have not disengaged publicly from this group. Indeed, political authorities in totalitarian regimes are not fooled by people who hide their loyalty to a forbidden group. They are often forced to confess publicly to their belonging to the forbidden group and to renounce any affiliation with it officially. In the history of religion, too, one finds many examples in which people who belonged to a persecuted religious group had to abjure their faith publicly.

Many individual and family therapists understand invisible loyalties as unconscious loyalties, meaning that we are pushed to express our loyalty to people for motives that are unconscious, but in general, they do not define what these unconscious motives may be. In contextual therapy, the only strictly unconscious aspect of loyalty comes from its psychological unconscious determinant, i.e. the unconscious guilt that is triggered by the unconsciously internalized message of our parents, i.e. that our move toward autonomy could hurt them (counterautonomous superego). It is true that in many cases, we are not aware of the origin of self-defeating behaviors that decrease our chance to reach our own goals, or to engage in successful relationships. Indeed, they can be triggered by this unconscious guilt, and here we can speak of a true unconscious expression of loyalty to our parents.

In contextual therapy, invisible loyalties are best understood as indirect loyalties, or in a new terminology, *invisible loyalties* can be understood as implicit loyalties in contrast to direct loyalties, which could be described as explicit loyalties. Originally, Boszormenyi-Nagy coined the term invisible loyalties while working to understand the behaviors of patients who were diagnosed with schizophrenia. He and his team members discovered that some of the weird behaviors of their psychotic patients that appeared very discouraging to their parents could be understood as invisible manifestations of loyalty.

Example

Consider the example of Rita one more time. One day the family arrived at the office for therapy just as another teen was leaving the waiting room with his family. He was dressed in baggy clothes, with his cap turned backward on his head, and his attitude was quite provocative. As soon as the therapy session began, the parents said in a same voice: "We are so lucky that our daughter is not like all these teens who give trouble to their parents." As soon as the sentence came out of their mouths, they realized the enormity of what they had just said. Of course, they would never say that Rita was loyal to them by being psychotic, but they were clearly saying that it was better for them to deal with a sick daughter than with a rebellious teenager. Hence, implicitly, Rita was more loyal to her parents by remaining sick than by getting better, or in other words, her psychotic symptom could be understood as a form of invisible loyalty to her parents, even if there were many factors, including biological ones, that led to her psychotic breakdown.

Parents who have a hard time to separate from their children often struggle to accept their children's marriage. In this case, an affair that endangers the marriage may become an invisible expression of loyalty. In many cases, the cheated spouse may ask for a divorce, and the unfaithful spouse may begin to feel regrets and begin to experience difficulties in the relationship with his or her lover. At this end, this unfaithful child may end up alone and more available to his or her parents than during the marriage, and this could be understood as an invisible expression of loyalty to the parents. However, in this case, all of them lose. It is very unlikely that the parents would recognize the affair as an expression of filial loyalty. On the contrary, they may be very vocal about the immorality of their son or daughter's behavior. The cheated spouse is the biggest loser, and the lover often loses, too. And even if the affair ended up in a marriage, there are no guarantees that this second marriage would succeed if the parents were still very ambivalent about any marriage. Here, it is necessary that children find ways to respond to the needs of their parents in a way that is more direct and less costly, for instance by reassuring them that no matter whether they marry or not, they will always give them an important place in their lives.

Invisible loyalties as indirect loyalties

As already discussed, invisible loyalties can also be understood as indirect expressions of loyalty. People may be pushed to express their loyalty indirectly and invisibly, for various reasons. Adults may believe that their parents do not deserve their loyalty. For instance, people who have parents who have failed to meet their parental obligation may not feel bound by filial loyalty. Consequently, when the parents grow older and begin to need help, they may refuse to provide them the assistance that other children who do not feel short-changed would be happy to offer. However, people who refuse to show loyalty to their parents out of resentment for their shortcomings can rarely afford to become entirely disloyal to them because of the determinants of loyalty that lay outside the dimension of relational ethics, especially the determinants of loyalty that belong to the dimension of psychology: their remaining unconscious attachment to their parents or their remaining feelings of guilt.

Consequently, they may express this loyalty indirectly by sabotaging the relationships that could have led to detaching themselves further from their parents. For instance, the person who is determined to cut off a parent from his or her life out of anger may at the same time sabotage a friendship that could have evolved into a marriage.

Another example comes from Jane's story and her journey toward the exoneration of her mother. What was not discussed before is that during her treatment, she had often expressed the wish to move as far away as possible from her hometown. She felt that as long as she was remaining in the area, she would still be forced to deal with her mother at least on some occasions. Since she had a good job, she did not want to leave the company she was working for but try to obtain a transfer to another city. This would have required a promotion to a new position and, for reasons that she could not explained, she was sabotaging her chances to meet the criteria that were required to obtain it. In other words, she was sabotaging her chances to leave her mother. Things changed once she started to see her mother in a different light and to exonerate her. She was finally able to do what was required to obtain the transfer she wanted. Furthermore, as she was preparing her move, she even told her mother that she would return occasionally to visit her and the family. Here, Jane's story is a good example of the negative consequences of invisible loyalties and the benefits of direct expressions of loyalty.

Invisible loyalties in the case of complete cut-off from biological parents

We have seen that children seem to have the need to remain loyal to their biological parents, whether or not they merit this loyalty. The understanding is that the children's loyalty is based on a specific need to maintain a link with their genitors as a very special source of Self-Other delineation. As already discussed, when the biological parents are unknown or when the cut-off is permanent, the children cannot bring them into their lives through direct interactions. Children who are in placement can still prepare gifts for a parent who never visits, hoping that one day their parent will show up. However, this form of direct loyalty is not available if the children have been adopted. In addition, when nothing is known about the parents, the children do not even have the option to show their loyalty by doing things that their absent parents could have approved. Consequently, their only option is to show them loyalty indirectly, in a way that is invisible to their parents who will never know that they are trying to remain loyal to them. Some adopted children may do this by trying to get their adoptive parents out of their lives. Other children may take the side of their biological parents if their adoptive parents or the professionals who care for them indicate in one way or another that they have a very negative opinion of these absent parents.

To begin with the situation of children who try to push their adoptive parents out of their lives: they can become so aggressive toward their adoptive parents and their family that they have to be removed from their home and placed in residential treatment facilities. Other children may begin to refuse to receive anything from their adoptive parents and instead, they may steal from them while not stealing from anyone else. These behaviors can become so hurtful to the adoptive parents that they may give up on the relationship and ask social services to place them in foster care.

Once these children are in placement, the distance from the biological parents will decrease, not because they are actually getting closer to them but because they have managed to push away their adoptive parents. Hence, their behavior can be understood as an indirect and invisible expression of loyalty to these biological parents. In these cases, no one wins: the adoptive parents are heartbroken, the children deprived from the care of dedicated parents, and the biological parents do not gain anything since they will never know what is happening in their children's lives.

In some situations, there is not a total lack of information about the biological parents but only a negative one pertaining to the reasons for the adoption: information about a parent who was addicted to drugs, who was incarcerated, or about a mother who engaged in sex very early and got pregnant as a teen. Consequently, the adoptive parents and the professionals who are involved in their care often develop a very negative view of these biological parents. In many cases, it is expressed in a rather blunt way: "You better watch to not end up like your parents." In addition, very often, the adoptive parents and the professionals have a mistaken understanding of loyalties: they are convinced that these children are doomed to repeat their parents' behaviors because they need to remain loyal to them. Consequently, they do all they can to prevent this from happening.

For instance, the adoptive parents who have a very negative opinion of a biological mother who got pregnant as a teen may believe that out loyalty to her mother, their adoptive daughter could end pregnant like her. Consequently, they will try to prevent her from having contact with boys or, as soon as she reaches puberty, they may demand that her doctor puts her on birth control. Even if the adoptive parents do not say anything, she will understand her adoptive parents' actions as an incrimination of her mother as a bad person whom she should not imitate. At this moment, it is likely that she will start to show her loyalty to her absent mother by taking her side against her adoptive parents. Having no contact with her mother and no information about her life besides the fact that she got pregnant as a teen, she can only show her loyalty to her in an indirect way by defying her adoptive parents. If she indeed becomes pregnant as they feared she would, this would be the result of an invisible or indirect loyalty, not the result of a direct loyalty as many people would think. Why? Because if her mother had a chance to speak with her daughter, it is very likely that she would tell her that she has not made the sacrifice of giving her up for adoption to see her making the same mistakes she did. She may even tell her that she fully endorses the measures that her adoptive parents are trying to put in place to prevent her to become a teen mother.

The best solution to prevent these kinds of sad situations is to help adoptive parents to find out if any positive elements can be identified in the information that is available about the biological parents. More and more frequently, social services and adoption agencies ask people who give up their children for adoption to give some information about their personal and family history. Some countries have now moved to require similar information from anonymous donors. From a contextual point of view, adoption workers should strive to ask these parents about the positive things that they had been able to accomplish and about special skills, or hobbies. They should also enquire about positive elements in their families of origin, even if these families had serious shortcomings. In this way, even if the children may not have access to the full identity of these parents, they would hopefully get enough positive information to show them their loyalty directly. When adoptive parents are willing to help their children to express their loyalty to their biological parents constructively, it will not change anything in the lives of these people, since they will never hear about what their children do. However, it will change much in the lives of the adoptive parents and children. The adoptive parents' goodwill will earn them constructive entitlement, and the children will be free to offer them their loyalty without having to feel disloyal to their biological parents.

Example

Consider the example of Tony and his adoptive family (see Ducommun-Nagy, 2002, for the full case story). *Tony was born in the USA, where he was adopted by a couple of European descent. He could easily pass as their biological son. He had a younger adoptive sister, who was of African American descent. The adoptive agency worried that she could have trouble adjusting to her adoptive family because she looked so different from her adoptive parents, but she did very well. This was not the case for Tony. One possible explanation is that her appearance already brought her closer to her family of origin than to her adoptive parents, while Tony had to find a way to create a link with his own biological parents and did it by pushing his adoptive parents away. When he reached his teens, he had to be removed from his home due to an increasing level of violence toward his adoptive parents. He was admitted to a residential treatment program with a diagnosis of conduct disorder. There, his violence decreased, and he was able to develop a good relationship with some of the staff members. Soon, it became obvious that Tony's violence toward his parents was not the result of a violent temperament but that it had a purpose: it was aimed at pushing them out of his life. At the time, he did not know anything about his biological parents. His adoptive parents had some information about them, but they did not want to disclose it to Tony for fear that he would become even more distant after learning more about his biological family. However, with the encouragement of Tony's psychiatrist, they eventually accepted to share the little they knew with their son. They had a good amount of information about the mother because she had kept in touch with them to get news about her son. Her calls stopped when she got married, probably because she did not want to disclose her teen pregnancy to her husband. They did not have any precise information* about Tony's father, but they were under the impression that he was of Italian descent. As soon as Tony heard that, he asked to wear dress pants instead of jeans "because Italian men dress nice". The adoptive parents decided to let him buy new pants. Once Tony was able to hear positive things about his biological parents and allowed to identify with his biological father, he quickly lost the urge to push away his adoptive parents and he was able to return to their home.

Intergenerational repetitions of negative behaviors and loyalties

Too often professionals jump to the notion of loyalty to explain the repetition of detrimental behaviors generation after generation. We have already examined how the exploitation of children can go on over three or more generations. The ingredients of this repetition are the destructive entitlement of the parents, the loyalty of the children who try to meet the needs of their parents, their parentification, and consequently, their own destructive entitlement and then the parentification of the next generation. Another cause of repetition is what has been discussed above: the indirect loyalty of children who take the side of their parent against the criticism of others. However, we should not forget that people may repeat the behaviors of their parents for reasons that can relate to more than one dimension of relational reality.

We can consider the issue of alcoholism, and the same would apply to any kind of drug addiction. Often people who have alcoholic parents end up drinking or marrying people who are drinkers. However, it would be an over-simplification to attribute this to a direct loyalty to the alcoholic parent: many parents who are alcoholic do not feel good about their dependence and would much prefer it if their children never drank. Therefore, it is always necessary to consider all the determinants that can be involved in alcoholism. A factual element of the repetition is that some people seem to be genetically more likely to develop an alcohol dependence than others are. People who lived in families faced with poverty, discrimination, or violence generation after generation may experience the same emotional stressors and the same need to use alcohol or drugs as self-medication over several generations. From a transactional point of view, they may learn that drinking together is the only way to bring people to connect or that the violence triggered by drinking is acceptable. Generation after generation, they may accumulate the same destructive entitlement, with its same consequences: not caring about the needs of others, getting drunk or high to escape responsibilities, or parentifying their children.

While drinking should not be understood as a simple expression of direct loyalty, it can still be an expression of indirect loyalty for the reasons we have already explored. If the parent who was alcoholic is despised by the other parent, or seen as a bad person by other people, there is indeed a risk that children may begin to drink as a way to take this parent's side against the attack of others. Other people do not engage in any drinking but they end up engaging in a relationship with someone who has the same alcohol dependence. This too can be an expression of indirect loyalty: by choosing a partner who drinks, they elevate the alcoholic parent who has failed them to an ordinary parent: "Everybody drinks, so my parent is not different from anyone else." In this case, the danger exists that this person could unconsciously sabotage the efforts of a partner who would try to reach sobriety by joining an organization like Alcoholic Anonymous because it would then put a new negative light on the dependent parent, a parent who did not try to do that.

As in all the other situations involving invisible and indirect loyalties, the path to avert the repetition of detrimental behaviors over the generations is the same and it is twofold. It entails helping people to find the way to express their loyalty to parents who have serious shortcomings directly and non-sacrificially rather than indirectly. It also entails helping people to engage in the process of trying to exonerate them, i.e. by learning to requalify their actions as the result of their own attempt to seek justice.

Chapter 12

Special Issues Pertaining to Family and Group Loyalties

Divided loyalties and intergroup conflicts

The term *divided loyalty*, which may be more familiar to the general public than *split loyalties*, is used by authors who have discussed the predicaments of people who are forced to choose between two camps during wars, civil wars, changes of political regimes, or interethnic feuds. In these circumstances, people who have a double affiliation and dual loyalties due to a dual citizenship, mixed ethnic origin, mixed marriages, mixed religious backgrounds, etc. are indeed often put in a terrible predicament. They are often expected to kill people of groups in which they have relatives or friends. In addition, when they are of mixed origin, they may become the target of attacks by both groups. As individuals, people may find very different solutions to their horrible dilemma. Some may refuse to join their group in killing people who belong to a group with whom they have some affiliation through family ties or old friendships, even at the risk of their own lives. Others may decide that the group they are expecting to fight with has a valid reason to attack the other group and come to terms with the situation in that way. Some others may try to flee far away from the area to escape their dilemma, or some may even choose to escape this dilemma by committing suicide.

In all these situations which have repeated themselves in the course of history all over the world, the only true solution to escape the dilemma of divided loyalties is the re-establishment of peace and the reconciliation between the feuding parties. History shows this process may take years and may remain imperfect. This has been demonstrated for example by the South Africa Commission for Truth and Reconciliation. Hence, we need to remain realistic about the possible contributions of contextual therapy in intergroup conflicts and peacebuilding. Ideally, multidirected partiality, which is so central to contextual therapy, should serve as a guideline to all people who are in charge of mediating discussions between the representatives of groups who are engaged in a peace or reconciliation process. However, the actual success of these negotiations depends on a multitude of factors that have little to do with what contextual therapy can offer.

Loyalty conflicts and invisible loyalties in clashes between family expectations and societal expectations

When adults who represent the authorities impose rules that contradict the parents' values and religion, the parents have little leverage to reach an agreement with these people, and it can place their children in a serious loyalty conflict. In some situations, the only way to express their loyalty to their parents is to reject the people and the society that impose these rules. It can happen when children are discouraged or prevented to use the language spoken by their parents, or when children are prevented to display physical evidence of their belonging to an ethnic or religious group. For instance, teachers in public school may have the task to prevent children from talking in their native tongue, not only in classes, but also with each other in the courtyard. This happens not only in many places in the world where there is discrimination against a minority, but also in countries that admit immigrants and refugees. In these countries, authorities may believe that the best way to promote the integration of children from immigrant families or refugee children is to put them in classes where they will immediately be forced to use the national language of the host country. Children who are forced to abandon the language of their family may feel disloyal to their parents even when the parents themselves may see some benefits in the acquisition of a new language or new habits.

Besides language, other things can become sources of loyalty conflicts. Public school in France prevents children from wearing any signs of religion: no visible cross, no kippa, no headscarf. Also, many schools, not only in France, may not offer food choices to their students. They may be forced to eat food that is not allowed by their religion or else skip meals with the risk of being scolded by the school personnel. Some parents are able to send their children to private schools that accommodate their religious requirements, but most people cannot. In all these cases, children who are prevented to express their loyalty to their families by abiding by their customs may express it indirectly by not responding to the expectations of adults outside of their families. Young children may refuse to talk to people outside of their family and may be diagnosed with elective mutism. Some older children may refuse to pay attention to their teachers as a form of invisible loyalty to their parents. Consequently, they may get a diagnosis of learning disabilities. Teens not only may feel disloyal to their family, but also often experience some degree of discrimination at school and some degree of rejection by society, and because of these injustices, they may accumulate destructive entitlement. Consequently, they may become disruptive in class and aggressive toward their peers and teachers. They may also skip school. In short, they may present with behaviors that meet the criteria for a conduct disorder.

Here, professionals who are informed by contextual therapy are better prepared to deal with situations in which youths present with symptoms that can be related to these kinds of loyalty conflicts. Also, these professionals can play a role in informing colleagues and people in authority about the detrimental consequences of avoidable loyalty conflicts. For instance, if they are members of a school board, they may be able to convince the other board members to introduce a greater variety of food choices in the school cafeteria. It may cost some extra money but may go a long way in improving the behaviors of children who were acting out because they felt discriminated against. This would save the school money since there would be less need for the intervention of school personnel, including school psychologists.

Unfortunately, it is much harder to convince governments about the detrimental effects of general policies that can generate serious loyalty conflicts. For instance, in France and some other parts of Europe, women are not allowed to wear a headscarf when they work for the government in any capacity, for instance as teachers. When the parents are victims of discriminations and other kinds of social injustices, they too may express their loyalty to their ethnic and religious groups by rejecting the values of the society that imposes these rules. They may isolate themselves from the surrounding society and adopt more fundamental and rigid forms of religious practices. Instead of promoting integration, these kinds of bans can even push some people toward actual radicalization, especially youths who experience discrimination at school and in addition see their parents experiencing discrimination at work.

A significant number of youths who present with a conduct disorder that is often triggered by an exposure to repeated injustices end up engaging first in antisocial actions and later in criminal activities that can bring them to jail. It is well-known, in France especially, that many of the people who got radicalized and later joined terrorist organizations like ISIS got radicalized under the influence of other inmates. Hence, one of the forms of prevention of this type of radicalization could come from contextual therapy and from intervening soon enough to help the youths who present with a conduct disorder to rediscover the benefits of giving and caring about others before they engage in not just antisocial activities but true criminal actions. Also, often young people who feel that their family and their religion and culture are under attack can become an easy prey for recruitment by terrorist organizations like ISIS and join the Jihad against the whole society that they perceive as rejecting them.

From the point of view of contextual therapy, the best way to promote the integration of ethnic and religious minorities or the integration of new immigrants is to allow them to express their loyalty to these groups positively and constructively. This would prevent them from the need of expressing their loyalty indirectly by rejecting the rules and values of the dominant group or the host country. This can also be a first step in preventing actual terrorism.

Group loyalties and intergroup solidarity: 'Us versus them' or 'all of us'?

One of the first questions that is asked in discussing the issue of group loyalty and intergroup solidarity is the following: if indeed loyalty entails a selective/discriminatory element and behooves us to give priority to the interest of our families and the groups to which we belong before the interests of any other groups, is there still a space for intergroup solidarity, or does loyalty push us to automatically to a 'us versus them attitude'? The answer may be that, in fact, our ability to be loyal to our groups may open the door to intergroup solidarity.

Globalization and its rapid acceleration have made us aware of how great our interdependence with others is. Any event can quicky affect the entire world. We already know about the worldwide spread of the Covid-19 pandemic and its dreadful consequences for millions of people all around the world. More recently, the Russian attack on Ukraine not only led to devastating consequences for its inhabitants but also affected the entire world in terms of political and economic changes, including an increased risk of famine in certain parts of the world. A trivial incident like the drifting of a container ship in the Suez Canal in 2021 led to a temporary disruption of supplies all around the world. All of this should be enough to convince us of our interdependence on a global level. This should lead us to show solidarity with the people who suffer most from these situations and hope to escape them by trying to migrate to more secure or more affluent countries.

However, we also know that globalization has resulted in an increase of xenophobia and insularism. One of the problems is that we believe that globalization threatens our individual, group, and national identities. As we already know, one way to maintain the homeostasis of the group we belong to is to rally against common enemies or to create a barrier between our group and all the groups that could threaten its integrity by adopting an 'us versus them' attitude. Both solutions to maintain our group identity then become a very serious obstacle to intergroup solidarity. However, group loyalty can also become a resource. If we find a way to express our group or national loyalty directly and constructively, this loyalty will contribute to the group's stability. Consequently, the group will be less threatened, and the group members will become freer to express solidarity with outsiders without feeling disloyal to their own ethnic group or national group. For instance, the joint pride in the achievements of a national team during international competitions like the Olympic Games or the Soccer World Cup can serve as a cement for group or national identity. The same would be true of a successful launch of a rocket on the moon or on Mars. Individuals can also contribute to their ethnic, religious or national group pride through a variety of achievements. In short, there are many ways in which benign expressions of loyalty can serve to reinforce the stability of ethnic, religious and national groups, which can greatly decrease the risk that these groups try to maintain their integrity through violent confrontations with other ethnic groups or nations. This means that while there is no quick move from a 'us versus them' to a 'all of us human beings' attitude, surprisingly, group and national loyalty expressed in a direct and constructive way can bring up closer to that.

Chapter 13

The Theory of Change in Contextual Therapy: Treatment Goals and Strategies

Obviously, a complete presentation of contextual therapy should include a presentation of the strategies used by contextual therapists and a description of the therapeutic process that is involved in this approach. In many ways, this has already been achieved through the many examples that have been given throughout this section in connection with specific themes, for instance destructive entitlement and parentification, or in the discussion of family and group loyalties. Also, many issues concerning the evaluation, role, and activities of the therapist have already been covered. The same is true of the issue of the integration of various therapeutic modalities with the practice of contextual therapy. Furthermore, the description of the process involved in contextually inspired pastoral care is one of the central themes of Section II of this book. However, this does not mean that this is entirely sufficient. A discussion of the theory of change proposed in the approach and a discussion of research and teaching need to be added. Beginning with the issue of research is one of the ways to approach these subjects.

Two of the biggest issues faced by contemporary contextual therapists are the issue of research and the issue of standardization of the approach. For several reasons, formal outcome research in contextual therapy has lagged far behind the research done in many other schools of family therapy. Fortunately, this is changing, thanks to the efforts of a younger generation of contextual therapists and other professionals who are interested in the approach. A good example of this new research is the research done by Gangamma, Bartle-Haring, Holowacz, Hartwell and Glebova (2015) on relational ethics, depressive symptoms and relational satisfaction in couples.

One of the big requirements in any kind of outcome research in couple and family therapy is that the subjects of any research need to be comparable and that the interventions to address the symptoms or the problems that these subjects present are consistent. The first requirement, the comparability between the subjects, is very difficult to meet since couples and families may seek treatment for a similar problem but the variables in each of these couples and families are so numerous that it becomes difficult to ascertain if they are indeed comparable as subjects of a research. Also, it is difficult to ascertain that the interventions used to help them are comparable and consistent with stated treatment goals. Also, these goals need to be set consistently. This requires the establishment of a treatment protocol that all the therapists involved in the outcome research should follow. To achieve this, there is a movement to manualize couple and family therapy approaches, meaning to create manuals that could be followed by the practitioners of the given approach. However, is it possible to manualize contextual therapy or not, and if yes, what would a model of contextual therapy look like?

Can contextual therapy be standardized?

To answer this question, Van der Meiden (2019) proceeded to analyze video-tape sessions of Boszormenyi-Nagy's consultations with families using an encoding system to categorize his interventions. Here, it is important to be attentive to a specific element of this analysis: it pertains to Boszormenyi-Nagy's demonstration interviews that he led during his teaching activities, not to actual treatment sessions in his private practice. He also analyzed the results of the responses of a series of practicing contextual therapists who were asked to describe their own way of working.

Based on all the information that he gathered from this extensive research, Van der Meiden proposes a model for contextual therapy that focuses on "strengthening or restoring past, current, and future connectedness". His model includes three phases: an exploration phase, a modifying, and a reinforcing of connectedness in close relationships. He describes the goals that therapists need to accomplish in each of these phases. He also offers a list of core interventions and goals pertaining to each of these phases. This model can serve as a useful guideline for beginner therapists, and it also provides a useful blueprint for a discussion among all the contextual therapists who are interested in developing models for the approach. Here it is important to mention the work of Heyndrickx (2016), who has been interested in this issue for a long time and agrees about the need of some standardization in the practice of contextual therapy. At the same time, he proposes that he would not like to see such models used much beyond a use as training tools (Heyndrickx, De Loof, Knip, Van Herck & Van Klaveren, 2022).

Now, how should the efforts of all these contextual therapists be reconciled with the statement that Boszormenyi-Nagy made years ago in Holland: "I do not have a theory"? Hanneke Meulink-Korf, who was present at the time, reports that this statement stirred a strong reaction in the audience: "You do have a theory. How can you say that you do not have one"? She also reminds us of Martin Buber's statement: "I have no doctrine. I only point out something... I take him who listens to me at his hand and lead him to the window. I push open the window and point outside. I have no doctrine; I carry on a dialogue" (Buber, 1965, transl. in M. Friedman, 1996). Here, Buber's view is very consistent with Boszormenyi-Nagy's view on his approach. He believes that his approach should serve as a source of inspiration to therapists and other professionals, and that he did not expect professionals who were attending his teachings to suddenly adopt contextual therapy as a theory and a fixed model for their own interventions. He believed that what he was presenting should not be taken as directives but as a source of inspiration. He was not interested in coming up with a simple theory and a simple method of intervention. What he strived for was to address the complexity of human relationships for which he proposed a multidimensional model. He also strived to define what the therapeutic moment in contextual therapy was. He concluded that it is the moment in a relationship when one person makes a gesture toward the other that leads to a double gain, an indirect gain for the giver and a direct gain for the beneficiary of this gesture. At the same time, he did not see this as a theory but as an empirical finding. Only then, reaching this therapeutic moment became a central goal in his approach.

Contextual therapy: A dialogue of giving and receiving

There is one possible way to reconcile Boszormenyi-Nagy's statement that he has no theory with the idea of a model for contextual therapy that would define the restoration of connectedness as a central goal of this approach. This is possible if going back to the notion of the dialogue that is so central in Buber's work and in the writings of the many contextual therapists who see 'rejunction' as a central goal in contextual therapy. What they mean by this term it that this dialogue should be understood as a dialogue that restores connectedness in families and close relationships. However, it can also be understood as a dialogue that is in line with the definition of the therapeutic moment in contextual therapy: a dialogue of giving and receiving. To return to the example of the mother who agreed to write to the judge about renouncing her rights to visit her son after he had told her that it was too difficult for him to have any contact with her, one can see that both gained from her gesture. Her willingness to consider her son's needs for the first time became a source of constructive entitlement for her, and her gesture was a real gift to her son. However, clearly, this therapeutic moment was not meant to reinforce their connectedness, since the mother's willingness to consider her son's needs effectively ended their relationship.

The restoration of the dialogue understood as a dialogue of giving and receiving should take a central place in the work of contextual therapists and other professionals who are working with people who have been the victims of severe injustices. It can be the individual situational injustices that come from suffering from a severe mental illness, the situational injustices inflicted on families who were the victims of poverty, discrimination, or other adverse life circumstances, and, in connection with all these injustices, the relational injustices caused by parentification that has its own multigenerational consequences. As we know, all these situational and relational injustices can become sources of destructive entitlement, which has detrimental consequences in close relationships, especially in the parent-child relationship. In ordinary situations, giving flows from the generation of the parents to the generation of the children, even if children are happy to do things for their parents, of course. However, in parentification, the flow is reversed: giving flows from the children to the parents. Hence, one of the central goals of therapy is to return the flow of giving and receiving between the generations to its normal course by helping parents to discover that they can gain from showing generosity to their children when they refrain from trying to get what they did not receive from the past generations.

A theory of change: The therapeutic moment as a moment of bifurcation

We have already seen that the therapeutic moment is a moment of double benefit for the giver and the receiver, but how does this connect to a theory of change? In the classical systemic model, the notion of circularity and negative feedback explains why it is very difficult for families to change. For instance, in a family, giving by one person may trigger a counterreaction in the other, a refusal to receive. From a systemic point of view, this reaction would be understood as negative feedback, a reaction that could prevent real changes in the family relationships. This can also happen during couple therapy when one of the partners tries to show generosity to the other and the other refuses to acknowledge it. Here, each school of couple or family therapy has its own view of what could bring actual lasting desirable changes in relationships. Important in contextual therapy is that the action of giving is an act that has consequences in the dimension of relational ethics, not only in the systemic dimension. Through the act of giving, the giver earns constructive entitlement, and this indirect return does not depend on the response of the one toward whom this act is directed. Also, it will not diminish the credit of the giver. Whether or not the beneficiary of the gesture accepts it, the giver is still able to experience an increase in self-worth and an increase in inner freedom that can lead the giver to new actions and to changes in family relationships that are not affected by the possible negative reaction of the receiver. Furthermore, if the dismissive beneficiary of the gesture can be helped to recognize at least some goodwill in the attitude of the giver, this person will also begin to earn constructive entitlement, and this in turn can become a source of changes in relationships.

It is very important to note that when people have accumulated much destructive entitlement, it becomes difficult for them to accept to receive from others or to recognize their contributions. This is true not only in families and close relationships, but also in society in general. This may sound strange. In general, people should be happy to receive from others, and their destructive entitlement should decrease if they become the beneficiaries of a generous gesture or if they receive acknowledgment for past injustices. However, there is some logic to their attitude. Often people who have been wronged have lost trust in others and they are never sure that people are truly motivated to help them. Hence, to them, it may appear safer to refuse to receive and keep their claim for redress open than to recognize the goodwill of others. For these reasons, the professional needs to be ready to show partiality to the family members who are not able to recognize the contribution of others by acknowledging their predicament and see then if this helps them to take the risk to accept receiving.

In the process of therapy, the moment in a session in which someone chooses to give rather than take can be seen as a bifurcation, a model of change that is associated with the work of M. Elkaïm (1985). To explain this idea simply, one can choose the image of a bifurcation on a road. The person who gives chooses to engage in one road instead of the other, and after the bifurcation, the landscape changes. The beneficiary, too, needs to decide which road to take, the road of accepting to receive or the road of refusing to do so. In short, no matter what option people choose, in the dimension of relational ethics, there are no feedback mechanisms, only feed forward ones, changes that lead to new changes.

This model of change from bifurcation to bifurcation requires great attention on the part of the therapist. The moments of choice come and go very fast in treatment sessions and in life. Here, it is very important to note that in many cases, therapeutic moments can occur outside of the therapy room, outside of the counseling session. In many instances, professionals who meet families around a concrete situation may find more options to elicit such a moment than the therapist or the counselor in the therapy room. Here is the example of a social worker who needed to talk to a parent who was always late to pick up a child who was attending an afterschool program. The child was getting angry for always arriving late at home, and not having time to play with her friend. When the parent was asked about this lateness, the answer was: "Well this is the best I can do." This could be the end of the conversation, but the social worker could ask: "If I could help you to find other ways of getting to the center and arrive sooner, would you accept my help?" This would then place this parent in front of an option: accepting this help, which would be also giving to the child, or refusing it. And, even if the parent refuses this help, the question brings a change. The parent has to return home knowing that not only he or she has not met the child's need but in addition refused help to do so. This can work in the parent as a sense of discomfort that could result in a change of mind about this help.

So, one of the first task of the contextual therapist or the contextually oriented professional is to help people slow down so that they can consider the consequences of their response before they act, like the driver who needs to slow down to avoid missing an intersection. And if they miss one bifurcation, they still have the option to take the road of giving at the next intersection. In couple therapy, one partner can respond very quicky to the other: "Why should I do this for you?" and move on to the next phrase. The therapist can come back to this statement even in the next session, for instance by asking: "I remember that in the last session, you said that you did not know why you should do what you partner had asked for. What would be needed for you to think differently?" and then go from there into helping both partners to re-engage in a dialogue about what they expect and what they are willing or not to do for the other.

Contextual therapists, especially beginners, wonder about what questions they could ask to bring people to engage in a discussion of matters that are relevant for the dimension of relational ethics, for instance, a discussion of giving and receiving, a discussion of family loyalties, a discussion of parentification, a talk about giving and receiving between themselves or between the generations. As already discussed, Michard (2017) provides useful lists of questions, but one problem is that these questions can easily detract therapists from listening to what people bring spontaneously to the sessions. It is rare that people do not talk about what is relevant in the dimension of relational ethics already very early in a session. Another problem is that many therapists tend to return to questions that connect much more to the dimension of psychology than to the dimension of relational ethics. Here is a small example in the treatment of a family that was seen because the younger son, Bobby, was aggressive and disruptive at school and at home. One complaint was that he kept disturbing his older brother, John, by keeping opening and closing the door of his room. The family therapist asked Bobby: "What do have to say about your brother's complaint?" Bobby answered: "I know it is not right because he always helps me to do my own homework." Bobby simply could have answered: "I know it is not right." What he added had to do with fairness. However, the therapist overlooked this and simply asked him: "What do you think makes you do that?" This is a perfectly acceptable question, but from the point of view of contextual therapy, it is a question that opened a door into the dimension of psychology, not into the dimension of relational ethics. A more productive question to follow up on Bobby's statement would have been to ask him: "It seems that you are saying that that you are unfair to you brother, have you ever told him that you appreciate his help?" Then the therapist could have turned to the parents and to John and asked: "Did you know that Bobby cares about fairness?"

Learning to recognize these moments and learning to intervene to take advantage of them requires much training and practice. One way for practitioners to improve their skills in this area is to watch videotapes of past sessions and to try to look for these moments on the tape, and then think about what could have been said to take advantage of them. As already discussed, it is always possible to come back to a past session with clients. It shows them not only that the therapist takes his or her work very seriously, but also that one can always return to something that was missed. This leads to another method, which is to ask the clients about the prior session: did they feel that there is something they would have liked to add, something that they regretted to have said? Did they sleep well after the last meeting, or did they toss and turn in their beds, worrying about what they had said? This question is also important to assess if the sessions triggered guilt about disloyalty or not.

The genogram as a tool to explore the sources of injustices

We have already seen that destructive entitlement is one of the main obstacles that prevent people from finding the freedom to engage in a dialogue of giving and receiving and that one of the sources of their destructive entitlement often lies in parentification, a result of the destructive entitlement of their own parents. We also know that when clients can realize that their parents too were seeking redress for past injustices, and not simply acting out of callousness, they will be more likely to be able to enter the process of exoneration that has been described in detail earlier. Hence, therapists want to help their clients to learn about their parents' history, the history of their family of origin, and about all possible injustices that could have been at the source of their parents' destructive entitlement. To reach this goal, therapists may ask their clients to try to obtain as much information as possible from their family members or other people about the illnesses, losses, life-changing events, and socio-historical circumstances that may have affected their family.

Contextual therapists, like the vast majority of couple and family therapists, use genograms as a tool for recording information about families. The genogram is a graphic representation of a family, which has analogy with a family tree, except that in the family tree the ancestors who are at the source of the family are drawn first and all their descendants with the various branches of the family are drawn above them. Although there are many ways to draw a genogram, in most cases, the therapists start with the person or the family members who seek help, placing the members from the past generation above them, and their children below them. Some professionals draw this genogram as part of their treatment notes. Other professionals ask their clients to participate in the establishment of this genogram, which is drawn in such a way that everyone can see it. Then, they use it to engage the family members in a discussion of their family relationships. Readers who are not familiar with the establishment of genograms can be referred to the work of McGoldrick and her colleagues (see McGoldrick, Gerson & Petry, 2020). In standard genograms, lines are used to represent the type of relationships family members have with each other. For instance, broken lines to indicate relational conflicts or double lines to indicate enmeshment and these genograms are often used to evidence of patterns of interactions that have been repeated over several generations and are believed to cause individual or relational pathologies.

Contextual therapists use the genogram to explore the dimension of relational ethics. They want to record who has been giving to whom, who has shown loyalty to whom, who has been the victim of an injustice and of what kind, for instance who has been parentified and by whom, etc. But the most important point is that contextual therapists do not use the genogram just to evidence relational problems like most therapists do, but they also use it to search for relational resources that may have been overlooked. As already discussed, they may use it to evidence the situational injustices that could have been at the source of relational injustices, something that can help in the process of exoneration. But they can also use it to help people realizing that even if they did not receive much from their parents, they may have received a lot from other people. This realization often brings them the strength to let go of some of their destructive claims to redress.

The five dimensions of the genogram and the five dimensions of relational reality

The effort to introduce a new method to establish a genogram came from trying to solve a problem encountered by all professionals: it is often hard to establish a genogram that includes all the family members of their clients and all the people who have played a significant role in the lives of their clients without ending with a rather confusing document. Here, the idea is to begin with a standard genogram drawn in a black pen that does not contain any of the lines used in standard genograms to represent relationships. This genogram should start with the generation of the parents, in some cases an anonymous donor or a surrogate mother and continues with the prior generations as much as possible to the generation of the great grandparents if not further when information is available. The next step is to add all the other people who have played a parental role in a given family, also with a black pen. Once this initial step has been completed, the professional who is in charge of the genogram session asks the person who presents his or her genogram to encircle the people who are identified as parental figures using five specific colors, one for each of the five dimensions of relational reality. The relevant colored pens are passed one at a time to the person who presents, and the person is asked to make sure not to have forgotten anyone before moving to the next dimension. The color blue represents Dimension I and is used to encircle the biological parents. The color red represents Dimension II, the dimension of psychology and is used to encircle people who are figures of attachment and who have been internalized as parental figures. The color brown represents Dimension III, the dimension of transaction and is used to represent people who have exerted parental authority. The color green represents Dimension IV, the dimension of relational ethics, and is used to represent people who have been committed to offer their care. The color violet represents Dimension V, the ontic dimension, and is used to represent people who have been fundamental as a source of Self-Other delineation.

This multidimensional genogram is also very useful to visualize people with regard to the five dimensions of loyalties: who are the people toward whom these clients are loyal because of blood ties; the people toward whom they are loyal because they are attachment figures; the people who are using their power to demand their loyalty; the people who truly deserve their loyalty as an expression of gratitude for their commitment and care; the people whom they need as source of Self-Other delineation? The use of these colors can also help to evidence what are the determinants of loyalties in situations of loyalty conflicts, split loyalties or invisible loyalties.

When people have been raised entirely by their own biological parents and when these parents have been reliable as providers of affection, structure and care, these two parents will most likely be encircled in all the five colors since they have functioned as parents in all the dimensions, i.e. as biological parents, figures of attachment, figures of authority, responsible and committed caregivers, and as a special source of Self-Other delineation. To that extent, the addition of these colors may not add much to the original standard genogram. This changes when the biological parents have not exerted all these functions, and when some of these functions were exerted by other people. The person who has been adopted will have to add the adoptive parents to the genogram. They will not be encircled with the color blue that is reserved to the biological parents. However, since they are most likely figures of attachment, figures of authority, responsible caregivers, and an important source of Self-Other delineation, they will need to be encircled with all the other colors. Besides being encircled with blue for biological ties, the biological parents will also be encircled with violet since they remain a special source of Self-Other delineation.

A very important point is that it is the person who works on his or her genogram who decides whom to encircle, what color to use for whom, not the professional who is leading the genogram session. People should be allowed to use their own imagination. For instance, people may want to use a broken green line to encircle a biological parent who has always been in their lives but not as a fully reliable parent. Some people choose to add the pet that plays a crucial role in their lives. Some people have encircled the drawing of a Bible or a Quran in violet, the color of the ontic dimension, to signify that for them God or Allah is the main source of Self-Other delineation. One person even drew the word God and encircled it with all the five colors, which makes perfect sense if someone sees God as the source of everything. At the end of their presentation, they should be asked to reflect on the changes that the use of these colors have brought to their understanding of their past and present relationships. They should also be asked to reflect on the possible impact of these changes on the next generations.

In many instances, this special genogram can be very useful to help people remember the many people who may have contributed to their lives as parental figures besides their biological parents. They can be forgotten easily. It can be a nanny, or a devoted teacher, a guardian who assumed the parental authority, or even peers who were available to offer support when the parents were not available. All should be drawn into the genogram and encircled with the color corresponding to the dimension in which they played a role.

As already discussed in the prologue, since 2010 this genogram has been a didactical tool to help professionals to get familiar with the five dimensions of relational reality and the five dimensions of loyalties. By now, some two or three hundred professionals in Europe have had the occasion to build their own genograms in this fashion. At the end of these seminars, the vast majority of the participants expressed that this new approach to the genogram had been very helpful to them at a personal level. But it is difficult to estimate how many of them have then used it in their practice. By now, several therapists have reported that they have used it as a tool in individual therapy and some have used it in couple therapy, but most are still hesitant to use it in family therapy. One of the fears is that the presence of family members would restrain the freedom of people to use or not use the colors as they see fit. For instance, someone may choose to refrain from encircling a parent in green, the color of relational ethics if this parent had been neglectful. But if this parent is present during the genogram session, this person may be pushed to encircle this parent in green anyway to avoid an argument. For the therapist, the best way to overcome these kinds of obstacles is to use multidirected partiality as a tool to help the family members to begin a dialogue around the use of these colors.

In short, this five-dimensional genogram offers therapeutic resources that are not found in other forms of genogram. The hope is that the professionals, including pastoral caregivers and counselors, who have had a didactical experience of this genogram will now start to use it in their practice and will publish treatment outcomes that are based on its use.

Session timing and termination of treatment

In all forms of therapy and counseling, professionals and clients need to come to an agreement on who will be involved in the sessions, at what frequency they will occur, and what criteria will be used to set the time of termination. This is true for contextual therapists and pastoral counselors. Here we shall discuss situations in which people engage in contextual therapy without the addition of any other treatment modalities by the therapist. However, still each situation may need some adjustment to the guidelines that are proposed here.

Contextual therapists should strive to include as many family members as possible in their sessions, at least at the beginning of therapy. At the same time, contextual therapists should not refuse to meet a family if one of the members who was listed to attend the session is missing. As we know, contextual therapists intend to offer their partiality to people who are affected by their interventions, whether they are present or not. Regarding the interval between sessions, the idea is that they must be frequent enough to avoid spending half of the time of a new session reviewing all that has happened after the last one. This is best achieved with weekly or bi-weekly sessions that should be scheduled, if possible, at a same convenient time of the week over time so that one does not need to come back to the issue of scheduling at the end of each session. Usually, the sessions are set to last an hour, and the therapist needs to make sure that people do not run over the time agreed upon. Offering longer sessions appears helpful when working with large families, but the risk is that both the family members and the therapist lose their focus. Therefore, it is better to see these sessions as part of a process that continues from session to session, not as single units that need to have their own finished course. Clients should be told that they are entirely free to decide to stop therapy at any time, but it would be best to address the issue of termination during a treatment session, since the family members may have different views and needs, some being ready to stop therapy, some not. At the beginning of therapy, the therapist needs to use multidirected partiality to help family members to come to an agreement about treatment goals. At the end of therapy, the same multidirected partiality is needed to help people to come to an agreement about termination. For the contextual therapists, the criteria for termination are the same as the ones used in other forms of therapy: a decrease in individual symptoms, a decrease in individual suffering, and an improvement in relationships. However, in contextual therapy, one of the most relevant criteria for termination is the increased ability of the family members to engage in a fair dialogue with one another without the help of the therapist. Experience has shown that families who have made excellent progress in this regard can still experience problems when they meet new life challenges. For this reason, at the time of termination, therapists should offer their clients the resource of returning for further sessions later if necessary.

Concluding messages

As a conclusion to this section, the message is that the most central goal of contextual therapy remains the restoration of the proper direction of the flow of giving between the generations, meaning restoring the ability of the generation of the parents to give to the generation of the children. When this is not possible, contextual therapists need to see what can still be done to protect the younger generations from unfair burdens. In short, prevention should be the true goal of any contextual therapist.

SECTION II

THE CONTEXTUAL APPROACH IN THE PASTORAL PROCESS AND INTERCULTURAL ENCOUNTERS

HANNEKE MEULINK-KORF & GRETEKE DE VRIES

Prologue to Section II

Inspiration from contextual therapy and theory has become widespread in the fields of social work, youth care, and education, among others. It has also become significant for the two interrelated areas highlighted in this section of the book, namely that of pastoral work and practical theology and that of interreligious studies and intercultural encounters. Its inspiration contributes to the challenges met by chaplains, congregational leaders, and spiritual directors. A fairly recent practice is being developed in service of multireligious and multicultural settings with its scope on 'fair bridging'. The interpretation and reinterpretation of contextual theory and therapy for the pastoral field and practical theology (see Van Rhijn & Meulink-Korf, 2019) has a decades-long history of interdisciplinary engagement in line with the long-developed integrative framework of Boszormenyi-Nagy. In both areas, the contextual approach opens up insights for intra- and interdisciplinary practice theory, practices, and transdisciplinary research (see also Thesnaar, 2022).

The clustering of relational variables in five dimensions, presented in detail in Section I, provides pastors, spiritual counselors, and leaders in pluralistic networks with a strong framework for dealing extensively with the complex relational issues they encounter in their work in diverse settings. At least, this is the experience on which we base our confidence.

In Section II, the focus of our approach is the dimension of relational ethics, or: ethics of caring. We must be aware of the risk of confusing relational ethics with value or virtue ethics based on religion or culture. Although the next chapters deal with religion, spirituality, and culture, the main focus of relational ethics lies in what we believe are universal features in unique human encounters.

We hope that this second section can speak not only to contextual therapists and other practitioners who are involved in religion and spirituality but also to professionals who are not familiar with these areas or who are even very hesitant to consider the religious and spiritual dimension as a potential resource in their clients' lives and in their work.

PART 1

Hanneke Meulink-Korf

Chapter 1
Contextual Pastoral Care and Counseling (CPCC) and the Dialogical Intergenerational Pastoral Process (DIPP)

Introduction

Personal experiences may lead to acknowledging the importance of the contextual approach. I want to begin this part on a personal note.

When I was 17 years old, I lost my mother, who suddenly died of cardiac arrest. It was shortly before my final exams. The minister of the church that I attended, who had led the funeral service of my mother, took me out for an afternoon in the woods and for tea in a nice restaurant. She did not question my feelings about my mother, nor did she mention God. In a kind way, she made small talk. She respected my needs for remote sympathy, and she respected my loyalty to my mother by not showing any mother-like concern. Some weeks later she invited me to her office, and we had a good conversation about my fragile faith in a merciful God and my concerns for my younger sisters and my father. I could tell her about my hesitations to leave home and my family to go to university. The fact that I chose to study theology is absolutely connected to these precious meetings.

Were these conversations a form of pastoral care? Yes, they were. I shall explain why. However, first: often, this adjective 'pastoral' to 'care' is interchangeable with 'religious' or 'spiritual', but not always. Later in this chapter, I shall comment on the origins and the scope of the word 'pastoral', referring to the work of shepherds. Nowadays, in practical theology, one speaks of 'pastoral care-and-counseling', a combination of terms that refers to a plurality of practices and, metaphorically speaking, not only to keeping sheep to the flock, and protecting their souls.

Even more than in psychotherapy, there is not one particular spiritual or religious domain or application that represents all pastoral or spiritual practices. To be sure, there is not a standard procedure for pastoral or spiritual care and counseling that fits all situations that spiritual counselors, congregational leaders, or institutional chaplains are dealing with. Therefore, I will only give suggestions and recommendations that the readers themselves may add to their practices.

The term 'pastoral care and counseling' is a complex one. Pastoral and spiritual *care* extends to several professional services and not only to leading faith communities. This care is also about assisting individuals to express their spiritual needs, to find their religious orientation, or to reflect on their existential questions about life and death. It covers praying, singing, and reading texts. It involves giving consultations about personal issues and advice about moral choices. It refers to comforting, offering a shoulder to lean on, showing compassion, encouraging, perhaps criticizing, and just being present, being a witness. Special rituals and their preparations are also part of pastoral or spiritual care, for instance performing a wedding ceremony or a funeral. Frequently other rituals are assisting to rejoice in the birth of a child, accept a new member into a community, and guide a dying person, family, and friends to say farewell.

Pastoral or spiritual *counseling*, as a collaborative effort to help people navigate life's challenges, is specifically mentioned in combination with pastoral *care*. The reason is that at the background of any pastoral or spiritual counseling, there is always some form of care for persons that is embedded in a world of wisdom related to traditions, communities, institutions perhaps, rituals, specific assignments, and special ministries.

In the meaningful informal pastoral meeting that occurred in my youth, the symbolic role of the minister was important to me, referring not only to my religious community as a social group that I belonged to, but also to its beliefs, so somehow to God and the Bible. The minister did not counsel me; she was just present, and her presence as a minister was all the pastoral care that I really needed in those days.

How did I go from this personal experience to developing contextual pastoral care? With a master's degree in theology, and with some experience as a social worker, I became a client-centered Rogerian psychotherapist. My training seemed broad. However, when I began to work with young single parents in residential care, I noticed how inadequate I was prepared. I shall explain this. Some of the clients in the residential home were pregnant because of abuse, many of them were neglected as children, and most came from socially disadvantaged backgrounds. The residential home presented itself as an opportunity for them to escape the circumstances in which they had grown up and to leave the people from their past behind. In the counseling sessions I offered, I often asked: what do you like to do with your life? Implicitly, I gave the message: I mean *you*, and not you in the context of your not-so-nice family of origin. This individualistic approach was a rather common practice in the sixties and seventies in the Netherlands. I lacked knowledge and awareness of the essential meaning of relationships. However, something happened that opened my eyes. It came out that some of our clients were visiting their families without mentioning these visits to us at all. Then we realized that our narrow-minded individualistic ideology was leading us astray. We had to help our clients *in* their family relationships, and not deny these or work against them. Our practices broadened and deepened when we learnt more about the approach of Boszormenyi-Nagy and were trained in contextual therapy.

A decade later, I changed jobs and became a university lecturer in Practical Theology. Together with my colleague Mr Aat van Rhijn (1930-2002), I was eager to study a possible interplay between contextual therapy and pastoral care and counseling. We learnt that the contextual multigenerational approach is aimed at understanding legacies, expectations, and motivations. The intention is not to blame ancestors for possible symptoms of their offspring. It rather draws attention to fairness and attends to justice and maybe even mercy. We also learnt about the inclusiveness of the attitude of multidirected partiality. All these notions and instruments are derived from observing people in their relationships, in real life. These are by no means idealistic standards.

This approach of human reality as relational indeed proved to be compatible with biblical notions. It also challenged new interpretations of wisdom traditions, and it still does. We found that it corresponds with some traditional dogmatics and rituals that are familiar in the toolkit of many pastoral counselors.

We studied the interplay between contextual theory and the dialogical philosophy of especially Martin Buber, as well as Emmanuel Levinas's 'philosophy of the Other'. We were aware that Ivan Boszormenyi-Nagy objected against being annexed by disciplines outside the field of mental health. He often emphasized: "I am not a philosopher, let alone a theologian." However, nevertheless, at many meetings he wondered about what we would find and write. This enterprise of transposing, adapting, and reinterpreting of the theory of contextual therapy on behalf of pastoral care and counseling is a continuation process. Each reader is invited to join in this process.

In the past decade, I got the opportunity to give some classes on contextual pastoral care at Stellenbosch University. There, I witnessed specific South African pastoral practices and theology being developed. Therefore, in this book, the reader will find some specific attention to South Africa. It is not self-evident that a theologian from the Global North is entitled to bring her experience and reflections to this other part of the world. The risk is indeed of being guilty of white arrogance or of cultural appropriation. Yet, I gave it a try, because C. Thesnaar, the author of the Foreword, leader of the program Dialogical Intergenerational Pastoral Process, invited me to contribute to this program.

Of course, this approach to pastoral care-and-counseling, just like contextual therapy, does not propose a context-free application for the whole world and for all circumstances. On the contrary, in relational contexts of specific persons and groups, in concrete acts of trust and fairness, the particulars must be sought and found. South African pastoral practitioners work with persons and communities deeply affected by various serious injustices, including the ongoing effects of apartheid. Their specific insights and their inspirations from African philosophies, some partly related to the contextual theory, are only modestly referred to in this text. However, their challenging views on transgenerational wisdom, social and relational justice, and an inclusive philosophy of life, are relevant to contextual practitioners elsewhere.

The reader will notice that this whole section is complex, as the texts are composed of more than one discipline and subdisciplines and of more sources of knowledge on relationships than those of the contextual approach. Next to and partly overlapping with the indispensable principles and the original conceptual framework of contextual therapy, there are here and there (including in South Africa) collected assumptions that influence my view of relationships and the aforementioned process of transposition on behalf of pastoral care and counseling. These play a role, sometimes in the background, in this part of this book. I mean assumptions like these: human life as given from beyond; autonomy through heteronomy; personal suffering because of the suffering of others; the other/Other as a disturbing countenance for genuine humane encounters; patience and perseverance as relevant for a pastoral relation with someone who suffers; asymmetry in reciprocity as prior to symmetry; responsibility and respond-ability.

Therefore, the following two chapters, especially this first one, are also dedicated to the influence of contextual theory on an inclusive anthropological theological thinking, to broaden the framework of pastoral, religious and interreligious practices.

The scope of practice and reflection by congregational leaders, pastoral counselors, chaplains, and spiritual healers extends well beyond the scope of common therapeutic counseling practices, in particular when the presence of God or of any transcending 'being' is evoked. There is a kind of 'beyond and above' present in all pastoral care and counseling. I sometimes refer to the notion '*coram Deo*'. I do not search for the presence of God in an explicit manner in this text.

Since most of my personal experiences relate to Christian theology, I cannot avoid or hide that in my writings. Nevertheless, I hope to inspire and inform the work of pastoral and spiritual practitioners of any faith tradition, as well as that of those who adhere to a secular philosophy. I am sure we can all learn from each other's ways and ideas about fair connecting, both by listening and speaking.

A contextual intergenerational approach for pastoral care and theology

Pastoral practice and practitioners, in short

For many therapists and other professionals in psychosocial health care, the concept of pastoral care may refer to a rather vague domain. For them, religion has become suspect, or at least irrelevant. Keep in mind that this text is not a defense of religious doctrines or spiritual ideals. It is intended to elicit an exchange of experiences with a theory open to dialogue.

This will be obvious: pastoral care and counseling is different from therapy. What does it provide? It may involve counseling an individual, a couple, or a family, including the young, adults, and senior citizens. It may be a telephone counseling service, or counseling via video conference or e-mail. Often, it includes visiting sick persons, prisoners, and displaced persons. Often, it provides guidance to theme-centered peer groups, for example on mourning after the loss of a loved one, loss of work or health, on divorce, on raising young children, on sexual behavior, on living in a residential home, on the personal and relational effect of migration. It may also involve the prevention of estrangement between family members, or the reconstruction of their connection. It may offer support and inspiration from sources like rituals, sermons, religious texts, and other narratives. It can also provide support during challenging times as well as during joyful celebrations. In principle, this type of caregiving addresses the whole path of life of an individual in his or her unique relational reality. It is not appropriate to set a standard for how long a pastoral practitioner stays involved with a particular person or family. Each pastoral process is unique and is never a standard procedure.

It is always a complex challenge, presumably for all pastoral practitioners, to align the pastoral care they may provide with the requirements of the present human world, combined with an awareness of a trans-psychological realm of 'beyond' or '*coram Deo*', with consideration of the consequences of their interventions for future people, guarding their professional and personal legacies. However, this task is not without limits. There are limits that are set by the client or parishioner who, for example, leaves the community after some time or ends the pastoral relationship for another reason. The limits also have to do with the practitioner's own situation, regarding his or her professional skills and responsibility for self-care including care for the relations with family and friends. As part of the professionalism, a practitioner needs to be aware of the possible destructive consequences of transference and countertransference and of the possibility of being parentified in a pastoral relationship. Pastoral care often extends to a person who lives or works in the same community, mental institution, or care facility as the professional with whom they also share a common belief. These and many other pastoral situations require special awareness and fitting tools. We also need to consider the plurality of the background of pastoral practitioners and of their clients. In all these cases, the theory of contextual therapy can be surprisingly helpful.

A professional pastoral practitioner often is a theologian with an academic education, especially an education in Practical Theology, who in most cases has received a mission by a church official of a religious institution. He or she may be an academic in humanistic studies. In some cases, pastoral practitioners prefer to function without a specific mission and work with an agreement on the basis of appropriate education in combination with professional experience.

'Pastoral' and a definition of pastoral care

For the professional most frequently discussed in this part, we shall use the terms chaplain, minister, congregational leader, pastor, or pastoral counselor alternatively. For practical and situational reasons, these terms will also often be replaced by 'pastoral practitioner'. We also use several terms for the person to whom this care is provided: parishioner, member of the congregation, client, and sometimes a more extensive description.

Why the term *pastoral*? Using the metaphor of a shepherd ('pastor') when we refer to religious and spiritual practices as well as practitioners, we are in line with several religious traditions. The term may sound old-fashioned and even patronizing; however, for Jews and Christians, the term 'pastoral' bears biblical connotations, for instance with Psalm 23, "The Lord is my shepherd" or with the parable of the good shepherd from the Gospel of John (John 10). We also find a parable of a shepherd in the Quran, calling to someone who must listen to the message instead of only hearing a scream (Surah Al Baqarah 2).[1] Nowadays, 'Pastoral Counseling' is included in the curriculum of several Islamic studies. Some Buddhist meditation centers also offer 'Pastoral Care'. The same is true for the education of non-religious chaplaincy, with the term 'Humanist Pastoral Support'. Hindu pandits often use the term 'pastoral care' for the chaplaincy they provide in hospitals and detention centers. Thus, the origin of using the pastor metaphor lies in the Semitic world. Other traditions adapted and also use this term.

Many professionals use the term 'spiritual care'. In most models of 'spiritual care', attention is given to 'mystagogy', meaning the initiation of individuals into mystic beliefs, and the healing power of sacraments. Notwithstanding differences, there is an overlap in the meaning and understanding of pastoral care and spiritual care.

Regarding the definition of pastoral care, we adhere to many traditions when we follow this community-directed general definition:

> The personal, relational, social, and spiritual support that people give to each other in a religious community or an institution and to others outside this group (Lindijer, no date: 2).

In this description, a reciprocity of concern is seen as basis. The definition aims to include members with mental retardation, mental illness and/or physical limitations, and people from outside the community. Moreover, in this definition, no distinction is made between professionals and lay-persons. However, in this book, although we know how well many lay volunteers are involved as leaders or helpers in pastoral care and chaplaincy, we primarily focus on professionals.

In line with the above definition, we add some general comments:

- There has to be an orientation on the relational reality of a parishioner or client, in all her or his being, not only on a separate spiritual aspect.

---

[1] https://quranonline.net/al-baqarah

- The care and counseling should never reduce the responsibility of the parishioner or client, or in another way neglect this person's care and concern for other people.
- Each practitioner should take care of his or her personal relational resources in a dialogical mindset toward the own relatives of different generations.
- Each practitioner should guard or renew his or her personal spiritual wisdom by studying one's own holy scriptures or other sources of belief. Care for one's own sources of inspiration helps in 'not doing the job on the automatic pilot'.

Later in this chapter, we pay some attention to the plurality of 'schools' in this field, but for the sake of clarity, we now move to the origins of *contextual* pastoral care.

Some history: Theologians inspired by contextual therapy theory

After the USA, the Netherlands was the first country where 'family therapy' was introduced. In 1967, Ivan Boszormenyi-Nagy and some colleagues, David Rubinstein and Gerald Zuk, presented an extensive course in Leiden. They were invited by a national institute for mental health, on the intervention of one of the first Dutch family therapists, Ammy van Heusden. Then Boszormenyi-Nagy began to visit the Netherlands rather frequently, lecturing especially contextual therapy. These lectures brought new insights into approaching families. According to contextual therapy, it appeared that it is not so much the structural characteristics of a parent-child relationship (in terms of hierarchy, subsystem, coalitions) that determine personal mental health and family well-being. It is rather the trustworthiness that a parent demonstrates and his or her ability to exonerate others and to acknowledge the point of view of the child and the significant others even in the midst of a serious family conflict. Even in a family with an overburdened parent, it is still possible for this parent to demonstrate trustworthiness to her or his child(ren). The expectations of reciprocity and justice have to be addressed throughout the generations, including grandparents and other ancestry.

In the early lectures, many participants were personally touched and professionally influenced by this new approach, not in the least by the possibility of finding relational resources beyond pathology. After the Netherlands and Flanders, lectures and workshops followed in other West European countries (such as Switzerland, France, Norway). Boszormenyi-Nagy also worked with professionals from other disciplines and domains, including theologians.

Theologians were especially drawn to two interconnected topics: the possibility of an exchange of contextual theory with notions of Biblical theology, and the inspiration linked to Martin Buber's dialogical thinking that Boszormenyi-Nagy showed.

Here again, I make a personal remark. Since the time that I participated in workshops with Boszormenyi-Nagy and began to study his approach, I have been truly strengthened by the fruitfulness of an exchange between the contextual theory and biblical wisdom. The contextual approach helped me recognize biblical themes more than before as 'close to my skin', as truly, deeply human. And the other way around, my trust in a God who in the Bible is presented as righteous and merciful, helped me in my work as a counselor and therapist to look for openings to transformation, to renewing dialogue. Together, these inspirations helped me move away from a slightly cynical powerless stance or indifference or total despair about relational entanglements. It opened my eyes to 'hope without illusions' (see Van Rhijn, 1992, passim). I learnt to view justice as an orientation for a fair dialogical process and not as a fixed obtainable goal.

Many theologians recognized the influence of Martin Buber with enthusiasm. Buber's dialogical thinking had strengthened the work of Boszormenyi-Nagy that was already a dialectical way of thinking itself. Boszormenyi-Nagy's attention to dialectics in reciprocity merged with a dialogical approach. For example, one may regard the giving of a person to another as receiving, too, and his or her receiving from another may be regarded as giving.

So, the study by Boszormenyi-Nagy, a psychiatrist and family therapist, of Buber's *I and Thou* (1923, in: Buber, 1947, 2002), of Buber's lecture *Guilt and guilt feelings* (1957, in: Buber, 1998) and of the short text *Healing through meeting* (1951, in: Buber, 1967), was exciting for theologians. Boszormenyi-Nagy's 'application' of these texts provided many practical incentives. Theoretically, it provided the impetus for philosophical and theological investigations. The work of Maurice Friedman (1921-2012), a world-famous expert on Buber's work and a friend of Boszormenyi-Nagy and Krasner, helped in establishing the connection with dialogical philosophy (Friedman, 1992). Although Boszormenyi-Nagy never studied the position of Emmanuel Levinas, Levinas' attention to responsibility for the Other and to a radical asymmetry between the one and the other person, became a source for further reflections on Boszormenyi-Nagy's thinking (Van Rhijn & Meulink-Korf, 2019).

Organized dissemination

In accordance with these anthropological views, we offered in the Netherlands a course in 'contextual pastoral care', primarily a week-long course. Since 1989, a post-academical extended course is offered (Van Rhijn & Meulink-Korf, 2019). Many theologians from Holland and Belgium have participated as students or teachers, trainers, and supervisors in the development of programs and projects based on this approach.[2] Later, some of these programs were attended by colleagues from Central Europe. Their participation led to new initiatives, and similar courses were offered in Hungary and Transylvania (Rumania), mostly led by the theology professors M. Kocsev and J. Kiss. Appropriate books and articles were translated into Hungarian, and original Hungarian texts on contextual pastoral care were written and published. Initiatives followed in the Czech Republic and Germany.

---

2 www.contextueelpastoraat.nl

Over a period of several years, introductory courses in Contextual Pastoral Care and Counseling (CPCC) were presented in South Africa. At the cradle was the Dutch Reverend Nel van Doorn, who has been in contact with colleagues from Stellenbosch since 2002 (Van Doorn, 2020). Being a teacher and trainer in CPCC herself, she included me, and together with F. Marais, senior researcher in practical theology (Stellenbosch), we founded the Zebra Foundation.[3]

The Zebra foundation facilitates short courses for mixed groups of ministers, chaplains, and other spiritual leaders from both South Africa and the Netherlands. Based on CPCC, a pilot project was organized in Wellington, where C. Thesnaar was participating. The courses are preceded by one or two weeks of exposure to the life and work setting of a colleague with whom they will participate in the course. The intention of the project is to give students an opportunity to perceive differences without judgmental comparison, through meeting others and otherness. A decentering experience entails the awareness that 'I' am not the center of the universe. Philosopher Gabriel Marcel expressed this notion as follows: "A human life has always its center outside itself" (in: Boszormenyi-Nagy & Framo, 1965, 2015: 36). This decentering process facilitated by the Zebra-project is often very necessary. There are many reasons why human beings become prejudiced and distrustful of others and trapped inside themselves. Sometimes, a shock helps to deconstruct these reasons. With the help of others, I recognized such a prejudice in myself.

I had to learn how the rituals that are used in meetings of 'Healing of Memories' contributed to reconciliation in the South African context. I knew that since the 1990s, The Institute for Healing of Memories (IHOM)[4] "seeks to contribute to lasting individual and collective healing that makes possible a more peaceful and just future". At first, when I saw a video of such a meeting, I was shocked by what I thought was religious enthusiasm without real attention to relational ethics. Thanks to an emotional conversation with colleagues from local communities, and only after some reactive anger and shame on my side, I understood my own habit of relying on a fast intellectual judgement and dichotomizing ethics and mystics/rituals. For me, this was a decentering and liberating experience that helped me to have a more patient and open attitude. I presume this also helped me grow in my professional capacity for multidirected partiality.

As an extension of these courses, as an academical deepening and adaptation, a master's program at the Faculty of Theology at Stellenbosch University was instituted in 2017 and led by Prof C. Thesnaar. The program is consistent with postgraduate programs elsewhere, combined with new academic and practical inspirations. Participants in this postgraduate course are expected to have sufficient practical experience. Many of them follow a clinical route with an internship in a hospital, a detention facility, or an institute for residential care. Others will develop their academical competences in particular but

---

3   www.stichtingzebra.nl
4   healing-memories.org

always in contact with pastoral practices. A key aspect of the learning experience is the ecumenical community created by the students in the course. This learning community, characterized by its diversity, matches the objectives of the master's-program,[5] among other things: "To establish a multidirected pastoral sensitivity in care and counseling/ To develop a sensitivity for other people's suffering and enjoyment of life, Coram Deo ('in the presence of God'), in awareness of their relational entanglements/To cultivate an attentive acceptance of the richness of cultural diversity/To read and interpret the Bible text from an ethical relational perspective". The purpose of the program is to assist students to develop dialogical intergenerational pastoral knowledge and skills through the integration of theory and practice. Linked to this program, research projects were begun and resulted in the writing of master's thesis and other publications on religious, social, and relational practices, inspired by contextual theory.

According to Thesnaar (Thesnaar, 2022), further development of an African contextual pastoral theory would require a transdisciplinary approach. In a dialogue with scholars and practitioners from the social, medical, and economical sciences, and the contribution of practical theologians inspired by the contextual approach may develop a hopeful perspective on human relations in current and future societies. This could challenge people to adopt a 'not-give-up' patient attitude, and to believe in the possibility of transformation in situations of injustice and despair. Hope can be an existential motivation and is at the center of religious life: "neither naive nor innocently optimistic. It seeks to include hopelessness and despair as a part of hope" (Anderson, 1990, referring to Jürgen Moltmann's theology of hope).

New input and new terminology

Different geographical and language-regions with their own word connotations may call for variations in professional language. Sometimes a setting needs its own language to help the counselors who support people in their own specific reality. Therefore, C. Thesnaar in South Africa coined the name 'Dialogical Intergenerational Pastoral Process' (abbr. DIPP) as a substitute for CPCC.

'Context' in *contextual theology*, as it is mainly developed in South American and African theology, means the influence of the interconnectedness of culture in place and social position, and religion. In other words: the intertwining of the cultural situation and personal and public theology. More specifically, the influence of local religion on (inter) human conduct is examined.

This terminology, namely 'contextual' theology, may be confusing for those who have studied in the USA and Europe where there is a distinction between contextual therapy, contextual pastoral care and counseling on the one hand and contextual theology on the other hand. The meaning of 'context' in contextual theology is not similar to what is meant

---

5   http://www.sun.ac.za./english/theology

by 'context' in the writings of Boszormenyi-Nagy and his colleagues. In contextual therapy, it refers to the relational reality of a person as described in five dimensions. It focuses on the ethical dimension of a person's relationships, including past and future relations, with threads of giving and receiving that weave a fabric of dependence and interdependence between people. Thus, the main reason for choosing and using the name DIPP was to avoid confusion of concepts.

A new term and a new language do bring new inspiration and at the same time refresh the 'old' term 'contextual pastoral care' and its meaning. The words in the acronym DIPP reverberate a relational ethical definition and content. 'Dialogical' and 'intergenerational' are central words in contextual therapy. The term 'pastoral' was reviewed earlier in this chapter. What about the expression 'process'?

The DIPP program takes a process approach in study, training, practice, and research, and this is clearly indicated in its name. Without including the notion 'process', it could be assumed that pre-defined objectives are the most relevant elements guiding interventions. However, empirically, pre-defined goals are an abstraction. At the beginning of a concrete pastoral contact, one rarely knows what objectives one wants to achieve, except in very general terms. During this contact, in the process, one will constantly find and adjust goals. Levers for constructive change, for the sake of fairness and justice, are described and reflected in the program. Moreover, there is another relevant reason for the term 'process' in DIPP. This has to do with the importance of patience, or perseverance, in the pastoral relationship that seeks *intersubjectivity* or dialogue amidst the multigenerational history of the relational, societal, and political *objectification* of many people being objectified by racism, slavery, and apartheid. Since 1994, the legacy of transgenerational trauma in South African society has been acknowledged, but it still needs to be addressed in its complexity. Many communities, families and individuals in South Africa suffer in a "state of frozenness" (Thesnaar, 2019) about whom to trust, especially outside their own inner circle. This stagnation in the transformation process has serious implications for building interhuman trust and personal growth. Especially when people live for generations in non-privileged circumstances, many people are filled with mistrust. Unfulfilled personal and political promises increase the destructive entitlement of persons and groups. "The failure to deal with the past traumas could lead to an eruption of the suppressed anger, violence, and vengeance at any moment" (Thesnaar, 2019).

Stagnation in restoring justice is a predicament that leads to a double frozenness of the trauma. There is the original injustice and damage, frozen into trauma, and then there are the injustices in society afterwards, caused by indifference, and by misunderstanding or downplaying what had happened. This harsh situation, which extends over several generations, must be addressed through long-term unfreezing processes. The notion 'loyalty' turns out to be very relevant in dealing with the sometimes-overwhelming problems and their transgenerational transmission.

Enduring reliability

This approach, CPCC and DIPP, relates to both major life events and people's daily lives and requires a special focus on family ties, including the transmission of trust and faith. In this respect, the pastoral involvement with a person or a family will often be a contact of lasting reliability. Pastoral care, unlike therapy, has similarities with liturgy, in its original Greek etymological meaning as *leitourgia*, the work for a community which is done 'for free'. The one that serves does not get a direct reward, perhaps none. This resembles the 'normal' sympathy among neighbors. There may be an expectation of reciprocity, but reciprocity is not a condition. "This work has no aim but hope ... for the kingship of God, of which 'only the patience is certain' (Levinas)" (Meulink-Korf & Van Rhijn, 2016: 158).

This patience also applies to the expectation of a pastor that the parishioner seeks personal and relational improvement. A pastor will show respect for the parishioner's own timing, without ceasing to address the other's accountability for seeking improvement in the relations with family members. This respect also refers to a process of hope without certainty of success.

Multigenerational homes of wisdom

In a text about "What is 'African' in Africa", Louw (2018: 147-148) does not deny the often-overwhelming problems affecting the African continent. However, he is looking for a constructive paradigm, away from the more usual deficiency and problem paradigms. He quotes Kenneth Kaunda, the politician who led Zambia to independence: "Let the West have its technology and Asia its Mysticism! Africa's gift to world culture must be in the realm of Humane Relationships" (in: Louw, 2018: 148). However, 'the world culture' has to be aware that this gift can become romanticized and idealized, as sometimes happens with 'Africa' itself. When a concept is idealized, there is a great risk that the real life of human beings is neglected or misused. Aware of this danger, we need to investigate what Kaunda called the gift of Africa.

The theologies of the African scholars Mugambi, Gathogo and Mkhize, are at the source of the development of DIPP (Thesnaar, 2019). In their writings, spirituality forms a main resource for both identity and community-building. Jesse Mugambi (University of Nairobi, Kenya) emphasizes the importance of family life and the need for reconstruction of society. He also argues that the Hebrew Bible and the Christian New Testament, read anew, are relevant sources for relational ethics and social justice. The "myth of a vanishing people" must be replaced by the narrative of "a resurgent, or resilient people" (Mugambi, 1995). And the same applies to hunger in Africa, there must be hopeful narratives of people capable of feeding themselves and one another (Mugambi, 1995).

In these thinkers, as in many African philosophies, the meaning of hospitality is central in addition to interconnectedness of humanity across generations. Julius Gathogo (Kenyatta University, Kenya) sees *Ubuntu* philosophy as the best illustration of African hospitality.

Ubuntu, meaning 'humanity' or 'I am, because of you', is not a romantic but a critical, demanding concept. "True Ubuntu […] requires an authentic respect for individual rights and values and an honest appreciation of diversities amongst the people. This stance allows the self to feel the other, and to stand within the other's historical circumstances in order to evoke a sense of shared humanity across time and place" (Thesnaar, 2019). This includes one's respect for the self.

When the Europeans came to Africa, they were often received with generous hospitality. Therefore, it was a huge injustice that many of them and especially their leaders (for instance Cecil John Rhodes) stole from their hosts. They deprived the indigenous peoples from their land, their way of living, their ways of expressing themselves in traditional stories and rituals. The social alienation of people from themselves and their humanity is one of the worst predicaments. Gathogo (2012) therefore calls 'reconciliation' "a minor but critical paradigm [that] is inevitable". He provides us with a profound definition (with the help of 19th-century political theorist Karl Marx) on reconciliation: "the movement that makes estrangement (Entfremdung) disappear" on interpersonal and intergroup levels (Gathogo, 2012).

Learning from African scholars and teachers entails the awareness of a history of injustice and lack of hospitality, especially from the Western side. Many white Europeans and Americans nowadays are happily surprised by the generous hospitality they encounter in Africa and at the same time, they feel badly ashamed. Is this a mirror, reflecting a permanent lack of generosity? In each case, it does reflect their possible abuse of the generosity of others. So, this uneasiness is primarily about justice. Heirs from European history especially should acknowledge the pitfall of a continuing lack of awareness and attention. They cannot simply incorporate notions such as *Ubuntu* in their own models. Talking about mutual trust and the African hospitality, being inspired by *Ubuntu* entails indebtedness and it has to include relational, societal, and political justice.

In the process of designing DIPP as a master's program, there was an expert meeting in Stellenbosch in 2016. In highlighting what one should learn from African culture, its traditions, and values, Velaphi Mkhize uncovered a rich source of knowledge. In his quest for restoring an Africa-centered approach, he mentioned *Umsamo*. This concept comes from the Nguni, a collective name for several Bantu ethnic groups in Southern Africa. *Umsamo* means a place in a Nguni hut where some ancestral spirits reside. This is the home of ancestral wisdom. Throughout history, this home was severely threatened. Mkhize talked about the misunderstandings and injustices that were done to this kind of wisdom. Imposing a Western rationalistic view on personal and communal life meant the exclusion of an Africa philosophy of life. All categories that were considered less rational, such as traditional spirituality, were excluded from the official discourse by colonialism. Mkhize is one of the scholars who want to change the Western views on life that were forced on Africa. He claims the freedom to choose topics for research and to pursue intellectual and spiritual paths that are not dictated by outsiders: "Theologians have no business telling

African people that they will reach heaven only if they see Jesus Christ as the one and only mediating spirit between them and God" (Mkhize, 2016). A listening attitude toward non-living ancestors is relevant for the relationship of persons and their community with God. These ancestral spirits are part of a person's relational reality. They are not to be worshipped but must be respected as parents and co-creators of wisdom for the future. According to Mkhize, this traditional African life orientation is not the same as but congenial with the contextual theory. "Boszormenyi-Nagy's theory on relational ethics speaks and makes perfect sense to the contemporary Zulu experience [...] it resonates pretty well with how in our culture as in so many other African cultures in Southern Africa, we view the idea of living a life that is interlinked to that of others through various chains of loyalties based on direct and indirect kinships" (Mkhize, 2016). We see here one of the fundamentals of the contextual approach in pastoral care and counseling.

A plurality of approaches

The shift to relationality that led to a formulation of CPCC and DIPP may be an enriching source for pastoral theory and practices in general. Before coming to this very relevant topic, we need to briefly consider the plurality of pastoral care theories. For this overview, we adopt a theme-centered categorization as used particularly in Western Christian pastoral studies. The contributions of African and Asian scholars are hardly included in this overview. Partly, this neglect comes from accustomed Western 'blind spots', but also from Western classical categories (based on explicit propositional logical knowledge) that are not fitting enough for a more inclusive overview. Until now, I am not sure if this is a shortcoming that should be repaired in the future, or that an increasing awareness of the global diversity of approaches will command us, for reasons of fairness, to waive overviewing schemes. Any such scheme, including the following overview, tends to compare what is incomparable.

We can distinguish the 'kerygmatic' school, based on proclamation of the Gospel to the individual, the 'client-centered' school (sometimes called: the 'therapeutic' school, with a personal growth-model based on humanistic psychology in line with Carl Rogers), and thirdly the 'hermeneutic-narrative' school that pays special attention to methodological interpretation and understanding the perspective of other persons, such as the client or parishioner. In the hermeneutic school, the dynamics of interpretation (i.e. to find meaning) were directed to communication with the other person as 'a living human document'. Through the years, this hermeneutic school developed into a narrative approach. It is rooted in theology but open for perspectives from other disciplines such as humanities, philosophical anthropology, social and medical sciences, and economics. So, the investigations of human reality by several disciplines are used to find meaning in life and fate. The goal is the growth of the parishioners' self-understanding and an increase in their freedom to live their lives in accordance with God and their neighbors. The client or parishioner is the expert. The pastor or chaplain takes a position of 'not knowing'. Much attention is given to the individual consequences of trauma, loss, grief, tragedy, and therefore to traumatizing religious experiences, too. D. Louw (Stellenbosch) has made many contributions to pastoral hermeneutics. He emphasizes pastoral care as meeting with a fellow believer within the space of the congregation as *communio sanctorum*, a mystical transgenerational bond of both the living and the dead, in a confirmed hope and love. Moreover, Louw adds systemic insights, emphasizing the notion that "spirituality should be understood in terms of human relationships" (Louw, 2008: 53). In several contributions of the hermeneutic-narrative approach, systemic family therapy theory is followed for example by rabbi E.H. Friedman (Friedman, 1985, not to be confused with M. Friedman), in line with Murray Bowen. Their focus is on helping people to reach individuation by getting freedom from family entanglements. Differentiation of the pastor from the members of the congregation is viewed in this same light. This approach, although a systemic one, differs from contextual theory. In contextual theory, individuation happens through relating. As far as I can see, reflection on the dimension of relational ethics is missing in this hermeneutic-narrative approach, as is the case for the dimension of an ontic dependence. Nevertheless, the book *Generation to generation* (Friedman, 1985) offers wisdom for congregational leaders, because of the important issue of a differentiated position of the pastor, as not coinciding with the needs and wishes of the parishioners.

Throughout the years, each of these approaches has influenced the others. Moreover, there are other important insights, for example the theory of not-knowing as a principle in 'a ministry of presence' that considers simply active-reflective listening as a healing force.

In CPCC and DIPP, we do not intend to offer an alternative 'school' or 'model'. Mentioning the contextual pastoral approach, we mean a specific attitude (multidirected partiality) toward all who may be affected by the interventions in a pastoral process that can be characterized not only as hermeneutics but also as 'heuristics' (from the Greek word for 'to find'). The concept of heuristics refers to less formal, more intuitive ways of understanding and possibly of transformation. Amidst concrete intergenerational reality, marked with concerns, conflicts, and injustices, one may find a person's 'tacit knowledge'. With this idea of implicit knowledge, the Hungarian-British scientist and philosopher Michael Polanyi emphasizes the need to share conscious experiences in order to pass on personal insights and wisdom. "We did know more than we could tell" (Polanyi, 1983: 5). There are many things one knows how to handle, but one does not know how to explain this ability. It goes from driving a car, enduring pain, all the way to raising a child. The practitioner may help the client or parishioner to find old but hidden, as well as new, personal, and relational perspectives including resources for justice, trust, and faith. For this patient process, there is much to learn from African scholars who transcend the reduction of knowledge to systems of logic and linear causality, for example by paying attention to transgenerational wisdom (Mkhize, 2016). The same applies to insights into the intertwining of personal and cultural traumas and its risk for persons and groups, including churches, of being captured in the past. For example, in post-apartheid South Africa, this danger requests a process of developing a collective memory in dealing with the trauma. Here is a task for "a collective pastoral hermeneutics" (Thesnaar, 2013).

Concluding: the wisdom and skills of any contextual chaplain can be enriched by insights and tools of several approaches. Let us refer to the "all-encompassing respect of the [contextual] approach for other therapeutic modes and rationales" (Boszormenyi-Nagy, 1987, 2014: 319). In short, pastoral practitioners need to be open to the contributions of other theories, provided that the contextual hermeneutics of the pastoral process as intergenerationally and dialogically directed and orientated on justice, remains at the center.

Amidst diversity of pastoral settings

In newer chaplaincy services

The insights of contextual therapy, CPCC, and of DIPP are of benefit in the work of congregational leaders and chaplains, with their various beliefs or life-orientations, and in many different settings. The most experience of applying these insights so far has been in situations of institutional work (in congregations, parishes, hospitals, and schools with a religious affiliation). However, pastoral care and pastoral counseling are not limited to institutional church-connected work. It is obvious that in places where modernization of society, economic development, and technological advancement in general lead to less institutionalized forms of religion, traditional pastoral practice also recedes. However, the need for pastoral or spiritual guidance seems to remain or to revive. Forms of 'secular chaplaincy' and 'humanistic chaplaincy' begin to appear and are appealing to many people.

"As church attendance ... declines nationally, the need for chaplains will only increase," says Shelly Rambo, an associate professor at Boston University School of Theology. The rise of chaplains is not necessarily a Christian trend, or even a religious one. Other faith traditions are adopting the term chaplain, says Preeta Banerjee, a Hindu adviser in the University Chaplaincy at Tufts University. She was given this role because there is now a need for chaplaincy for different faiths, she says, as well as for people who do not belong to a religion, often called "the nones" (Fitzgerald, 2021). In August 2021, the *New York Times* mentioned the appointment of a humanist chaplain, Greg Epstein, as president of the chaplains at Harvard University. Apparently, his appointment was not yet self-evident for all, but it was met with the warm consent of many religious chaplains. Instead of the roots that traditional pastoral care finds in theology, these secular chaplaincies find inspiration in humanities (poetics, philosophy) and often in ecological notions ('healing', 'wholeness'). These chaplaincies may also benefit from the relational view offered by contextual therapy.

In the previous years, CPCC has indeed expanded to several new chaplaincy services. Here, chaplains are not always involved with a specific person or family for a longer period, as is often the case in more traditional settings like congregations. Take, for example, the chaplaincy of a major airport, where the encounters are short-lived.

Evelyn, a non-theistic humanistic believer, employed as an airport-chaplain in a multireligious team, was schooled in contextual pastoral care. In a meeting with her supervisor, she indicated: "Much of the stories of passengers-in-transit are about relational problems. In my work, I hardly have the opportunity for sessions with a family, nor for more than one session with a person. Nevertheless, sometimes merely one good question, one single question, can be helpful. Last week a man came to me in our little chapel. He burnt a candle, and asked: 'Reverend, what can I do? I have abandoned my son. I am on my way to work in the USA, and now he lives with his mother and stepfather in Asia, without me. What have I done? How can I ever be happy again?' I said: 'I do not know anything about you and your family. Would it be possible for you to tell your son by phone or mail that you burnt this candle, and what you hope for him?' After a while, the visitor said: 'I shall tell him. And I shall light another candle for his little half-sister, too. My son loves this baby a lot, and that is doing him good'. He stayed for no longer than a quarter of an hour and then left for his flight."

This is an example of how a single intervention, based on contextual theory, in an environment with a religious atmosphere and the possibility of a ritual referring to an intangible world (the candle!), may offer support. Without knowing which of these aspects helped most, we assume that it was also the chaplain who encouraged the passenger with a few words. She did not explain her own position, being a chaplain but not an ordained minister or priest. She did not ask many questions. She did not go into the details of this man's factual situation, e.g. his economic situation, nor asked about his feelings, probably unhappiness and ambivalence. She refrained from going into the systemic background of his migration, perhaps connected with the divorce and the new blended family of his ex-wife including their son. Instead of using these interventions, the chaplain encouraged the client's active concern for his son and for his son's baby sister. She acknowledged this concern as a form of caring, a gift to his son. Her attitude was based on multidirected partiality.

In this short case, one finds some of the key notions of contextual pastoral counseling: encouraging a person to focus on relational resources, supporting a person in vitalizing these relationships by giving. The visitor at the airport chapel was in visible despair. By helping him to reconnect with his son through some actions that were a form of giving, the chaplain was able to alleviate his suffering.

In all contextual interventions, the healing moment is defined as one of giving and receiving. The relief of suffering is defined relationally. The son may never know the gesture of his father, but even then, this gesture of the father would bring some relief of suffering to the father.

Suffering is not the same as experiencing problems or deficiencies

The role of therapy, including contextual therapy, is to help the client to find solutions for problems he or she is facing. In general, a therapist does not address human suffering as such. This is different for a pastor or chaplain. Newer pastoral services may require even more reflection on suffering, because in secularized societies, so many persons seem to be suffering without definable problems. Do they need someone to address their concerns, and get some guidance, someone outside the circle of family or friends from whom to receive some consideration? Over the past years in contact with many people, I have become convinced of this.

How do you view the suffering of a person who comes to a pastoral practitioner? Although this subject does not belong to the domain of contextual therapy, here is much to learn from contextual theory. If the person who has caused harm to others suffers from shame or from a bad conscience, this person may accept to re-examine his or her responsibility. The focus in contextual pastoral practice will be on the guilty person's earning relational trust, more than on reduction of suffering. Guilt, taken seriously, requests long-enduring relational action (see: Buber, 1998, on the subject of guilt and guilt feelings). A contextual pastor may be of assistance in this process.

However, there are other 'types' of suffering next to suffering because of a bad conscience. Sometimes the suffering cannot be cured, but the vindication of the suffering must be deleted.

For a deeper approach, we turn to the philosopher Emmanuel Levinas. He describes suffering as intrinsically useless, as "for nothing" (Levinas, 1988: 158). Of course, he does not deny the effect of suffering. On the contrary. Undergoing severe physical pain may deeply limit a person's freedom. In this state, for the sufferer, no activity against this pain seems to be possible. This imposed passive state can be stronger than any diversion or other mental resistance against physical pain. The same can be true for emotional pain. Especially when someone's suffering is neglected by others or vindicated as a *catharsis* or as an obligated penance, this may block a person's sensitivity for others. In terms of contextual theory: this can lead to a destructive entitlement.

Levinas warns against any justification of suffering. Such justification would amount to totally abandoning another in his or her pain: "certainly the source of all immorality" (Levinas, 1988: 163). 'I' am never entitled to see the suffering of another person as useful or justified. Levinas's objection against a justifying interpretation of the suffering of others is especially challenging Christian theology and theodicy, for in Christian thinking, but not only there, suffering sometimes is idealized wrongly as a high moral goal or as God's pedagogical instrument.

Investigating suffering, Levinas raises very important considerations. Thinking about the cruelties of the 20th century, with "two world wars, Hitlerism and Stalinism, Hiroshima, the Gulag, and the genocides of Auschwitz and Cambodia", and (we add) apartheid, he writes about the "just suffering" in 'me' for the unjustifiable suffering of the other (Levinas, 1988: 162).

My suffering because of the suffering of another may bring me to solidarity. The suffering of the other commands me to help and to show compassion. Levinas connects this with the interhuman order that "lies in a non-indifference of one to another, in a responsibility of one for another" (Levinas, 1988: 165).

The direct personal experience of suffering may give a person a sensitivity for the pain or burden of others. For instance, a man who lays awake at night, unable to sleep, may feel for others who are in the same predicament. He may even pray for them.

Nevertheless, nobody should try to convince a man or woman that his suffering might be meaningful.

What about someone's justification of his or her own suffering? For example, an older woman who was in severe pain communicated to her pastor that she perceived her situation as the reimbursement for the "good enough life" that she had lived until recently. Another example: a man, mourning after the sudden death of his young spouse, told his minister about his belief that "God in his mysterious way is perfecting him".

Here is another example:

A man in his fifties has been living in Europe for many years. He is suffering for his relatives in Morocco. These former neighbors and especially their offspring are poor. They seem to have few opportunities for jobs and are unhappy about this. The man has tried to encourage them during phone calls and has sent money on several occasions. Because of their own modest financial situation, his wife is sometimes angry about these gifts. While this man is temporarily in hospital, he opens his heart to the Muslim chaplain, not asking for release of his burden but longing for some understanding. He seems to expect that the chaplain will reproof him for living a European prosperous life and not sharing enough with his family of origin. Maybe the imam will see his suffering as a punishment from Allah.

The response of a pastoral counselor who is involved in any of these situations will depend on several factors. However, more specifically, one needs to consider this issue: is the worry of the person (the client) an obstacle in her or his fair relating with others, or not? The counselor may be of assistance by exploring the important relationships in the suffering person's life, without minimizing any of his or her concerns. Such concerns indicate the opposite of indifference, namely non-indifference, and responsibility. When clients suffer because of worries about others, a counselor should respect this disquieting concern, instead of dismissing it with the phrase that is used too often: "Do not worry so much about others. You have already enough to bear in your own life", or something like that. Instead, the counselor should try to support the suffering person while, if possible, also including the one(s) for or with whom this person suffers. Such an attitude of inclusiveness requires neither to see the suffering as a pathological problem, nor to seek solutions. This kind of suffering does not belong to the field of problems from which a person has to be liberated. Compassion, or suffering-because-of-the-suffering of another, may be a discomfort that happens to someone. Being moved (by another, by the suffering of another) is not a deliberate choice. However, let us not forget to see it as a "divine discomfort" (Meulink-Korf & Van Rhijn, 2016: 44, with quotation of Levinas. See also Thesnaar, 2019). On the part of the counselor, patience, perseverance, and acknowledgement are needed, as ever with an attitude of multidirected partiality.

In the case of the man of Moroccan origin, the chaplain helped him to discuss with his European wife and adult children if and how he could continue to send money to Morocco without being unfair to them in financial and other issues. The chaplain encouraged the wife and the children to explore in which way they could cooperate in helping the former neighbors and relatives of their husband and father. The organized meeting with his family did not stop the suffering or worrying of the client. However, it made him open to dialogue with his European family members and it included them in his concern instead of ignoring them. His adult children even succeeded in coordinating a town twinning association between their town and the Moroccan village.

No pastor has the right to object to a person's concerns about the suffering of others. After all, this worry, or suffering is a valid relational ethical concern. Sometimes this happens as "the most profound adventure of subjectivity" (Levinas, 1988: 163). It can be a rupture in a quiet daily life that seems to be enough in itself, self-sufficient. This experience is coming from outside, it is an advent. It may meet me from up front, from a time-to-be. Advent is not the same as the future that can be extrapolated from the past. The subject to whom this happens, is moved as *sub-iectus* (Latin, in English: put under, exposed to). This 'adventure' is probably not a general daily event, but it deserves acknowledgement.

Being patient and compassionate with the pain of the other and persevering in this, is what persons can do for one another on a more daily basis. Just like suffering from one's own pain, it may bring the sufferer into solidarity with others. Many people indeed are undergoing this and are doing this.

Compassionate perseverance is also part of a pastoral process. Sometimes this includes encouraging the suffering person to hold on to the not-so-easy belief in a God who is an ally instead of a punishing, rejecting power.

Co-suffering with a suffering client is not an adequate response. As a professional, a pastoral counselor will try to help people to bear their sufferings including the other people's burdens and notice with respect when amid suffering, a person undergoes some relational ethical transformation. A suffering person may be 'subject' in the utmost sense. In this way, her or his suffering might no longer, or not always, be useless, but it may bring this person into compassion and solidarity.

Ethics of caring

Based on empirical work and on reflections, contextual theory proposes "a mutual constitutive interdependence of being" in human relationships (Boszormenyi-Nagy, 1987, 2014: XVI). On a very fundamental level, human beings depend on one another for many aspects of their survival, and also for the mutual establishment of their Self ('the ontic dependence', see Section I), which is a relational process. Human relationships have at least these two fundamental characteristics: people expect reciprocity in relationships, and they have an innate tendency to offer care to others and take responsibility for them. In short, human beings have an expectation of fairness and a capacity to be fair.

This can be demonstrated in the particular relational context of a concrete person in which the concrete acts of giving and receiving are connected with past generations as well as with future ones through threads of consequences. There is often a great degree of relational commitment in the attitude of many people. However, there may be serious shortcomings, too, due to many variables. Then a pastoral practitioner may try to be of assistance.

How should one help and give support and sometimes comfort a specific person in his or her unique relational reality? How should help, and what help, be given in the diversity of persons and groups? In both the Global South and the Global North, contextual pastoral processes aim to help people who are suffering from relational disconnection by promoting healing dialogues between individuals and groups. Next to a basic insight into anthropology, including the above-mentioned interhuman structure, professionals are required to have an awareness of the diversity of relational injustices as well as of situational injustices such as huge socio-economic inequalities.

Thus, trying to give help and/or support also requires a cultural sensitivity, and certainly a capacity for the attitude of multidirected partiality. Above all, the counselor must be accountable to all persons affected by the consequences of the counseling. Boszormenyi-Nagy (1987, 2014: 319) calls this accountability the "ethics of caring". Applying this ethics should be a common mandate in all forms of psychotherapy and counseling, including CPCC and DIPP.

Heuristics of hope

An unawareness of the consequences of the differences between human beings based on their relations, situations, and predicaments, would lead to an attitude of indifference to the human world. The 'ethics of caring' as the accountability and responsibility of the professional, means the opposite of indifference and cynicism. 'Ethics of caring' in the contextual approach implies a commitment to the (re)building of interpersonal trust in a concrete situation. To illustrate this, I refer to a rather common experience. Often, in meetings and dialogues with students and colleagues from different regions in the world and with diverse cultural and ethnic backgrounds, as well as in counseling sessions, one finds people with a like-minded hopeful motivation to improve relationships. It is a wonderful experience: to share hope for a better understanding of family relationships, especially in terms of reciprocity and fairness, and for restoring justice in hurt human relationships. It is amazing to see how many young students and senior professionals are motivated to help and support others. Altruism is not the only motive here; the need to meet others and be of service to them is also self-interested. Here is an example.

Theodore, a young, not very self-confident student, in a South African DIPP-class, told how he was helped by giving practical support to non-privileged and often troublesome children in a slum. Theodore lives far away from his family and had been feeling very lonely for some time. "I am merely helping these kids playing football, but for me, my weekly afternoons with the children are also a spiritual experience. I see girls and boys grow when I give them some honest comments with hope for their future. And after a while, some of them let me know that they would help me if I had a problem … They grow in self-esteem, I think." Later in his course, he wrote a paper on reciprocity and trust building in a congregation.

In any pastoral counseling session and any other pastoral activity, inducing hope may strengthen the client's motivation for earning relational trust. Hope turns out to be much more crucial than empathy-with-possible-despair. Receiving hope often means regaining motivation for personal growth and becoming more trustworthy and reliable. This also applies to giving hope, passing on hope. It is amazing to see how altruism and motives of self-interest overlap. What happened between Theodore and the children also influenced the dimension of relational ethics. The relationship was asymmetrical in terms of responsibility, yet there was a reciprocity of giving and receiving between Theodore and several children. This experience of reciprocity may have reinforced hope for the future in both the children and the student.

Before proceeding to the practical framework of the contextual pastoral process in relation to religion and spiritualty presented in the next chapter, the following paragraphs provides facts and considerations relevant to the development of contextually inspired practices in pastoral care and counseling, including academic programs. The meaning of these facts and reflections for new situations must be reconsidered repeatedly. Just like the departments of psychology, psychiatry and the domains of therapy and therapists, the Department of Practical Theology and the domains of pastoral practices and practitioners, are dynamic. In the background, one can see a process of globalization, as a multi-layered phenomenon. The disconnectedness between people of different social groups and different generations seems to increase. At the same time, there seems to be a growing awareness of global destiny, among many different people, old and young, along with an increasing moral consciousness (Meulink-Korf & Noorlander, 2012). It is an urgent human and professional possibility to use a dialogical intergenerational perspective as "hope for this hour" (Buber, 1957, 1990: 255). This hope includes fear and despair over the lack of dialogue.

Buber was not in the least naïve about hope. He saw the urgent and overriding importance of what is at stake, namely "the conflict between mistrust and trust of man conceals the conflict between the mistrust and trust of eternity" (Buber, 1957, 1990: 264).

Heuristics of hope and heuristics of fear are connected.

Hans Jonas's heuristics of fear

Here we make a brief excursion to the work of Hans Jonas, who strongly has criticized the often too easy or naive thinking about hope.

Jonas, a Jewish American-German philosopher, was like his lifelong friend and colleague, Hannah Arendt, a refugee. Jonas was motivated by a concern for ethical issues in biological sciences, and especially, after the terror of Nazism, by a deep concern for the survival of truly relational human life. By this he meant human life free from oppression and slavery, including slavery through the forced manipulation of genes.

Jonas analyzed the unjustifiable confidence in more and more advanced technology that would make a better world for people. Optimism would be irresponsible. Boszormenyi-Nagy noticed Jonas's concern as congenial. With reference to Hans Jonas, Boszormenyi-Nagy writes: "In order to survive, humanity needs a new, appropriately effective ethics of responsibility to thwart its likely destructive consequences to posterity" (Boszormenyi-Nagy, 1987, 2014: 301). Hans Jonas proposed this imperative: "Act so that the effects of your action are compatible with the permanence of genuine human life" (Jonas, 1984, passim).

According to Jonas, humankind must track down the danger before it is too late. If not, the potential disappearance of the human species will become a reality and will mean irreversible destruction. Jonas's idea of responsibility implies what he calls a non-reciprocity, a fundamental asymmetry, because humanity bears responsibility for 'the not yet', in terms of its duty to newborn and yet-to-be-born children. In this asymmetry lies the prototype of all responsible action, which fortunately does not need to be derived from a principle, because it is powerfully implanted in us by nature (Jonas, 1984). According to Jonas, responsibility includes a transgenerational sacrifice, the sacrifice that people living today are willing to protect future generations which implies accepting limitations in economic and technical growth. The earth must be respected rather than exploited if we are to save the human species and humanity.

We must remember, and now I quote Boszormenyi-Nagy again: "The future is unilaterally, thus captively exposed to the consequences of the present reality" (Boszormenyi-Nagy & Krasner, 1986, 2014).

At the end of his book, Jonas presents modesty as one of the most important admonitions of responsible ethics. Now, decades after Hans Jonas, we may call modesty a key to what is now called sustainability. Thanks to Jonas's 'heuristic of fears', we human beings can orient ourselves toward hope.

Working with a dialogical intergenerational perspective

A discipline with a broad orientation

Usually, pastoral practitioners like chaplains and congregational leaders are not specialists in psychiatry or in psychology. However, they are acquainted with the use of several lenses. In their academic curricula, they learn about religion, spirituality, ethics, dialectics, hermeneutics, literature, psychology, and other cultural and social sciences. This broad orientation can be an advantage for a sensible approach to the interpersonal reality.

Academically, the theory of the pastoral process belongs to practical theology. This broad discipline provides practical, empirically underpinned theories. The scope is multi-layered. Pastoral practitioners often are familiar with systemic thinking and functional roles. Most pastors meet not only individuals but also families, as members in the congregation or as relatives of the patient in an institution. Often, they are familiar with more than one family generation. They know about the need for dialogue between family members and have a mandate to guide family members with partly conflicting interests. They may have learnt about views with multiple perspectives, for example about time and eternity, or God's presence and God's absence, or predestination and responsibility. Thus, they may be prepared to understand the dialectical theory of personality and the dialectical view of relationships developed by Boszormenyi-Nagy (Boszormenyi-Nagy, 1987, 2014).

Moreover, pastoral practitioners know about correlations, such as the correlation between fairness in family relationships and justice in society. They know about correlations between relational (un)fairness and (in)justice in society. These may be viewed as converging in the justice of the order of being (Buber, 1957, 1998); in other words, in being human as orientated on and commanded to justice. No wonder that in their search for practical theory, they see a huge relevance in the findings of Boszormenyi-Nagy. These findings fit in with pastoral experiences of reciprocity and fairness as cornerstones of communities, such as contained in the Christian concept *communio*. We have already pointed out the compatibility of the fundamentals of contextual theory with biblical notions. These foundations also fit into other traditional (meta-) narratives of human existence, often expressed in novels and films.

Each person's unique relational reality needs a broad-based approach. As stated above, contextual theory applies five dimensions to face relational reality, as interwoven options for care and support. Moreover, in the contextual pastoral approach, the spiritual viewpoint plays a role, connected with the other dimensions, but is never reducible to any of them. As we shall see more in detail later in this text, religion, or spirituality in someone's relational life, is a possible resource in relational ethics. However, it will also be viewed as a possible obstacle to fair relating.

Therapists and pastoral counselors/chaplains: Different domains

CPCC and DIPP are unthinkable without the influence of contextual therapy, not only regarding its origins but also for its further development. However, it would be a mistake to reduce the contextual pastoral process to contextual therapy, or vice versa. Each professional domain has its own content and scope. Pastoral care is not deficiency- or pathology-centered. Nevertheless, pastoral practitioners may learn from specialists in the field of therapy. When a client presents his or her suffering as caused by a religious issue, this might be primarily a religious problem indeed, but not necessarily. Sometimes the situation of a client requires the help of a specialist in any of the five dimensions of relational reality. For instance, parishioners with an ongoing story of financial debts may need pastoral counseling but also some extra support from a social worker. In other cases, they may need therapy. Therefore, it is important for each contextual practitioner to know some good therapists, if possible contextual therapists for consultation, cooperation, or referral. The possibility of consulting a psychiatrist is important as well. How actively the pastor will stay involved when the professional of another discipline supports the client, should be discussed with the client. This is also an issue of consideration between the pastor and the other professional.

The contact between pastors and therapists is not *per se* a one-way street. In meetings with pastors and in some discussions of theological or spiritual insights that pastors bring, therapists can be nourished, too. It may need both a pastor and a psychiatrist to differentiate moving spiritual experiences from hallucinations, and to decide what is the best help that this person could receive. Both domains, therapy and pastoral care, have their own inspirational potential for other professionals. Interdisciplinary consultation may help all professionals involved to gain a broader perspective.

Some themes are of specific relevance to pastoral practitioners, in distinction to therapy. Adjacent to the theme of 'spirituality' or religious belief as more or less explicit in a pastoral conversation, other elements can be relevant, too, such as the following:

- Often a pastoral practitioner is connected with a religious community or institution.
- In general, there is 'natural' access to family members or neighbors, since pastors often visit people at home, or they meet them unintentionally in the neighborhood, in the supermarket, at the park, at a political meeting. These chance encounters influence the contact between pastor and parishioner.
- A pastoral practitioner has the possibility of giving support in the form of attention or 'presence', even when there seems to be no improvement in the presented problem of the parishioner or client.
- The contractual aspect of the relationship differs from therapy, connected with 'who pays'. It may be the client, the insurance company, the state, or the church.
- According to the laws of specific countries, regulations concerning confidentiality, mandatory reporting of abuse or incest, and a right to remain silent in court, may be different for psychotherapists and pastoral counselors.

- The prestige of a pastor may be lower than the prestige of a therapist. Depending on the social and political environment, the goodwill and rating of these two professionals may be different.
- However, the authority of the pastor for many people often is increased by her or his religious calling or ordination. Members of the congregation may regard a minister in a congregation as a man or woman of God, in closer proximity to God than others. A Roman Catholic or orthodox priest has even more authority, because of the theologies that underline the priest's special position. A *shaman*, too, would have a very special position.

All these factors influence pastoral relationships. To understand how this works, and to reinforce its benefits, we shall focus on two related themes: the responsibility of the pastor in the faith community as the leader of an intergenerational network of relationships, and the theme of proximity and distance, especially the boundaries in this professional relationship. In connection with these topics, we shall discuss the case where a pastor accompanies believers from his or her own community and how this affects the attitude of multidirected partiality.

Relational life care in the community and the pastoral practitioner's attitude

Multidirected partiality and its possible limitations in a pastoral relationship

In CPCC and DIPP, *cura animarum* or soul care means relational life care. This includes much more than just a conversation in which the pastor comforts or challenges an individual client or parishioner. At the heart of this care is the attitude of multidirected partiality. This functions throughout the whole attendance of pastoral practitioners, not only in pastoral conversations and consultations. These practitioners will reach people with or without family members, at home and in church and in hospital, in the neighborhood of their community, through counseling, rituals, teaching, preaching, organizing, guiding of volunteers, and more. This broad professional domain and the authority that often is attributed to them demand awareness concerning the special character of their relationship with the parishioners or clients, and its consequences at the beginning of a specific pastoral process such as counseling. Why is this awareness necessary?

Often, there is already some familiarity between the pastor and the parishioner, and this contact has its consequences when the two are meeting in a more specific professional way. After all, pastors meet many parishioners in a personal way because they belong to the same congregation. For example, it happens that the wife of the pastor befriended the spouse of the parishioner to whom the pastor now may offer counseling. Pastors and parishioners may live in the same neighborhood. Perhaps their children are friends. It also happens that a person who seeks pastoral counseling from the pastor is a member of the board who advises on the salary of this same pastor. A chaplain may be in touch with a patient and her family members for many years. If this chaplain begins counseling the patient, the parent, or both together, what does this mean for the counseling relationship and also for her or his relationship with the others?

These situations may be problematic. The professional herself or himself may be involved as a party. However, multidirected partiality presumes a certain distance. Between friends or good acquaintances, a full attitude of multidirected partiality is therefore not an option. In this case, there are at least two other options: first, referral to a colleague-pastoral practitioner or a therapist who is less or not familiar with this parishioner or patient. This may often be preferable.

If no suitable colleague or therapist is available, for example in remote areas, the professional faces a dilemma. He or she may refrain from acting as a counselor for this parishioner and her family. In this case, the consequence will be that the pastor will leave them without the necessary professional help. The second possibility is that the pastor will offer some counseling sessions and will do his or her best to maintain a professional attitude aimed at fair multilaterality. Then, the pastoral counselor will set new relational boundaries in the pastoral contact as a counseling relationship. Without fully using the method of multidirected partiality, as in contextual therapy, the counselor who chooses the second option needs to come to a fair multilateral exploration of the relationships of the parishioner. This orientation toward multidirected fairness (or fair multilaterality, see Boszormenyi-Nagy, 1987, 2014) requires honesty and self-reflection of the counselor. 'Am I free to work with this specific person as a professional counselor?' This also includes a discussion of the counselor's dilemma with the client; i.e. the concern about the effect of their prior relationship on the counseling process. If possible, the counseling pastor or chaplain should be supervised to ensure that he or she maintains the utmost integrity during the counseling process.

If the pastor or chaplain who lacks an alternative for referral, chooses to begin and proceed with counseling, the change in the relationship may lead to distrust and is a threat to the 'old' familiarity between the pastor and the parishioner or the pastor and the clients' family, and even between the family members. However, if the counselor is able to facilitate a growing dialogue between the family members, they will eventually realize that they have benefited from this change in the relationship with the professional.

A human disposition for multilaterality

As a strong orientation, multidirected partiality is the most important attitude and it needs to be learnt. For several reasons, it may not always come easily. However, there is a disposition for multilaterality within most people. "The concept of multilaterality, as examined and proposed by Nagy, assumes an underlying psychical 'structure'. Each of us is intrinsically involved in more than one other. The quantity and quality of these involvements are of course diverse. Nagy was not the only one and not the first to think along these lines. A number of psychoanalysts, especially of the generations after Sigmund Freud [...] have enabled elaborating on this meta-psychologically and enabled psychological-empirical research into relational life – being relational not as something that is added, but as existential, constitutive of being human" (Meulink-Korf & Van Rhijn, 2016: 114).

The assumption of an intrapsychic multilateral disposition may be perceived as puzzling or naïve, and this misunderstanding is often the case in Western culture. This negative perception undermines trust in relationality as the basis of individuation and individualized care for others. Despite the great work of dialogic philosophy and contextual thinking, an ego-centered monological view of personal motivations often seems dominant, especially in Western mindsets. However, a one-sided view will see only one-sided motivations. Therefore, as a prerequisite for multidirected partiality, practitioners must renew their faith in a human intrapsychic tendency to multilaterality and acquire a multi-person perspective. No contextual practitioner can do without this trust.

The importance of a multi-person perspective

Faith, a talented adolescent in Cape Town, has problems with her parents, who blame her for studying Arts. The parental condemnation makes her sad and uncertain, and now she is doubting her choice. Both her mother and her father emphasize the need for educated nurses and medical doctors in their rather poor community. "Nobody is getting better by tales about paintings," they say. The parents consult the minister of their congregation, expecting him to reprimand their daughter for her "selfish conduct" by not choosing a medical career. However, the minister tells them to respect the choice of their daughter: "She has to fulfil her potential as a gift of God, and she deserves your permission, the lack of that is the only problem." He says he will pray for them that they can give Faith their blessings. When somewhat later the minister meets Faith, and she shares something about her uncertainty and doubts, he invites her to take part in a religious program for young adults, in which he is the leader. He is disappointed when after two sessions Faith quits the program and avoids further contact with him. In a consultation, he tells his supervisor that he feels inspired by the work of the psychologist Alice Miller ('The drama of the gifted child') and by the insights of Aaron Beck's cognitive behavior therapy. "I work hard in trying to understand and support God's way with each specific child ... I must assume that Faith's parents are wanting the best for their daughter, so respecting her freedom will be the best for them, too ... Good people, but obviously these parents are not in the least as talented as their daughter ... Probably they will never understand her. It was they who influenced her decision to leave my class."

Albert, the minister and pastor of Faith and her family, lacked a consistent view on the intertwining of multi-person motivations. He saw some complexity in the parent-child relationship, but he did not recognize the loyalty dynamics in Faith's family or the lack of consistency in his own attitude. Partly, a religious interpretation blocked his view of relational reality. His perception of a God who has a special way with each individual child, as separated: "free" from the family of origin, blinded him for considering individuation as a relational process. Although his intentions were good, no one in this family was helped by him.

A supervisor examined with Albert his (Albert's) relationship with his parents and especially his psychological needs. The term 'helper syndrome' was used. Albert's tendency to take the position of helper was also examined. Later in his career, during his DIPP-training, Albert learnt about multidirected partiality as an attitude that requires accountability to all those potentially affected by the interventions. As mentioned earlier, this attitude requires taking the side of each of the people involved sequentially, considering the consequences for each, including people who are personally unknown to the pastor. Even when the pastor accompanies a person without being able to meet the family members or other close people, it remains possible and very relevant for the pastor to include these absentees through multidirected partiality.

Regarding Faith, Albert had been in professional contact with her parents, but he neglected to be partial to them. In this case, it was not his personal involvement with the parents that could have made him 'a party' in the conflict, and therefore not capable of a really inclusive attitude. A serious misunderstanding of parent-child relationships blinded him for a long time. For Faith, this meant that her side was also neglected. What Albert should have addressed was her loyalty to her parents. However, instead, Albert interpreted her concern for them as an immature dependency that she had to overcome. Therefore, Albert could not help her find another channel to express her loyalty to her parents other than fulfilling her parents' wish. The possibility of another way did not occur to him. Although his intention was to help Faith on her path to autonomy, Albert did not do so.

Contextual theory offers a multi-person view of motivations. It focuses on the dynamics of justice and the ways of expressing loyalty in families. It does this not by defining what would be good for society or morally just, but by bringing family members or significant neighbors into a dialogue where they can learn about their respective needs and expectations (Ducommun-Nagy, 2018).

Such a learning dialogical process would have helped Faith and her parents. This could have included the needs of the community. Even if Faith was not engaged in a medical profession, she might be able to contribute to her community in another way, for instance by giving art-classes to deprived children. In this way, she would have been loyal to her parents in a visible manner since they were expecting her to contribute to her community. At the same time, she would have been able to earn constructive entitlement.

Participation in the community, a relational opportunity

The fact that pastors and chaplains are members of a religious community can be a resource for people who are seeking support. The community of the counselor, thus the congregation, parish, or institution, is usually open to the participation of the client and his or her family members. Religious communities can be a great source of support by providing practical care, by mediating and nurturing faith and trust, and by providing opportunities for the members of the congregation to give and receive. This can also apply to care centers.

An old man died after nearly ten years of suffering from diseases and illnesses, among them dementia. During the last months of his life, he lived in a nursing home. His mourning widow, who had visited him only irregularly, was invited by the chaplain of the home to remain present as a helper in the Sunday services of this home. After a while, she also began to work in the kitchen of the home as a volunteer during the week. She had suffered from "feelings of guilt and self-contempt", as she formulated, because she had given up caring for her husband at home, and because she felt relieved by his death. She was trying to channel her guilt feelings by doing more and more for the home. The chaplain, who saw that her tendency to over-give had become problematic to the staff, did not discourage her from wanting to help. He encouraged her to find ways in which she could continue to perceive herself as a reliable resource for others, without having to impose her presence in a manner that had already become a headache for the staff members. In this way, her guilt was still alleviated and at the same time, she was still able to earn constructive entitlement without the danger of being asked to stop her activities altogether.

In summary, the presence of a community or an institution where one is welcome as both a giver and a receiver provides opportunities to relate to others in a way that can be a great resource. Unfortunately, this potential relational benefit sometimes comes too late, because of so many situational injustices. Most religious communities cannot live up to the values and expectations they convey. A client may remember a family member who was treated unfairly by church officials. In such cases, family loyalty may lead people to distrust anyone associated with the church. Loyalty may also lead people to question the trustworthiness of the clergy, including a counselor.

Here is one example of injustice in the history of churches. As scholars in the history of South Africa found: "the Christian church played no major role in ending slavery at the Cape" while this church was proclaiming freedom and interhuman equivalence (Giliomee & Mbenga, 2007: 93). What does such an ambiguity mean for family dynamics and group loyalty? Does the church community deserve your attendance when the same church abandoned your ancestors? Does the present pastor or chaplain deserve your trust? Does she or he understand the intergenerational transmission of mistrust? Understanding the reasons for mistrust instead of downplaying these as merely stories of the past may help to restore trust.

If someone is treated unfairly by a family member ('relational injustice') during situational injustices, the mistrust is doubled. Obviously, this is true for the relationship of church members with their pastors. Just one current unfair relational experience in addition to past situational injustices can lead to great resentment and to serious harm to the trust in the pastoral relationship and in the community.

When Anna and Gilbert, a not-so-young couple, had a child after two miscarriages, it turned out that their son James was born with a condition that would lead to a permanent physical handicap and to mental retardation. When their chaplain visited the parents, he proclaimed that this was the benevolent will of God. According to the parents, he did not look at the child at any moment. They felt abandoned in their responsibility for their child, and their growing bond of love for their little James was ignored. The pastor could have shown interest in what the baby already had given to them. The pastor could have given attention to what it meant to them, and to their own parents that James would always need help and would never have the chance to have offspring himself. Earlier, this couple had hoped to raise a large family that would live and be free, without the burdens of being second-rate citizens as their ancestors had experienced as black people living under apartheid. The pastor could have explored the motivation of Anna and Gilbert to be part of a chain of offspring. No such pastoral care happened. Six months after this visit, this small family left the congregation. Their decision caused difficulties with their families of origin. Consequently, they felt more isolated than ever before. Furthermore, when a colleague of the pastor proposed a visit "to restore contact" in a very insensitive way, they refused to receive her since they had lost trust in the help pastors could give.

Abuse by a pastor or chaplain and the relational and social effects

Probably even more so than neglecting or downplaying the needs of parishioners, boundary transgressions by a pastor or chaplain reactivate experiences of loss of trust and of abandonment. These transgressions can include sexual abuse, financial problems, chaotic social behavior, and other social transgressions. The transgressions can have far-reaching consequences for the victim and her or his family, especially in the case of sexual offences. The abused person deserves good professional help. Usually, help from within the community, however well-intentioned, is not enough. There may be denial or other inadequate responses in the community, even victim-blaming. Or, on the contrary, the pastor-offender may be seen as a criminal and hunted down. These reactions from others are not helpful at all. They add unfair and isolating experiences for the primary victim and her or his family members.

There is often a loyalty aspect in the history of the victim's relationship with the offending pastor. For example, this pastor used to support a parent of the offended person positively, and later the adult daughter shows her loyalty to the parent by allowing the offending pastor a secret intimate approach. This indirect loyalty may have coincided with psychological or sexual needs of the daughter. However, this is no excuse at all for the pastor's behavior. The abuse began as a comforting kind of friendship but became more and more inappropriate given the asymmetry of the pastoral relationship. The stealth underlined the inappropriate nature. Ultimately, the aforementioned pastor exploited the daughter's feelings of loyalty to him. Loyalty aspects in transgressive behavior by a pastor require careful attention (Van den Berg, 2015).

Moreover, group loyalty must be considered. The relationship of the victim with the community needs attention, too. Abuse by clergy affects relational trust and the community members' faith in God. For this discomfort, they may blame the victim. Practice shows that in most cases, victims of abuse by a pastor will leave the local religious community, even if the transgressing pastor has been transferred to another congregation or is in detention. The departure of the victim and often of the victim's family can be a sad and disappointing outcome for well-meaning community members. Nevertheless, it shows the strength of the victim who wants to make a new beginning elsewhere. This may show her or his restored capacity for self-delineation and self-validation (Van den Berg, 2015).

Restoring trust between affected community members, including the lay leaders, requires careful contextual guidance from an external professional who can advise the congregation's lay leaders on how to restore safety, trust, and confidence in the harmed community. More and more religious communities and institutions have clear procedures for dealing with misconduct by a pastor or chaplain. They also include names of competent outsider professionals who can be called in. The pastor who was guilty should at least comply with the procedures, including cooperation, therapy, transfer, or removal from ministry. Often, the pastor's family also needs therapy. The primary orientation for any intervention, in procedures and in counseling or therapy, should be on fairness and on justice for the victim.

An asymmetric responsibility for the client's relational reality

Cases of abuse underline how the issue of 'distance and relating' deserves special attention. Evidently, a professional distance between counselor and client is needed for the attitude of multidirected partiality, and moreover, it is a basic condition to establish professional asymmetry-in-responsibility.

However, the importance of distance is not always self-evident. Therefore, systemic thinker rabbi E.H. Friedman advises spiritual leaders to develop a style of interaction especially marked by differentiation. A well-differentiated leader will be non-anxious present with each of those he or she is guiding (E.H. Friedman, 1985).

As already mentioned, there is much wisdom in this systemic approach. However, as far as relationality is concerned, it is not entirely satisfactory. It neglects relational ethics, including the dynamics of loyalty, in the complexity of a pastoral relationship. After all, the pastor or chaplain and the client are in a relationship that involves a certain reciprocity in giving and receiving. Yet the professional is the one who must maintain a meta-position concerning the relationship. Responsibility in a pastoral relationship has an incommensurable asymmetric character.

We call this asymmetric, because there is no equivalence between the participants in this relation (pastor and client). The nature of this responsibility varies because each human being differs from others and can be seen as unique. The responsibility of the pastor toward the one is not comparable to the responsibility toward the other. One element does not change: preserving an appropriate distance is important.

How does this condition relate to proximity? The pastoral relationship means in se the possibility of spiritual proximity in confidentiality. However, this intimacy is not a closed privacy or a *secrecy à deux*. Intrinsically, the pastoral relation requires that the counselor also gives attention to the relatives of the parishioner, whether they are visibly present or not. The attitude of multidirected partiality prevents the risk that the pastor tries to endorse roles that do not belong to him, for instance the role of a dear friend, a 'better' parent, or a (more) committed adult child. Taking the place of a loved one in the client's life, as a substitute, is an unprofessional act that is unfair to all concerned. Especially when this violation seems to result in a reduction of symptoms, the client or parishioner may be burdened with feelings of guilt due to feelings of disloyalty toward the real loved ones. His or her need to express loyalty to the real relatives has been neglected by the violator.

This risk is particularly relevant in relation to children (Boszormenyi-Nagy, 1987). The chaplain in a psychiatric unit who has warm contact with a hospitalized child, may understand some current needs of the child better than the parent may. However, it is precisely then that the chaplain must express concern and respect for the parent as the person with whom the child is relating in the first place. Because of the attitude of multidirected partiality, to assist the client, whether child or adult, a professional distance must be maintained.

Philosophical and theological outlines

Inspiration comes from several sources

So far, this chapter has been about the contextual inspiration in the developments in pastoral theory. Now, we shall draw some outlines from philosophical and theological backgrounds.

The philosophy of Martin Buber played an inspirational role in the founding of CPCC. This concerns primarily Buber's dialogical thinking, on I-Thou next to I-It, on healing through meeting, existential guilt, and justice of the order of being. More in the background, there is Buber's exegetical work as translator of the Hebrew Bible and his work on Chassidism. The reflection on Buber's dialogical work by Boszormenyi-Nagy, who derived the term 'relational ethics' from Buber's work, became the center of this inspiration.

In CPCC and DIPP, attention is also given to the philosophy of Emmanuel Levinas, which includes an ethics of Otherness and a critique of the totalizing tendency of Western thinking.

According to Levinas, in Western thinking, another is often made an object of comparative classifications, measured as different against the same, and deprived of uniqueness. In approaching the other as a call for responsibility I follow Levinas in often using the capital O. Another being is not 'just' different from me, but Other.

For many professionals, the philosophical perspectives of Buber (dialogical ethics) and Levinas (radical ethics) have become a relevant part of the contextual approach (relational ethics connected with the relational definition of the Self).

However, to study and be inspired by these aforementioned philosophers is not a condition for contextual practice and reflection. Colleagues from other traditions and from other parts of the world may receive inspiration from other sources, other philosophies of life that will sustain their motivation to engage in CPCC or DIPP.

As mentioned, in Africa, *Ubuntu* has great inspirational meaning (Ramose, 1999, 2005). *Ubuntu* is the abbreviation of an aphorism with different sounds in several African languages, as Zulu, Xhosa, and Ndbele: *Umuntu Ngumuntu Ngabantu*. The meaning is that a person is a person because of or through others. In DIPP, the *Ubuntu*-tradition is a truly relevant support. It may become enriching for practitioners of CPCC, too.

Therefore, instead of imposing or preaching a specific philosophy of life to one another, contextual practitioners could be sharing their dissimilar sources of inspiration for the sake of enriching one another with new points of view on personal life and relationships. This sharing as a resource is not always self-evident. In society, the differences between life orientations often become a cause of estrangement, for example when some people feel threatened by immigrants and their lifestyle. A comparable estrangement may happen when immigrants are hardly allowed to show loyalty to their original faith or culture. Communication about life orientations by diverse groups may contribute to connectedness in society. Under certain conditions, a contextual practitioner with the attitude of multidirected partiality could function as the leader of such a communication process. (For this sharing and healing through meeting, see part II of this section.)

Therefore, there are no good reasons for imposing any specific philosophy of life as a prerequisite for engaging in CPCC or DIPP. On the contrary. However, there is one condition: this engagement requires understanding of relational ethics.

Relational ethics come first

Relational ethics should be seen as *prima philosophia*, 'first philosophy'. When it comes to the compatibility of any given philosophical anthropological view with the contextual theory, this is the condition. Following Levinas, this means ethics as a category sui generis and responsibility as a kind of commandment that cannot be reduced to something else (see Van Rhijn & Meulink-Korf, 2019: 161). In other words: it is "an interpretive, phenomenological description of the rise and repetition of the face-to-face encounter, or the intersubjective relation at its precognitive core; viz. being called by another and responding to that other" (B. Bergo, quoted in Thesnaar, 2019). Relational ethics are neither the result of psychological factors, nor the product of value ethics or theological values. This primal ethics corresponds with an anthropology in which relationality is at the beginning of being, and in which the ethical dimension is intrinsically linked to an order or command to practice justice and fairness and to provide care.

Consequently, CPCC and DIPP are compatible with any philosophy of life that has a main place for fair giving-and-receiving in and between the generations. In other words, the concrete accountability of one human being toward another, which includes the responsibility for even more others and for their relations, counts as the first philosophy. This is primal to any '-logic', such as psycho-logic or socio-logic or theo-logic. For the purpose of pastoral care and counseling, the challenge is how to connect this with theology.

To a theological relational anthropology

Now moving a little further in the direction of theology, I hope to encourage readers coming from the field of theology and chaplaincy to engage their own thoughts along these lines. Also, nonbelievers are invited to reflect on these points. Perhaps some will recognize similarities from their own humanistic philosophies. What follows is a framework in line with relational thinking and especially contextual theory.

Let us consider the work of diverse thinkers for examples of related theo-anthropological findings. Of course, these specific voices from Islam, Judaism and Christianity cannot be representative of theology in general, but it can nevertheless create a connection when we see how thinkers, coming from different religious and philosophical backgrounds, underline human existence as inseparable from a call to responsibility by a transcendent God or 'exteriority'. In the interior of the Self, this call is experienced as an often-disquieting presence of the Other.

In Belgium, Reyhan Kayikci (2019) studied how female Muslim volunteers experienced responsibility. These women were both embedded in a Muslim tradition and in a liberal secular context. They saw their volunteer work, taking responsibility for others in society, as something that brought these two worlds together. According to these women, dedication to society means dedication to God. In their ontology, responsibility is based on a theological foundation. Reyhan Kayikci relates this to Levinas' approach to God as a condition higher than the self, which binds the self in a responsible relationship with the others in his/her world.

Rabbi Jonathan Sacks' book, *To Heal a Fractured World: The Ethics of Responsibility* (Sacks, 2005), focuses on the notion of mending the world. Every human being is invited by God to be God's partner "in the work of creation", in particular to help repair the breach between God's essence and his indwelling presence (*Shekhinah*) that is currently in exile (Sacks, 2005: 1). All human beings are invited to participate in this responsibility, which means: to choose life, over and over again.

As theologians, we may see this in relation to living in response to an unheard call, living under a call (see also Caputo, Moody et al., 2015), without knowing for sure whether there is really a call for 'me'. For Caputo, in his own words a postmodern Catholic, God means an invitation to responsibility for the earth as creation, and especially for other human beings. This includes responsibility for the interpersonal relationship and even 'my' responsibility to not take over another's responsibility for the self and others.

The call for justice has priority

The core criterion of compatibility between a theological anthropology or a philosophy of life and the contextual theory lies in the notion of relational ethics. This is not surprising, even if the dominant culture does not see this perspective as self-evident, in part because of natural sciences, where the notion of determinism is accepted broadly. This does not leave much space for the notion of human free will or free action. In the perspective of determinism, human actions and feelings are merely the inevitable consequences of 'how it is'. In theological anthropology, these radical deterministic and monocausal theories are not acceptable.

Here is yet another impasse in the Western culture, namely the belief in a free independent individual. Based on this assumption, people may have to deal with societal obligations, but they are making their own choices about how to be involved with the well-being of others. Often, especially in the western and northern regions of the world, one is indeed convinced that responsibility follows freedom. According to that, I would have to be free before choosing what kind of conduct and what kind of responsibilities suits 'me'.

This way of thinking seems to ignore that such autonomy does not exist. Already at birth, a human being participates in a network of relationships that includes expectations and obligations. Even a young child may show some responsible conduct, not to be confused with knowing morals, or with merely obeying the will of the parents. Nevertheless, the idea of responsibility as dependent on freedom has become widely influential. Unfortunately, this leads more and more to arbitrariness, unfairness, and egotism. If the criterion for what belongs to my responsibility depends on my free judgement of this call, i.e. whether this call suits me or not, then I would be at a loss for any order other than my own. My life would constantly revolve around my self-preservation, and my need to care for others would remain without direction.

This would result in chaos that is destructive for myself and violent to others. I would remain imprisoned in myself and keep others captured.

Therefore, neither radical determinism nor the idea of the free independent individual is a viable approach. Therefore, we must find another way to discuss freedom or unfreedom. In this new way, the autonomy of the subject means: not being deaf to the call of others. As far as the relational life of each person in its empirical concreteness is concerned, freedom lies in the fact that one responds to the other. Here lies 'my' liberation.

This is not an easy demand. I might wish that another person would be called, or that God or a god could replace me. The call of the other to 'me' is often disconcerting in part because more calls may come at the same time and so I must rank them. No God or god can absolve me of this responsibility. I must choose. Here, paradoxically, lies my autonomy, which can also be called heteronomy. It is the Other or otherness that promotes my freedom. This freed consciousness requires justice regarding several different others (the third, fourth etc.).

The call or 'epiphany' of the other(s) may be the revelation of God. In the relation with others, I hear a command or order, as God's Word. The order is also an offer, a gift that liberates my freedom from the arbitrariness (see also Van Riessen, 2019). In a kind of shorthand, one can name this assumption of the human condition: the relational reality before God, *coram Deo*. Reflecting on contextual theory as a source of inspiration for pastoral hermeneutics and theo-anthropological thinking, the following quote may be helpful: "We believe that a person always stands before God, hand in hand with others, and at the same time with others before God" (Meulink-Korf & Van Rhijn, 2016: 32). Intentionally, this expression does not say anything about God separately. The phrase is a relational one in itself. 'Before God' or 'before the face of God' is a metaphor for being encountered by transcendence, and for command-without-coercion; therefore, without threat of violence. It expresses a sense of theonomous living: in the presence of a faithful God, under a certain authority of an external being, and to be called to the honor and glory of this God. Paradoxically, this heteronomy may be the most autonomous and relational mode of human existence.

How is responsiveness possible? On respond-ability

Let us come back to, in particular, phenomenological terms. Empirical reality shows that human beings have the receptiveness to hear others and respond to them. However, it is obvious that this receptiveness and responsiveness do not always happen. Sometimes to a great extent, people are occupied with their own destructive entitlement and therefore deaf and blind to others. Contextual theory explains much of how this seeming blindness works in and between people and is focused on how people can be helped to hear the other(s) and to respond to the other(s).

What makes this human responsiveness possible? Boszormenyi-Nagy sometimes spoke of an "innate" tendency to care for others (Boszormenyi-Nagy & Krasner, 1986, 2014: 78). However, even if this innate tendency really exists, from where comes the human openness to hear the specific needs of the other who needs to be cared for? Responding to a more or less unwanted call does not come naturally from my own personality. Of course, 'I' am busy with many things regarding myself, including caring for different people. Therefore, the call of that particular other person to me often disturbs me. Maybe it does not suit me at all. Maybe I am busy with someone else, or I need to rest. So, the voice of my inner self is not the source of responsiveness. Relational ethics come from outside.

This human condition of being called and being responsive gives direction to my freedom. However, the how and when and to whom of my response remains my freedom, my consciousness as an individual, as a separate being. It is I who must act (or refrain from acting). It concerns me (Buber, 1998). This trust is perhaps the only certainty I have. I may be called, but for what, for action, for passivity? Perhaps in 'this' special case I should refrain and give space to others. Nobody knows in advance what kind of response to an actual call is the right one. It may be a call for help, care, or hospitality or being-left-alone or something else. It may be a call for togetherness, for intimacy, or for enjoyment. The call can be a call for *Mitfreude*.

Let us take a closer look at this phenomenon. The unusual German word *Mitfreude* translates as 'joy-with', a generous display of empathy with the well-being and joy of the other. Friedrich Nietzsche coined this word after focusing for several years on *Mitleid* (suffering-with) as opposed to *Schadenfreude*, malicious joy (Nietzsche, 1986). Although Nietzsche states that *Mitfreude* will be empirically rare, one can doubt whether this is true. Many people, including children, do show their joy for the sake of others. This phenomenon is not invisible, but it often remains unseen. Sometimes the culprit for this blindness is a psychological theory. For some, psychology reduces interpersonal behavior to egoism, and then ego-driven actions are particularly seen (for this criticism, see also Bregman, 2019). In some cases, theology can be the culprit, especially when it posits all activities as merely payment for an individual debt to God. There can be a combination of these two 'logics', one stemming from a certain individualistic psychology and the other from a guilt-oriented theology. Deconstructing *Mitfreude* in this way as merely a mask, a cover for destructive intentions, leads to a serious neglect of a relevant phenomenon. The special human reaction of *Mitfreude* deserves positive attention instead of deconstruction.

In any case, the call of the other to me is a gift. My presence is required. I am in the position to say: "Here am I", available for another. My freedom is liberated. This is where it all begins, the human give-and-take, the giving and receiving, the relational entanglements. The response to the call of others does not originate from morals, or merely from my psychological needs or my personal virtues, but from life as thoroughly relational. With an allusion to Descartes' *Cogito*, the philosopher F. Heinemann formulated: *respondeo ergo sum* – I answer, therefore I am (Heinemann, quoted in Boszormenyi-Nagy, 1987, 2014: 95).

Again, responding does not come naturally from personal goodness. My responses presuppose another who has already addressed me, with or without words. Often, I shall be blind and deaf or refuse to see and hear. However, the body may respond before the conscious mind knows. Here is an example from literature:

An old woman gave a hated enemy a drink, even before she knew what her hands were doing. The story is from *Life and Fate*, by the Russian writer Vasily Grossman (1905-1964). Levinas often referred to this novel as a source of important insights (Levinas, 1997). Although the woman in the story acted actively, it happened to her passively. For a moment she could not not-do this, she could not resist. She could not refuse to give the hated soldier some water. Grossman and Levinas refer to this as "a small kindness". A similar kindness can be seen in the immediate renunciation of a destructive redemption: 'I cannot do this'. This human behavior out of the blue, face-to-face, happens unintentionally, pre-cognitively. According to the novelist Grossman, goodness without conditions does exist (Grossman, 1995). It is clear that such an occurrence is not a daily, natural experience. However, just like *Mitfreude*, it deserves attention. The memory of a small goodness can have a contagious effect as a reminder of respond-ability.

So far, these sketches of a theological anthropology that sees responsibility as responding to the other(s) and that sees a trace of God in the vulnerable call of the other(s) to me. However, there is something else that deserves attention: the phenomenon of trust.

Trust without guarantee

Trust is a key concept in the hermeneutics of Maurice Friedman. Being addressed by another, responding to the other, and my trust that the other will trust my response – these three phenomena are connected. And the same goes for: I address another, I trust that the other will respond, and I trust the response. For the sake of clarity: trust does not mean having blind faith, being manipulated into trusting, acting as an obedient child, or as a parentified innocent-naive adult. On the contrary, trust presupposes individualized integrity. That is why Maurice Friedman emphasizes that no one could take over another's responsibility, and that this should not be attempted either. Of course, this creates dilemmas such as: how can one be sure of the sincere trustworthiness of another when there is no guarantee? In fact, one often cannot be sure whether there will be a genuine answer. To quote Friedman: "The courage to respond is not the courage of blind faith but the courage of really entering into a relationship" (Friedman, 1992: 10).

What is challenged the most is not an intellectual creed or a religious belief, but "an ... attitude of trust – a sense of being at home in the universe" (Friedman, 1992: 7). How do we deal with this challenge, and what is the significance of religion in this context? Some existential insecurities have diminished in many parts of the modern world, especially in places where there is a social security system run by the government. On the other hand, as became clear in times of Covid-19, there is still much insecurity, and feelings of unsafety can be everywhere. There are still so many reasons to be afraid and not feel at home, to feel left to one's own means and to trust few people. Sometimes people who try to avoid their own fears and distrust tend to seek refuge in religion, away from the world and away from the realm of insecurity. Others, and sometimes the same people, are motivated by their feeling or conviction that distrust will get them nowhere, and that the human world deserves better.

They seek God for talking, praying, maybe quarrelling. They seek God not primarily or not only as a refuge but as a partner in dialogue, addressing God with their complaints, for the purpose of fairness. Amidst situations of insecurity, fairness and justice are at stake. They refuse to accept that justice in the human world is lost. This trust without guarantee has to do with what Caputo phrases as hoping without hope, or against hope. "Hoping against hope calls believers and nonbelievers alike to participate in the praxis of the kingdom of God, which [...] we must pursue without why" (Caputo, 2015, Preface).

Summarizing these theo-anthropological outlines, human reality is a thoroughly relational reality, oriented on fairness, calling for justice. It is clear that the human condition is more than the use of others by individuals to maintain themselves. It means caring for others. It is the other, the Other, that summons me to responsibility, a heteronomous responsibility. Giving to others is often without direct reward. However, there can be, as an indirect reward, a certain trust that, in this way, one contributes to the well-being of one's neighbor and to a more just human world. This trust applies to people on a personal level, but also on a professional level.

Chapter 2
A Practical Framework, Related to Religion and Spirituality

The first chapter was mainly about basic principles and hermeneutics. Now we come to contextual pastoral care in practice, with attention to religion-related issues.

The effect of relationality

Spiritual counseling is not enough

The main questions for the practice of CPCC and DIPP are the same as for contextual therapy. What makes it work? How can someone move toward healing, toward (re-)building fairness, toward faith and (inter-)human meaningfulness, trust instead of getting stuck in destructive entitlement and the vindication of one's own rights? How can a professional be of help in these entanglements?

Often, the offering of religious interpretations and rituals by the practitioner as an interpretative guide is not enough, just as an incitement to stricter adherence to certain religious values is not appropriate. Spiritual counseling of the individual with attention to emotional healing and growing of faith, may be a support for individual well-being. However, when one aims at helping a person to heal in his or her relational reality, with attention to all dimensions, including the relational consequences of material facts, merely spiritual counseling of the individual is not sufficient.

CPCC- and DIPP practitioners are oriented to basic anthropological discoveries such as the existential interdependence of living creatures and these two structures in human life: a certain reciprocity in relationships and a tendency to responsibility and caring. Therefore they will work methodically with multidirected partiality as part of a relational focus. Now, for the sake of good practices, let us have a closer look at the relational focus in CPCC and DIPP practices.

A relational focus for approaching the human reality coram Deo

No counselor has quick-fix solutions. Nevertheless, a contextual pastor or chaplain does not stand with empty hands. What is needed for pastoral care at least is active listening to feelings, observing patterns of conduct, adequately reflecting, and using some specific tools and tales concerning beliefs and spirituality, sympathizing with someone's suffering; in other words, compassion, as well as empathizing with someone's well-being and joy of living (*Mitfreude*). Although this may seem already a long list, it may fail to meet its duties. It lacks a discussion of what a relational focus requires throughout the pastoral process.

Learning this relational focus in life and work

How does one learn a professional relational approach to the interpersonal reality?

To become a contextual pastor or chaplain, empirical sensitivity to one's own reality is paramount. We experience this reality as the relational complexity within and between ourselves, our family and neighbors, our clients, patients, and parishioners. Metaphorically speaking, threads of giving, taking, and receiving weave a fabric. Texts in context create a texture, and each texture is interwoven with some others. Each person's relational reality is unique, and at the same time, it exists only with others. A sensitivity to this interdependence can connect to responsible awareness. This may be the main root for contextual professionality.

Then there are the written sources. Literature about human life deals with relationships and is instructive in itself. The same applies to many song lyrics (see Hendriks, 2020).

Pastors and chaplains read culturally elemental texts, religious and non-religious, fiction and novels, prose and poetry. Such sources may also vitalize their thinking about relationships.

For example, John Donne (1572-1631), in his poem *No man is an island*, impressively expresses the fundamental human condition, including *coram Deo* without mentioning God.

> No man is an island,
>
> entire of itself,
>
> every man is a piece of the continent,
>
> a part of the main.
>
> If a clod be washed away by the sea,
>
> Europe is the less,
>
> as well as if a promontory were,
>
> as well as if a manor of thy friend's
>
> or of thine own were.
>
> Any man's death diminishes me,
>
> because I am involved in mankind.
>
> And therefore never send to know for whom the bell tolls;
>
> It tolls for thee.
>
> (MEDITATION XVII, Devotions upon Emergent Occasions)

Thus, the bell tolls for 'me', to be a responsible fellow-human and to be a responsible helper: *Mea res agitur:* "it concerns me", adapted by Buber from the Roman poet Horace, in his (Buber's) article on guilt and guilt feelings (Buber, 1957, 1998). Here too is the notion that my responsibility lies in my human reality as relational reality. This is what a person, including the professional, receives as a primary lesson from others, not once but repeatedly, as in this verse: *Tua res agitur*, it concerns you!

Thus, the pastoral counselor can learn and acquire this orientation through experiences in his or her own relational reality through inspiration from numerous sources, through training, through reflection and self-reflection on his or her personal life and work, in dialogue with others, intergenerationally.

For a relational orientation, this learning cycle is indispensable throughout life. It is a non-moralizing focus. I would add that high moral values can prevent pastoral education programs from addressing the risk of violating professional ethical codes. Awareness of the urgency of addressing this risk is important.

On burdens, resources, and a reversal in the counselor's mind

Before applying the relational focus to practical guidelines, we need to think about the burdens and resources of the client. Do 'burdens' in this regard refer to suffering of a special kind? Sometimes, the suffering is visible in serious symptoms and requires the aid of a psychiatrist or another professional specialist. However, usually, the relational hardships that someone brings into a conversation with a chaplain or pastor are not vastly different from the entanglements described in Section I of this book (which is not specifically about pastoral practice).

Certainly, those who prefer a pastor often expect more religious words, and these persons may use a different frame of reference than persons in secular circumstances. However, in addition to motives of familiarity, practicality, feasibility and availability, the choice of a helper depends on trust. People seek help or advice from a professional they can trust when sharing their hardships.

Are these worries always relational? Sometimes, what burdens someone has a very specific origin or individual character, for example, a negative health condition, irrational fears, an enduring grief, a bitter envy of the happiness of others, a search for gender identity, the loss of work, or a crisis of faith.

Yet all these worries would require a relational perspective. They connect to the lives of others through relational and social consequences. Especially when the person seems blocked in giving, the situation calls for relational care. Therefore, a contextual pastor or chaplain must go beyond the search for psychological explanations, and beyond offering comforting support. He or she will explore relational resources and find ways to mobilize them. It may be relevant to help a person engage in a process of exoneration. Reconnecting estranged family members is an important goal of CPCC and DIPP. All those involved, for example, the person who exhibits psychiatric symptoms or bad behavior and the persons who live near her or him, can benefit from rejoining each other in responsible dialogue (Boszormenyi-Nagy & Krasner, 1986, 2014), and the person with the (seemingly) individual problems will benefit.

The balances of giving, taking, and receiving may become fairer. This process from estrangement, disconnection, or disruption to reconnection, often is amazingly helpful for the whole being of each person.

Yet, a reconnection will not put an end to all burdens of the client. To be concerned with others often means hardship. Levinas calls this a divine discomfort. Dealing with worries and anxiety about the lives and fates of others, being patient, withholding the temptation to violate the other, are not comfortable. It means effort. The efforts are not always rewarded by positive results. The discomfort may be perceived as unfair. Partly, this is unavoidable. When the relationship is asymmetrical, the responsibility of one person to another cannot be balanced by a similar offer of responsibility (see also Ducommun-Nagy, 2008, in line with Levinas).

Why would this discomfort be divine? The answer to this question is that I meet in these burdens my responsibility as an infinite command to care for "the holiness of the Other/others" (Thesnaar, 2019).

However, here the dilemma of entitlement is relevant. There may be facts in my history that make me entitled *not* to care about anything other than what I consider as me or mine. On the other hand, I may choose to be responsible and bear new burdens in caring for others. Here lies a difficult freedom (Levinas, 1997). As we learn from contextual theory and research, in choosing to be responsible, earning constructive entitlement, my level of self-validation increases and eventually I may heal from the wounds that were at the root of my destructive entitlement.

My responsibility will not vanish then or be paid off. In some ways, it seems the opposite. Responsibility has the tendency to grow when it is taken seriously. Responsibility may be infinite, but my carrying capacity, energy and time are not! Therefore, this responsibility needs delineation. It brings with it the daily task of comparing the claims that are placed on me by several people, claims that are in principal incommensurable. The relational work of setting priorities is demanding and rarely easy. My presence may be demanded by different parties, who often have conflicting interests. To whom do I respond first? That is up to me. Without any exaggeration, this freedom is a difficult freedom. It brings with it a burden of worry and responsibility.

The counselor should never try to liberate the client from this freedom but will encourage this person to display and maintain concern for others as the core of humaneness. We discussed this in the previous chapter, reviewing suffering. Consider the following example from the practice of a prison chaplain:

A Dutch chaplain, working in a detention center, visited a young man, Ian, who was convicted for robbery. Ian was blatantly non-cooperative in the institution. In their first meeting, the chaplain asked him about whom he was concerned. Ian answered: "Of course about me. I do not deserve such a sentence, such a long term in prison, I never had a fair chance in life." The chaplain counseled him for some time. At some point, Ian came back to the question: "I am concerned about my mom, I feel so troubled, ... better to forget her." Spontaneously, the chaplain answered: "I am so glad you are! Let us talk about what you can do for her." This chaplain told his supervisor that this incident became a first step in Ian's repentance. Ian began to write to his mother regularly. He also attended group sessions and helped a visually impaired fellow prisoner. Although his more constructive attitude did not shorten the length of his incarceration, his gain was earning constructive entitlement. In Ian's own words: "I am becoming a better person, and I feel better too, although it is still difficult for me to get along with others."

It is notable that the chaplain did not merely focus on the prisoner's need to be understood, by asking "Who is concerned about you?", or "From whom did you get understanding in your not so easy life?" The chaplain changed the focus of his interview from questions about receiving to questions about giving. "The reversal has to start in the counselor's own mind" (Boszormenyi-Nagy, non-published remark).

The chaplain called the prisoner's new giving attitude a touchstone for humanity. In any case, when not applied in a moralistic prescriptive sense, the reversal in the counselor's perception of the client as a person who cares for others can become a lever. It helps the client to re-engage in giving, in constructive interactions. This means a reopening of relational resources.

Connecting listening, connecting speech, re-engagement in giving

Introduction

Concern means connection, or at least longing for connection. The term 'connection' is related to 'rejunction', which is mentioned as a special goal in contextual therapy and in the pastoral approach (Boszormenyi-Nagy, 1987, 2014; Meulink-Korf & Van Rhijn, 2016: 142). This is not the same as restoring harmony. It has to do with a re-engagement in giving of and by family members and possibly other people who were once important to one another. Connecting (or connective) listening is about the practitioner and means not only hearing the other's words, but also hearing the silence of the other(s). The pastoral practitioner who listens and asks questions and talks in a connecting way will be committed to what is said and what may be withheld. The term 'connecting' for pastoral practice is about two goals: rejunction of the clients with each other, and about the courage of the client to connect with his or her relational needs. The ultimate goal is the client's resumption of giving to others.

By connecting listening and speech, the counselor will encourage the client to take the risk of direct address and re-engaging. This means to speak directly and (re-)start giving to others (see also Heyndrickx, 2016).

Erica and the J.B. family, a pastoral process

The following example describes the practices of a contextual pastoral practitioner, especially of a pastoral counseling process. Please remember that each relational situation is unique.

Erica, a protestant minister in Belgium, was called by Mrs J.B., who asked for a consultation regarding the marriage of her and Mr J. (both 60 years old). Erica had known the couple for five years. They were members of the congregation, where Mr J. was more involved than his wife was. On occasions, Erica had also met their only child, a son, together with his wife. She knew that they lived with three grandchildren in a nearby city. Mrs J.B. complained that she and her husband "do not communicate, we grow apart. I do not understand why he is so stuck ... I feel lonely." She sounded exhausted.

By consulting her supervisor after this unexpected phone call, Erica reflected on the best way to help these people. For mainly practical reasons, she decided not to refer them to another professional. Erica went to their home to meet them both. She had been there before for meetings of the congregational finance commission, of which Mr J. was a member. Once she also had made a pastoral home visit, but at the time she got the impression that the couple did not appreciate her visit very much. This time Erica briefly inquired about their expectations of this planned conversation and explored the concerns of each. She also asked about their family. "I have good hope for your relationship as a couple and with your relatives," she said during this visit. They did not talk about a fee for the sessions, since members of a congregation together pay the minister's salary, some more, some less. Each member can consult the minister 'for free'.

Not to mix up Erica's different roles as their pastor, it was agreed that the next sessions should be held in Erica's office. This was not obvious because Mrs J.B. was disabled and staying at home was the most comfortable situation for her. The fact that during this visit she agreed immediately to come to the office seemed to surprise her husband positively. Erica did not comment to the surprise of the husband, but merely underlined the cooperation as a contribution. The couple and the minister agreed on a number of 5 or 6 meetings, for themselves and maybe also some together with relatives. Thus began the counseling process.

In the first session at her office, Erica explored in more detail the couple's relational stories, by listening and sequentially siding with each of them. Although Erica knew Mr J. as an active conversational contributor in the congregational organization, now he was rather withdrawn. He usually referred to his wife instead of answering Erica's questions himself. Erica asked about their shared relational history: "What did it mean to you to become a father?" Mr J.: "My wife took care of our son, that was because I went to work." Mrs J.B.: "Yes that was our situation, I was at home with Jake, he was a nice child." Erica insisted on questioning Mr J., who began to tell about his love for their son. Mrs J.B. said that being at home was a happy time for her during Jake's youth. "Then he left home and for his studies he went to the United States. No complaints, but that was the same year I was diagnosed with multiple scleroses." Erica: "That must have been hard for you. I think it is an injustice, that you as a rather young woman was struck by this hard fate. How did you cope with this diagnosis? And being without your son?" Mrs J.B.: "I had to. Jake and his family are back in Belgium now, but he is very busy. And I cannot help them with their children." Erica: "How does your husband help you in your difficult situation?" Mrs J.B. looked at her husband, and Mr J answered: "I cannot replace my son." Mrs J.B.: "That is not what I need, I need you. Not only your concern about my health condition. I like to share your concerns about your work, and the political world, and ... moreover, I do not want to intrude in the life of Jake, I do not want to be a meddlesome mother. I want my husband." It appeared that Mr J. was burdened with worries about his business, but he had not shared these concerns with his wife so as not to frighten her. "Otherwise, she's going to worry a lot about me and about our finances in the future." At the next meeting, the couple told Erica that at home, they were now able to talk to each other more directly than before.

At the beginning of this second session, Mr J. clarified that he had donated to a children's fund to compensate for the sessions with Erica. This gesture seemed to please his wife. Erica asked them about the relationships with their relatives, exploring their relational resources. Mrs J.B. talked about her only living sister: "We do not have much contact, and only by phone. She lives far away from here. But in the last years I miss the contact." Mr J.: "I never noticed that you miss her. But that is sad." He himself had no siblings, but his old father was still alive. "I regularly make sure that he is well taken care of, I do not know if he appreciates my involvement."

The third session was with Mr J and his father. Mr J. was able to tell his father about his business problems, and the father responded with interest and without over-concern or reproach. Mr J. cried when his father assured him that he valued his son's care. His father said he loved him, as his son and not as a successful professional. Mr J. told his father that he trusted his love. They never met like this before, according to both son and father.

The fourth session included Mrs J.B. and her sister. Through the years, the relationship between the sisters had become rather distant. Each of them had spared the other her own troubles, especially health problems. The sister said: "Our parents taught us not to exert ourselves too much, not to exhaust oneself. They were kind people. But since long, I do not believe this sort of care is the best parental message. I should have learnt to behave more solid, braver." Mrs J.B. was able to talk about her feelings of loneliness. The sister expressed her thankfulness that Mrs J.B. had invited her here. They planned to have more regular contact.

After two weeks, there was the fifth session, with the couple, and shortly thereafter a sixth one with the couple and the son and daughter-in-law. The son told his parents about his guilt feelings in the relationship, especially with his mother. In this long session, he also shared his and his wife's concerns about their 14-year-old daughter. The daughter-in-law reproved her parents in law: "Why do you never inquire about Elizabeth?" This girl had told her parents recently that she was distressed because of her gender identity confusion. Mrs J.B. did not react to the reproof but said instead: "Maybe she needs some other help, but she has to know that for us, whatever identity she is choosing, she would be accepted by us in any case. What matters to me is how can I cheer her up, she is a brave person." Mrs J.B. showed her interest in her granddaughter with a new generosity. Erica noticed how Mrs J.B. used the word 'brave' that was also spoken by her sister, about what they had not received in their youth. Erica communicated this lightly, in a connecting way: "Last month, your sister said that braveness was not encouraged by your very concerned parents. I see that you acknowledge the braveness in your grandchild." Mrs J.B.: "My parents came both from poor families in which a child had died at a very young age. They protected us. But times have changed." After the last session, the son phoned Erica and asked her for some advice regarding his daughter. Erica referred him to a psychologist whose qualities as a contextual practitioner she valued highly.

And between these sessions? Erica and the couple had met in church, not discussing the counseling contact. Shortly after the last counseling session, Mrs J.B. said to Erica: "My prayers are more grateful now, Reverend Erica." She emphasized with a big smile the word 'reverend'. During the sessions, they used only first names.

What attitude and skills were the so called levers Erica used to facilitate this process?

Erica's expression of hope for them may have been received as an encouragement. Above all, the couple's commitment to the process was strengthened by Erica's attitude of multidirected partiality and her acknowledgement of the disease of Mrs J.B. as a situational injustice. By refraining from commenting on what she saw in the couple's communication toward each other, Erica's counseling created a safe atmosphere. In the first meeting she could have asked directly: "Why now?" She did not do this, assessing the couple's trust in her as fragile. Erica acknowledged only lightly the first contributions of both partners (Mrs J.B.'s offer to come to the office, and Mr J.'s financial gift to the fund). However, her appreciation helped to install in both wife and husband a new esteem for the other. Erica's sequential partiality facilitated the exploration of destructive entitlement and the development of constructive entitlement instead. The counselor's identification of the father and the sister as relational resources helped to revitalize these relationships. Erica facilitated that they shared their problems (Mrs J.B. with her sister), received the offered help (Mr J. and his father), and offered support (both parents in relation to their son and his family). Grandmother's clear interest in her granddaughter became a source of confidence between the grandparents and the young couple. In the case of the sisters and their parents, Erica did not address the loyalty issues, at least not explicitly. She merely supported how Mrs J.B. exonerated her parents.

As for the couple, Erica's attention to how one helped the other in the history of their marriage, strengthened each of them in their daring to express what one needed from the other. The self-delineation and self-validation by each of them were stimulated. At the end of this counseling process, Mr J. and Mrs J.B. had begun to re-engage with each other, not in the least by seeking the other's attention. They also took the risk of being more active in their care for their son and his family.

Here ends this account of a counseling process by the clients' minister who also became their counselor. Of course, this was not the end of all burdens on the lives of these people. Erica remained available for a new consultation and pastoral conversations.

Some guidelines as suggestions

In this paragraph, I share some suggestions for (one or more sessions of) a counseling process, as in the case of the J.B. family. Some of these actions, certainly not all, were present in Erica's counseling. The list is not about a standard procedure; it is a list of possible recommendations (see also Meulink-Korf & Van Rhijn, 2016).

- Listen actively to facts and feelings and be attentive to the couple's interactions, without commenting on them.
- Enquire whether there are, or have been, others involved as listeners or counselors. Ask what the partners expect or hope from this current conversation.
- Ask for concrete examples: "You tell me that you are disappointed in your husband. What is disappointing you?"; "What is your biggest concern?"; "What do you worry about the most?"
- Explore the balance of fairness between the partners and pay attention to what is or was not fair. Explore the balance of trust with attention to each one's expectations for the future.
- Each of the partners must be invited and supported to present, one after the other, their own perspective (multidirected partiality by the counselor). This sharing does not need to be 'the whole story'. Any effort to make a sincere contribution to this consultation (through direct address, real presence, as opposed to a seeming presence) must be recognized as help.
- When you as the counselor feel that the client is coming with a hidden agenda or is feigning to be open, try to communicate your impression in a non-blaming way. For instance, you may ask: "Is there something that blocks you from opening your heart?"
- Offer the possibility of one or more separate sessions with each of the partners. Here the main reason is to avoid the risk of disloyalty to their families of origin.

- Ask about other relatives, particularly children and parents (inclusiveness of the multidirected partiality, also asking questions about relational resources).
- Try to think about more than two family generations of the persons involved. This will lead to a better understanding of what may motivate each person.
- Ask "Are you worried about someone in particular?"
- Ask not only: "What does this important person mean to you?" but also: "Do you know what you mean for this person?" Compare the reversal in the example of the prisoner.
- Make sure that you help the client to give credit to the person(s) who, in the past or currently, have helped him or her.
- "How did your wife try to help you?" is often a more trust building question than "Did she help you?" The counselor, by using connecting speech, assumes that people in long-term relationships are still available to help each other, even if only sporadically.
- Pay attention to the relationships within the families of origin. Be aware that the description of these relationships by a person about his or her own family has more relational weight than told by the spouse who is the in-law because this in-law is not bound by the same loyalty to this family.
- Acknowledge a spouse's concern about in-laws.
- Acknowledge the concern of the wife for the husband's relationship with her family and of the husband's concern for the relationship of the wife with his family.
- Explore possibly stagnant relationships and sources of destructive entitlement in the history of each one's family of origin, which may require separate sessions.
- Ask about religious faith or another form of spirituality as a resource, and (how) the partners share this.
- Ask about sexual intimacy as a resource, and how the partners deal with this.
- Encourage a real exchange about a just and equitable balance of giving and receiving and its dynamics over the years.
- Sometimes it is good to have a conversation about the often-unavoidable non-synchronicity between people. Relatives, including spouses, do not always live in the same Now. For one partner, for example, this Now is a time of saying goodbye to her dying father; for the husband, although often a compassionate partner, these same weeks mean that he Now finally gets a well-deserved promotion at work.
- Discuss whether there are severe loyalty conflicts and other deadlocks. For example, what do irreconcilable legacies mean for mutual trust?
- Express appreciation (give credit) for taking the step of requesting help for their problems (responsibility). No parishioner or client needs to be one hundred percent motivated or full of hope. It is the pastoral counselor who must communicate his or her hope that there is a way out of their entanglements.
- Close the session with words of hope, perhaps in the form of a prayer or a simple word of blessing. A search for 'the right words' sometimes also means finding silence and words that give meaning to the silence.
- Thank the parishioners or clients for the trust they have put in you.

The following indicators are intended as suggestions for pastoral visits or counseling sessions.

- Propose to agree on a certain number of subsequent appointments. If none are scheduled you must communicate that you as counselor will remain open for further contact if needed.
- In situations in which the pastor sees her- or himself as not competent or has other more urgent priorities, the pastor needs to help finding another pastoral counselor, preferably a contextual practitioner.
- Indicate and affirm the confidentiality of the conversation.

This list of specific and general suggestions is not intended as a blueprint or a standardized procedure. In the next sessions, there may be other pathways to follow. For example, relational education, possibly by religious rituals or texts, can be an adequate tool, if this does not contradict the counselor's multidirected partial stance (for examples, see also Van Doorn, 2020).

Often, the counselor will use a socio-genogram (a term coined and standardized in 1997, see Van Rhijn & Meulink-Korf, 2019; see also Meulink-Korf & Van Rhijn, 2016: 173). The socio-genogram is a special family tree-drawing, in which family members and significant others are recorded, over at least three generations and certainly with inclusion of the youngest generation. Socio-economic life events and circumstances are included. The counselor may draw this socio-genogram together with the client as the narrator, or the client will draw it at home and may ask a family member for more information. When the client indeed visits a family member who shows concern for the significance of this guest's visit, and especially when the family relations were neglected and the balance of giving and receiving is stagnated, this contact will make a difference. Sometimes it is not a family member but a near acquaintance of the family who may give new information from the past. The recorded facts often make it possible to see the emotional and interactional aspects of someone's relational reality in an ethical perspective, including the fifth dimension of the Self-Other delineation. In this way, it enhances the client's freedom to formulate an ethical redefinition of his or her relationships.

The counselor may encourage the client to bring a family member as participant to the session. When a family member participates in one or for a few meetings, it is important that this person can benefit from the counselor's multidirected partiality. The counselor will explore relational stagnation and will be especially attentive to the individual and relational resources, encouraging (a restoration of) dialogue. Sometimes this process leads to the client's reassessment of the other's resources, and maybe to a process of exoneration. The counselor will also be attentive to family members who will never be present (see also Van der Meiden, 2019).

Last but not least: a contextual practitioner should not forget to keep learning in practice and theory and not hesitate to ask for supervision.

Guidance in non-family in-group conflicts

The following paragraph is not about family relationships, but about conflicts within a group. Conflicts between groups have their own specific dynamics. Guiding conflicts between groups moreover requires historical insight that must include a knowledge of the economic situations of these groups as well as a deep awareness of the situational and relational injustices that these groups may have experienced. Many notions proposed by the contextual approach may be relevant to managing an intergroup conflict. Nevertheless, because of the limited practical experience of contextual pastoral practitioners with intergroup conflicts so far, I shall concentrate here on conflicts within groups.

Pastoral practitioners sometimes are consulted concerning conflicts in non-family groups, especially in church-related situations. There may be coinciding interests among the participants in a religious community, about for instance the survival of the community. In general, the community, represented by the board and the pastor, will listen to all the voices of its members and often also of people who are not full members, such as a refugee who does not yet know if he or she wants to become a member but who is interested in the future of the congregation anyway.

However, often there are also conflicting interests. There may be serious problems, creating obstacles to in- and outside group solidarity. Here is an example, based on a frequently occurring dilemma. In a village there are several church buildings, and one of the church buildings must be closed and sold, for financial or other reasons. Therefore, the question is which to choose? Another related example is the following situation: there is a lack of money, and no other related church in the neighborhood is available to form an association with in order to save the costs. The question is then: how to save money, and what are the consequences? Once the decision to sell a building is made, usually by the leaders of the congregation, how should they deal with the feelings of loss, pain and anger of those members who were attached to this religious home? Loyalty dynamics often play a role in these kinds of settings.

"This is not fair," said Mila. "My father was such an active member. Now he feels exploited, abandoned in his ideas about the future. The intended merger of churches in our town is for him a nightmare. Keep in mind that my father's father raised the funds for planting this specific church. And now the building will be sold, and the money goes to some youth-work program working with refugee-children." Mila is no longer a believer, and she does not attend church anymore. Nevertheless, she joined in a bellicose way an initiative to save this building as a church. Members of the board who were planning to sell the building took the position that she was not entitled at all to be included in the discussion.

Here the contextual theory can provide insights that are useful steps in dealing with meetings regarding a church-related conflict.

As 'work principles' (Brouwer, 2004), the counselor-facilitator in a group session with two or more parties in opposition, can use the following directives, which partly overlap:

- Invite everyone to respond to this question: "To whom or to what would you be or feel disloyal if you would shift your position?" and to listen to the responses of the other participants.
- Address in a considerate, connecting way the possibility of conflicting and split loyalties.
- Encourage a mindset of 'and-and', as preferable to 'either-or'.
- Try to 'hear back' the pain and desires of each of the parties involved. This is also called 'back-track-hearing' or 'reverse listening'. 'Hearing back' means that the counselor evokes what is not said and not directly heard by the members at this time of the conflict. The counselor tries to elicit trust in everyone's capacity for responsibility and reliability. When people in the community have lost trust in each other, it may be helpful to mention that most people share the same motivation to behave responsibly and reliably.
- Evoke mutual recognition of each person's entitlement to be involved in the problematic situation, and to make a constructive contribution. Encourage the participants to share with each other the basic assumption that each participant has the right to participate and to get the opportunity to express him or herself constructively.
- Invite each party to recognize its own destructive style of communication.
- Invite each party to commit to constructive, direct address and to dialogue. This includes willingness to ask straight forward questions, and to ask to whom it may concern rather than to speak in vague or general terms.
- Use connecting listening and connecting speech. Trust in constructive cooperation increases when there is direct communication instead of behavior based on images and ideas about the other party. The way one party in the community gives, takes, and receives, may be an indication of the possibility of working toward more fairness toward the other party (a more balanced fairness).
- Try to avoid weighty words such as reconciliation and forgiveness, especially at the beginning of a dialogue. These words should be used only when people are ready to contribute to fairness and justice for all involved.
- Give hope and be realistic. "Perhaps there is no solution for this conflict, but there may be a way forward for all" (Aat van Rhijn, oral remark).
- Work as inclusively as possible toward a trust-based future, searching with all involved for a way to deal with the conflict and the conflicting interests.

These above-mentioned directives can also be used to prevent conflicts.

Here are some additional guidelines that can be applied in the congregation before a conflict arises:

- Provide some informative lectures on relationships, including on loyalty dynamics, organize a discussion on the use of a multigenerational perspective in community issues, and on the benefits of lasting concerns for future generations (transgenerational solidarity).

- Provide some psycho and socio-education on mimesis, rivalry, and scapegoating mechanisms (Girard, 2004).

All these guidelines are compatible with core perspectives of Christianity. Most of these viewpoints are found also in other religions. For instance, traditional African religions have a similar orientation on 'living forward' with careful consideration of the past as beneficial for the community. This consideration means sometimes even a consultation with ancestors, as in the *Unsamo* gathering in the hut of the ancestors.

Another example comes from a non-religious culture. In Amor Towles' novel *A gentleman in Moscow*, the protagonist wants to protect his foster-daughter from the surrounding communist ideology. Therefore, he equips her with an attitude of respect for the past: "The principle here is that a new generation owes a measure of thanks to every member of the previous generation. Our elders planted fields and fought in wars, they advanced the arts and sciences, and generally made sacrifices on our behalf. So, by their efforts, however humble, they have earned a measure of our gratitude and respect" (Towles, 2017: 50). Viewpoints like this might be seen as merely conveying moral values, but they also can be seen as fostering relational ethics.

Can the spiritual dimension be a relational resource?

Introduction

Although they do not have exclusive access to this domain, all pastoral counselors will deal with the spiritual dimension of life, as a hope or a need for meaning and fulfilment, often expressed in terms of belief and faith. The spiritual sphere does not come separately in life. Buber is one of the thinkers who warned people not to put a so-called sacred sphere apart from a profane daily reality (Buber, 1998). In Judaism, as in traditional African religions and in other traditions, this seems to be obvious: one should not separate the transcendental sphere from the earthly one. After all, spiritual life is about unity, wholeness, or interdependence, in other words, about the opposite of compartmentalization of life. In Christian theology, one finds this related assumption: as human beings, we are soul, in all our functions and relationships. Human beings do not possess souls, they are soul (Louw, 2019). In this integrating sense, the spiritual dimension of life can be a rich resource for fair relating.

Relationality in spirituality and in religion

The 'spiritual dimension' refers to the related phenomena *spirituality* and *religion*. Spirituality has to do with feelings (longing for harmony, for connectedness with an encompassing entity, for an ultimate purpose in life) and values by which individuals are motivated in the depths of their being. A person may perceive her or himself as spiritual in one's "deepest inner self", seemingly without connection with what is exterior, namely the self of others, or otherness. In practice, this person may not value relationships any less than any religious or non-religious person.

In most religions, relationality is perceived as a fundamental notion, as a 'root note' in music. Religion is not only about individual beliefs or personal faith. It is also about belonging. Theoretically, the two aspects, believing and belonging, can be distinct. However, empirically, these two usually go together (Van Tubergen, 2020). The element of belonging is more than a mere social aspect. For religious believers, there is a relational motivation that arises intrinsically from belief. This should not be surprising. Most current etymology connects the word 'religion' with the Latin verb *religare*, to bind strongly. Through the times, there have also been references to a lost Latin verb *religere* that probably had to do with *obligere*, to oblige. Or as Cicero said, religion has to do with *relegere* (meaning: reading again, considering). All these related notions contribute to nourish the current concept of religion. Therefore, religion is inherently concerned with human reality as relational reality, which includes both a committed relation with God and with fellow human beings. It includes the notion of distance as an unavoidable condition of any relationship, and of proximity, especially with God as the Ultimate Other. Without distance there can be no relating, this is "a twofold principle of human life" (Buber, 1998: 54).

Interpretation of life and a transgenerational concern

As said, the interhuman relational characteristic is part of religion. The golden rule to treat others as you would like others to treat you, with its implication of reciprocity, is assumed to be universal. Overall, religious traditions give interpretations of fundamental life experiences to help or even to redeem persons. They address possible basic facts and experiences in the life of a concrete person, such as coming of age, sex and gender, friendship, illness, and death. There are experiences of harmony, affirming a person's basic trust and his or her ability for hope. However, often, life experiences are less reassuring. Migration, divorce, a pandemic threat, abuse, and violence (at times related to religion), may challenge a person's feeling at home in the world. When experienced more often, these events generate a loss of familiar meaning and meaningful interpretation of life. After such experiences and especially after relational losses, religions can offer restoration of trust and healing by exposing people to symbols of (a) God, n/Nature, or of another entity that transcends the limits of the self. In connection with their interpretative comments, religions offer rituals for mourning, for addressing and celebrating thankfulness, for understanding relational and social obligations, for penance, forgiveness, reconciliation, and more.

Religions are meant to be transmitted through generations. This is true even when a personal divine revelation is considered more important than a shared tradition. Usually, the transmission of religious narratives provides an idea about the future with attention to ethical consequences. It means the opposite of *après moi le déluge* ('after me, the flood'), the words attributed to Madame de Pompadour, at the court of Louis XV of France. This historical notion stands in contradiction with the story of so many people who tend to be concerned about others outside their own circles. They even do care about the fate and fortune of future human beings (see Bregman, 2019). We often see this attitude of transgenerational solidarity in religions. It is also found in traditional religions that are oriented to listening to the voices of the ancestral spirits or to praying for God's intercession. Regarding important decisions and moral values, these ancestral voices are valued as feeding-forward. They bring expectations of fairness and healing of sorrows, including the well-being of posterity. Thus, religions provide an awareness of posterity that is not limited to biological offspring. It concerns the posterity of humankind.

Intergenerational options for proximity and generosity

Transmission of religiosity in changing times, its implications for loyalty

"Religiosity tends to be rather stable over time and geographical areas" (Van Tubergen, 2020: 465). This 'stickiness' is not surprising from a multigenerational perspective. "Research shows that parental transmission of religion plays a major and enduring role in people's own religious group identity, practices, beliefs, and values" (Van Tubergen, 2020: 465). Nevertheless, in Africa, as in other continents, under the influence of modernization, religious transmission is not limited anymore to a transmission within the family or the ethnic group between one generation and the next (vertical diffusion). Now, this transmission occurs also within the same generation, outside of the familial line (horizontal diffusion, through peers). This has implications for loyalty dynamics and other aspects of family relationships.

Living in modern societies, we shall be aware of religious pluralism, within communities and within the individual. Nowadays, in the Western part of the world, for instance in Europe, people often engage in more than one spiritual movement ('patchwork-religion'), while other members of their family may stick to one single tradition. Because keeping a religious tradition can be a way of expressing one's loyalty to the previous generation, it is important to examine what happens when someone takes another route.

Karen is a Dutch single adult. Sometimes she visits a group of Buddhists in her neighborhood, and on an irregular basis she spends the weekend in a Roman Catholic monastery, where she participates in worship services. She tells: "I collect the most inspiring aspects of both religions. I am open about this, and nobody expects me to make a choice." In her youth, she was caught between the strict Calvinist church of her father, and the evangelical enthusiasm in the 'Free vineyard church' of her mother. "Now," she says: "I am myself, and honestly this is a deep relief."

People like Karen draw inspiration from heterogeneous sources in finding not only a foundation for their individual values, but also support for their relational lives. Karen's reliance on multiple sources for her inspiration and sense of belonging is not only a phase in a transition but may also provide her with a lasting home for her spiritual longings. Like Karen, many others are born in families in which the parents come from different traditions. When the parents are unable to agree on what tradition to pass on to their children, their children are placed in a loyalty conflict. Their offspring may escape the conflict by rejecting religion entirely or by engaging in a new religious path. Karen's choice may be perceived as disloyal to her parents. Yet, it can also be understood as an expression of indirect loyalty to the parents since she does not reject religiosity as such. Karen reported that she avoided guilt feelings by showing her loyalty to her parents in a different way. Initially, her new attitude to her parents was a bit artificial and affected overdone. However, she increasingly enjoyed the contact as, in her own words, a form of nearness. She takes constructive interest in their life by more frequent calls and in view of their ageing, she offers them practical support.

Here is another example, from the history of Judy and Eric, a couple with two little sons. They made the decision to leave the synagogal congregation in which Judy was rooted and where they together had celebrated their marriage. They had a good exit conversation with the board members of the community in which they had taken part.

"You know, our commitment is limited in time and energy. Participation in two groups is too much. This old synagogue in the city ... it takes too much time to walk here on Shabbat. We must choose, and we made our decision on a practical basis, for a more liberal religious group of young families in our neighborhood. This will be our way to be good Jewish parents for our children," said Eric and Judy.

In the exit interview, the couple also talked about how they were feeling disloyal to Judy's family. The rabbi who took part in the conversation suggested them to see a contextual counselor because their decision had consequences for their relationships with Judy's family. Indeed, they had a few sessions of therapy. It helped Judy to have a dialogue with her mother, exploring her mother's side. Her mother, a widow, expressed her hurt feelings. After World War II, her father, Judy's grandfather, had contributed to the rebuilding of the old synagogue. Therefore, to Judy's mother, this synagogue was a very special place. As a result of the counseling, Judy and her mother made plans to go to the USA to visit an old aunt. To Judy, the expensive trip, without her husband and sons, and away from her work, entailed a sacrifice. This gift of Judy for her mother and aunt was received by them as an unexpected gesture of generosity. After some time, Judy's mother told her daughter that she had accepted the new congregation as indeed more helpful for an appropriate transmission of Jewish tradition to the grandchildren.

In contrast to Judy's mother, Eric's parents were not really affected by their son and his spouse's decision. They seemed rather indifferent. Eric had converted to Judaism when he married Judy. Eric's parents were atheists. They might have been reassured by the decision of the couple to go to a more liberal religious community. In Eric and his parents' relationship, it could be relevant to have an exchange about what is spiritually important to each of them.

Changes in religious belonging and options for vitalizing relationships

During and after colonialism, in many regions of the world, we can find combinations of a traditional religion with its own rituals and mythology and of elements of the dominant religion of the previous conquerors. In this regard, the word 'syncretism' is often used. This term has a pejorative connotation. It is used mostly by the representatives of those religions that are based on a revelation instead of on a tradition, especially by Christians. Nonetheless, 'syncretism' often helps to increase tolerance and interest in the culture and beliefs of others.

In families, the non-synchronicity of the generations in these processes of change affects the relationships (see also Van Doorn, 2020). There may be feelings of alienation and mutual accusation of selfishness. When adult children belong to another religion or denomination, parents may feel abandoned and even cheated. Their loyalty to their own perhaps long-dead parents seems to be at stake. They blame not only modern society but also themselves and their children. It may help the relationships if adult children express their loyalty to their ancestry constructively, for instance by keeping elements of the 'old' religious family tradition amidst their current culture.

The following example is of a family with a complex history of religious belonging. It includes the counseling in which this family has engaged.

Fundile, a teacher of History and African Culture at a high school, came from a poor background. He was born in the nineties as the youngest child from Xhosa parents in the Eastern Cape (SA). At birth, he was given the name Fundile. He was still a baby when his parents separated. Shortly after that, his father died. At three, he was baptized and was given the name Andrew. He was raised by his mother and his much older half-sister, who both became professionals in healthcare. These women were intensively committed to a Calvinist community (Uniting Reformed Church of Southern Africa). They never talked extensively about what apartheid had meant to them. As a teenager, Andrew had found out that his father had been inspired by the Black Consciousness Movement. After this discovery he began to take part in meetings with the Izinyanya (a healer and diviner, in Zulu called sangoma). He longed for harmony with the dead and, according to his words: "a place for the pain". He changed his name back to Fundile. It took years before his mother and his sister agreed to use this name. They persevered in anger and guilt because he had "not really converted to Christianity". Later, when the minister of his mother's church invited Fundile to give a lecture on local history at the church, things changed. The family attended the lecture, and this became the starting point of a dialogue between Fundile and his family of origin. The family consulted the minister, David. David, who at that time was training to become a counselor, led the session with an attitude of multidirected partiality. Pastor David: "I see, mother, you raised two children. Both are well educated. You did a rather good job." A crucial moment occurred when David asked about Fundile's motivation: "Fundile, for whom did you become a history teacher?" Fundile, making an encompassing gesture including his mother and sister: "for all of you. You suffered so much before I was born, I wanted to know more about that time and tell this to others, to white kids too. And ... [crying] for my father."

The mother of Fundile received these words as a gift. Three meetings followed with Fundile and his sister, Angel. Angel said that she had carried a great burden by being the confidant of their mother who was always concerned about her brother, her mother's only son. For the first time, Fundile heard that his sister was suffering because she was the closest companion of their mother. He began to engage more actively with Angel. Angel refused to invite her mother to join a session with the pastor on this subject, but at home she spoke about it with her mother. Her mother showed that she understood her daughter. Now each member of this small family was increasingly able to take the position of the other(s) into consideration. In this way, they earned constructive entitlement. This was visible, for instance, in the fact that for the first time in her life Angel was able to engage in a realistic and loving commitment with a man. In a dialogue with her mother about their relationship, Angel could begin to speak about her plans to move out. The mother acknowledged her daughter for having been such a supportive companion. In doing so, the mother was validating herself. She could see herself as a committed parent who, in a situation of poverty, raised two children and gave them both the opportunity to study. Now that they were adults, she wanted to be a loving parent for them in a reliable and not guilt-inducing way. "I shall always give them food and shelter whenever they come. I love them. But I understand that they have a life of their own." In a personal manner, she gave both Angel and Fundile her blessings. She organized a small ritual that involved only the three of them. The mother shared with them her sense of guilt and her gratitude and offered them a prayer. This ritual underlined their common intention to keep the unity in the family in the face of unavoidable changes. Parental blessings mean so much! Not only Angel but also Fundile received their mother's prayer as a gift. Fundile did not have problems with the Calvinist terminology of the prayer. Fundile's choice of a more traditional religion was no longer seen as disloyalty by his family. His mother now could show her well-meant interest in his visits to an Izinyanya. Angel was increasingly able to engage in constructive relationships outside the family. The connecting interventions of pastor David, based on the attitude of multidirected partiality, helped to overcome the family's estrangement. He encouraged them all in their process of renewed giving to one another.

The beliefs of the professional and receptiveness to otherness

Pastoral counselors and chaplains have to take care of their own beliefs in the relationship with their clients. This does not require them to be explicit about them. However, if they wear external signs of their faith (a cross, a kippah, a headscarf, or another garb), they need to explain that their physical presentation does not imply that they could not be available to everyone. Sometimes such an explanation is not enough. For instance, if a Christian chaplain is counseling a Jewish person, out of consideration, the pastor may avoid wearing a visible cross.

At the same time, the pastoral practitioner has to strive for congruence. Congruence in communication means that what one thinks corresponds with what one actually says. Moreover, we listen to Louw (2018: 220), who states: "If pastoral care within a Christian paradigm becomes separated from the content of faith, it easily loses its unique character." In other spiritual paradigms, the same will be true. There are several ways in which a pastoral counselor can congruently display her or his faith. The wordings of the contextual pastor following the Calvinist theology will differ from the formulations of a chaplain with a purely humanistic philosophy of life. However, in any case, whether these beliefs are expressed directly or remain implicit, they must be consistent with relational ethics. No belief or conviction should prevent the counselor from being open to the client's motivations and beliefs, and to be multidirected partial to all involved. Responsible siding with diverse forms of religious belonging and believing of parishioners and their family members demands from the practitioner an openness toward what is unknown, toward what still may seem to be strange, in other words, it demands receptiveness to otherness.

Therefore, an integration of his or her own beliefs throughout the stages of life up to now, is important. Many pastors and chaplains were raised in a specific religious group and later in life they found their own path, different from their parents'. Of course, this had an effect on their family relationships. How these practitioners dealt and deal with feelings of guilt or anger to their own families will influence their position toward their patients or parishioners, and their reliability as colleagues. Are they still caught in a loyalty conflict and tend to avoid the difficult matters in their own family? Were they free to choose a religious community other than that of their parents? Were they pushed by their family to attend a theological school? They may recognize László's feelings, who says: *"Often I only feel loved because of my church career. My parents are proud of my profession as a minister, but what about me as a person?"* How are these practitioners dealing with their own parentification? In contact with a parishioner, are they emphasizing possible religious and spiritual issues as a resource? Are they even propagating them at the expense of being attentive to what is relationally burdening the parishioner? Are they receptive to peer cooperation instead of trying to earn the affection or admiration of their church members at the expense of colleagues?

Let us reflect on pastor David, who participated in group supervision.

At the time of his sessions with Fundile's family, David participated in a training program and learnt to reflect on his practices from a relational ethical point of view. It seemed to come quite naturally to him to follow the conditions for genuine dialogue between family members. In a group supervision, David shared with the other students his experiences with Fundile's family. As this happened, another trainee attacked him: "What about your loyalty to God? Your own Dad is a strict minister. We must proclaim that in Christ is all, as your father does. You have the obligation to discourage this young man Fundile from going to an Izinyanya. There is old dangerous superstition." David replied with the personal story of his searching for faith and trust amidst his parents who "belittled me in order to make me strong and at the same time a total sinner". The co-members of the supervision-group felt moved. The supervisor supported them in how to listen and talk to David with respect, instead of judging his theology.

In the next session of the supervision, David's opponent was asked to investigate for himself if there were some possible loyalty issues that could have triggered his unexpected harshness toward David. Then they talked about the content of his accusation: supporting superstition as opposed to being a person in partnership with God in a "theonomous reciprocity". They agreed on the necessity of a religious dialogue and on "never limiting God to our own convictions". They were all vitalized by what they believed was an inspiring, open meeting. The former opponent of David closed this session with a prayer of gratitude for what he called "a new sense of sister- and brotherhood that he was part of".

Shortly afterwards, David had a meeting with both his parents, and he told them about the supervision meetings, including what he had shared about the pain he had felt in the past. They listened to him and responded well. Three weeks later, David's father consulted David about his efforts in trying to accept the recent news that his daughter (David's sister) was attracted to persons of the same sex. David was moved by his father's openness to him. This meeting was a healing moment in the history of their relationship.

Loyalty to God?

In David's youth, his faith in God was intertwined with what his parents had told him about God and how they behaved in church and in daily life. They seemed to have expected a strict religious practice by their children without much attention to their relational needs. In his case, this caused a "feeling that I never am good enough". These rather bad experiences of *brokenness* were an obstacle in his becoming an adult who trusted himself and God and others. "But I always hoped for a loving God, and merely this hope helped me a lot.". At the time of the aforementioned counseling sessions, he describes himself as partially healed thanks to his faith in God and also to experiences with teachers, with friends and especially with his spouse. As a part-time chaplain in a psychiatric institution, next to his work as a pastor in the congregation, he refers to his strong affinity with severely suffering patients, as "the attitude of a wounded healer" (with a term of C.G. Jung, also used by Henri Nouwen). "I still have to work on my strong tendency to please others, to be the most empathic listener, and sometimes even by downplaying a colleague. And more important, as a parent I am still too soft on my own daughter. I am too permissive. Sometimes I feel that I cannot establish contact with her. But perhaps I am too much focused on my own side, trying to avoid the hard ways of my father and to be myself an excellent parent." David perceives his 'loyalty to God' more and more as being open to receive and to give love "in whatever form. It happens that I feel God's love in listening to music, and in sharing Holy communion. There are also such moments in my supervision group. Now I feel that I am a friend to some of my colleagues." Apparently, David is less focused on "working for God, pleasing God. God remains a mystery to me, but this does no longer scare me." At the same time, his relaxation and his growing trust in being 'good enough' reinforce his parental attitude.

The preferential character of loyalty, *in casu* my commitment to God over 'my' commitment to a certain fellow human being may be *de facto* not applicable to a 'loyalty to God' concept. When one's belief in God indicates that to serve this God is to be present for one's fellow human beings without being coerced to perfection, then there is not a not-preferred party that 'I' may disadvantage because of my choice for God. In this regard, the contextual thinking about loyalty does not apply to a relation with God. However, we shall not conclude that this diminishes the importance of the contextual approach. On the contrary, it may underline the relational character of religion. Primarily, this God refers to someone's relation with the other(s), as a personal difficult freedom. In other words: "the ethical relation as a religious relation" is "an exceptional relation: in it, contact with an external being, instead of compromising human sovereignty, institutes and invests it" (Levinas, 1997: 16).

We do not know a general answer to the issue of what room could remain for an unmediated dyadic relationship between a person and his or her God. I myself as a theologian only know that keeping these relations (to God, and to other human beings) apart from other people does not help me in my personal life neither my theological thinking nor in celebrating the liturgy or in any other expressions of my faith.

Religion and theology as an obstacle in relational ethics, and pitfalls in counseling

David saw his own pitfall. The exaggerated concentration on 'Christian virtues', as presented by his parents, made him unfree. Here lies a very serious threat to reciprocity and fairness. Christian morality tends to extol certain deeds and feelings such as loving other people, helping those in need and forgiving them for the wrong they did, promoting these as virtues a Christian must acquire.

Here lies the risk of self-centeredness. The *Ego* that never serves others sufficiently will not enough consider the perspective of others who also have a right to give and help. Sometimes, in a congregation in which the people abide by high moral standards, a leader indicates himself as a moral instance *par excellence*, with a special relation with God. This attitude may even stimulate a mimetic desire, a desire to be innocent or saintly under all circumstances (see Oughourlian, 1982, in line with René Girard).

A reflection on God-images is important. An image of God as the One who points out to the believer that only He is the One to whom the believer should turn to has a destructive potential for interhuman relationships.

The following are some examples of the pitfalls in counseling related to theology and, often, to religious moralism.

- The 'seeming'-aspect. Reverend Fritz is idealizing marriage as a holy covenant before God. Since childhood, his mother, a young widow, told him about her marital happiness. He himself is a mourning widower after a short happy marriage. When a parishioner comes to talk to him about his marital problems, Fritz's first assumption is that these problems cannot be severe. And if they are, it would mean that this parishioner must be an exceptionally serious sinner. Fritz seems to be caught in his perception, and this makes him at this moment more or less incapable of a genuine dialogue about marriage, both professionally and in private.
- Focusing merely on guilt feelings or on shame toward God, instead of exploring guilt and shame as primarily effects of interhuman entanglements.
- Focusing on forgiveness and reconciliation as an obligation in all circumstances. If forgiveness and reconciliation are imposed on someone as the main goal, from the point of view of relational ethics this does not help the people involved.
- Preaching 'cheap grace' (a concept of the German theologian D. Bonhoeffer). Instead of this, the release from existential guilt as a relational reality has to be connected with an "action demanded by the conscience" that fulfils itself in three events: "self-illumination, perseverance and reconciliation" (Buber, 1957, 1998). In other words: this process requests confession, enduring repentance, and deeds of fair compensation. This is not cheap or easy but a long enduring task.
- Reducing guilt to a personal matter, instead of making people aware that there are always others involved ('the unexpected third', Meulink-Korf & Van Rhijn, 2016). When a person has committed an injustice to another person, at the same time the trustworthiness of 'the human order' is also harmed (Buber, 1957, 1998). Buber extends the domain for 'reconciliation' from an interpersonal level to the human world. As long as a culprit lives, this guilty person can contribute to the justice of the human order, by taking up responsibilities for global well-being.
- When it is proclaimed in church that God and no one else is the main source of compensation for any injustice, this proclamation can induce or increase destructive entitlement. God, addressed in prayers does not always give a satisfying answer. Feelings of bitterness or indifference toward a disappointing God can be linked to the experience of interhuman unfairness.
- Imposing a religious conversion as the solution for whatever the problem is.
- Presenting God as a rival against whom nobody can win. A couple of European missionaries with 7 children lived in South America. The children were sent to foster homes in their homeland in Europe as soon as they were old enough to go to a secondary school. The parents were always busy, even exhausted, because of "the poor people we as Christians have to care for". They assumed that the children would understand this decision, and could even benefit from it. "What better example than parents who are working for God's Kingdom?" Once an adult, one of these children spoke with bitterness

of an impossible rivalry with God. He now shows a cynical attitude toward others. A similar result can occur in a marriage when one partner neglects the needs and merits of the other for a long time with the excuse that he or she is engaged in religious activities.

- Proclaiming that being human means to be always insufficient and sinful. When preached repeatedly, this statement is humiliating. "Of all the forms of trauma, humiliation has the greatest impact on people's psyches" (Thesnaar, 2019: 2). The transmission of religious humiliation through generations is a bad predicament and harms the future. When people experience shame, the consequences may be that they lock themselves up in a monological position.

Religion as a motivational resource for relational ethics

"Where are you?" (Genesis 3: 9)

Religion sometimes creates inhibitions in relational ethics. Religions, however, also give positive contributions to the relational reality of a believer. A religious existence *per se* is a relational reality, certainly where God is the one who points away from Him or Herself and refers to responsibility toward other people and to interpersonal relationships (see also: Van Doorn, 2020). Below are more experiences and ideas about how a relational ethical impulse from religion can work.

- Religion offers opportunities for expressing a person's loyalty to her or his parents. *Maria, from Bulgaria, married a Dutchman and went to live with him in Holland. She was forty years old. Until then, she had lived as an only child with her parents. The parents were happy with their daughter's happiness, but also sad that she would live so far away. Frequent travelling was not possible. Maria felt a bit like a traitor in leaving them and going to live in a materially more privileged environment. During the celebration of the marriage, Maria thanked her parents for their love and support. She gave them flowers and spoke at the ceremony about what she had learnt from them. The priest also paid attention to them and gave acknowledgment that they had raised their daughter "in a good Christian way". The service and especially her own expression of loyalty strengthened Maria's entitlement to enjoy her new life.*

In Western Europe, marriage often is an event with a small non-religious ceremony, many times followed by a big party. An increasing number of couples committed to a long-term relationship and to parenthood do not marry officially. Then there is no ceremony at all. In contrast, when Maria's wedding was celebrated in an Eastern European country, attention was paid to the loyalty implications. It proceeded in a way that has some similarities with the process of marriage in traditional African societies, which includes performances of prescribed rites at several stages of the ceremony.

Maria's wedding inspired a Dutch friend for her own wedding ceremony a few months later, to include a special moment of attention to both families of origin. The inclusion of loyalty issues in modern, less institutionalized forms of liturgy, such as in the rites of traditional culture, can reduce feelings of guilt arising from leaving the family of origin. In this way, the loyalty conflicts are less intense.

Maria went away without too much guilt. She found the entitlement to set her own terms for visiting her parents: on a biannual basis. With the full cooperation of her husband she manages to save money for these visits, including for material gifts. Her parents are glad when she visits and they do not reproach her choice to live abroad. "They know I am praying for them when I am in Holland," says Maria: "that means a lot to them and to me." Praying for the benefit of others is a form of giving. Knowing that somebody is praying for you often means receiving a gift. However, not always. *Maria's mother prayed for her daughter with the hope that she could become pregnant. The mother continued her prayers even after Maria had told her that, from a medical point of view, there was no chance for her to become pregnant. Maria had gradually learnt to accept this as a reality in her life, and therefore her mother's continued prayers became an obstacle to their relating. Maria felt guilty because of her inability to give her parents a grandchild. A Dutch chaplain helped them to have a dialogue about this. The mother now understood her daughter's situation and perspective. "From now on, I trust that God makes your life fulfilled." Trust was restored between Maria and her mother, and they could again rely on each other.*

- Other religious rituals (such as eucharist, anointing of sick people, mourning rituals) may also offer a space for expressing both family loyalties and commitment to neighbors. Religious rituals around children and young adults (baptism, initiation rites, confirmation) offer the older generation the opportunity to demonstrate intentions of transgenerational solidarity also outside family relationships.

- Religion has to do with believing and with belonging. Therefore, when someone feels guilty toward God and toward the parents for not having sufficient faith, there are many opportunities for this person to overcome these feelings of guilt. He or she may be a church member with practical commitment to other members. And when a person was raised in a religious family but stopped to attend church while on a personal level remaining a believer, this person can show loyalty to his or her parents by explaining this. Then the parents may be relieved to hear that their child has not lost his or her faith.

- In many congregations and institutions, the pastor organizes peer support groups. Belonging to such a group, may be meaningful for vitalizing someone's trust that he or she can be understood by others and has a capacity to understand others.

- By narratives and tales, religion may enhance the decentering realization that I am not the center of the universe and at the same time I am a unique human being with an unalienable right to be present for and with others.

- Faith in God may supply an address not only for complaints but also for confused feelings, and therefore it functions as a sublimation of unacceptable desires and impulses (for instance, aggressive impulses). Although repression of negative feelings may be pathological, it is also possible that this repression may have a positive result in as much as it could help people to refrain from negative actions and help them to abide by relational ethics.

- God as an address for anger and indignation may prevent a person from taking revenge on others. Trust in God's justice may give patience and even abstinence from violent repayment.

- Psychologically, religion may encourage the longing for an ethical redefinition of the relationship. This may lead to exoneration and maybe forgiveness.

- Trust in God can be an encouragement for dialogue and direct address. "Do not be afraid of them, for I am with you and will rescue you" (Jeremiah 1: 8). *Anna, a South African psychologist, said that this text helped her to take the risk of renewing contact with her parents. In her childhood, she experienced a great degree of unfairness in her relationship with them. "Maybe my parents are also rescued by my daring."* Bible scholars may say that this text refers to a totally different situation. However, that is not the point. The point is that this religious text was a resource for Anna that reconnected her with her parents. It encouraged her to meet her parents in a new perspective. Since it was her parents who had taught her about this text, she could conclude this was "one of the few gifts" that she had received from her parents.

- Pastoral care may entail diaconal care. Diaconal care (from the Greek word *Diakonia*, meaning service) is based on the call to serve oppressed, poor, and wounded people in a practical, often material way. This care is meant as helping without dominating. Although the responsibility for this care falls on the side of the professional, the professional will know that by helping the other, the self of the helper is helped, too. This is the opposite of, in German, *helfen ist herrschen* (meaning, to help means to exert power). It is also opposed to self-centeredness (focusing on 'my own goodness'), to indifference or social exclusion. In diaconal care, there are opportunities for fair relating.

- The 'call for being human' is not coercive but evocative. When religious belief is experienced in this evocative way, it may enhance the motivation for generosity in relationships and for promoting fairness and justice.

Relational presence activated by indebtedness

In any process of restoring wounded human justice, people can not only demonstrate their needs and rights, but also pass on to others and to future generations what they have received from the relational generosity of another. At the same time, there is a risk here that generosity is seen as a virtue to be pursued, focused on one's own goodness or so-called innocence. Such a non-relational orientation is a form of persistence in one's own being and continuation of the self. Breaking free from this ego-logical orientation as a non-dialogical mode of being, lies in assuming concrete accountability and responsibility for others.

In the dialogical process of what this will mean in concrete terms between persons in relational entanglements, contextual pastoral practitioners can offer guidance, support, and encouragement.

Aat van Rhijn, initiating contextual pastoral theory, framed that guilt or debt refers to the past in a habitus of passivity, but indebtedness activates to the now and the future. He used Dutch words in a wordplay: *schuld* (guilt/debt) and *verschuldigd-zijn* (indebtedness). Colleague Marianne Thans added: "Then the issue is: let's explore the options for action" (Thans, oral remark). This orientation on indebtedness, different from an ego-logic virtue or a social contract or strict mutuality but as a vitalizing motivation for the Self, is a widespread wisdom (see also Ducommun-Nagy, 2008). It is at the core of Christianity. Grace, in Christian belief, like *chèsèd* in the Hebrew Bible, is about not being tied up to guilt and obligations, nor to revenge. It is also about free generous giving, that often works contagiously, although not *per se* mutually. When one gives to another, the other may give not to this one but to other others.

For those in the position of a helper, counselor, pastor or chaplain, the issue is not how I dare to speak of relational healing in a world full of injustices. The better question is how to help families and individuals in the congregation or hospital or residential home with a dialogical process of healing. This dialogical process is not exclusively *à deux*. The responsibility is also referring to 'the thirds'.

Sometimes there was or is a personal debt or guilt; this book focuses on ways to help restore relational fairness by revitalizing one's giving. However, there are many injustices from the past and present that are not directly the fault of individuals today. In the situation where one group had profits while other groups and individuals were abused or disadvantaged, the term *collective indebtedness* as part of a pastoral hermeneutics helps to focus attention on what needs to be done. "Here I am" (as in Genesis 22: 1). This statement shows confidence that it makes a difference that I am present and respond. This is true for everyone. This trust is not naive, it is the basis of being human, for human reality is per se relational. Being accountable for lesser-known others, even across generations, even if we will never be able to have a real dialogue with each of them, contributes to processes of healing in society.

PART II

Greteke De Vries

Chapter 1
Fair Bridging: Ethics of Caring in Intercultural Worlds

Sensitivity to intercultural relations

In many parts of our planet, the need to nurture sensitivity to differences among individuals and communities is great. Developments in today's world are breaking down geographical and social barriers and are leading to societies with many cultures and complex relational situations. This is partly due to the emancipation of disadvantaged communities, imperialist and separatist violence, migratory flows, communication technologies, more widely available means of transportation, and more chances for individualization – people breaking out from their own social groups. In culturally, religiously, ethnically mixed societies, especially in immigration societies that have not dealt with pluralism to the extent as it is needed today, old-timers and newcomers, privileged and disadvantaged, conservatives and realists, all experience challenges. Organizing daily life, cooperating on a common cause or formulating plans for a common future become part of processes that may lead to discontent and collisions over different values (Sniderman & Hagendoorn, 2007). Family members struggle with changing relationships, communities disintegrate and they close borders. Many choose solutions to escape these problems that they base solely on their own interpretation of facts, their personal emotions, their desired social structures and on their own perception of relational fairness and unfairness. Where does that leave others?

Sensitivity to ethnic, cultural and religious differences should be important to contextual practitioners. By sensitivity, we mean not only valuing what is important to others, but also especially nurturing, the ability to be touched by situational and relational injustices, and by our human ability to contribute to fair relationships, both within one's own cultural group and outside of it. This goes beyond empathy by which one person tunes in to the feelings of another person in any given situation. Sensitivity involves developing an attitude of attentiveness to the dynamic balance between what people give and receive in a relationship and noticing the fair and unfair distribution of burdens. To be moved by relational injustice, to suffer because of the suffering of another is not a defect but a credit to us humans (see, among others: Buber, 1998). Through the vulnerability of another, we ourselves become vulnerable. If we do not close ourselves off but remain receptive to it, we can begin to see and hear who is appealing for our help or guidance. It is precisely this active ability to respond and thereby contribute to the repair of a hurting relational situation. In a distant way, this sensitivity is related to a phenomenon that psychologists and spiritual caregivers have recently described as 'moral injury' in soldiers, journalists, medical personnel: "The damage done to one's conscience or moral compass when that person perpetrates, witnesses, or fails to prevent acts that transgress one's own moral beliefs, values, or ethical codes of conduct" (Project Moral Injury, 2022).[1] Moral injury projects are developed at several universities throughout the world, in the Netherlands at the Radboud University in Nijmegen. The therapies that these projects provide to heal moral wounds are based on individual psychology and aim at helping people to come to terms with their moral injuries, first of all by self-forgiveness, acceptance, or self-compassion (Williamson et al., 2021).[2]

From an Africentric perspective, these therapies are criticized for not dealing with relationships, and social cleansing rituals are proposed instead (Nwoye, 2022).[3] From the point of view of contextual therapy, we shall ask why this 'moral injury' needs to be 'healed', since it points out to our precious human capacity to be sensitive to relational ethical questions.

In this book, we assume that contextual practitioners and other professionals are not hindered in their work by their relational ethical sensitivity but instead it inspires them to commit to bridging gaps between individuals and communities in multicultural worlds. Contextual practitioners who come to the aid of families, whether in migrant or established communities, must consider the social developments that cause hardships in relationships. Let us mention two: although Dutch society has a long history of people coming from the outside settling within its borders, this only began to become problematic a few decades ago when The Netherlands became a modern immigration country with migrant workers and refugees who brought new cultures and religions into society. A mere tolerance of minorities by majorities is no longer effective. What is needed to create cohesion in a multicultural society is that all residents must be included in its organization. To be able to collaborate together people need to accept the consequences of plurality. In The Netherlands this process leads to fierce debates about identity, integration and assimilation in parliament, in the marketplace and at home. Not so much in churches, though; perhaps also in The Netherlands, the most segregated hour of the week is Sunday morning? Responses to societal changes due to immigration range from showing interest in, respect for, and friendship with newcomers and adopting some cultural practices (food!), to racism, xenophobia in general, and Islamophobia

---

1 https://projectmoralinjury.nl/nw
2 https://www.thelancet.com/journals/lanpsy/article/PIIS2215-0366 (21)00113-9/fulltext
3 https://bit.ly/3LeI815

and antisemitism in particular. Consequently, there is much fear, pain, and resentment in families and neighborhoods, and at work, in the relation between the people and the government, and all of them use conflicting strategies to deal with it, as do contextual practitioners, pastors and intercultural leaders, who use their knowledge and wisdom to react to these tensions.

As for South Africa, today's traumatized society is struggling with problems resulting from colonialism and apartheid. These are deeply felt in families and social communities, such as universities and churches. At the Stellenbosch University, Prof Thesnaar organizes gatherings in an 'encouraging space' where brown, black and white students engage in often uncomfortable relational processes. Together, they discover the complexities of cross-cultural relationships, including economic injustices that affect their relationships. Once students interact, they begin to relate to each other, hear personal stories, learn to think honestly about the discrepancies (asymmetries) between them, and discover the survival mechanisms that they or their communities are using. Once they stop talking about others and stop objectifying each other, the healing process begins. Gradually, a mutual and presumably lasting trust grows. Prof Thesnaar is hopeful about this, although he speaks of a generations-long process. Becoming one nation, a cohesive society, cannot be reached with a quick fix. He sees that the younger generations are better at intercultural relations than the older generations whose personal and social identities were so much formed under the social system of apartheid.

I am sure that we can learn much from the intercultural processes that occur at the Stellenbosch University, especially from the dialogical intergenerational pastoral process (DIPP) that is taught there (see previous chapters by Hanneke Meulink-Korf). However, my chapters are written from my own, Dutch perspective. I shall draw on personal experiences, lately gained in the eastern part of Amsterdam, capital of The Netherlands, with its inhabitants of more than 175 different nationalities, where I am pastor of a traditional Protestant congregation. And I draw on lessons learnt from Emouna, an interfaith leadership program I attended a few years ago.

Personal situation

The need to broaden and deepen my education as a contextual practitioner began only a few years ago when I relocated to the Caribbean island of Bonaire and later to Amsterdam, the cosmopolitan capital of the Netherlands. As a Protestant congregational leader, highly influenced by the theory and practice of contextual therapy and contextual pastoral care and counseling, I discovered that I missed the resources needed to conduct my ministry appropriately and comfortably in these new situations.

So far, I had focused on relational ethics as such, now I needed to learn more about how factual and systemic variables affect the lives of individuals and communities in a multi-cultural world. The vignettes that illustrate my observations have been anonymized; however, the core of the stories is not altered.

What follows is an example of my own role and its limitations – due to my unfamiliarity with a specific funeral ritual, and my underestimation of the relational complexity of the family I met.

A Christian woman, Surinam by birth and culture, had died. She was a member of the congregation which I had recently begun to serve, and I was not aware that she was about to die. While terminally ill, she had asked her husband to ask me to lead the funeral service in the church. The husband, whom I had met only once, invited me to prepare the ceremony, together with the whole family. The couple had no children but brothers and sisters, nieces and nephews were present. Some relatives showed no interest in my role as a church minister and what I could offer, as they firmly expressed that they wanted a traditional ceremony to which I, as an outsider, was not allowed to be present. Other relatives inquired about my ideas of what should happen during the funeral service. The widower did not seem to care, as he was nervous and afraid that the discussion might turn into a family feud, which was the last thing he needed. When I asked, all confirmed that the situation was a bit tense but that all wanted to honor the deceased. I did not want to explore the tension as I did not feel comfortable enough to address it and besides this, we had to focus on organizing the funeral ceremony. Meanwhile, I had to juggle with many factors that I was not acquainted with, in an atmosphere that was unfamiliar to me. I was wondering: can I do justice to all involved and still remain faithful to my own position? We were able to find a middle ground, I thought, by splitting the ceremony into a traditional part in the morning that I would not attend and a public church service in the afternoon that all would attend. When the time came, to my surprise, only the husband and some family members attended the service. It felt that they had come because they wanted to please me, and not so much because they needed a Christian ceremony to honor the deceased and find comfort for themselves. The woman's body had already been buried in the morning. By all, by some? What had happened? I wondered if the preparatory meeting could have gone differently if I had encouraged a more open dialogue, but about what exactly? And what if I had been less unaware of what turned out to be so important to this family?

Here is a second example of an encounter that could have become more meaningful if I had been able to pay more attention to the relational complexities of this intercultural family.

As the new pastor of my church, I paid an introductory visit to a family who had recently moved into the neighborhood. The wife and three children had expressed interest in the church, and I went on a home visit to get to know them. The meaning of this visit was to begin a bond and to establish a foundation of trust with the family. Sometimes people immediately share with their new pastor what they are concerned about, and at other times, the pastor senses that something complicated is going on in the family and will inquire about it cautiously. When I visited the couple, the children were out. The woman told me she had been born and raised in an ethnic Dutch family; her husband also talked about his background. He had been born and raised in a Muslim family in a country of East Asia; subsequently, he had converted to Humanism. Then we chatted pleasantly about their new home, the neighborhood, her first experiences with the church community, their jobs, and the children's school. Everything went smoothly and we enjoyed each other's company. I asked about their religious differences, but since they had "no problems" with that, our conversation on this matter was not continued. Frankly, I did not want to bring differences and their consequences into the enjoyable conversation and perhaps disrupt the apparent harmony of the couple. And I was shy, afraid of my own inexperience, not knowing exactly what I could and could not ask.

A deeper awareness of the need to expand my professional skills came only later when I paid a closer look at the multicultural environment in East Amsterdam where my congregation is situated. All these people and their respective communities were affecting one another, interfering with others, and therefore I wondered: what makes it possible that there is cohesion in the neighborhood, at least some peaceful co-existence most of the time, and what makes it work? What are people's resources to strive for friendly connections and pleasant cooperation? And what would happen if all these neighbors who position themselves differently around so many aspects of life were to get tense with one another, nervous, perhaps even hostile?

I also thought about the consequences of this new awareness for my ministry in a diverse congregation. I started to wonder about the implications of this diversity for many of the activities of the congregation and for its organization.

Combination of perspectives

As a trained contextual practitioner, I already worked in my ministry from the perspective of relational ethics and the position of multidirected partiality. However, I sensed that I needed more. Fortunately, I was able to attend an interfaith leadership program (called Emouna, more about it later) that aimed at cooperation for a common cause by people from different (religious) backgrounds. The result of this combination, which I present in these chapters, strengthened my skills and may contribute to other contextual practitioners' competences, especially of those who work in a multicultural environment.

It is important to use a word of caution at this point. In this book, we do not advocate that contextual practitioners have to come from the same ethnic, religious or cultural background as their clients. In their conversations, the familiar can become unfamiliar, and that disturbance of a normality may in fact help both practitioner and client to reconsider a situation, an opinion or a custom that one or even both took for granted.

Here are openings to be found for the transformation of strained relations. However, we should not be naïve or presumptuous about client-practitioner relationships in a multicultural context. Astrid Roemer (Roemer, 1998), a famous Dutch-Surinam writer on psychological and relational suffering originating from colonialism and migration, warns unequivocally: "There is a gap between Western therapists on the one hand and migrants in psychological distress on the other. Those who have insufficient feeling with Moroccan, Turkish, Arab, Persian, African, Asian, Caribbean, or Latin American communities are not able to really help someone from those cultures. Not to recognize this is arrogant." Roemer was also a certified family therapist who in the nineties presented workshops on the meaning and use of Boszormenyi-Nagy's contextual approach for working with migrants and especially with the second or third generation. She then advised that professionals need to seek training in "transcultural competence at training institutions" to understand and alleviate migrant pain and migrant anxiety. A contextual practitioner who is attentive to a client's otherness, to his or her "subcultural context", will not forget to pay attention to "the migrant's world of experience" as fact, and the "articulation of and making meaning of this world by the migrant" (Roemer, 1998, translated by Greteke De Vries).

Connected to this attentiveness is the importance of both the dimension of facts and the dimension of transactions of the five-dimensional model of relational reality proposed in the contextual approach. The facts may be objective, but they certainly are not neutral. The facts in the lives of individuals and of groups are weighed and discussed, since they often determine the extent to which people can contribute to groups or societies, or not. It is also very important to take into account the systems in which people are involved (Dimension III). But many of the contextual practitioners I know are mostly focused on individual psychology and on the establishment of relational fairness (Dimension II and IV) They do not focus as much on facts and systemic mechanisms. However, these dimensions should never be ignored, and certainly not in a pluralistic world.

The *fourth dimension*, that of *relational ethics* does not seem to be at the forefront of organized interfaith encounters. For instance, in my experience, searching for relational fairness *as such* among the participants of these encounters is not the *explicit* motivation for interfaith or intercultural dialogues. If anyone leading intercultural encounters would give dimension IV the attention that is needed, it could change the interfaith methods of dialogue, put the importance of religious literacy into perspective, and raise questions about basing intercultural encounters on shared values.

A few more preliminary remarks

Perhaps needless to say, the premise of the entire book and of these chapters is that individuals do not exist on their own; relationship comes first. There are, have been, and always will be others. However, individuals are not defined either just by their family or their religious or cultural group. Every person is uniquely connected to others in his or her (intergenerational) networks of relationships by the dynamics of expectations, obligations and merits. Contextual practitioners need to develop a subtle and demanding skill for perceiving clients as concrete individuals who find personal freedom by contributing to important others in accordance with their own capabilities and needs.

We realize that in discussing intercultural relationships, we can create confusion with the term 'context'. In social sciences, *context* refers to the interrelated conditions in which something (or someone) exists or occurs; that is: the environment. Facts and circumstances in time and space influence relationships. 'Context' in the contextual approach refers to the whole dynamics of giving to and receiving from others in intergenerational networks of relationships. Therefore, the meaning of *context* in this approach is about *consequences* of facts and circumstances within relationships. In these chapters, the term *interreligious* is used for the academic interdisciplinary field that studies the interaction between different traditional religions, spiritualities, and philosophies of life, and their narratives, values, and practices. The term *interfaith* or *interpath* is used alternatively, especially in the context of dialogue and organized meetings. The term *intercultural* indicates interaction between people of different beliefs, ethnicities, and cultures.

Structure of the upcoming chapters

So far, this introduction has only hinted at the mutual inspiration of the contextual approach and academic interreligious studies and interfaith practices. I shall develop this further in the following chapters.

In Chapter 2, I shall discuss theory and methods for bridging religious, cultural and ethnic divides, that interreligious studies such as the European leadership training program of Emouna teaches against the backdrop of a popular though destructive narrative that supports separation of social identity groups (*clash of civilizations*). I shall provide these with comments based on the contextual approach that offers guidelines and practices for working with families which, I believe are also fitting to working with faith communities as such, and with any relationship in intercultural worlds.

In Chapter 3, I shall integrate these interfaith insights with the contextual approach. This integration is intended to deepen our explorations and discussions of perspectives of fairness and injustice in multicultural worlds, and this will contribute to the sensitivity of contextual practitioners and everyone who contributes to fair bridging.

For didactical purposes, in this chapter, we shall meet Margaret and Nasr, two people interested in interfaith meetings. We shall analyze the way they greet each other through the lenses of the five dimensions of relational reality and also give some attention to loyalty, destructive and constructive entitlement, enriched by observations of interreligious studies.

Chapter 2
Wisdom from Interreligious Studies

Worldwide

What can contextual practitioners learn from interreligious studies and the practice of interfaith encounters? Many universities throughout the world offer academic programs within the field of Interreligious, interfaith, and intercultural studies. In recent decades, multiple interfaith organizations have emerged in many parts of the world, expressing their aspiration to contribute to connecting people from different faiths by their specific goals, strategies and activities. They develop strategies and activities based on moral values with a universal claim. They also attract people who share these human values. Their students and participants are willing to learn from one another's religious resources, enter in dialogues for mutual understanding and enrichment, find common points of interests, and see the necessity of cross-boundary cooperation for a specific goal or cause.

A search on the Internet reveals an entire range of these organizations. For instance, *The Cape Town Interfaith Initiative* in the Western Cape of South Africa[1] is a "driving force in the pursuit of interreligious understanding and dialogue" and it envisions and embraces "a country and peoples unified by interreligious and spiritual understanding and respect". It promotes "interfaith understanding, harmony and co-operation, through both an awareness of universal spirituality and an honoring of the dignity of difference". Participants in the *Rwanda Interfaith Council on Health*, based in Kigali,[2] connect in their shared hope of a "healthy nation in which Religious-Based Organizations are united for health and peace". The *Interfaith Network for The United Kingdom*,[3] based in London, aspires to reflect in their work on: "Service to others, Integrity, Accountability, Trust, Consultative and cooperative working, Valuing diversity, Inclusiveness, Listening and openness, Courtesy, Mutual respect, Respecting dissent and people's right to express this". The vision that KAICIID pursues, *the King Abdullah bin Abdulaziz International Centre for Interreligious and Intercultural Dialogue,*[4] headquartered in Austria, is "a world where there is respect, understanding, and cooperation among people, justice, peace and reconciliation, and an end to the abuse of religion to justify oppression, violence, and conflict." The "spirit" of *The Elijah Interfaith Institute* with its *Center of Hope* in

---

1   https://capeinterfaith.org.za
2   https://www.rwandainterfaith.org
3   https://www.interfaith.org.uk
4   https://www.kaiciid.org

Jerusalem[5] is "wisdom, inspiration, friendship and hope across religious traditions. Elijah deepens understanding among religions. Elijah's mission is to foster unity in diversity, creating a harmonious world." The mission of *the Institute for Inter-Faith Dialogue* in Indonesia, situated in Yogyakarta,[6] is "to encourage and develop a pluralistic religious thinking through dialogue, to stimulate a dynamic network of dialogue and interreligious cooperation, to encourage religious transformation as a solution to humanitarian issues faced by the society". Through education and dialogue, participants are encouraged to discuss the topic of "pluralism, conflicts, and peace" in the Indonesian context. In Washington D.C., United States of America, *the Washington Interfaith Staff Community*,[7] stemming from the Civil Rights movement of the 1960s, puts into action "the values that cut across all faith traditions". *The Canadian Interfaith Conversation*, based in Richmond Hill, Ontario,[8] "was established to promote harmony and religious insight among religions and religious communities in Canada, strengthen our society's moral foundations, and work for greater realization of the fundamental freedom of conscience and religion for the sake of the common good and an engaged citizenship". In Kurdistan, Iraq, the *Dialogue and Culture Organization*[9] asks attention to "the beautiful dialogue" among different religious communities in Kurdistan, especially in Sulaimani, where people of eight faiths live in peace. The "attendees seek to contribute to tolerance and peaceful coexistence in the region". All of them are committed to end unnecessary conflicts and suffering and strive toward friendship across all faith traditions.

We shall now focus on the teachings of a European initiative called Emouna, already mentioned in the introduction, with which I am familiar.

Emouna[10]

Emouna is a European initiative that offers an educational interfaith leadership program. The Dutch branch is situated at the Free University (VU) in Amsterdam. In Semitic languages, *Emouna* means trust, commitment through acts, and reliability. Emouna in The Netherlands wants to work on constructive relationships between different faith traditions and communities, and to contribute to peace and inspiration in society. Its program presupposes that interreligious leaders accept diversity as a fact of modern life. They embrace the challenge of creating a society in which the richness of pluralism can contribute to answers to so many questions that require intense cooperation on a national and often global scale: health care, economic inequality, climate change, interracial conflicts, and human rights. Not one group or culture by itself can solve those issues.

---

5   https://elijah-interfaith.org/hope-center
6   https://bit.ly/40LwIaN
7   https://washingtoninterfaith.org
8   https://www.interfaithconversation.ca
9   https://dialogueculture.org
10 https://www.emoena.nl

Emouna's motivation is that cultural and religious communities need to work together to heal a fractured world (Moyaert, 2019).

Emouna's program goes against what seems to be worldwide tendencies of establishing and protecting fixed group identities. The program is based on the people's capacity to relate, meet, respect, tolerate, cooperate with others, become friends, *cross borders*. This resonates with a key perspective of the contextual approach, namely that it wants to evoke 'the motivational layer in which hope resides for repairing the hurt human justice' (Boszormenyi-Nagy, 1973, 1984). How should this innate human capacity to meet and cooperate be stimulated? What stands in the way? What can contextual practitioners learn about this from Emouna

The following background details are perhaps necessary to understand Emouna's ambition. Pauline Bebe, a female rabbi in France, established Emouna in 2015. The momentum for her initiative came after the January 2015 terrorist attacks in Paris that shook European society. Her deep motivation did not come from the terrorist attacks as such, but from her anger about the very sharp divides between the different worlds in her country, namely the religious communities, the government, and the universities. That had led to problematic forms of divisiveness in society. Bebe managed to begin her initiative in France, and from there, it expanded to other countries throughout Europe. In The Netherlands, it is connected to the Department of Theology and Religious Studies of VU Amsterdam. Since 2019, Marianne Moyaert, chair of the department, and her staff have been developing the program in accordance with Dutch circumstances.

Clashing of social identity groups

As a background to the necessity of interreligious learning, Moyaert reacts against the narrative of the so-called 'clash of civilizations'. This theory, which has been embraced and criticized, came from the late American political scientist and Harvard Professor Samuel P. Huntington (Huntington, 2019). He argues that the present battlefields are ethnic and religious identities and not so much political ideologies or economics. Moyaert: "When I listen to the media, both nationally and internationally, the song that keeps being repeated and that plays different social groups against each other is a song that connects religion with violence and oppressions. The song that tends to get the most air time is that of the clash of civilizations. Emouna suggests: it is about time we change the song!" (Moyaert, 2020).

Indeed, in its program, Emouna focuses on respecting diversity, practicing tolerance, overcoming hostility, trusting strangers, sharing the same public space, and cooperating together. It acknowledges a certain threat of group identities. These may exclude individuals who do not wholly match the frame, or who rather identify with another community or a different walk of life. Focusing on group identities for understanding or managing relationships may be a pitfall not only for conservative politicians and their followers or for emancipatory activists of minority groups. By focusing on group identity, even those who are actually trying to find a bridge between people of different life orientations can create resistance and unintentionally offend an individual or a group.

What follows is a story of a politician who addressed a multicultural group by using an all-inclusive umbrella term. His intention was to connect them all in a positive way. The following happened:

A secular politician in Amsterdam is invited to give the opening speech at a conference of leaders of several religious communities in the city. He appreciates the efforts by these religious leaders to contribute to the well-being of the city. In his endeavor to connect all even stronger with the city he calls the audience enthusiastically: "We, Amsterdammers". A young female Muslim leader of a women's organization, born, raised and living in Amsterdam, protests: "I'm not". The politician is astonished: "Why not?" Unfortunately, the program did not allow them to begin a dialogue about this perhaps eye-opening confrontation.

The proud reference by the politician had the intention to confirm that all are included, all leaders present at the conference need to feel they belong to this wonderful city. However, did the leaders doubt that? Did they need the politician's confirmation? Would he have said the same if the attendees were all of an ethnic Dutch background, albeit, for instance, of different economical or educational status?

The leader who objected to this generalizing term understood it as an imposed group identity marker that indicates a dismissal of their different cultural and religious identities, such as hers. She felt hurt because she did not want to conform to the liberal cultural norm of an "Amsterdammer". Of course, the woman was committed to the laws and the well-being of the city that had contributed so much to her life, while at the same time she was staying loyal to her religious community. Did the politician really respect the city's diversity? Was he interested in the urgent question of what all could contribute without first having to meet a dominant cultural standard? Apparently, the woman was not sure about that. What experiences with the city's politics did she have that caused her to immediately distance herself from the social equality that the politician so encouragingly supported? And how is it that he had not seen such a protest coming?

As individuals, we cannot live without others. The relationship between individuals and our own communities, and that of individuals in different networks that are friendly or hostilely connected to other networks, is complex and requires a wise consideration from politicians, interreligious leaders, and contextual practitioners.

Here, the difference between 'equality' and 'equivalency' (in Dutch: *gelijkheid* and *gelijkwaardigheid*) may play a role in misunderstandings. Administrators in Dutch society govern by the principle of equality: the government should treat everyone equally in equal situations. However, citizens may experience an injustice in this when their religious or cultural preferences are not honored. Their desires, their needs, their contributions are not equal to those of other cultural or religious groups; however, they perceive these to be of equivalent value. The composition of a family requires a different style of housing. People have different views on illness and death may call for different health care treatments. Religious duties require different holidays. Different life styles require different opening times of shops, and cultural preferences lead to the need for different recreational facilities. Any claim about 'sameness' by officials or by fellow citizens from other communities may expect the reaction 'I beg to differ'.

In short: clashes between individuals and between social identity groups occur. Although clashes can lead to new discoveries about self and others and therefore may contribute to creative processes, preventing or diminishing the unnecessary hardships of clashes is an important principle of Emouna's training program. It advocates that positive stories can be told about interreligious encounters, fruitful perspectives can be found in interreligious partnerships, and constructive cooperation can be developed. This needs practice, reflection and the ability to change.

Stereotypes and prejudices

Attention to the destructive narratives of clashes within multicultural worlds and the refusal to accept the notion of unbridgeable gaps between the members of different identity groups is a lesson that contextual practitioners may need to learn from interreligious studies. We shall now consider these clashes and gaps more closely. What systemic dynamics may lead to them?

Emouna stimulates its participants to investigate their personal prejudices that are based on stereotypes. These stand in the way of reciprocal learning. Stereotypes overstate characteristics and qualities of individuals and groups that often are not based on facts or on the self-understanding of people. Either because of ignorance, or antagonistic intentions, people are reduced to one attribute, one offensive label that limits or even ignores the whole of a person's identity or that of a group.

Everybody has prejudices. Prejudices are generalized judgements built from stereotypes about others in complex situations. They are part of communication patterns that impose roles on people, which turn them into mere categories and labels. Stereotypes and prejudices feed on our biased ideas without checks and balances. They can lead to discrimination and exclusion of individuals and groups.

Therefore, to overcome stereotypes and prejudices, participants in the Emouna program visit a variety of religious venues, do roleplaying in which they step into the shoes of others and learn to reflect on their personal preconceptions and biased ideas. They may then want to share what they learned about them in a personal dialogue with another participant, but they also can reflect on them privately in a log or diary or discuss them with a staff member. Contextual practitioners may consider reflecting on their own biases and discussing them with colleagues. Not with their clients!

Stereotypes and prejudices get in the way of learning about each other, and they also get in the way of fair relating. No person is a copy of another person, nor merely a carrier of an ideology, a member of an ethnic group, a culture, a religion, or of a group with a specific way of life.

In reality, of course, people do not live without images and ideas about others. It is impossible to live with others in the same world without concepts of others, without the names we call them, the peculiarities we emphasize, the stories we have heard, and the feelings we have developed. Stereotypes give an easy access to others. They help to structure reality according to our own ideas. However, people or situations, both strange and familiar, can always turn out differently than expected or than previously thought.

With their attitude of multidirected partiality, contextual practitioners are careful not to be driven by stereotypes and prejudices. They do not want to let preconceptions paralyze their creativity in finding ways for fair relating and will not allow their attention to the right of each person's own voice to wane.

An honest conversation to check prejudices and reassess them, usually helps people to connect or reconnect. However, people can also willfully adopt group stereotypes as part of their identity and find pride in them. This pride may encourage them to say things like:

"Say it out loud, I'm black and I'm proud" or:

"This is what we proud Latino's do!" or:

"Girl power!"

Nevertheless, everyone should be aware of the danger of de-individualizing and dehumanizing individuals and groups if one allows systemic stereotyping and openly accepts the expression of prejudice. Giving up prejudice can be a profound and lengthy process that needs much dialogue or positive encounters. However, it may also happen in the blink of an eye. A simple kind gesture and an honest appreciation can be all that is needed. The following example is about the elimination of a prejudice that took place during an interreligious conference in Amsterdam:

A Jewish woman attended an interreligious conference, where she noticed that she did not feel comfortable with the Muslim male participants, although she had not really met them yet. That day, the group went to a meeting on the third floor of an old Amsterdam building. While climbing the stairs, her bag fell and made a lot of noise. Someone behind her caught the bag, hurried with it to her and asked her friendly: "Shall I carry your bag further up the stairs?" She noticed it was one of the Muslim men who had made the offer. He not only was concerned about her bag, but he was also afraid that she would fall and get hurt. This kindness of a Muslim to a Jew made a great impression on her. She considered this short healing meeting the highlight of the conference.

Privileges

The obvious danger of holding on to stereotypes and prejudices is that they become part of the fabric of a system that tends to totalize people and classifies them into this or that category. A system, no matter how democratically organized (or just because of this!) will at some point ignore the unique situation of a person and her or his personal contributions and needs. Individuals and groups become trapped in systems when they even unconsciously adopt stereotypes and prejudices and act on them; then they conserve the order of the system, block change and clash with those who see and judge people and situations differently.

Therefore, stereotypes and prejudices are not only private issues that individuals may overcome by personal growth, but they are also a part of social codes that guide the rules in a society or group. Many of these rules are seen as part of a tacit knowledge that some have and others do not have. Behaving, dressing, communicating, appearing according to the rules of those who live by these codes is giving entrance to the privileges of a group or society. People stumble over codes when they cannot meet these requirements or when they are unwittingly crossing the do's and don'ts. By the way, people may also wittingly cross codes and regulations to make a statement about the discriminatory nature of a certain code.

Individuals and groups that conform to the standard rules of a greater whole are rewarded by chances to participate. They are called 'privileged' people. Here, we may be aware of the fact that all communities and networks entail more or less privileged people and more or less disadvantaged people.

Since the nineteen eighties of the last century, the term 'privileged' has become a well-known notion. This started when Peggy McIntosh, a women's-studies scholar at Wellesley, a women's liberal arts college in the State of Massachusetts in the USA introduced the term in seminars on feminism (Rothman, in The New Yorker, 2014).[11] The idea of 'privilege' indicates that "some people benefit from unearned, and largely unacknowledged, advantages, even when those advantages aren't discriminatory". McIntosh, in the Rothman interview in The New Yorker, indicated: "In order to understand the way privilege works, you have to be able to see patterns and systems in social life, but you also have to care about individual experiences." McIntosh believes that "everybody has a combination of unearned advantage and unearned disadvantage in life. Whiteness is just one of the many variables that one can look at. Others are, for example, one's place in the birth order, [...] or what is projected onto your religious or

---

[11] https://bit.ly/4oHMNhl

ethnic background." McIntosh further stated: "We are all put ahead and behind by the circumstances of our birth. We all have a combination of both. And it changes minute by minute, depending on where we are, who we are seeing, or what we're required to do." According to her: "psychology isn't very good at taking in the sociological view". It takes others "to find your inner history [and] understand that you are in systems, and that they are in you. It has to do with looking around yourself the way sociologists do and seeing the big patterns in the rest of society, while keeping a balance and really respecting your experience. Seeing the oppression of others is, of course, very important work. But so is seeing how the systems oppress oneself."

Privilege check

Emouna stimulates its participants to do a privilege check, for instance the buzzfeed test,[12] and discuss the outcome among themselves. Contextual practitioners may want to follow this advice. The check provides insights into the systemic position they personally hold in relation to their clients. Many quizzes can be found on the Internet with questions or statements to assess one's social status, one's competence to exercise one's human rights, or one's inaccessibility to do so. Of course, that tells much about someone's chances in society, one's access to amenities, one's problems, and one's comforts which often are not the result of personal choices but of systemic dynamics. Privilege tests consider personal and social characteristics such as appearance, class, gender, sexual orientation, access to socio-economic resources, education and physical or/and mental health. The scores of the tests indicate systemic privileges or disadvantages compared to other members in the same group of people.

However, in these quizzes, adherence to a certain religion does not seem to play much of a role in assessing societal benefits, which is strange for me because I believe that this plays an important role. The authors of the questionnaires may consider religion a choice, or they do not consider religion a decisive variable in discrimination or fair treatment. However, interreligious studies do rightfully ask attention to religious influences on someone's identity. We shall come back to this later under the heading 'Religious literacy'.

Both privileged contextual practitioners as well as contextual practitioners who come from an underprivileged background should ask themselves if they are alert enough to take notice of privilege issues their clients and they themselves are dealing with. Clients with continuing disadvantages know, as McIntosh observed, that "something out there is working against me". Do their practitioners know that, too? Will they understand that people who fear resistance by deviating from certain systemic dominant norms may be hesitant to intercultural encounters? For instance, they would like their children to marry within the same group. They prefer non-mixed schools, all-female swimming lessons, and nursing homes of a certain religious identity.

---

12 https://bit.ly/3n6Mm2G

Contextual practitioners need to realize, what surveys show, that clients with fewer privileges need to struggle harder to be accepted by or to participate in society. Their clients have to deal with more stress than privileged clients have to. They are on guard, prepared for possible prejudices or discrimination, anticipating who might turn against them, based on how they are seen and judged by others. Whatever their background is, they may be more ready than privileged clients are to blame others for their predicament. Disadvantaged persons may avoid situations in which they run the risk of not being taken seriously. They have experienced that what they have to give is undervalued, ignored or not appreciated. Therefore, they are experiencing systemic unfairness. Contextual practitioners need to be attentive to clients' positions and perspectives regarding systemic privileges and disadvantages.

Language

Language is also a fundamental systemic aspect that contributes to people's privileged or disadvantaged positions. Who benefits from knowing a dominant language well, who cannot express him/herself in this language comfortably or competently enough? Interreligious studies are well aware of the importance of linguistic competences regarding equitable communicative participation. Students and participants at interfaith conferences from different linguistic backgrounds must be able to choose a common language to communicate together. If not all can join the chosen language, this needs to be discussed first. Perhaps an interpreter is necessary? Teachers educating interreligious groups and leaders of interfaith encounters must use a welcoming language, inclusive and without jargon. Drawing, drama or music offer intercultural groups non-verbal communication tools – however, facilitators should know that not all religions allow all these forms of expression, especially when it comes to mixed-gender groups.

Contextual practitioners also need to pay attention to the language that is used in the client-practitioner contact as well as the language used in group sessions among clients. If there is someone who cannot express him- or herself well enough to be understood by others, the relational dynamics will be complicated, not only in terms of emotions but in terms of relational ethics. Children who may speak for their parents, fluent-speaking clients who may help people who are less fluent may end up neglecting their own needs, or they may speak for others, complete their sentences, making them even more insecure. Contextual practitioners must strive to find solutions if the language becomes an issue and limits the dialogue between people.

The following is an example of how creative language developed in the therapeutic world, which may be of help when there are obstacles to the communication:

A contextual practitioner is meeting a client who was born and raised in Africa and is a divorced father with three teenagers who were born in Amsterdam. This father is afraid that he will lose his children to the many negative sides of modern Western society, and he asks for advice. What can he do to protect his children and at the same time let them find their own way in this world? Since the father is not fluent in Dutch and the practitioner not fluent in French, the language of the father, the practitioner puts little plastic dolls on the table, amongst which are many black figurines. The father recognizes that the practitioner is trying to represent his family and accepts the use of these toys. By moving the figurines around, and also using red, white and green coasters and wooden cubes, the practitioner is able to communicate with the father about his concerns as a parent, the absence of the mother, the meddling of the family who has remained in Africa, and his troubled relationship with his children.

In the 1990s, a Dutch trauma therapist, Marleen Diekmann (1949-2007) developed a method based on the use of figurines in system therapy and called it: "Another language". She used it among refugees in a camp in Croatia, where she did not share the language of the families she was trying to help. Today, the use of these figurines as a second form of language is popular among Dutch contextual practitioners and they use them also in their work with clients who can communicate fluently with them. Visualizing relational processes with figurines and engaging in playing together with clients instead of simply talking, is seen as a very good tool for bridging language gaps and for opening unexpected new insights (Doornik, 2022).

Religious literacy

What we have learned so far from interreligious studies is that it is crucial that contextual practitioners pay attention to stereotypes, prejudices, intersecting privileges and disadvantages, and to the role of language in the therapeutic or pastoral conversation.

However, it is also important for contextual practitioners to acquire a pragmatic knowledge of their clients' religion, spirituality, or worldview. They certainly do not have to become religious experts, but they must have some basic ideas of the effects of these backgrounds on the way their clients experience their daily life. This knowledge can be gained for instance by studying some of the history of their clients' communities and by getting information about the social rules and regulations that apply to their clients' communities.

It is obvious that chaplains, spiritual guides, or congregational leaders pay more attention than other practitioners to their client's religious identity, but all practitioners can gain from having at least some practical religious and spiritual knowledge in general and of their clients specifically. This is the point where the notion of religious literacy comes in. Emouna's interfaith training pays close attention to mutual learning about faith traditions and about how participants personally relate to them.

Emouna does not deny the downsides that are part of every faith tradition, but it seeks what can provide the stones needed to build bridges, to connect people of different faiths. Therefore, the program emphasizes an 'appreciative knowledge' of people's faiths, which will help to begin the dialogue. This means: paying attention to the beautiful aspects of others' traditions and not so much to the problems or the mere facts. Starting a conversation with appreciative knowledge can contribute to build trust between the people. When professionals are familiar with some of the important aspects of their clients' faith and religious traditions, they may acknowledge the religious traditions of their clients by offering them for instance the propre wishes at the occasion of their religious holidays. They may say to them "Eid Mubarak", "Happy Holi", "Hanukkah Sameach" or "Merry Christmas". A kind and thoughtful gesture like this may contribute to increase the client's trust in the relationship with professionals.

Yet, as Emouna clearly indicated, knowledge about religions should not lead to generalizations about individuals. Within one religion, people follow different paths, based on family traditions, geographic locations of origin, and histories of migration. Within each religion there are strict and loose observants. Some abide strictly to the rules and regulations of their religion, others do not. Some people tend to have their own interpretation of daily life's restrictions and obligations, others do not. Some people focus on life in the here and now, others are oriented toward earning rewards for life hereafter.

The danger of superficial religious literacy is that it can lead to simplistic and inaccurate ideas that would prevent contextual practitioners from taking into account the uniqueness of their clients with regard to their practice of religion. Another serious problem occurs when a contextual practitioner follows a religion or is inspired by a spiritual movement that entails an intolerance to the religious or spiritual orientation of a client. In this case the practitioner can experience a loyalty conflict between his or her obligation to this client and his or her commitment to his or her religious group. Here, the interest of the client should obviously prevail.

All this connects to Emouna's method for stimulating *religious literacy*. This method is not based on lecturing on faith traditions in general, but it calls for specific attention to people's personal experiences of their religion or philosophy of life. As said, each person embodies his or her tradition differently. Rather than asking: "What is Judaism?" Emouna asks: "What does it mean for you as a female rabbi to be Jewish in France?" To the Hindu chaplain of Indian descent: "What rituals do you perform in Amsterdam?" To the homosexual protestant minister: "What does Protestantism mean to you?" Here religions and philosophies of life get a human face through personal stories. This approach to the religious identity of people calls at least for tolerance, and for the ability to not arrogantly equate an individual believer with his or her religion. Conversely, drawing conclusions about a whole religious community from a single personal story is also unfair. Here, religious literacy helps contextual practitioners to focus on how their clients' personal religious choices and positions influence fairness in their relationships.

A young man seeks help from his contextual counselor about a problem with his parents. He came from a Roman Catholic family where he received a lot of support from his parents and from the family's church. He later converted to the Baha'i faith. On one weekend, he visited his parents, and they invited him to accompany them to church, which he did. When his parents gestured to him to join them in the Holy Communion, he declined. For him, not attending the Eucharist since he had left the church was a way of showing that he was taking his parents' faith seriously. His parents did not understand his choice and perceived it the opposite way, meaning that he had lost his respect for their church and that he had made a break with them over such a precious aspect of their religious practice. They were hurt and since they were not able to begin a dialogue with their son, they could not give him credit for his good intentions. The young man examined with his counselor how he could show his parents that he still respected their religion. As a result of this discussion, he decided to offer them for their wedding anniversary a Bible in the most modern translation. They appreciated his gesture very much and it opened the way to a constructive dialogue between them.

Intersectionality

In addition, contextual practitioners may want to learn from the concept of *intersectionality* that Emouna incorporated in its program. The term 'intersectionality' was coined in 1989 by the American black feminist and scholar of Critical Race theory Kimberlé Crenshaw, who is also a civil rights advocate (Runyan, 2018).[13] She describes it as "a method and a disposition, a heuristic and analytical tool" that she used in court when defending her black female clients who got paid less for the same job than white women or black men, by stipulating that her clients' intersecting identities had contributed to an unfair treatment by their employers. Her metaphor relates to the image of a traffic junction: different roads converge at an intersection and cars from different directions meet at this intersection. In this sense, intersectionality raises awareness to the interconnectedness of the many factors that contribute to form a person's identity; for instance, the interconnectedness of race and gender; gender and abilities; race, gender and religion; gender and economical status; and race, poverty and education, etc. According to Runyan, Crenshaw argues "that this 'structural intersectionality' among forms of oppression based on race, gender, class, and national origin that emanated from both the state and intimate relations put immigrant women of color at most risk of violence".

An example of intersectionality comes from a European survey in 2016 indicating that 73% of Afghani-Dutch Muslim women in The Netherlands wearing a hijab reported experiencing discrimination on the basis of religion, compared with 11% of Afghani-Dutch Muslim women who did not wear a headscarf (Seta, 2016).[14] Another survey that takes intersectionality into account shows that around the world: "people of (darker) color have been systematically marginalized. They are disproportionately likely to live in

---

13   https://bit.ly/43ZuFme
14   https://bit.ly/422lBv3

poverty, suffer the impacts of climate change, experience hunger, die in childbirth, earn less, have unequal access to education, and be physically and economically impacted by Covid-19" (Bumb, Carlson & Iyer, 2020).[15]

Recognizing that we are all vessels of intersecting identity variables can help us to understand others. One may find similarities with persons of a different ethnicity, culture, or religion, which inspires to reducing social distances and bridging gaps. However, in comparing identity variables one can overlook the fact that in a given social system people with certain intersecting variables may face exclusion or discrimination while others do not. One of the most obvious variables that lead to discrimination are skin color and physical appearance. Sometimes comparing identity variables can also lead to a competition: "who is most disadvantaged" or "who is most privileged" which does not benefit anyone. Also, the phrase "Check your privilege" may be used as a reproach and an insult rather than an invitation to sincere dialogue.[16]

A native Dutch progressive politician was invited to say a few words at a Black Lives Matter meeting, to which he kindly agreed. In his attempt to show understanding and to empower his audience, he told a personal story about his family's suffering as Jewish immigrants from Russia in the early 20th century. After their arrival in The Netherlands, they became blue-collar workers. Living in a Roman Catholic environment, they were exposed to prejudices. They were also affected by the intergenerational transmission of anxieties. And now, a few generations later, he had reached the status of a respected member of society and was doing what he could to help disadvantaged people to move up in society. His message was: "Don't be a victim, take your life into your own hands!", and he backed his message by sharing his own experience: new generations do reverse social injustices by embodying the changes they wanted for themselves. However, many people in the audience did not appreciate his encouragements and told him as a reproach: "You're not of color, you don't have to deal with judgments based on your appearance". In turn, the politician felt that his identity had been reduced to only one characteristic, the whiteness of his skin. This had caused him great pain. Only later did he understand that he had focused on individual achievements and he had overlooked the social stigmas that are based on physical variables that result in systemic disadvantages. In overlooking that, he had contributed to a social status quo instead of contributing to desirable systemic changes.

Two types of dialogue

Accepting the responsibility to engage in the process of systemic transformation is a great motivation for engaging in the type of organized dialogues that interreligious studies and interfaith programs promote. This motivation and the trust in this type of dialogue is based on our belief in the fundamental capability of humans beings to giving attention

---

15 https://bit.ly/3VgUyM2
16 https://bit.ly/3He9kMf

and care to others, even when they are unfamiliar or perceived as potential antagonists. To be successful, these organized interfaith dialogues need to take place in groups, in a specific location, at a set time, and they need to entail an agreement on a theme or a topic. Through an open and 'appreciative' conversation, the participants get acquainted with each other primarily by sharing their personal cultural and religious experiences.

The late Rachel Reedijk, a Jewish Dutch anthropologist and writer, and one of the founders of Emouna Netherlands, published on the role, meaning and effectiveness of interreligious dialogue between Jews and Muslims (Reedijk, 2010). In her unpublished lecture at an Emouna meeting in 2019, she explained that she saw chances for an effective, successful dialogue when the participants shared a specific common goal or cause. According to Reedijk, this 'functional dialogue' needs to meet certain characteristics. In short: interfaith dialogue generally begins with an honest and attentive listening. It aims at a transformation of action and a change of perception in the people who engage in this dialogue. Such a dialogue can take place only when this dialogue is based on true reciprocity and when dialogue partners see each other as equals. Furthermore, this dialogue can only occur if the participants have the freedom to engage in it: forced dialogues do not exist. The dialogue partners need to feel safe. They need to be able to trust each other. They need to be given the time to tell stories and the freedom to find their own solutions. Other conditions for dialogue are preparedness, warmth, curiosity, humor, and self-mockery. Once these conditions are met, they can begin their dialogue, with or without a dialogue leader.

These functional dialogues aim at more than getting people acquainted with each other by acquiring knowledge about their respective faith traditions. People engage in these kind of dialogues when they want to work on a common goal or cause. Together, they agree to organize themselves around specific projects. It could be the prevention of a conflict in a neighborhood, the establishment of a youth center, the maintenance of a public space, or the attempt to make a factory stop its air pollution. While doing this, they may also want to contribute to necessary changes in the culture, organization, or society they belong to. We know that religious or spiritual beliefs can contribute to conflict among dialogue partners; however, faith traditions can also enrich the shared wisdom of these dialogue partners and help them to overcome the obstacles they may encounter in dealing with each other.

From the perspective of the contextual approach, organized dialogues seem to overlook the notion of relational fairness between dialogue partners. While an aspiration to fair relationships might be implicitly present in the theory and practice of interfaith dialogues, as far as I know, this is not mentioned explicitly in interreligious studies or training programs. Obviously, interfaith dialogues require an attention to each of the participants' perspectives and an attentiveness to possible misunderstandings. They are also based on valuing the idea that each participant has the right to have a personal position and to defend it. By contrast, in the contextual approach, the interpersonal dialogue is based on relational ethics which explicitly aims at promoting fairness between the relating partners. Here the dialogue is an interpersonal process in which one gives weight to one's perspectives and interests while at the same time making space for the perspective and interest of all other participants in the dialogue. The dialogue in relational ethics is based not so much on shared values and a willingness to learn from others, but on the powerful human capacity to discuss fairness and unfairness in relationships. Therefore, participants may need to share the inconvenient truths that may be brought up by their dialogue. They need to be able to acknowledge relational debts and relational contribution. They need to search for ways forward that are fair to all. Here, the biggest challenge is to respect those who, for unknown motives, do not understand or know in what way they can contribute to the dialogue. Showing patience, accepting to wait, keeping hope for what may still happen are stones that help to build a bridge between the participants in the dialogue. According to the philosopher Martin Buber, the dialogue is always characterized by its unpredictability. This dialogue may change direction when a new perspective demands attention or when those who had thus far remained silent demand the attention of others.

This dialogue can then result in a shift in ideas about oneself and others and in a readiness for an active change. The participants in this dialogue may succeed in removing the most difficult obstacles to their relationship. They may be more able to differentiate themselves from others ("We do not have to be or think the same, I am I and you are you"). They may also be more ready to respect or tolerate different points of view. They also may be freer to discuss without any fear whether they want to stay connected or not, whether they want to continue to cooperate together on a common cause or prefer to end their relationship. At the minimum this dialogue may be useful to avert the escalation of potential conflicts.

No dialogue

Sometimes there are good reasons for not going into any organized form of dialogue. People have responsibilities to their own faith communities, which prevents them from searching for the stepping stones that can help bridge the gap between them and others. Not entering a dialogue does not always have to originate from power plays by privileged parties, nor from apathy, fear, or indifference by disadvantaged people. It may originate from staying faithful to one's identity and personal points of view; it can be an expression of loyalty to a community and its heritage. Forcing a dialogue may induce expressions of hatred and contempt, which can move a situation from neutral to bad and to worse. In cases of violence between opposing partners, other measures should be taken first, such as discussing the points of conflict separately with the respective parties.

Sometimes, a moratorium on any kind of dialogue that has already begun can contribute to the delay of violence among the dialogue partners. Here is an example of an intercultural dialogue that failed because the involved partners did not pay attention to relational ethics.

For more than 20 years, two Christian congregations have shared the same church building. One is liberal protestant, respecting individual human rights, the other is a so-called evangelical international church, believing in obedience of its members to a strict religious doctrine. The first consists of many senior believers of Dutch origin, the other is composed of Christians with backgrounds in West Africa who came to Europe as refugees in the 1990s. For a few years, the congregations got along well in terms of celebrating Pentecost together and in meetings between the leadership of the two congregations. This cooperation ended after the Dutch congregation appointed a gay minister. The evangelical congregation decided to stop participating in the celebration of Pentecost, because "propagating homosexuality" is too great a sin to condone. The liberal board reacted with anger: "Do not judge us, keep your hands off from our LGBTQI minister and members, and shame on you for your faith that prohibits people from being who they are."

Both parties became too angry to enter a dialogue about fairness. They had no interest in learning more about the others' values and convictions. They felt that they knew enough. Still, both parties agreed to wait and pray. Both decided to take the time to see what move the other one would make. Since the board members of the liberal congregation assumed that any congregation entails people with same-sex preferences, they hoped that a change would occur if only one of the members of the evangelical congregation would openly condone this type of sexual preference. Conversely, the leaders of the evangelical congregation started to say prayers wishing that the liberals would turn into real Christians who condemn homosexuality. Two years passed without any dialogue between the two boards.

Meanwhile, the two communities still shared the same amenities in the church building. People were not showing any hostility toward each other; on the contrary, they kept making friendly gestures toward each other when crossing paths in the building. One of the possible explanation is that no one wanted to enter into a contentious discussion that could escalate to a complete break because both communities had too much to lose if they had to break the owner/tenant agreement that regulated their shared use of the church building. A more optimistic interpretation of the situation is that no one wanted to cause further damage to the remaining reciprocal trust that had been built during the decades of shared use of the church building. Whether and when this dialogue may resume is impossible to predict, but the current situation can be understood as a form of moratorium that keeps the door open for a future dialogue while at the same time preventing the risk of a serious escalation of the conflict.

Chapter 3

Exploring Intercultural Encounters

So far, we have discussed the important insights and practical tools that interreligious studies offer to address the complexities of intercultural encounters. However, sharing certain relational values, an interest in knowing more about the religion or culture of others, and acquiring skills for intercultural dialogues may not be sufficient to respond to situations of discomfort and conflict that may occur in these encounters. This chapter will contribute to the analysis of obstacles as well as bridges in intercultural encounters by using some of the tools offered by the contextual approach. Here I will specifically rely on the five-dimensional model of relational reality to show all the factors that can play a role in intercultural encounters. I believe that not only leaders who organize these encounters can benefit from this analytical model but also contextual practitioners who work in a multicultural environment. A very short meeting of two people from different backgrounds will serve here as a case to study the many elements that have played a role in the way these people were able to bridge their differences. We will call them Margaret and Nasr.

A simple greeting

Margaret and Nasr are two people who were interested in learning about interfaith relationships and they choose to attend an interfaith meeting. Margaret is a middle aged Christian woman and a protestant minister of a congregation in the cosmopolitan city of Rotterdam. She enters the room where she is expected to meet the other participants. In the Netherlands people who attend these kinds of meetings are expected to shake hands and exchange names (this was in the pre-covid 19 time). She approaches a dark-skin Muslim man, in his thirties, dressed traditionally. He sees her, walks up to her, smiles and before she can extend her hand to him, he says kindly: "I don't shake hands with women, but I greet you like this". He nods his head and crosses his right hand in front of his chest. "My name is Nasr, who are you?" Margaret immediately accepts his greetings with a small bow, she smiles in return and tells him her name.

Margaret and Nasr knew from the start they were going to meet people from other religions, they also knew they were going to be confronted with unfamiliar ideas and behaviors. They encountered each other on the basis of values such as mutual respect and consideration for people's possible vulnerabilities. This very moment, however, could have been the beginning of a conflict instead of the starting point of a respectful relationship. What would have happened if Nasr and Margaret had not been able to meet and greet like they did? What would have happened if they had not been able to recognize each other's good will?

This short vignette shows us the danger of simply assuming that people who meet in the course of interreligious activities will always be able to work together because of their shared values. In fact, many factors could prevent people from adjusting to their respective needs. Here we can use the framework of the five dimensions proposed in the contextual approach to list the possible variables that can become an obstacle but also a resource in relationships.

A five-dimension perspective on Margaret and Nasr meeting

In our example, Margaret comes from a family where her parents were committed to her welfare and gave her all what she needed to develop successfully. She comes from the dominant middle class of her country and had never suffered from any social, political, or religious discrimination. Time and again she had experienced the privilege of being accepted and protected by the institutions of her society. Whenever anything out of the ordinary happened, it made her curious rather than unsettled. She had always felt safe enough to speak up and was used to being heard. She had also been raised with the value of equal rights for all people and respecting differences. The setting of the interreligious conference contributed to her ideals that people from different backgrounds could basically meet freely as friends and fellow citizens. This all played a role in the way she responded to Nasr's greeting.

Nasr came to the Netherlands from Egypt when he was five. He comes from a loving and committed family, but his family was limited in what support they could offer to him as a growing child. His family struggled to find its place as both Muslims and people of color, in a predominantly white and Christian village in a rural area of the Netherlands. His experiences had made him cautious meeting new people. But as time went by, Nasr adopted the wisdom of Islam, and his faith gave him courage. He had learned to understand that his religious task was to surrender to Allah by living the exemplary life as once the prophet Mohammed had lived. Even if Nasr did not understand all the rules and regulations of his religion, he wanted to follow them, no matter how people may react to him. He believed his intentions were pure and he hoped that others could sense that. It is with these ideas he went to the interreligious conference and greeted Margaret.

Dimension I: Facts

The dimension of facts includes all the givens of one own's life such as the time and place of our birth, the socio-historical circumstances in which we are born which can determine the language we are using or the religion that we are following.

In our example, the factual variables that are part of Margret and Nasr's relational reality are rather obvious: their sex difference, their age difference, their physical appearance, their native background: Dutch/Moroccan, their native language, and their religion: Christian/Muslim. All these factual elements have played a central role in their encounter.

These could not be changed but what made the difference was the way in which Margret and Nasr dealt with them.

Contextual practitioners and interfaith leaders need to pay attention to these factual variables. They cannot change them, but they need to know that facts are as important determinants of our behaviors as is our psyche, our place in our family and other social systems, and our expectation of fairness in relationships. Also, as I have already discussed in my paragraphs on privileges, disadvantages, and intersecting identities, factual elements like the color of our skin can lead to particular benefits or disadvantages in the systems we are part of. Here, the interpretation of these facts and their intersections may have consequences for the way Nasr and Margaret perceive each other.

Dimension II: Psychology

The dimension of psychology entails all the determinants of our psychological functioning: conscious and unconscious needs and reactions, types of emotions, intellectual abilities, and the various unconscious mechanisms that influence the way we perceive others and the world.

In the situation of Margret and Nasr, psychological factors leading to their acceptance of each other could have been their intellectual curiosity i.e. their interest in meeting different people, their self-confidence, their ability to trust others, etc. Margaret could have reminded Nasr of the older Christian woman from the village who gave him cookies and tea, which would evoke pleasant feelings toward her. Nasr's eyes could have reminded Margret of a nice past boyfriend which would have also evoked positive feelings in her.

Conversely, many psychological factors could have played a negative role in their encounter. Many people may have a simple fear of the unknown. Some may suffer from a lack of self-esteem. If this would have been the case for Margaret, she would have immediately experienced Nasr's refusal to shake hands with her as evidence of rejection. She could also have been scared of Nasr because he shares features with people who are considered dangerous by some parts of society. Nasr himself could have been retraumatized by meeting Margaret if she was reminding him of a domineering Dutch teacher who had ignored him in class. This would have retriggered his sense of exclusion as an immigrant.

We need to be aware that conscious and unconscious psychological factors do play a big role in relationships. These factors can prevent people from being comfortable with each other in interreligious meetings, or from really hearing each other. We need to take the psychological elements that can form an obstacle in relationships seriously. Again, we should not simply assume that people can work together just because of their common values. We need to be attentive to the possibility that people may experience difficulties in meeting other people that are related to their individual psychological features, and to past experiences, especially past traumatic experiences.

In intercultural groups, leaders should be prepared to notice when people have negative emotional reactions to others. They do not have the mission to resolve the psychological difficulties of group members, but they should at least acknowledge the person's struggle and offer to make space for a discussion whether the person who struggles and the group members who are affected by the situation accept this offer or not. Contextual professionals do not focus their interventions directly on this dimension of psychology, but they too need to know about the psychological factors that influence people's reactions to each other.

Dimension III: Transactions and systems

The dimension of transactions or the systemic dimension entails all the supra-individual determinants of our behaviors that are connected to our belonging to larger systems like the family system, our local community, our religious community, etc. This dimension entails all the variables that are related to the functioning of these systems. Important variables are the power structures of any given system, the observed transaction patterns, or styles of communication, the shared myths and rituals, the shared narratives, or the shared values that bring people together.

When people from different backgrounds come to an interfaith meeting, they may attend out of their own personal interests, or they may attend as a delegate of a specific group. They also come with their own individual characteristics, personal ideas, and personal goals. Nonetheless, whether they are sent by a group or come just as interested individuals, in any case they are part of larger systems that have an influence on their behaviors, and on the way they treat each other.

In Margaret's and Nasr's situation, there is an asymmetry between Margaret's position as a member of several privileged systems and Nasr's position as a member of a social and religious minority group with fewer privileges. Margaret follows the rules and values of her family and church, which promote equal rights and tolerance between people. As a member of the dominant social system Margaret has more power in society than Nasr. This could have contributed to her acceptance of Nasr's way of greeting her because she knew that no matter how people are treating her it would not threaten her position in society. On the other hand, if she was part of a militant feminist group, she would have refused to acknowledge his offer because accepting it would have been an acceptance of male dominance (accepting his way of greeting rather than imposing hers). If Margaret would have been part of anti-immigrant political party, she would have interpreted Nasr's gesture as an unacceptable form of social transaction in her society.

For Nasr shaking hands was not an option because this was contrary to the rules and regulations of his religion that he wanted to follow. At the same time, his position as a man who is a member of minority and underprivileged groups makes him much more dependent on the reaction of people from majority groups than they depend on his reaction to them.

An in-depth discussion among professionals in a multicultural world about the systemic factors that are involved in people's encounters could broaden their awareness of the systemic powers exercised by privileged people, who are able to include and exclude other people. These privileged people can do this by having access to various resources such as language skills, education, communication tools and positions higher in the hierarchy of the system. This awareness can spark necessary discussions about submissive or subversive responses of less privileged people to a system, which they can express in mild and radical forms of protest, in withdrawal from this system by no longer wanting to take responsibility for it, in indifference, in seeking refuge in radical religious or political movements, etc. Contextual practitioners should pay attention to all these elements whether they are called to the aid of a couple, a family, colleagues or neighbors.

Contextual practitioners are supposed to be able to recognize the systemic influences on their clients and help them to discuss these. It adds to the professionality of interfaith leaders if they also would be able to recognize systemic factors that lead to social differences that contribute to gaps between people. All need to realize that no matter how much Margaret and Nasr would have learned about each other's traditions and no matter how many exercises they would have done to try to put themselves in the shoes of the other, still Margaret would have to decide if she recognized Nasr's way of greeting her as a form of giving or if she will insist on her right to have her needs met. This brings us to the discussion of the dimension of relational ethics.

Dimension IV: Relational ethics

The dimension of relational ethics is at the very heart of the contextual approach. As already discussed, relational ethics are not based on values, individual virtues, or religious codes of conduct. Relational ethics refer to a form of ethics that requires that people treat each other in accordance with an understanding of the direct impact of their behavior on others, not in accordance with preset moral or religious guidelines. The dimension of relational ethics is based on our fundamental characteristic as human beings, which is that we expect reciprocity, fairness, and loyalty in relationships. This dimension also entails the discussion of the relational consequences of injustices.

What is fair in a relationship can never be defined absolutely. What people experience as fair or unfair is determined by how each of them weighs their own contributions to the relationship and those of the others. We need to be aware that the assessment of the fairness does not just depend on people's subjective valuation of what they have given and received in the given relationship. It also depends on the value that they have learned to attribute to specific gestures and behaviors in the community they are coming from, for instance their religious community. This subjective valuation also depends on people's past experiences of injustices, for instance the experience of having been short-changed, ignored, exploited, or subjected to any other form of injustices.

In the example of Margaret and Nasr, we can easily assume that Nasr had no intention to hurt Margaret and that he considered his way of greeting with his hand on his heart and a bow of his head was certainly a way to convey respect to her and a form of giving. It seems that indeed Margaret could recognize this. Her capacity to give credit to Nasr for treating her with respect may have come from her experience of giving and receiving trust in her own family.

It is important to remember that this assessment of fairness and unfairness often happens in just a split second. It occurs before people have time to think about the consequences of their behavior (body language or a word spoken too quickly) for the future of the relationship. Contextual professionals can help people make a second assessment by inviting them to engage in a dialogue which may lead to a more correct assessment. Or to confirmation of the spontaneous assessment of the other's behavior as 'fair'.

In order to discuss fairness and injustices in social systems it is important to raise awareness about institutionalized injustices and to find leverages for social transformations. In a Western democratic society as The Netherlands, however pluralistic, the premise is that all citizens have the equal right to be treated fairly by the system, and all have the right to contribute to the common good according to the requirements of the system and to their individual ability and capacity. However, this is theory. In practice, people of minority groups are likely to experience unfairness when for instance their specific contributions to the system are not recognized enough or when they face the risk of being excluded by their 'foreign' family name or the wrong zip code of their address.

In this multicultural world, contextual practitioners and interfaith leaders can offer to organize intercultural dialogues that discuss both expectations of fairness and systemic injustices. The objective of a dialogue about relational ethics is that it should help the participants to discover that all of them can gain more from generosity toward others than from insisting on their own rights without compromise. But here one has to pay attention to the position of the non-privileged participants who need to be offered an added attention and possibly an added support in this type of dialogue.

At the same time, contextual practitioners and interfaith leaders may teach that agreement and harmony are never expected to last, since life is ever changing. Diversity of people forms the basis under these ongoing and ever-changing relational dynamics. The issue of relational justice is here an important driver. Questions such as 'What is fair?' or an exclamation such as 'This is not fair!' signals these relational dynamics and the need for dialogue. Both the contextual approach and interreligious studies provide the hope that people of any background are willing to defer violence and to find bridges to overcome the differences that keep them apart.

Dimension V: The ontic dimension

The fifth dimension pertains to the relational definition of the self, and the relational definition of autonomy. As presented in the first section of this book, in the view of Boszormenyi-Nagy, the Self can only be defined in relationship with its counterpart, the Other. The mutual dependence of the Self and the Other is defined as an ontic dependence. This dependence is inherent to the relational definition of the self, and not depending on any kind of psychological needs. In Section I, there is a detailed discussion of the different modes through which the delineation of the Self and the Other occurs. For the purpose of the discussion of the meeting between Margaret and Nasr, I will focus only on the two modes described by M. Buber for the establishment of the Self and the Other, the I-Thou, and the I-It mode.

In most cases, people meet because they have specific needs and expectations that bring them into a relationship. This means that in most cases, the meeting takes the form of an I-It meeting, in which each party serves a function for the other in fulfilling their needs and expectations. This is the case with Margaret and Nasr. Margaret's main need is to learn from members of other faiths to improve her competences in providing services to the neighborhood where her congregation is situated. Nasr has similar needs to learn about other religions, and in addition, he was hoping that he could also be a spokesperson for his faith as he felt that people have no or wrong ideas about Islam. Both served a function for the other as a mutual source of information about their respective religions.

This function could have been taken by someone else, another Christian minister, or another representative of the Muslim faith. The fact that their meeting entails a functional element, i.e. that they use each other as a source of information results in an I-It form of encounter. However, this does not mean that the relationship is exploitative since there is mutuality in the role that both play for each other. The relationship would become exploitative only if one was trying to use the other as a source of information without accepting to reciprocate. It also would become destructive if Margaret and Nasr were stereotyping each other. "He is ...". "She is ...". This kind of disparaging characterization would of course lead to hostility.

In any situation, contextual practitioners and interfaith leaders can help people to become attentive to their mutual interdependence and teach them about the difference between a functional relationship and an exploitative relationship. A dialogue about the nature of a relationship is necessary when one experiences the other's behavior as exploitative, even while the other experiences the relationship merely as an agreement on how to fulfil each other's needs. A dialogue about these two relational modes may also be necessary as a wakeup call in case people have the unrealistic expectation that they never want to serve a function for the other. No matter how fair the relationship is, it always entails elements of functionality.

The I-Thou meeting refers to a rare level of meeting in which both people are able to meet each other for a brief moment in the fullness of their humanity. In the case of Margaret and Nasr, the moment when Margaret and Nasr met through their smiles, they did encounter each other as two unique human beings.

Up to now we have examined the greeting of Margaret and Nasr from five different angles. Two other concepts that are central to the contextual approach also deserve attention: *loyalty* and *constructive and destructive entitlement.*

Loyalty

Recognizing loyalty as a factor that influences emotions (Dimension II), systems (Dimension III), and the degree of fairness in relationships (Dimension IV) is always important, and even more so in intercultural relationships. This is because cultures and religions can lead to polarization: the idea of 'us' and 'them'. In relationships that are more monocultural, what could potentially cause divides often remains hidden. Thus, by learning from intercultural relationships, contextual practitioners may become more sensitive to diversity in situations where differences are less obvious.

In the contextual approach, loyalty is not only a moral commitment or a pledge to abide to traditions. Loyalty is a commitment based on mutual expectations, merits, and obligations, which contribute to complex dynamics in the triadic configuration of individuals, their intergenerational communities, and outsiders/other communities. We become especially aware of our loyalties in the face of hurtful questions and derogatory criticism by influential others of a more dominant community, the public opinion, the tacit agreement of a group about what is good and desirable and what is not. Customs, ideas, traditions, or beliefs to which we ourselves are attached by birth or choice may be unfamiliar, strange, obscure, or threatening to others. Outsiders who are unfamiliar with our religious or cultural idiosyncrasies may challenge us to discuss and defend them. Hidden or overt hostilities from outside and inside can jeopardize but also strengthen the stability and survival of a community. Even members who have chosen a different religion or adopted a different culture may stand up and defend the community in which they grew up: "Don't touch my people, my country, my culture, or my former religion!" Criticism from within and new insights or preferences can also threaten the unity of our own group.

When, where and why do we set our boundaries as members of a certain community? Loyalty conflicts can be difficult to discern by contextual practitioners who are not familiar with certain tensions in a community or between groups. Whom and what are they defending against which attacker? What relational injustices by whom are they experiencing? Here, we are reminded of the requirements for contextual practitioners to which Astrid Roemer's warning applies (see Chapter 1). A dialogue about relational ethics with critical friends, for instance friends or acquaintances from other communities, will help us to better understand our own loyalties and our own position in relation to those who challenge us.

How did loyalty play a role in Nasr's and Margaret's meeting? As long as others respect Nasr's obligations to his family members and to his faith community, as long as he is not prevented from fulfilling them, Nasr is at peace. Margaret, who does not challenge Nasr's preferred greeting gesture, does not force him to choose between her world and his world. By his manner of greeting, Nasr honors the religious tradition he prefers, and this prevents him from experiencing distress. His fellow believers are not going to challenge him, which they might have done had Nasr given in to Margaret's insistence to greet her the way she had wanted. Nasr also fulfils his commitment to his parents by being courteous and kind to strangers; that is how they raised him and that is what he himself values too. His wife is as committed to his religious tradition as he is, so he has not betrayed her by his behavior either.

In short, Nasr's greeting could potentially create a conflict with Margaret, but also a loyalty conflict with his religious tradition and with his family members. It is to be expected that Nasr considers: to whom am I primarily bound? As for his way of greeting women, his religious tradition wins. Perhaps he considers his choice as a sign of his confidence in and a compliment to the social institutions that allow him to express his individual preferences and his loyalty to his religious tradition. At the same time, treating women respectfully as he did here is a form of loyalty to both his family and religious values and at the same time a loyalty to the value of the society he lives in now. This is an example of a bridge that can be built through direct and constructive expressions of loyalty.

As for Margaret, her loyalty to her 'own people' could have been strengthened, had she dismissed Nasr's way of greeting as a signal of loyalty to his Islamic and North-African community against her Christian and Western community. However, since Margaret grew up in a spiritual and socially tolerant environment, she shows her loyalty to her family, church and society by acting on their values by responding to Nasr's greeting cordially. In doing so, she built a similar bridge as Nasr through her own direct and constructive expression of loyalty.

Destructive entitlement

In section I of this book, we find an extensive discussion of the concept of destructive entitlement. In brief, when we have been wronged, we expect redress. If it does not come from the people who have caused us a tort, we may turn to other people with the hope that they can compensate us for the damages that were not repaired by the culprit. Our claim to compensation is justified but expecting people to repair injustices that they did not cause is destructive to the relationship, hence the concept of destructive entitlement. In other words, people are entitled to obtain redress, but they have no right to cause harm to others in seeking it.

While giving is clearly a source of constructive entitlement, over-giving can lead to destructive entitlement when the over-givers expect an added recognition for their extra giving. In Margaret's case the risk of over-giving could come from extending tolerance toward others, beyond the limit of her own needs but then expecting that people reciprocate at the same level. Which is an unfair disposition on them.

It is very likely that Nasr has accumulated destructive entitlement from his experience of discrimination while he was growing up. Systemically disadvantaged people face multiple problems and have to muster an unfair amount of personal strength to combat, overcome, or perhaps accept these. In Nasr's situation this could have led to a revengeful attitude toward members of the dominant society which includes Margaret. But instead, his religious background and motivations have protected him from acting in a negative manner toward her.

Constructive entitlement

As already described in Section I of this book, in the contextual approach, the healing moment is defined relationally. It is the moment when a person is able to show generosity to another one by trying to meet this person's needs. When a person can show generosity to another person, both sides benefit. For the beneficiary of the gesture, the gain is obvious: it is whatever the giver has offered. At the same moment, the giver experiences an indirect benefit from his or her action in the form of what contextual therapists call *constructive entitlement*. It is marked by an increase in self-worth, self-esteem, and self-definition, and it does not depend on the reaction of the beneficiary of the gesture. In other words, we need others in our life to gain the special relevance that comes from our ability to contribute positively to the lives of other people. When we care about the needs of others and can be generous toward them, our positive gestures bring us increased human value, and increased inner security (constructive entitlement).

In the example of Margaret and Nasr, Margaret had earned entitlement by offering a smile to Nasr instead of dismissing him as a man who does not treat her the right way. Nasr himself had gained constructive entitlement when he gave Margaret a sign of respect by bowing his head toward her instead of simply refusing to shake hands. Nasr was not forcing Margaret to accept his greeting offer, and Margaret did not act superior to Nasr, nor did she behave like a victim who had no choice but to accept his greeting. They showed receptivity to the needs of the other, they received credit from the other as a result, and this exchange of trust paved the way for the continuation of their encounter. It also became part of a new narrative in their respective communities that laid the foundation for others to engage in intercultural meetings, as the stone that is thrown into the pond creates expanding waves. At home and in the mosque Nasr spoke of Margaret with much appreciation, just as Margaret spoke well of Nasr to her parents, friends, and church members. The two did not only bridge a gap between themselves but they inspired others to meet people from outside their communities with interest and even trust. These responses came on top of the merits the two had already earned, which gave them even more freedom to continue reaching out to yet unknown people and to be good to strangers. And that, of course, is a characteristic of relational justice.

We are now about to say goodbye to Nasr and Margaret. We are pleased that they were able to show us how their intercultural encounter culminated in a form of *fair bridging* which led to a reliable relationship that affected others and contributed a small step to a more just society they both are part of.

Chapter 4

Final Remarks

Sensitivity to ethnic, cultural, and religious differences in multicultural societies has been the main focus of all my chapters. I first drew on my personal experiences. As discussed already, I discovered that I missed the resources needed to conduct my ministry appropriately and comfortably in the new situation of a multicultural congregation and that I needed to acquire the necessary intercultural skills to carry out my ministry more adequately. In sharing my experience, I am inviting contextual practitioners and interreligious leaders to reflect as well on their own intercultural competencies and possible shortcomings. Writing these chapters has also helped me to bring aspects of the contextual approach and interreligious studies together which may serve as guiding principles for all professionals who work in multicultural contexts. Now it is time to draw some conclusions.

Insights

When I visited the grieving Surinamese family to prepare the funeral service, we could have all benefited from shared knowledge of Surinamese ideas about life and death and the community's funeral traditions. Yet the preparation could have been more effective if I had dared to think and speak about our differences: our ethnic, cultural, or religious differences (Dimension I) and our systemic differences in terms of my power as a minister with the privilege of leading the meeting (Dimension III). However, the cultural taboo that I had internalized, the taboo on addressing differences, which I believe is part of a democratic ideology about the equality of all people, and my loyalty to this democratic ideology made me apprehensive to do so. The cultural convention to not pay attention to differences prevented me from seeing these conflicts. Understanding that we need to break down *the taboo of not inquiring* may be the most important gain and I want to share this important insight with the reader. In recent years, I have come to realize that asking about differences and seizing the opportunity to acknowledge the different wants and needs of others can become the starting point for an open conversation about what constitutes relational justice in a given situation. This can then lead to a better mutual understanding and to improved relationships.

In the situation of the intercultural couple, I came for an introductory visit. The conversation was aimed at mutual acquaintance and establishing a bond of trust. At the same time, my mandate as a minister gave me the opportunity to inquire about their relationship as a couple, and to ask them questions about their children and their extended families. Looking back, I could have invited this couple to share something with me about the kind of enrichment they must have experienced from learning about their respective background and differences, and the cultural gaps they had not bridged yet. I would now consider asking them how their intercultural marriage and their loyalties to their respective families and religious groups have influenced, for example, the organization of their household and the education of their children. I would now listen more attentively to what they may have wanted to say about the influences of racism and discrimination, of systemic stereotyping, prejudices, privileges and disadvantages on their family life, their hopes and fears, their struggles, and how they earn constructive entitlement. Again, avoiding conversations about differences as a taboo becomes a real obstacle when people from different backgrounds want to get to know each other and wish to build a relationship with each other.

However, in the situation of the mourning family, my inquiries about differences could have been resented by the family because in this case it would have forced to address conflicts around cultural issues that they were not prepared to discuss, including my own position. Here, perhaps I did not ask them too little, but rather too much!

Regarding the congregation that I still serve in East Amsterdam, I became aware that while it is becoming increasingly multicultural over the years, the intercultural faith exchange that would be necessary in this changing situation is not really taking place. Here also, the fear of conflict over different religious beliefs seems currently greater than the desire for dialogue. However, members are interested in each other and here lies the prospect for future meetings. The quality of relations among members can also improve by no longer considering those who have immigrated to the Netherlands as *guests* but as equal individuals with different backgrounds. Sharing responsibility for governance and policy also contributes to fair relating. This calls for accommodation on the part of members who have long been in charge. What do they need to do to give space to others? Here the congregation could learn from my example of the meeting with Nasr and Margaret, and the use of the five- dimensional model of relational reality as a resource in addressing complex situations.

Recommendations

Interfaith studies and the contextual approach are based on the hope and experience that people care about others, across borders. Contextual practitioners can broaden their knowledge of the complexity of human relationships and societies and also sharpen their understanding of multidirected partiality by learning from interfaith studies, by joining intercultural networks and organized dialogues and by visiting religious communities or participating in cultural events outside of their familiar world. In these chapters, using my intuition and personal experience, I have shown that it is possible to transfer knowledge about relational ethics and ethics of care from families to intercultural encounters. However, this is a new endeavor and it needs to be pursued by further discussions and research.

Contextual training programs should include an attention to multiculturality and intersectionality. I recommend developing these programs with an ethnically, culturally, and religiously mixed group of contextual practitioners. This kind of intercultural training programs should obviously be anchored in the dimension of relational ethics but they should also focus on Dimension I (the interpretation of facts), Dimension II (critical self-reflection), on Dimension III (the influence of social systems on relationships) and on Dimension V (the risk of instrumentalization leading to an I – It dialogue).

Exploring diversity and helping to bridge gaps draws our attention to a paradox: acknowledging individual differences or even standing up for human rights as a commendable goal in therapy or social work can unintentionally disconnect individuals from their religious, cultural, ethnical context. A question that needs answers is: does acknowledging individual differences necessarily lead to the breaking up of generations-long lasting relationships that were kept together by the dynamics of giving and receiving care, motivated by shared narratives, values, rituals, practices? Contextual therapy proposes that it remains possible that people who have joined a new social identity group can stay connected to their communities of origin by expressing their loyalty in various, old and new, constructive ways. This would be an answer to the defenders of cultural and religious communities who see individualism as a threat to the communities they want to preserve.

Urgent global commitment

There are more issues relating to multicultural worlds that need reflection by contextual practitioners, and it is done best in interdisciplinary settings together with religious and cultural leaders. This book shows that a good number of religious individuals, among them leaders from many religious denominations, have a desire for genuine encounters with people from different cultural, religious, and professional horizons. They are committed to learn from others. They are able to recognize that other people have different perspectives on reality than they themselves and make different assessments of situations. More importantly, they can process input from communities other than their own, while cooperating with others to make the world a better place.

Marianne Moyaert of Emouna Netherlands stated in a lecture that "ignoring the social capital of faith-based communities sends the message that these communities have no real bearing on society at large or on the common good. This may lead these communities to invest mainly or even solely in their own 'constituency' or their own 'adherents'." This "does not enhance their 'bridged social capital', which is outward faced and all about working together across lines of difference" (Moyaert, 2020).

Rituals and words can be found in any faith and spiritual tradition to express the deepest respect for all present, past and future human beings and for our natural environment. In interfaith studies and interfaith encounters, participants can learn together about the diversity of their worldviews, work together on a common goal and change cultural narratives of unavoidable and ongoing clashes between ethnic, religious and cultural communities. In intercultural conflicts the contextual approach can support steps toward reconciliation with its relational-ethical guidelines and relational insights. In fact, in my opinion, the contextual approach and interfaith programs must join forces to revitalize stalled or hostile relationships. Fair bridging aims at connecting and not assimilating, differentiating and not equalizing.

Contributing to fair bridging between people and their different communities in this complex multicultural world is not an option but a fundamental human engagement. It is the sincere wish of the three authors that both sections of this book contribute to this urgent global commitment.

Bibliography

Anderson, H. 1990. The congregation as a healing resource. In: D.S. Browning, Th. Jobe & I.E. Evinson (eds.), *Religious and ethical factors in psychiatric practice*. Chicago, IL: Nelson-Hall, 264-286.

Berzin, A. 1998. *Developing balanced sensitivity: practical Buddhist exercises for daily life*. Ithaca, NY: Snow Lion.

Berzin, A. & Ducommun-Nagy, C. 2019. *Dependent arising of the Self in terms of relation with others*. https://bit.ly/41BNytS (Accessed 30 December 2022).

Boszormenyi-Nagy, I. 1987. *Foundations of contextual therapy: Collected papers of Ivan Boszormenyi-Nagy*, MD. Reprint 2014, New York, NY: Routledge. https://doi.org/10.4324/9781315803852

Boszormenyi-Nagy, I. 1996. Relational ethics in contextual therapy. In: M. Friedman (ed.), *Martin Buber and the human sciences*. Albany, NY: SUNY Press, 371-382.

Boszormenyi-Nagy, I. & Framo, J.L. (eds.) 1965. *Intensive family therapy. Theoretical and practical aspects*. Reprint 2015, New York, NY: Routledge.

Boszormenyi-Nagy, I. & Krasner, B. 1986. *Between give and take*. Reprint 2014, New York, NY: Routledge. https://doi.org/10.4324/9780203776315

Boszormenyi-Nagy, I. & Spark, G.M. 1973. *Invisible loyalties*. Reprint 2014, New York, NY: Routledge. https://doi.org/10.4324/9781315825939

Bregman, R. 2020. *Humankind. A hopeful history*. New York, NY: Little Brown and Company.

Brouwer, R. 2004. Conflict in contextueel perspectief. *Nieuwsbrief Werkverband Kerkelijk Opbouwwerk*, 55: 13-16.

Buber, M. 1947. *Between man and man* (R. Gregor-Smith, transl.). Reprint 2002, London: Routledge. https://doi.org/10.4324/9780203220092

Buber, M. 1957. *Pointing the way. Collected essays* (M. Friedman, transl.). Reprint 1990, Amherst, NY: Humanity Books.

Buber, M. 1965. *Das dialogische Prinzip*. Heidelberg: Lambrecht Schneider.

Buber, M. 1967. *A believing Humanism: my testament, 1902-1965* (M. Friedman, transl.). New York, NY: Simon & Schuster.

Buber, M. 1970. *I and Thou* (W. Kaufman, transl.). New York, NY: Scribner. (First published in German, 1923).

Buber, M. 1998. *The knowledge of man. Selected essays* (M. Friedman & R. Gregor Smith, transl.). Amherst, NY: Humanity Books.

Bumb, N., Carlson, C. & Iyer, L. 2020. Change the world – for whom? Why addressing racism must be a top corporate priority. In: *Fortune*, September 21. https://bit.ly/3AAb4vo (Accessed 21 July 2022).

Burns, J.H. & Hart, H.L.A. (eds.) 1970. The Collected works of Jeremy Bentham: An Introduction to the Principles of Morals and legislation. London: Athlone Press.

Caputo, J.D. 2015. *Hoping against hope*. Minneapolis, MN: 1517 Media. https://doi.org/10.2307/j.ctt155j2ts

Caputo, J.D., Moody, K.S., DeLay, T., Pennock, R., Purnell, M., Hardt, J., Harris, J., Crockett, C., Preis, L.E. & Keller, C. 2015. *It spooks: Living in response to an unheard call – responses to a paper by John D. Caputo*. Rapid City, SD: Shelter 50.

Carr, L., Iacobani, M., Dubeau, M-C., Mazziotta, J.C. & Lenzi, G.L. 2003. Neural mechanisms of empathy in humans: A relay from neural systems for imitation to limbic areas. *Proceedings of the National Academy of Sciences*, 100: 5497-5502. https://doi.org/10.1073/pnas.0935845100

Changeux, J-P., Damasio, A., Singer, W. & Christen, Y. 2005. *Neurobiology of human values*. Berlin: Springer. https://doi.org/10.1007/3-540-29803-7

Dalai Lama 2012. *Toward a true kinship of faiths: How the world's religions can come together*. New York, NY: Harmony Books.

Dawkins, R. 1976. *The selfish gene*. Oxford: Oxford University Press.

De Vries, G.A. 2010. *Meer dan voldoende te eten en een vrolijk hart. Aat van Rhijn, dominee en therapeut in het spoor van Nagy en Levinas*. Vught: Skandalon.

De Waal, F. 1996. *Good natured. The origins of right and wrong in humans and other animals*. Cambridge, MA: Harvard University Press. https://doi.org/10.4159/9780674033177

De Waal, F. 2006. *Primates and philosophers. How morality evolved*. Princeton, NJ: Princeton University Press. https://doi.org/10.1515/9781400830336

Dillen, A. 2004. *Ongehoord vertrouwen. Ethische perspectieven vanuit het contextuele denken van Ivan Boszormenyi-Nagy*. Antwerpen: Garant.

Ducommun-Nagy, C. 1999. Contextual therapy. In: D. Lawson & F. Prevatt (eds.), *The casebook in family therapy*. Pacific Grove, CA: Brook/Cole, 1-26. https://doi.org/10.1007/978-3-319-15877-8_361-1

Ducommun-Nagy, C. 2002. Contextual Therapy. In: F. Kaslow (ed.), *Comprehensive handbook of psychotherapy*, Vol. III. New York, NY: John Willey and Sons, 463-487.

Ducommun-Nagy, C. 2003. Can giving heal? Contextual therapy and biological psychiatry. In: D. Keith & P. Prosky (eds.), *Family therapy as an alternative to medication, an appraisal of Pharmland*. New York, NY: Brunner-Routledge, 111-138.

Ducommun-Nagy, C. 2006. *Ces loyautés qui nous libèrent*. Paris: J-C. Lattès.

Ducommun-Nagy, C. 2010a. Les cinq dimensions du génogramme. L'apport de la thérapie contextuelle pour la compréhension des relations familiales. [Unpublished plenary presentation]. 11èmes Journées Francophones de Thérapie Familiale Systémique de Lyon. Lyon, France, 20 May.

Ducommun-Nagy, C. 2010b. Forgiveness and relational ethics: The perspective of the contextual therapist. In: A. Kalayjian & R. Paloutzian (eds.), *Forgiveness and reconciliation. Psychological pathways to conflict transformation and peace building*. New York, NY: Springer, 33-54. https://doi.org/10.1007/978-1-4419-0181-1_3

Ducommun-Nagy, C. 2014. *Lojalitás*. (J. Kiss, transl.) Cluj-Napoca: EXIT.

Ducommun-Nagy, C. 2018. Contextual therapy. In: A. Chambers, D. Breunlin & J. Lebow (eds.), *Encyclopedia of couple and family therapy*. New-York, NY: Springer International Publishing. https://doi.org/10.1007/978-3-319-15877-8_361-1

Ducommun-Nagy C. 2021. Loyalty and transgenerational solidarity. Unpublished plenary presentation. Seeking for Hope (On-line Webinar). Stellenbosch: Stellenbosch University, Department of theology, South Africa, 26 May.

Elkaïm, M. 1985. From general laws to singularities. *Family Process*, 24(2): 115-164. https://doi.org/10.1111/j.1545-5300.1985.00151.x

Fitzgerald, J.D. 2021. *Chaplains and the rise of on demand spiritual support*. https://bit.ly/41JhEM3 (Accessed 25 January 2023).

Fivaz-Depeursinge, E. & Philipp, D.A. 2014. *The baby and the couple*. New York, NY: Routledge. https://doi.org/10.4324/9781315779775

Freud, S. 1930. Civilization and its discontents. Reprint, New York, NY: Norton, 1961.

Friedman, E.H. 1985. *Generation to generation: Family process in church and synagogue*. New York, NY: Guilford.

Friedman, M. 1992. *Religion and psychology: A dialogical approach*. New York, NY: Paragon House.

Friedman, M. 1996. *Martin Buber and the human sciences*. Albany, NY: SUNY Press.

Gangamma, R., Bartle-Haring, S., Holowacz, E., Hartwell E.E. & Glebova, T. 2015. Relational ethics, depressive symptoms, and relationship satisfaction in couples in therapy. *Journal of Marital and Family Therapy*, 41(3): 354-366. https://doi.org/10.1111/jmft.12070

Gathogo, J. 2008. Some expressions of African hospitality today. *Scriptura*, 99: 275-287. https://doi.org/10.7833/99-0-669

Gathogo, J. 2012. Reconciliation paradigm in post-colonial Africa: A critical analysis. *Religion & Theology*, 19: 74-91. https://doi.org/10.1163/15743012-12341235

Gert, B. 2013. Loyalty and morality. In: S. Levinson, P. Woodruff & J. Parker (eds.), *Loyalty*. New York, NY: NYU Press.

Giliomee, H. & Mbenga, B. (eds.) 2007. *New history of South Africa*. Cape Town: Tafelberg.

Girard, R. 2004. *Oedipus unbound: Selected writings on rivalry and desire*. Stanford, CA: Stanford University Press. https://doi.org/10.1515/9781503624139

Given, L.M. (ed.) 2008. *The Sage encyclopedia of qualitative research methods*. Thousand Oaks, CA: Sage. https://doi.org/10.4135/9781412963909

Godbout, J. & Caillé, A. 2016. *The world of the gift* (D. Winkler, transl.). Montreal: McGill and Queen's University Press.

Goleman, D. & Davidson, R.J. 2017. *Altered traits: Science reveals how meditation changes your mind, brain, and body*. New York, NY: Avery Publishing.

Graham, E., Walton, H. & Ward, F. 2005. *Theological reflection: Methods*. London: SCM. https://doi.org/10.1080/13520806.2005.11759006

Grossman, V. 1995. *Life and fate* (R. Chandler transl.). London: Collins Harvill.

Hargrave, T.D. & Pfitzer, F. 2011. *Restoration therapy. Understanding and guiding healing in marriage and family therapy*. New York, NY: Routledge. https://doi.org/10.4324/9780203817247

Hargrave, T.D. & Sell, J.N. 1998. Forgiveness: A review of the theoretical and empirical literature. *Journal of Family Therapy*, 20: 21-36. https://doi.org/10.1111/1467-6427.00066

Hargrave, T.D. & Zasowski, E. 2016. *Families and forgiveness. Healing wounds in the intergenerational family* (Second edition). New York, NY: Routledge. https://doi.org/10.4324/9781315650708

Heath-Thornton, D. 2018. "restorative justice". *Encyclopedia Britannica*. https://bit.ly/3Lx6NPy (Accessed 15 December 2022).

Hendriks, B. 2020. *Sense of wonder. Encountering Van Morrison*. Published by the author.

Heyndrickx, P. 2016. *Contextuele counseling in de praktijk. Het risico nemen opnieuw te geven*. Antwerpen: Garant.

Heyndrickx, P., De Loof, L., Knip, R., Van Herck, A. & Van Klaveren, W. 2022. *Contextuele hulpverlening*. Kalmthout: Pelckmans.

Higgins, K.M. 2013. Loyalty from a Confucian perspective. In: S. Levinson, P. Woodruff, & J. Parker (eds.), *Loyalty*. New York, NY: NYU Press.

Huntington, S.P. 1996. *The clash of civilizations and the remaking of the world order*. Reprint 2011, New York: Simon and Schuster Paperback, (Dutch transl.) J. Bos, 2019. Amsterdam: Hollands Diep.

Inagaki, T., Ross, K. & Laurent, P. 2018. Neural correlates of giving social support: Differences between giving targeted versus untargeted support. *Psychosomatic Medicine*, 80(8): 724-732. https://doi.org/10.1097/PSY.0000000000000623

Jonas, H. 1984. *The imperative of responsibility. In search of an ethics for the technological age*. Chicago, IL: The University of Chicago Press.

Kaplan Thaler, L. & Koval, R. 2006. *The power of nice: How to conquer the business world with kindness.* New York, NY: Reed Elsevier.

Kleingeld, P. & Anderson, J. 2014. Justice as a family value: How a commitment to fairness is compatible with love. *Hypatia: A Journal of Feminist Philosophy*, 29(2): 320-336. https://doi.org/10.1111/hypa.12048

Knight, K. 2014.Theories of distributive justice and post-apartheid South Africa. *Politikon*, 41-1: 23-38. https://doi.org/10.1080/02589346.2014.885669

Krasner, B.R. & Joyce, A.J. 1995. *Truth, trust, and relationships. Healing Interventions in contextual therapy.* Reprint 2015, New York, NY: Routledge.

Levinas, E. 1988. Useless suffering (R. Cohen transl.). In: R. Bernasconi & D. Wood (eds.), *The provocation of Levinas. Rethinking the other.* London: Routledge, 156-167.

Levinas, E. 1997. *Difficult freedom: Essays on Judaism* (S. Hand, transl.). Baltimore: JHUP.

Levinas, E. 2018. *De l'Unicité.* (Preface by Danielle Cohen-Levinas). Paris: Payot-Rivages.

Lindijer, C.H. College-materiaal inleiding Pastoraat. (Unpublished papers). Amsterdam: University of Amsterdam.

Louw, D. 2018. *Cura vitae. Illness and the healing of life.* Cape Town: Lux Verbi.

Louw, D. 2019. Pastoral encounters as appealing spaces of meeting and healing, Preface. In: A. Van Rhijn & H. Meulink-Korf (eds.), *Appealing spaces, the ethics of humane networking: The interplay between justice and relational healing in caregiving* (D. Louw, transl., preface, adapt.). Wellington: Biblemedia, 9-24.

Mauss, M. 1925. *The gift: The form and reason of exchanges in archaic societies* (J.I. Guyer, transl.). Reprint 2016, Chicago: University of Chicago Press.

McGoldrick, M., Gerson R. & Petry S. 2020. *Genograms.* New York, NY: Norton.

Meulink-Korf, H. & Noorlander, W. 2012. Resourcing trust in a fragmenting world. The social-economical dimension and relational ethics in the track of Boszormenyi-Nagy. *European Journal of Mental Health*, 7(2): 157-183. https://doi.org/10.5708/EJMH.7.2012.2.1

Meulink-Korf, H. & Van Rhijn, A. 2016. *The unexpected third. Contextual pastoral care, counseling and ministry: An introduction and reflection* (N. Visser, transl.). Wellington: CLF.

Michard, P. 2017. *La thérapie contextuelle de Boszormenyi-Nagy.* Brussels: De Boeck. https://doi.org/10.3917/dbu.micha.2017.01

Miller, W.I. 2009. *An eye for an eye.* Cambridge, MA: Cambridge University Press.

Mkhize, V.V.O. 2016. The seven universal guardian spirits of Umsamo and their influence with the healing wisdom of Africa. [Oral presentation/unpublished paper]. Symposium on Africanizing Contextual Pastoral Care. Stellenbosch, Stellenbosch University, Department of Theology, South Africa, 18-19 July.

Moyaert, M. 2019. Emoena – Leiderschap in een multireligieuze context. [Unpublished lecture]. Inaugural day of the Dutch Emoena program. Amsterdam, the Netherlands, 18 October.

Moyaert, M. 2020. Emoena – Toward a pedagogy of interfaith leadership. [Unpublished lecture]. Symposium for Rabbi Awraham Soetendorp. The Hague, The Netherlands, 19 November.

Mugambi, J.N.K. 1995. *From liberation to reconstruction. African Christian Theology after the Cold War.* Nairobi: EAEP.

Mugambi, J.N.K. 2012. Justice, participation and sustainability as prerequisites for peaceful coexistence. In: J.N.K. Mugambi & D.W. Lutz (eds.), *Applied ethics in religion and culture.* Nairobi: Acton, 9-29.

Nietzsche, F. 1986. *Human, all too human.* (R. Hollingdale, transl.). New York: Cambridge University Press. (First published in German, 1887).

Nwoye, A. 2022. *Rituals of cleansing and repossession: An Africentric approach to treatment of moral injury. African psychology, the emergence of a tradition.* Oxford: University Press, 448-464. https://doi.org/10.1093/oso/9780190932497.003.0019

Oughourlian, J-M. 1982. *Un mime nommé désir.* Paris: Grasset.

Polanyi, M. 1983. *The tacit dimension.* Gloucester, MA: Peter Smith.

Prieur, N. 2021. *Les trahisons nécessaires. S'autoriser à être soi.* Paris: Robert Laffont.

Project Moral Injury. 2022. *Een NWO NWA-project van de Radboud Universiteit Nijmegen, de Nederlandse Defensie Academie, de Politieacademie, het Nederlands Veteraneninstituut en het ARQ Nationaal Psychotrauma Centrum.* https://bit.ly/3LznH00 (Accessed 21 July 2022).

Qur'an. *Al-Baqarah, Surah 2.* https://bit.ly/3Azcere (Accessed 28 July 2022). https://doi.org/10.56672/alwasathiyah.v2i1.53

Ramose, M. 1999. *African philosophy through Ubuntu.* Harare: Mond Books.

Rawls, J. 1999. *A Theory of Justice.* Oxford: Oxford University Press. (Revised edition). https://doi.org/10.4159/9780674042582

Reedijk, R. 2010. *Roots and routes. Identity construction and the Jewish-Christian-Muslim dialogue.* Amsterdam: Rodopi. https://doi.org/10.1163/9789042028401

Reyhan Kayikci, M. 2019. Relational ethics: Volunteering and the responsibilities of the good Muslim. *Religions*, 10, 150. (An open- access journal from mdpi). https://bit.ly/3NgZc9e (Accessed 30 July 2022). https://doi.org/10.3390/rel10030150

Ricard, M. 2015. *The science and the psychology of kindness.* New York, NY: Little, Brown and Company.

Ridley, M. 1996. *The origins of virtue. Human instinct and the evolution of cooperation.* New York, NY: Penguin.

Ridley, M. 2004. *The agile gene. How nature turns on nurture.* New York, NY: Perennial.

Roemer, A.H. 1998. Migrantenhulpverlening in contextueel perspectief. In: M. Michielsen, W. van Mulligen & L. Hermkens (eds.), *Leren over leven in loyaliteit. Over contextuele hulpverlening.* Leuven: Acco, 259-277.

Rogers, C.R. 1951. *Client-centered therapy. Its current practice, implications, and theory.* Boston, MA: Houghton Mifflin.

Rosenstock-Huessy, E. 1981. *The origin of speech.* Norwich, VT: Argo Books. Rothman, J. 2014. The origins of 'Privilege'. In: *The New Yorker*, 12 May. https://bit.ly/40HMNhI (Accessed 22 July 2022).

Runyan, A.S. 2019. What is intersectionality and why is it important? Building solidarity in the fight for social justice. In: *Reports & Publications of the American Association of University Professors*, November-December 2019. https://bit.ly/43ZuFme (Accessed 21 July 2022).

Sacks, J. 2007. *To heal a fractured world: The ethics of responsibility.* New York, NY: Schocken Books.

Seta, D. 2016. *Forgotten women: The impact of Islamophobia on Muslim women.* Research report by European Network against racism. https://bit.ly/422lBv3 (Accessed 21 July 2022).

Sniderman, P.M. & Hagendoorn, L. 2007. *When ways of life collide. Multiculturalism and its discontents in the Netherlands.* Princeton, NJ: University Press.

The Holy Bible. *New International Version, 1978.* (Ref for Genesis, Jeremiah, Psalm 23, and the Gospel of John). London: Biblica.

Thesnaar, C.H. 2001. *Die Proses van heling en versoening: pastoraal-hermeneutiese ondersoek van die dinamika tussen slagoffer en oortreder binnen post-WVK periode.* PhD thesis. Stellenbosch: Stellenbosch Universiteit.

Thesnaar, C.H. 2013. Embodying collective memory: Toward responsible engagement with the 'Other'. *Scriptura*, 112: 1-15. https://doi.org/10.7833/112-0-75

Thesnaar, C.H. 2019. *Divine discomfort: A relational encounter with multi-generational and multi-layered trauma.* Inaugural Lecture. Stellenbosch: Stellenbosch University.

Thesnaar, C.H. 2022. Dialogical Intergenerational Pastoral Process: A transdisciplinary research approach. In: J. Cilliers (ed.), *Moving methodologies. Doing practical and missional theology in an African context.* Wellington: Bybelmedia, 167-190.

Theunissen, M. 1984. *The Other* (C. Macann transl.). Cambridge, MA: The MIT Press.

Towles, A. 2017. *A gentleman in Moscow.* New York, NY: Penguin Books.

Trivers, R. 1971. *The evolution of reciprocal altruism.* Quarterly Review of Biology, 46: 35-57. https://doi.org/10.1086/406755

Tutu, D. & Tutu, M. 2014. *The book of forgiveness. The fourfold path for healing ourselves and our world.* New York, NY: HarperCollins.

Van den Berg-Seiffert, C. 2015. *Ik sta erbuiten - maar ik sta wel te kijken. De relationele dynamiek in geloofsgemeenschappen na seksuele grensoverschrijding in een pastorale relatie vanuit het perspectief van primaire slachtoffers.* Zoetermeer: Boekencentrum Academic.

Van der Meiden, J. 2019. *Where hope resides. A qualitative study of the contextual theory and therapy of Ivan Boszormenyi-Nagy and its applicability for therapy and social work.* Utrecht: University of Humanistic Studies.

Van Doorn, N. 2020. *Encouraging encounters: Reframing time by dialogue in the intergenerational pastoral process* (D. Louw transl.). Wellington: Bible Media.

Van Doornik, A. 2022. *Een taal erbij. Het handboek voor systemisch werken met poppetjes.* Leuven: Acco Learn.

Van Rhijn, A. 1992. *Door de hemel uit de droom geholpen. Afscheidscollege.* Amsterdam: Hogeschool van Amsterdam.

Van Rhijn, A. & Meulink-Korf, H. 2019. *Appealing spaces, the ethics of humane networking. The interplay between justice and relational healing in caregiving* (D. Louw, transl., preface, adapt.). Wellington: Bible Media.

Van Riessen, R. 2019. *Van zichzelf bevrijd. Levinas over transcendentie en nabijheid.* Amsterdam: Sjibbolet.

Van Tubergen, F. 2020. *Introduction to sociology.* New York, NY: Routledge. https://doi.org/10.4324/9781351134958

Von Bertalanffy, L. 1968. *General system theory: Foundations, development, applications.* New York: George Braziller.

Von Foerster, H. 1995. *Cybernetics of cybernetics. Or the control of control and the communication of communication* (Second edition). Minneapolis, MN: Future Systems.

Von Foerster, H., Mead, M. & Teuber, H.L. (eds.) 1951. *Cybernetics, circular causal and feedback mechanisms in biological and social systems: transactions of the seventh conference, March 23-24, 1950.* New York, NY: Josiah Macy Jr. Foundation.

Wiggins Frame, M. 2004. The challenges of intercultural marriage: Strategies for pastoral care. *Pastoral Psychology*, 52(3): 219-232. https://doi.org/10.1023/B:PASP.0000010024.32499.32

Williamson, V., Murphy, D., Phelps A., Forbes, D. & Greenberg N. 2021. Moral injury: the effect on mental health and implications for treatment. *Lancet Psychiatry*, 8-6: 453-455. https://bit.ly/3Hkti7U (Accessed 21 July 2022). https://doi.org/10.1016/S2215-0366(21)00113-9

Worthington, E.L., Jr., Griffin, B.J. & Provencher, C. 2018. Forgiveness. In: J.E. Maddux (ed.), *Subjective well-being and life satisfaction.* New York, NY: Routledge/Taylor & Francis Group, 148-167. https://bit.ly/3NfoeWr (Accessed 30 December 2022). https://doi.org/10.4324/9781351231879-7

Website references

Interfaith Organizations (All accessed 21 July 2022):

Canadian Interfaith Conversation, Richmond Hill, Ontario. https://bit.ly/3Vb5xVC

Cape Town Interfaith Initiative, Western Cape of South Africa. https://bit.ly/3V8yOjP

Dialogue and Culture Organization, Sulaimani, Kurdistan Iraq. https://bit.ly/3LJyvJn

Elijah Interfaith Institute, Center of Hope, Jerusalem. https://bit.ly/3V9yb9M

Emoena, Amsterdam, Netherlands. https://bit.ly/3Hjujgv

IHOM – the Institute for Healing of Memories, healing-memories.org. https://bit.ly/3V9E2f8 (Accessed 24 July 2022).

Institute for Inter-Faith Dialogue, Yogyakarta, Indonesia. https://bit.ly/44babHt

Interfaith Network, The United Kingdom, London. https://bit.ly/41ItC8O

King Abdullah bin Abdulaziz International Center for Interreligious and Intercultural Dialogue, Lisbon, Portugal. https://bit.ly/3HigdvY

Rwanda Interfaith Council on Health, Kigali. https://bit.ly/40KMzGG

Stellenbosch University, Faculty of Theology. https://bit.ly/3VegdDa (Accessed 30 July 2022).

Stichting Contextueel Pastoraat in Nederland. https://bit.ly/3Hfm2KA (Accessed 30 July 2022).

Washington Interfaith Staff Community, Washington D.C., United States of America. https://bit.ly/3Niw953

Zebra foundation.https://bit.ly/3Lz9KPK (Accessed 30 July 2022).

www.ingramcontent.com/pod-product-compliance
Lightning Source LLC
Chambersburg PA
CBHW081202170426
43197CB00018B/2899